R&B

RHYTHM AND BUSINESS

THE POLITICAL ECONOMY OF BLACK MUSIC

EDITED BY NORMAN KELLEY

Akashic Books
New York

Published by Akashic Books
©2002 Norman Kelley

Design and layout by Robert Perino
Additional design assistance by Jason Farrell

ISBN: 1-888451-26-2
Library of Congress Control Number: 2001097214
All rights reserved
First printing
Printed in Canada

Akashic Books
PO Box 1456
New York, NY 10009
Akashic7@aol.com
www.akashicbooks.com

In Memoriam:

DAVID EARL JACKSON
March 19, 1950–August 15, 2001

*Writer, journalist, radio producer, poet, musicman,
raconteur, educator, bibliophile, conjureman,
friend, cook, cultural generalist, and the first
and last of the down-home sophisticates.
Peace, brother.*

Acknowledgments

Rhythm & Business would like to thank the following people who have assisted in the writing and production of this book. First, the original-crew contributors: Mike Roberts, Yvonne Bynoe, William Phillips, David Sanjek, and Karl Hagstrom Miller.

Next, the second-generation contributors (i.e., contributors whose articles have been previously published): Danny Goldberg, Stephen Calt, Reebee Garofalo ("godfather" of the study of the political economy of music), Brian Ward, Mark Anthony Neal, Adam Mansbach, Chuck D, Charles Mann, Richard B. Woodward, Wendy Day, Courtney Love, and the late Frank Kofsky.

Also, James Murray of the NAACP, Jenny Toomey of the Future of Music Coalition, Rose Robinson of the University of California Press, Barbara Bowman of Pathfinder Press, Walter Leaphart, Jolyn Matsumuro, James Barber, Art Kara, and Frederick T. Courtright.

At Akashic Books: Johnny Temple, Johanna Ingalls, Justin Vogt, and Amira Pierce.

And special thanks to the Miller/Dominati/Baruchel family: Riel, Isabell, Noé, David, and Olivia, who allowed the editor to stay with them in Paris and Les Arcs. *Merci beacoup.*

TABLE OF CONTENTS

TABLE OF CONTENTS (CONT'D)

The price one pays for pursuing any profession or one's calling is an intimate knowledge of its ugly side.
—JAMES BALDWIN, NOBODY KNOWS MY NAME

INTRODUCTION

The idea for this book originated in an article I wrote, titled "Rhythm Nation: The Political Economy of Black Music." "Rhythm Nation" was first posted on from-left-field.com and subsequently printed in the New York University publication, *Black Renaissance/Noir*, and in *Doula*, a hip hop journal. People from out of nowhere began contacting me by phone and email with messages of appreciation. Black Radical Congress later posted the essay, and a database firm purchased the rights to license it for one of their informational wares. Previously, I had wanted to devote an entire book to an exploration of this essential question: Why is it that blacks have developed many musical genres yet have no real control or ownership in the recording industry? Instead, they are for the most part glorified employees.

Neither literary agents nor editors saw this question as having any publishing merit; the sole exception that I encountered was the publisher of this volume, Akashic Books. Not having the kind of financial support that warranted time for extensive research, writing, and reflection, I took the easy way out. I decided to use my essay as an organizing theme and asked a few writers to develop original articles around the idea of the political economy of black music. I also culled previously published material from books and other sources that touched upon the themes of music production, control, and distribution, and that examined the lack of wealth and power among African-Americans in an industry that fundamentally depends on black musical talent.

Rhythm & Business: The Political Economy of Black Music is the first anthology that explores the economic relationship between black music and the record industry. In another way, this book is really about black economic development—or lack thereof. Most books that focus on black music tend to look at the content or form of the music, but curiously neglect its economic aspects. It is not unusual to find books that "interrogate" the "site of blackness" or the "tropes" of black identity or the "black public sphere," but few investigate the political economy of black music. Odder still is that such works have been written by black academics—so-called black public intellectuals seduced by the postmodernese of the times.

Black non-academic writers like Nelson George (*The Death of Rhythm & Blues*) and white academic and non-academic writers like Reebee Garofalo (*Rock and Roll Is Here to Pay*; *Rockin' the Boat*; *Rockin' Out*) and Russell and David Sanjek

(*American Popular Music Business in the Twentieth Century*) have created a framework for this investigation. However, because such an opportunity comes dressed in coveralls and looks like work, such digging has not been picked up by any of today's Talented Tenth. It is easier to find theoretical constructs about the blues, or to purchase a spoken-word album from a cultural-studies professor than it is to encounter critical analysis of how African-American musical talent has laid the foundation for a multi-billion-dollar music industry that profits at the expense of the artists. Rarely have so many theorized about so much, but said so little.

R&B focuses primarily on how black music and talent (i.e., labor) is channeled into the $14-billion American music industry ($40 billion worldwide). This volume also tries to answer the question posed by a popular late-twentieth-century social philosopher, Marvin Gaye: *What's going on?*

R&B is divided into five sections after this introduction. Part One, "The Structure of Stealing," is essentially an overview of the music industry—present and past—and begins with my essay, "Notes on the Political Economy of Black Music." Mike Roberts's "Papa's Got a Brand-New Bag" presents to the reader the shifting trends that engulf the industry and confront musicians, union and non-union alike. Roberts also examines how the industry has moved to a "post-Fordist" model of production, transferring much of the grunt-work of production to "independent" labels. The next selection, the NAACP's 1987 report "The Discordant Sound of Music," is one of the few documents from an ostensibly black organization addressing the racial inequities in the music industry. "Tell Me Something I Don't Already Know: The Harvard Report on Soul Music Revisited" is David Sanjek's analysis of a document that has been much talked about, but until now not widely available. Commissioned by then–CBS Records (now Sony), the Harvard University Business School was asked to conduct a report on the profitability of the "soul-music market" of the sixties and seventies. The university's scholars came to an obvious conclusion: Black music is profitable. Danny Goldberg, an industry insider, closes this section with his views about the predicament of musicians who don't have mega-careers in "The Ballad of the Mid-Level Artist."

"The Politics of Race Music," Part Two, tracks the rise and transformation of "race music" into R&B and soul, as well as its politics and contradictions. This section begins with Stephen Calt's "Anatomy of a 'Race' Music Label," which focuses on Paramount Records, one of the original "race" labels. "Crossing Over" by Reebee Garofalo looks at how race music (black music) crossed over into a white buying market, and how white musicians and labels reacted by covering black hits, resulting in a loss of revenue and recognition for black artists. Brian Ward explores the convergence of black entrepreneurs and the civil rights era, as well as the commerce of "soul power," in "All for One, and One for All: Black Enterprise, Racial Politics, and the Business of Soul." Marc Anthony Neal's "Soul for Sale" examines the commodification of soul, or "blackness."

The third section, "Do Plaintains Go with Collard Greens? The Political Economy of Jazz and Salsa," begins with an investigation of the recording industry's relationship with jazz in the late Frank Kofsky's "If You're Black Get Back: Double Standards in the Recording Industry." This is followed by "Kind of Blue" by Richard Woodward, which looks at the double-edged sword of claiming jazz as America's "classical music." Karl Hagstrom Miller's "Crossover Schemes: New York Salsa as Politics, Culture, and Commerce" analyzes the interstices of these three distinct realms as they pertain to Puerto Rican nationalism, Boricua culture, and the dictates and tastes of the music industry as it searched for a new flavor after tasting hot-buttered soul.

Part Four, "The Politics of the Noise," begins with Yvonne Bynoe's "Money, Power, and Respect." Bynoe casts a critical eye on the most dynamic genre in the biz, namely hip hop, and looks at how various factors—class, education, and the music industry's commercial needs—influence hip hop artists and the music they produce. "How Not to Get Jerked!" is a roundtable discussion with several playas led by Adam Mansbach. Wendy Day, director of Rap Coalition, offers her views on the industry in an interview that I conducted with her, and Chuck D's "Death of a Nation" zeroes in on what is and what ain't happening in the hip hop nation.

The last section, "The Future of Music," moves beyond issues of black and white and focuses on the technological repercussions of the Internet on the music industry. Charles Mann muses about the modern industry in this extremely high-tech era in "The Heavenly Juke Box," and William Phillips presents the new players, issues, technologies, and strategies in "Music and the New Technology." We also present the testimony of the Future of Music Coalition to the United States Congress, before concluding the anthology with Courtney Love's call to her fellow artists to literally band together to challenge the practices of the five fingers of the music business.

NORMAN KELLEY
August 2001
Paris

Part 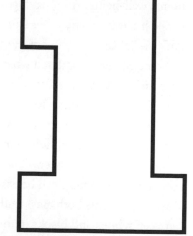 1

The Structure of Stealing

Notes on the Political Economy of Black Music
BY NORMAN KELLEY

> *No race that has anything to contribute to the markets of the world is long,*
> *in any degree, ostracized.* —BOOKER T. WASHINGTON

> *Black culture is too significant in American culture for blacks to be glorified employees.*
> —RUSSELL SIMMONS, DEF JAM RECORDS

When the Bush Administration issued an official proclamation honoring Black Music Month in June 2001, it did so at the *end* of the month. "Two measly days to celebrate Black Music Month?" decried *Slate's* Timothy Noah.[1] No malicious slight was intended, but unconsciously, this reflected the natural order of things with regard to a specific group's contributions to this nation's cultural heritage and economic well-being. After paying tribute to various black artists and noting how black music has told "many other stories, in many styles," Mr. Bush concluded that black music is "always easy to enjoy, yet impossible to imitate."[2]

Some citizens wondered what planet the president had been residing on, particularly since the phrase "always easy to enjoy" seemed somehow more suited to describing a soft drink. To be sure, black music is not a soft drink, but like one of today's multiculti flavors, it has become a commodity that is indeed easy—easy to exploit. This is largely due to the fact that blacks, America's foremost *forced* immigrants, have always been economically weak and thereby politically vulnerable. Although black music can be easy to enjoy due to phat beats and wicked hooks, Mr. Bush's comments both mask and underscore the fundamental economic relationship between whites and blacks in this society.

Through various modes of production and avenues of exchange, the relationship between the two races has historically rested on whites' ability to exploit and domi-

---

1. Timothy Noah, "Who Stole Black Music Month?" Slate.MSN.com/default.aspx?id=1007921.
2. Office of the Press Secretary, White House, "Remarks by the President in honor of Black History Month," June 29, 2001, whitehouse.gov/news/releases/2001/06/20010629-8.html.

nate blacks' bodies, images, and cultures. In the case of music, black artists have rarely received the just benefits of their work, especially in comparison to their white counterparts and those who control the music industry.

This state of affairs shouldn't exist given the prodigious talents of African-Americans in the realm of music. No other group in this nation has left a deeper stamp or a greater repertoire of styles and genres in America's storehouse of cultural heritage than African-Americans. When people worldwide refer to *American* music, they often mean, by way of shorthand, *black* music, due to the simple but largely unrecognized fact that black music is, essentially, America's *mainstream* music. African-Americans, collectively and individually, have set the standards for both performance and expressivity in American popular music, and, to a certain degree, in popular culture in general.

It is the contention of this essay that black music operates within a "structure of stealing" that dates back to the time when the ancestors of today's African-Americans began arriving to this country as slaves. Blacks served as commodities—objects purchased, controlled, and sold by others—while their labor was valued as an instrument in the production of cotton and other goods and services. Their heritage and transforming culture, however, were either ignored or exploited with impunity—or ridiculed, as in the case of black-faced minstrel music performed by whites in the middle of the nineteenth century. Needless to say, the dominant race would imbue greater value in the music of its own European heritage, while deriving ample enjoyment from the zany antics of the "others": Zip Coon, Sambo, and Beulah.

The structure of stealing that has evolved since the slavery period has allowed both whites and blacks to ignore the critical roles of black music and black *labor* in the American music industry. Another factor has been the racial hierarchy of caste-coding blacks. Through a process of stigmatization, almost any endeavor by African-Americans—in sports, music, dance, etc.—is of less consideration than of that by whites, because it is seen as merely the by-product of "natural talent," rather than the result of sustained learning, practice, discipline, and, most importantly, intelligence. "Natural talent" is like air: forever abundant and there for the taking.

Today's recording industry is less focused on the physical production of music—searching for new artists, recording innovative music, nurturing talent for the future—and is more concentrated on the marketing and distribution of existing stars. Five music companies, represented before the three branches of the government by the Recording Industry Association of America (RIAA) in matters pertaining to the trade, have increasingly subcontracted much of the production of music to so-called "independent" record labels not bound by union contracts. At the bottom of this $14-billion domestic music industry is a disrespected pool of black talent: America's colonized Rhythm Nation.

To be sure, of the five major conglomerates that control approximately eighty-five percent of recording, production, and distribution in the music industry—AOL Time Warner, Vivendi/Universal, BMG Distribution, Sony Music Entertainment, and EMI Distribution (see chart on pages 34–35)—not one is black-owned. Rap moguls such as Def Jam's Russell Simmons and Bad Boy Entertainment's Sean "P-Diddy" Combs are either showcased or touted as model entrepreneurs in today's hip hop–driven industry. What is often overlooked (if not patently ignored), however, is that their companies cannot distribute their music effectively without going through one of the five major conglomerates. Often, black subsidiaries are set up merely to respond to a parent company's demand for a marketable product. In turn, the parent company responds to a young white audience that purchases sixty-six percent of rap music, as reported by the RIAA.

A primary example of how black artists have been colonized by the major recording companies—aided and abetted by blacks—is the case of Tupac. The multitalented rapper was originally under contract with Interscope Records, founded by Jimmy Iovine and Ted Field (heir to the Marshall Field fortune). Allegedly, Tupac was later "handed over" to Death Row Records' Marion "Suge" Knight when the *enfant terrible* of rap was locked in a New York State penitentiary. While Death Row Records was the creation of Knight and Dr. Dre, it practically owed its existence to Interscope, and, some say, to a drug dealer named Michael "Harry-O" Harris. Desperate to get out of jail, reports document, Tupac signed an onerous agreement with Death Row that locked David Kenner (a Death Row attorney at that time, who also happens to be white) into the role of his counsel and manager—a direct and unmistakable conflict of interest. According to Connie Bruck, in her July 7, 1997 *New Yorker* article, "The Takedown of Tupac," the artist was trying to extricate himself from Death Row when he was killed on September 7, 1996.

Those who run the American recording industry understand the importance of black music for both its domestic and international markets. The five major recording companies, according to the RIAA, provided retail outlets with ninety percent of the music that the American public purchased in 2000. Rock music accounted for twenty-five percent of the total music sales, and rap/hip hop was the second most popular genre, with 12.9 percent, more than $1.8 billion.[3] On the international level, writes Harold Vogel, "recorded music generates aggregate worldwide revenues of some $40 billion per year. But because it is the most easily personalized and accessible form of entertainment, it readily pervades virtually every culture and every level of society. As such, it may be considered as the most fundamental of the entertainment businesses."[4]

There has been a growing awareness by blacks that something is amiss in the relationship between African-American artists and the recording industry. In *The History of Black Business in America,* Juliet Walker explains, "The huge profits the industry has earned from black artists have prompted some people to reach back into history for an appropriate term to describe the limited benefit that blacks have received and their general status in the industry; and so, one critic has surmised that record-industry blacks work under 'plantation-like conditions.'"[5]

During the civil rights period, executives at major labels, looking at the success of the Motown and Stax labels with black artists, began asking themselves, *is black music profitable?* In the early seventies, CBS Records commissioned the Harvard University Business School to analyze this question. The university's researchers returned with an affirmative answer, and with a tantalizing and insightful nugget: "Soul music is one of the very few basic art forms which is indigenous to America, although its own roots may be traced to Africa. It has been and probably will continue to be a vital and influential force on contemporary music. And Soul is by no means a static music form. It too will change."[6]

Enter rap/hip hop, the post–civil rights, postmodern continuation of African-American musical forms, a direct descendant of soul, R&B, gospel, and blues, a product of America's urban Bantustans. While rap music, like sports, has provided a few working-class blacks with a way out of the ghetto, it has given the music industry a constant source of cheap and talented labor.

3. Recording Industry Association of America, 2000 Consumer Profile, "Rap/Hip Hop Music Buyers Become Second Largest Segment, Record Stores, Mass Merchandisers Market Share Gap Narrows," March 13, 2001.

4. Harold L. Vogel, *Entertainment Industry Economics,* 5th edition, (Cambridge: Cambridge University Press, 2001) p.148. Michael Pfahl has cited worldwide music sales at $236.9 billion; see Michael Pfahl, "Giving Away Music to Make Money: Independent Musicians on the Internet," www.firstmonday.org/issues/issue6-8/pfahl/index.html.

5. Juliet E. K. Walker, *The History of Black Business in America: Capitalism, Race, Entrepreneurship* (New York: Macmillian, 1998), p. 322.

6. Harvard Report ("A Study of the Soul Music Environment Prepared for Columbia Records Group"), May 11, 1972, p. 18.

Despite the likes of Russell Simmons and Sean Combs, black-owned record firms have practically ceased to exist as independent forces in the realm of music. Motown has disappeared from *Black Enterprise's* annual roster of the top one hundred black businesses in America.[7] After all, Motown is now a subsidiary of Vivendi/ Universal, a giant French conglomerate; the label had to either merge or perish years ago. According to the June 2001 *Black Enterprise* roster, Simmons's Rush Communications had slid down from the fifteenth to the thirty-third spot in just a year. Even so, Rush Communications was the *only* ostensibly entertainment-based firm on the *B.E.* list. The former home of Def Jam records, Rush Communications had sales of $100 million during the previous year. The sales figure for the *entire* black entertainment industry for that period, as detailed by *Black Enterprise*, was $189.75 million. But rap music alone generated $1.8 *billion* in sales.

In classic colonialism, products were produced in a raw periphery and sent back to the imperial motherland to be manufactured into commodities, then sold in metropolitan centers or back to the colonies. The outcome for the colony was stunted economic growth, as it was stripped of its ability to manufacture products for its own needs.

Many black communities in the inner cities of America share some of these traditional characteristics of a colony: low per-capita income, high birth rate, high infant-mortality rate, low rate of capital formation and domestic savings, a small or weak middle class, economic dependence on external markets, labor as a major export, land and businesses owned by foreigners, and a tremendous demand for commodities that will be consumed by wealthier communities.

When applied to the music industry, this neo-colonial model has to take into account the relative wealth and health of African-Americans as a group. The per-capita income of African-Americans, notes economist Amartya Sen in *Development as Freedom*, is "considerably lower" than that of white Americans, but African-Americans are "very many times richer in income terms" than the people of China or India. African-Americans tend to fare better than these groups in terms of infant mortality. Yet African-Americans tend not to live as long as their fellow citizens in the United States, or those in China and India. In the words of Sen, while:

> American blacks suffer from *relative* deprivation in terms of income per head vis-à-vis American whites, they also are *absolutely* more deprived than the low-income

7. *Black Enterprise*, June 2001, Vol. 31, No.11: p. 104.

Indians in Kerala (for both men and women), and the Chinese (in the case of men), in the terms of living to ripe old ages.[8] [original emphasis]

As reported elsewhere, men in Bangladesh have a better chance of reaching the age of forty than black men in Harlem.[9]

African-Americans are essentially trapped in a state of relative *underdevelopment* in this market-driven society. This anomaly is due to the fact that blacks have been deprived of what Sen calls the five instrumental freedoms: political freedoms, economic facilities, social opportunities, transparency guarantees, and protective securities. In order for individuals to live to their fullest capacities in a marketplace society, they need a full complement of these interconnecting freedoms.

With rap music, the inner cities have become the raw sites of cultural production, and the music, once packaged, is sold to the suburbs, to white youths who feel they can relate to those of the urban Bantustans (but don't have to pay the social consequences of being black in a predominantly white society). If there is indeed a struggle for the control of rap, it is merely a battle between black gnats. The war for the control of black music was won many years ago by corporate America, facilitated by a black leadership that has never fully understood the economic significance of its own culture.

In the latter part of the nineteenth century and in the early years of the twentieth century, the black elite worldview was molded on a white, bourgeois, Victorian model, as noted by Kevin K. Gaines in *Uplifting the Race*. Black leaders—educators, racial spokespersons, intellectuals, etc.—have historically had a condescending attitude toward the black lower class, both urban and rural. Even though the black elite was outraged by whites' lucrative expropriation of black culture, Eurocentric images and ideals of respectability were nonetheless central to the black elite's aesthetic tastes.[10]

Black leaders' ideas about "racial uplift" were based on differentiating themselves from the black lower classes, who were seen as "bringing down the race." Even today's black "public intellectuals" use various codes to disassociate the "good black middle class"—themselves—from the "bad black underclass," which is populated in part by those who identify with rap music and hip hop culture. Randall

8. Amartya Sen, *Development as Freedom* (Oxford: Oxford University Press, 1999), pp. 21–22.
9. *Ibid*, p.23.
10. Kevin K. Gaines, *Uplifting the Race: Black Leadership, Politics, Race and Culture in the Twentieth Century* (Chapel Hill: University of North Carolina Press, 1996), p. 76.

Kennedy's feature, "My Race Problem and Ours," in the May 1997 issue of *Atlantic Monthly* is a modern-day spin on racial uplift; now, the racial extrication is based even more on class positioning. Such elitist attitudes throughout American history have prevented middle-class blacks and black leadership from seeing the worth of their own folk culture that spawned the blues and other musical forms that grew from the lower classes. Music from those "raw" Negores, in fact, now forms the base—the very foundation—of the $14-billion music industry in the United States.

Black musical genres emanating from the lower classes have been the "juice" that has long driven American musical expression—and whites have grown rich off of it. The black middle class has been too economically incompetent to champion and exploit (in the best sense of the word) its own folk culture and nurture the geniuses who have created the music. Black music has never had an enlightened leadership to give it a proper business footing. There has been no A. Philip Randolph or Thurgood Marshall in black music, visionaries who could organize musical artists or educate them about copyrights and contract law. In *Sound Effects*, Simon Frith notes one of many resulting dynamics:

> The pop industry is organized around music as composition—American copyright law protects composers rather than performers. It is songwriters who get royalties when records are sold or broadcast, not their performers, and black singers who were popular in the 1920s and 1930s were systematically cheated out of their due returns. Their music, however distinct, was in a legal sense "composerless," and it was white publishers who rushed to copyright the resulting "spontaneous" compositions. Such exploitation of black musicians by publishers and record companies continued into the 1960s . . .[11]

The history of black music has been a continuous replay of the uncontested and lucrative expropriation of black cultural forms by whites. This variegated structure of stealing developed through the minstrel shows of pre–Civil War America, to segregating black music as "race music," to white composers copping black jazz styles, to white rockers covering black R&B songs, to publishers stealing copyrights, to the nonpayment of royalties due to black artists by record companies. All the while, black musical forms have comprised the backbone of American music, though

11. Simon Frith, *Sound Effects: Youth, Leisure, and the Politics of Rock 'n' Roll* (New York: Pantheon Books, 1981), p. 17.

blacks themselves, brought over to the New World as bodies for work, have been widely portrayed as having no culture worthy of respect in a civilized society. As slaves, they were "socially dead" and could thus be depicted as coons, pickaninnies, and Sambos.

This is the basis of the structure of stealing in which other national groups—principally Anglo-Saxons (slavery), Irish (minstrelsy), Jews (Hollywood, the record industry), and Italians (through mob influence)—have participated. With the exception of Anglo-Saxons, the other ethnic groups were not originally considered "white," but through a process of Americanization eventually came to be viewed as such. Upon assuming the credentials (or badge) of "whiteness," these new Americans could begin exploiting a class of Americans who had been born in the United States prior to their own arrival, namely blacks. America's racial hierarchy and its politics of stigmatization would offer these groups—the newly "whitened" Americans—the means and the rationale to take advantage of an outsider class. However, it should also be noted that blacks, too, have engaged in the structure of stealing, as reflected in the history of black music. Within the hip hop community, the term "black-on-black crime" often refers to black label owners who fleece today's artists, and to one mogul in particular.

This structure of stealing, as Harold Cruse pointed out in 1967, is based on an *open* but unexamined network of interconnected operations, businesses, business practices, and social ties that mostly understand blacks as "talent," i.e., labor. Although Cruse used the jazz musician as an example in *The Crisis of the Negro Intellectual*, the same situation has always existed for black artists in blues, rock, R&B, soul, and hip hop. Beneath this structure, Cruse writes, is a:

> whole history of organized duplicity and exploitation of the Negro jazz artist—the complicated tie-in between booking agencies, the musicians' union, the recording companies, the music publishers, the managers, the agents, the theater owners, the night-club owners, the crooks, shysters, and racketeers. The Negro creative intellectuals have to look into the question of how is it possible for a Negro jazz musician to walk around the streets of large cities, jobless, starving, while a record that he cut with a music company is selling well, both in the United States and in Europe. They have to examine why a Negro jazz musician can be forced to pay dues to unions that get him no work, and that operate with the same discriminatory practices

as clubs, halls, and theaters. The impact of the cultural tradition of Afro-American folk music demands that the racially corrupt practices of the music-publishing field be investigated.[12]

In sum, Cruse argues, "the individual Negro has, proportionately, very few rights indeed because his ethnic group (whether or not he actually identifies with it) has very little political, economic, or social power (beyond moral grounds) to wield."[13]

The expropriation of black music has been so blatant and widespread that a Rhythm & Blues Foundation was set up in 1994, with $1 million contributed by the Atlantic Foundation (of Atlantic Records) and other music-industry organizations. The foundation was designed to assist R&B artists of the forties, fifties, and sixties who had been "victims of poor business practices, bad management, and unscrupulous record companies," according to the *New York Times*. Though well-intentioned, this program hardly provided a structural solution to the impoverishment of black artists. Because African-American leaders essentially ignored the early years of black music development in the United States, others moved in and established a foothold. Even during slavery, whites were dissing black folks while simultaneously taking advantage of them with the emergence of minstrelsy. Whites couldn't ignore the creativity of blacks, and figured out "how to grow rich off of black fun," as one minstrel poseur put it.

Over the years, sniping about Jews "controlling" the music business has obscured how blacks often ignored the "cultural-capital" potential of blues, jazz, and R&B until it was too late. The same can be said about rap music. It was independent labels, primarily white-owned (e.g., Tommy Boy Records, owned by Tommy Silverman; Wild Pitch Records, owned by Stu Fine; Profile Records, owned by Corey Robbins), not Motown, that produced the initial rap acts. The major labels rushed in only when they saw the staying power of the music and the young white audience, the desired demographic, that was buying it.

In his book *Blues People*, Amiri Baraka suggests that when Harry Pace, owner of Black Swan Records, began selling recorded blues music, he was castigated by the black middle class for not selling music that was more *racially uplifting*, meaning *not* sounding like music by lower-class Negroes. When jazz began circulating through

12. Harold Cruse, *The Crisis of Negro Intellectual* (New York: Quill, 1967), p. 110.
13. *Ibid*, p. 8.

the speakeasies of America during the twenties, and via the new communication technology of the day, radio, the "big-brain" denizens of the Harlem Renaissance couldn't figure it out. As noted by Nathan Huggins in his book *Harlem Renaissance*:

> Harlem intellectuals promoted Negro art, but one thing is very curious. Except for Langston Hughes, none of them took jazz—the new music—seriously. Of course, they all mentioned it as background, as descriptive of Harlem life. All said it was important in the definition of the New Negro. But none thought enough about it to try and figure out what was happening. They tended to view it as a folk art—like the spirituals and the dance—the unrefined source for the new art. Men like James Weldon Johnson and Alain Locke expected some race genius to appear who would transform that source into high culture . . . [T]he promoters of the Harlem Renaissance were so fixed on a vision of high culture that they did not look very hard or well at jazz.[14]

The black intelligentsia of that era could no more accept the reality of its own folk culture than the white intelligentsia could accept the black basis of American culture. American society has always been *creolized*, long predating "multiculturalism." Jazz and blues music were urban and rural expressions of working-class blacks, but the black intelligentsia, trained in the aesthetics of the dominant society and unable to produce a cultural philosophy of its own, neglected this very vital art in the hope that the music would evolve in a different direction. There was certainly a market for "race music," as blacks bought five to six million records in 1925.[15] In 1926 the record business reached a peak of $128 million in sales, a mark that wasn't again attained until after the Second World War.

Another reason that the economic potential of black music was not readily considered by the established black leadership was that the organization at the forefront of agitating for black inclusion in the American way of life—the NAACP—had a policy of *non-economic liberalism*. This policy was predicated on the ridiculous notion that African-Americans need not develop their own program of economic development in a marketplace society. After all, it was thought, if blacks could actually integrate, they would have free and unfettered access to the country's economic system. The Depression of the 1930s exposed the fallacy of the NAACP's position,

14. Nathan Huggins, *Harlem Renaissance* (New York: Oxford University Press, 1971) pp. 10–11.
15. William Barlow, "Cashing In: 1900–1939," Jannette L. Dates and William Barlow, editors, *Split Image: African Americans in the Mass Media* (Washington, D.C.: Howard University Press, 1990), p. 40.

though the organization was saved from having to revamp its priorities by Franklin D. Roosevelt's New Deal.

The premier civil rights organization has never had to consider the merits of a comprehensive economic program. What passes for one today is a program centered merely around home ownership and small business development ("Home Ownership and Business Initiative"). It was W.E.B. DuBois, while still an active member of the NAACP, who pressed for an effective program ("Cooperative Commonwealth"), but he did so after having taken issue, years earlier, with Booker T. Washington's emphasis on economics over politics.

While both men were economic nationalists, DuBois criticized what he saw as the Wizard of Tuskegee's neglect of political and social issues. The irony is that both men were right: Washington's commitment to economic development could only have been strengthened by political action—DuBois's focus—given that white Americans had a history of enacting laws to limit the economic activity of slaves and freed blacks before the Civil War, and that of black entrepreneurs after 1865.[16]

Curiously, despite the legacies of such prominent black economic thinkers as Washington, DuBois, Marcus Garvey, and Elijah Muhammad, the post–civil rights, post–Black Power generation has not produced any credible economic thinkers. Conversely, black popular culture, by and large, has been gripped by a black orthodoxy that tends not to critically examine economic issues. The culture has become locked into a *110-percent-blackness* ideology, and warped by fantasies springing from Afrocentric and conspiracy-driven thinking. While the black public is vaguely aware of the relationship between African-Americans and the recording industry, it has rarely been offered a historical overview or even economic strategies to help rectify the situation. Thus, some of rap's most embarrassing vulgarities and its glorification of social pathologies are indirect payback for the black leadership's record of benign neglect of its own cultural patrimony.

There is no comprehensive historical analysis of how black music became part of a process of cultural expropriation of black culture. This informal process gave rise to the more systematic neocolonialization of black music that occurred during the industrial era of the late twentieth century, and which now feeds into today's music industry.

16. Juliet E. K. Walker, *The History of Black Business in America: Capitalism, Race, Entrepreneurship* (New York: Macmillan, 1998), pp. 72–82, 122–126, 189–191.

Worse still is a lack of knowledge about the history of black entrepreneurship in the music industry. How did blacks fare prior to Motown?

In today's world, the development, production, marketing, and distribution of popular music receives little attention from black public intellectuals, particularly those who claim to be cultural critics. Instead, Henry Louis Gates Jr., Cornel West, Michael Eric Dyson (whose recitation of rap is much stronger than his analysis of the music industry), bell hooks, and Tricia Rose seek to decipher or decode "black cultural expressivity" or "representation." Music is either praised for its spiritual or cultural affirmations with regard to black struggle, or genres such as rap are mined for analytical nuggets before academic confabs.

Analyzing black music as part of the consumption/commodification process is the hip and lazy way out for most new-jack intellectuals. Through Frankfurt School theory, black culture is squeezed into the bankrupt paradigm of "cultural studies." These intellectuals reveal minimal historical understanding of the role of black music in American culture and offer no compelling analysis of how black music undergirds the record business. Rather than exploring the nuts-and-bolts trajectory of black music through the music industry, today's intellectuals have been more interested in discussing or breaking down the high/low distinctions of culture. They are driven to "interrogate" certain "privileged discourses." Left unexamined are many critical issues, including:

- how artists are recruited
- how record companies contractually ensure maximum profits
- how much money firms actually spend on the production of an artist's CD
- how musicians lose the copyrights to their music
- the paucity of royalty payments
- the overall effects of industry monopolization by the Big Five
- the absence of health-insurance coverage for the majority of recording artists

Interestingly, it has been rappers who have most clearly articulated their keen awareness of the lopsided condition of black creativity and the lack of economic rewards. Some of these artists understand the force of nationalism and the economic potential of black music—more so than the intellectuals who accrue a living by interpreting black music and culture for white audiences. Few people expect blacks to control their own resources; they have accepted white/corporate domination as the natural order of things.

While black scholars seem to be asleep at the wheel, some whites are at least cognizant of the issue of commercialization and exploitation of music and its creators, as evidenced in the following works: *Rock and Roll is Here to Pay* by Steve Chapple and Reebee Garofalo; *Rockonomics* by Marc Eliot; *The Rise and Fall of Popular Music* by Donald Clarke; *Hit Men* by Frederic Dannen; *Stiffed* by William Knoedelseder; *American Popular Music Business in the 20th Century* by Russell Sanjek and David Sanjek; and *Mansion on a Hill* by Fred Goodman. Still, with the exception of *Rock and Roll is Here to Pay*, none of these books explores the economic exploitation of black music as a main subject. (Chapple and Garofalo's book, to their credit, has one chapter on the topic.) But at least these books contain information about and in-depth investigations of the seedy underside of the business.

In 1994, at the then-annual New Music Seminar, Public Enemy's Chuck D made an astute observation: "If we don't get up on the good foot—I'm talking to my people— then we're going to be behind the eight-ball again." Chuck D also noted that "white businesses have built themselves up and blacks are still working for the white businesses." This absence of scrutiny by black intellectuals of the political economy of black music allows hip hop to be treated as another "black problem" or something that needs to be contained through efforts by moral commissars. How the music industry is structured, and the role of blacks within it, is never openly questioned or subjected to debate or critical inquiry.

In the lexicon of some black intellectuals, musicians are considered "cultural workers"; as such, their creative endeavors are fed into the culture industry. If these artists are indeed cultural workers—and their output is no more privileged than any other form of work and is subjected to the same vicissitudes of the marketplace— then perhaps they should be organized into collective-bargaining units when facing the music industry. After all, the industry is represented by two trade associations, nationally and internationally: the Recording Industry Association of America (RIAA) and the International Federation of the Phonographic Industry (IFPI). What do rappers have? Very little—several exceptions being a fledgling watchdog group called Rap Coalition, formed in 1992, and two unions, the American Federation of Musicians (AFM) and the American Federation of Television and Radio Artists (AFTRA), both of which have been widely criticized for ignoring the needs of rap artists. Rappers are a bit like a free-floating sweatshop posse; but unlike their Third-World sisters who produce the footwear of choice, Nike, many rappers actually live large for a brief moment before disappearing from public consciousness.

In a March 1997 issue of *Newsweek*, rap was once again blamed for the ills of black America. But in the report, the white-controlled industry was nowhere to be found, nor were the white youths who buy sixty-six percent of rap music. As critic Leslie Fiedler observed, "Born theoretically white, we are permitted to pass our childhood as imaginary Indians, our adolescence as imaginary Negroes, and only then are expected to settle down to being what we are told we really are: white once more."[17]

Then there's the rebellion factor, also known as commodifying dissent. "People resonate with the strong anti-oppression messages of rap, and the alienation of blacks," said Ivan Juzang of Motivational Educational Entertainment, in *American Demographic* magazine. "All young people buy into the rebellion in general, as part of rebelling against parental authority." On the one hand, this amounts to a sort of vicarious emotional pimping for whites. Blacks serve as the "other," who are allowed to "act out," since they are beyond the bounds of "civilization." Marketers who want to appeal to white teenagers often start with the black community, targeting the inner city before moving on to the black middle class. Says Juzang: "If [marketers] develop the hardest-core element, we reach middle-class blacks and then there's a ripple effect. If you don't target the hard-core, you don't get the suburbs."[18] In other words, blacks are unwitting trendsetters, whose tastes and talents are observed, detailed, and crunched as marketing points to music and fashion companies, a phenomenon aptly described by Malcolm Galdwell in his article "The Coolhunt" in a March 1997 issue of the *New Yorker.*

This marketing strategy has some particularly nasty ramifications. Black creation (music, fashion, "attitude") is taken up as a style by whites, "wiggas," who have accessed it through an intermediary source—rappers and music videos. This purchased "style" has the desired effect of boosting record sales. To some degree, the success of rap and hip hop culture represents a pervasive hollowing out of black culture itself. The urban folkways, musical expressions, and various styles of African-Americans have become grist for music, fashion, and media markets. Marketers know

17. Leslie A. Fiedler, *Waiting for the End* (New York: Stein and Day, 1964), p. 134.
18. Mark Spiegler, "Marketing Street Culture: Bringing Hip Hop Style to the Mainstream," *American Demographic*, November 1996, pp.28–34.

that if black kids—the naïve-but-sophisticated urban authenticators of postmodern American taste—can be induced to consume massive quanities of whatever is being sold, they, the marketers, can once again attract demographically desirable young whites to follow suit. To a certain degree, blacks have become the "accessorized other," whose culture, through commodification, can be sampled and discarded, or used as a reference point for authentification. Even more pervasive is the economic incentive for young blacks to act and perform in ways that conform to white buyers' concept of "blackness." Rap music is supposed to be *about* "blackness," as argued by some rappers, yet still plays into to a market-based expectation or interpretation of the term. Jay-Z's niggatude in "Izzo (H.O.V.A.)" offers an example of the kind of thrill no real wigga can resist:

> *Holla at me . . .*
> *I do this for my culture*
> *To let 'em know what a nigga look like*
> *When a nigga in a roaster*
> *Show 'em how to move in a room full of vultures*
> *Industry shady it need to be taken over*
> *Label owners hate me I'm raisin' the status quo up . . .*

And Jay-Z, according to Kelefa Sanneh in the *New Yorker's* August 2001 music issue, is the "greatest of the corporate rappers."

* * *

Since the days when illiterate blues musicians were robbed of their royalties and publishing rights, black leaders have been virtually silent on the music industry's dubious business practices. It is much easier for the Reverend Jesse Jackson to complain about blacks not getting enough Academy Award nominations, or for Kweisi Mfume to address minority underrespresentation on television, than it is to systematically take the music industry to task.

With the NAACP reconsidering the efficacy of busing and other remedies to segregation, the whole policy of integration now appears to be faltering—due to the simple fact that black leaders rushed into the arena without adequately considering the economic consequences of integration. African-American leaders failed to develop a coherent plan to build a black economic base; integration was to be the salvation of blacks, especially the poor. The Bureau of Labor's 1999 statistics show blacks representing a $360-billion segment of the US economy, but that money, spent by black consumers, is largely directed toward and circulated into the dominant economy, not into African-American communities. Now, with the slow chipping away of affirmative-action programs and minority set-asides, blacks are beginning to think, "*Uh-oh . . .*"

W.E.B. DuBois once proposed that blacks strategically engage in self-segregation— in order to tackle certain problems that society would not voluntarily address in the black community—and then *re-integrate* into the majority society from a position of strength. He argued in *Dusk of Dawn* that a black economy was not yet complete but was nonetheless critical to the development of black communities:

> It is quite possible that it could never cover more than the smaller part of the economic activities of Negroes. Nevertheless, it is also possible that this *smaller part could be so important and wield so much power* that its influence upon the total economy of Negroes and the total industrial organization of the United States would be decisive for the great ends toward which the Negro moves.[19] [emphasis added]

This essay contends that the "smaller part" that could wield so much power and influence is, in fact, black music. However, given a historical combination of factors— racism, black leadership indifference, economic and legal barriers—black music is now an essential and integral piece in a corporate structure that is primarily owned and operated by whites for the benefit of white shareholders. Understanding this particular set of circumstances has not been high on the list of black intellectuals who have been schooled in the likes of Foucault, Derrida, and Lacan. "Foreigners who have not studied economics but have studied Negroes," observed Carter G. Woodson, "take up this business and grow rich."[20] This observation invariably leads into a discussion about the "black economy," which is now a moot point. Granted, there have always been major structural impediments for blacks in business generally, and in the music

---

19. W.E.B. DuBois, *Dusk of Dawn: An Essay Toward an Autobiography of Race* (New Brunswick: Transaction Publishers, 1995), p. 198.
20. Carter G. Woodson, *The Mis-Education of the Negro* (Washington: The Associated Publishers [1933] 1969), p. 5.

business specifically: lack of credit, undercapitalization, poor distribution, inability to advertise, and white opposition. Intellectuals have often scoffed at the possibility of a so-called black economy, but, as Cruse has written:

> The black economy is a myth only because a *truly viable* black economy does not exist. It does not exist simply because Negroes as a group never came together to create one, which does not mean that it would be a simple matter to create a black economy. But it could be done—with the aid of attributes the Negro has never developed, i.e., discipline, self-denial, cooperative organization, and knowledge of economic science.[21] [original emphasis]

But the development of a black economy, as Cruse further argues, would take a:

> [c]ertain community point of view, a conditioned climate, in order to exert impact (political, economic, and cultural) on the white economy. It means the studied creation of new economic forms—a new institutionalism, one that can intelligently blend privately owned, collectively owned, and cooperatively owned, as well as state-sponsored, economic organizations. It means mobilizing the ghetto populations and organizing them through education and persuasion (if not through authoritarian measures from above).[22]

Consequently, black leaders have never been able to educate black talent about protecting their rights as musicians and artists, about earning a living from their crafts. If black music had been nurtured and understood as a source of cultural pride and cultural capital, African-Americans would have been able to more fully develop an entrepreneurial class of artists, businessmen and women, lawyers, and accountants, creating and supporting their own institutions. Today's black leadership has difficulty relating to those who are now the engines of a $1.8-billion genre in a multi-billion-dollar industry. Such an estrangement is a self-inflicted cultural, political, and economic dead-end road. African-American leaders have bought into a whole set of assumptions about blacks based on white beliefs and the corporate-American rules of the game.

In other words, black music could have been used to help build a reasonably self-sufficient artistic- and middle-class that would have been unafraid to express its own

---

21. Cruse, *The Crisis of the Negro Intellectual*, p. 310.
22. *Ibid*, p. 314.

nationalism and build some level of group economic strength on the talent of its own people. Such a development would have entailed educating black workers and artists about how they are deeply enmeshed in a specific economic system, one that they have to deal with—and *should* do so by organizing on their own terms and interests, rather than focusing solely on racial solidarity. Blacks, like the Jews who played key roles in the creation of Hollywood, could have had "an empire of their own," as Neal Gabler argues in his aptly titled book. African-American music could have been the force behind a black-led music industry with all the necessary contradictions of capital and labor. Despite the vision proferred by hip hop architect Russell Simmons in the statement that opened this essay, blacks remain glorified and underpaid employees in American Culture, Inc.

Norman Kelley is the author of three "politique noir" thrillers featuring Nina Halligan: *Black Heat* (Amistad/ HarperCollins), *The Big Mango* (Akashic Books), and *A Phat Death* (Amistad/HarperCollins; forthcoming in 2003). A former producer at WBAI radio, he has written for *The Black Star News, New Politics, The Bedford Stuyvesant Current*, Word.com, *Newsday*, and *New York Press*. He was also a contributing writer to *Gig: Americans Talk about their Jobs at the Turn of the Millennium* (Random House). An earlier version of this article appeared in *Black Renaissance/Noir* (Summer 1999) and *Doula* (Winter 2001) under the title "Rhythm Nation."

Papa's Got a Brand-New Bag: Big Music's Post-Fordist Regime and the Role of Independent Music Labels
BY MICHAEL ROBERTS

Introduction

There is a commonly held notion in the record industry—much the same as in the film industry—that the most creative artistic work takes place at the margins of the industry, a place occupied by relatively small production companies that are understood to be *separate* from the larger companies. According to this view, it has become the role of small, "independent" record companies (also called "indies") to provide the entertainment industry with new, cutting-edge aesthetics.[1] The independents, unlike the "Big Five" record labels (also known as the "majors"; see chart on pages 34–35), are able to produce novel sounds and interesting music because they are free from the marketing juggernaut that propels the music produced by the mainstream industry.[2] The majors will embrace any formula that sells records until it stops working. As a result, the corporate machine cannot deliver an adequate diversity of sounds, only a homogenized, prepackaged product. The indies, on the other hand, are known for their "legitimate" musicians who care about the artistic quality of their product, rather than its "exchange value" or its appeal to a mass audience of mostly teenage consumers. Consequently, the indies are often seen as a collective form of resistance to the corporate regime that dominates the record industry and the entertainment industry as a whole. The indies, so the story goes, represent a collective refusal to "sell out," a refusal to allow the marketing wizards of the corporate establishment to reduce their art to mass-produced commodities void of any compelling aesthetic value.

1. See for example, Rick Kennedy and Randy McNutt, *Little Labels, Big Sound* (Indiana Press, 1999). See also the numerous special issues published each year by *Billboard* that are dedicated to the smaller, "indie" record labels.
2. The "Big Five" refers to the five multinational corporate conglomerates that dominate the recording industry. Technically, the term "major" refers to a record company that owns its own manufacturing plants, distribution outlets, and recording studios. Major record companies usually have their own publishing companies as well as marketing and A&R (Artist and Repertoire) departments. All of the major record labels in the sixties—Columbia, RCA, Decca, Capitol, MGM, and Mercury—have been purchased and swallowed up by giant corporate conglomerates. Today's five corporate conglomerates are Sony, AOL Time Warner, Vivendi/Universal, Bertelsmann AG, and EMI. It was rumored last year that the Big Five would soon become the Big Four as both Bertelsmann and AOL Time Warner were looking to merge with EMI. That merger, however, collapsed due to speculation that the European Commission would reject the joint venture over concerns about AOL Time Warner controlling too much of the online music distribution channels (see *Billboard* [October 5, 2000]).

It has also been pointed out that some of the actual content of indie records (CDs) is an explicit critique of the cultural/economic status quo in the US. You don't have to look far to find an indie record that criticizes the racist, sexist, capitalist establishment in the United States. When indie record labels begin to sell lots of CDs—as is the case with punk and "grunge" rock, as well as with rap, hip hop music, and, to a lesser extent, blues and jazz—it is seen as a fortunate turn of events that the mass audience has developed an ear for "alternative" music. Indie labels are known for allowing musicians to have more control over the creative process, and royalty deals are often better than those offered by the majors. Unlike at major labels, where the musician is a small cog in a giant machine, where decisions about the music's content are made in faraway places, musicians at independent labels can often work closely with those who manage the label.

Nobody can deny that the recording industry has been taken over by a corporate regime—large conglomerates controlling approximately ninety percent of US market share in an industry with annual revenues of more than $14 billion dollars. And few would claim that it's a good thing that a corporation known primarily as a producer of liquor (Seagram, which itself is now owned by the French utilities, media, and telecom company Vivendi) controls twenty percent of the market for CDs.[3] The high rate of profit generated per CD adds to the questionable moral status of the corporations that rule over the industry. According to various sources, it costs about $3.50 to manufacture and distribute a CD,[4] which allows for a healthy profit margin on a product that retails for around $15. In short, the music business represents an enormous cash cow for the conglomerates. The annual earnings (profits, not revenues) of the major record-label groups are mind-boggling. Universal Music Group (UMG includes the MCA, Mercury, Motown, A&M, Island, Def Jam, Interscope, and Geffen labels), the largest music company in the world, now owned by Vivendi, had "earnings" of over $1 billion last year.[5] UMG was the first major record label to post profits over $1 billion, but the other label groups, Warner Music Group (WMG), Sony Music, Electrical and Musical Industries (EMI), and Bertelsmann Music Group (BMG), aren't far behind. Each of these has an

3. Sales in the global market for recorded music have reached $38.5 billion. These figures are based on data published by the Recording Industry Association of America (RIAA) and *Billboard*.
4. See Geoffrey Hull, *The Recording Industry* (Boston: Allyn and Bacon, 1999), Michael Fink, *Inside the Music Industry* (New York: Schirmer Books, 1996), and Donald S. Passman, *All You Need to Know About the Music Business* (New York: Simon and Schuster, 1998).
5. In contrast to earnings or profits, UMG's revenues last year topped $6 billion. See *Billboard* (August 26, 2000 and June 15, 2000).

annual operating revenue hovering around $6 billion.[6] Such a staggering level of market concentration in just a handful of firms makes it very difficult for new sounds to be heard. In sum, there are good reasons to question the corporate control of the recording industry.

Nevertheless, the role of independent labels in the music industry is more complex—and less uniformly positive—than it might seem at first glance. Ironically, the indies, through their active contribution to a "post-industrial" pattern of production, have actually weakened the role of many professional musicans working in the industry. After all, it is precisely this group of labels that are considered to be "radical," or "outside the corporate establishment," that play an integral role in the corporate strategy to outsource production. When musicians sign a contract with an indie label, they are possibly undermining the organization that was formed to protect their interests and their rights, the American Federation of Musicians (AFM), the union that represents professional musicians in the US and Canada. Most of the indie labels do not have labor agreements (contracts) with the AFM, so whenever a musician works for an indie label, she or he is essentially working as a scab, because these labels don't pay union-scale wages and don't contribute royalty payments to the union. In many cases, musicians at the indie labels don't realize they are working as scabs, and union musicians, for their part, often can't keep up with the changing structure of the music recording industry that encourages scabbing.

The indies are a key ingredient in the post-Fordist, post-industrial production patterns that have emerged in the music recording industry. The shift to this form of production is the hallmark of the so-called "new economy," dating back to the early 1970s. According to one school of thought, "post-industrialism" refers to the decline of the manufacturing sectors of the US economy, with less and less material goods produced here in the US as companies search for cheaper labor across the border. But dispersed production occurs within the US also, as companies move from north to south, where labor costs are cheaper due to the low rates of unionization among workers in the Southern states. Post-industrialism also refers to a declining commitment by the federal government to support unions and workers' rights. Ever since the Reagan administration, the government has abandoned the idea that unions are necessary partners in the quest for industrial stability and amicable labor relations among

6. These figures can be found in the *Annual Report 2000* for each of the corporations.

employers and employees. "Post-Fordism" refers to the vertical disintegration of corporations and market specialization, along with the progressive decline in mass production and mass consumption. Henry Ford's idea of centralized production and wage-led economic growth no longer has the same influence over economists and policymakers that it once did. Unlike the Fordist model, in which unions are seen as vital to the economy because they raise wage levels, increase the purchasing power of consumers, and therefore aggregate demand, unions today are viewed as a drag on the economy.

The new economy does not bode well for unionized workers, and workers in general, including professional musicians. In the music recording industry, sales are not down as much as in other industries, but for professional musicians, the shift in production patterns is just as detrimental as it is for workers in other industries. The post-Fordist model almost invariably translates into poorer working conditions and less pay.

In essence, the majors are using the indies as subcontractors to cut back on production costs, principally labor costs, a strategy that mimics a widespread pattern of farming out production that cuts across almost every industry in the United States. As with other industries, most of the subcontracting companies in the recording industry use non-union workers—in this case, musicians—and just as in other industries, the subcontracting music companies do not honor terms and conditions required by the union's labor contract, which is held by the larger contracting company. When a record company signs a labor agreement or labor contract with the American Federation of Musicians, it is referred to as a "signatory" company. The AFM has three contracts with the major labels that it uses to regulate wages and working conditions throughout the industry. The first contract is the Phonograph Record Labor Agreement, which regulates wage scales and health and pension funds for AFM members. The other two contracts are the Phonograph Record Trust Agreement and the Special Payments Fund, both of which raise monies to be used for AFM members and for free public concerts.

According to a well-known industry lawyer, "All of the majors are signatories, whereas most independent record companies are not."[7] As the market share of the indie labels increases as a result of major-label outsourcing of production, the number of non-signatory labels rises in proportion to the signatory ones. The AFM

7. This quote above is from Lawrence J. Blake, and can be found in *The Musician's Business and Legal Guide*, compiled and edited by Mark Holloran, Esq. (Prentice-Hall, NJ: 1996).

contracts are intended to protect both royalty musicians (those who earn money from a small percentage of record sales) and session musicians (the musicians who make a living playing as "extras" in the recording studios). In addition to creating the conditions for the erosion or reduction of pay scales for musicians, the increasing use of the indies by the majors is draining money from two of the union's funds, the Music Performance Trust Fund and the Special Payments Fund. Union avoidance is made possible by US labor law, which states that a corporation with a labor contract can outsource or transfer some of its operations to another company without being legally obligated to ensure that the other, usually smaller company enforces the conditions and terms of the labor contract. US labor law even allows for a union signatory company to own as much as fifty percent of another company and not be obligated to ensure that the subsidiary honors the terms of the labor agreements.[8] In other industries, it's clear that corporate subcontracting and outsourcing is an assault on organized union labor. In the record industry, however, it can be difficult to find out just how indie labels are connected to the majors, and the collective representation of the indies as "anti-establishment" blurs their role as non-union subcontractors.

At the point of *consumption*, it may seem like the "independent" record labels are part of an anti-corporate project, but at the point of *production*, the indies are often indirectly part of a reactionary, "pro-establishment" project. Indeed, this is part of the problem for analysis: Music is usually understood as an object of consumption rather than an object that is *produced*. Trade journalists, academics, and rock critics alike often view music as it's consumed, and as a result, music is rarely framed as a question of labor.[9] In the following pages, I will examine the music industry as a problem of and for labor, and further reveal how the recording industry is beginning a transition to a "post-industrial" or "post-Fordist" pattern of production, the hallmark of which is the corporate attack on unions. These shifts in the greater American economy are largely responsible for the widespread decline in real wages

8. These conditions were first written into law with the passage of the Taft-Hartley Act in 1947, and subsequent case law.
9. The trade journals are dominated by the perspectives of the majors, and most of the information that you can get from sources such as *Billboard* deal with sales data and marketing news. In academia, analyses of music are of two types: musicological and sociological. The former focuses on the "high culture" aesthetic, and the latter on the relationship of popular music to youth culture. Beginning in the early sixties, the consumption of rock music among deviant youths became a favorite object of analysis for sociologists. In the various circles of rock-music criticism, the spotlight is on the content of the songs, and how much or how little that content represents some kind of resistance to the cultural status quo. In all these forms of criticism, labor is an absent variable, a gaping blind spot in what are sometimes astute analyses.

for the average working person, as well as for the erosion of workplace safety regulations and vacation time.[10]

Profiles of Professional Musicians in the United States

Professional musicians, as a group, occupy a relatively small place in the occupational grid of workers nationwide. According to the US Department of Labor's Bureau of Labor Statistics, there were approximately 273,000 jobs held by professional musicians in 1999. Of that group, slightly over two out of every five were self-employed. Due to the nature of the business, however, most musicians have to find other jobs to supplement the income they make from playing music. Regular paying gigs are hard to come by, as most musicians scrape by on the occasional engagements they are able to find. Roughly three-quarters of professional musicians have part-time schedules. Many professional musicians are forced to accept full-time employment in different occupations in order to make ends meet. In the words of the Bureau, "intermittent unemployment" is common among professional musicians. They work in a variety of settings, including restaurants, nightclubs, weddings, theaters, parades, musicals, operas, orchestras, and, of course, in the recording industry, which is concentrated in New York, Los Angeles, and Nashville. The median annual income for a professional musician in 1998 was around $30,000. The most successful musicians earn far more than the median, while those who find only part-time employment earn less. If a musician is lucky enough to get a steady job in an orchestra, the annual salary can reach $95,000. Another stable source of work that musicians find is as session players in studio recordings. The most successful musicians in the recording industry are the relatively small number of royalty musicians who can make big money if they are lucky enough to have a hit record. While union density (the percentage of all US workers that are members of unions) nationwide has dropped precipitously from a high of thirty-three percent in the late 1960s to just over fourteen percent today,

10. The nationwide trend in declining wages, which began in 1973, continues today despite several years of sustained economic growth. In the midst of robust economic growth that began in 1994, wages for the bottom sixty percent of income earners declined steadily from 1989 through 1998. Wages for the median worker in the US were 3.1 percent less in 1998 than in 1989, after adjusting for inflation. If you look further back to 1973, you'll find that the average working American earns twenty percent less today, after adjusting for inflation. To make matters worse, working hours have increased and vacation time has dwindled to the lowest numbers since the Depression. Since 1969, the average American family has added six weeks to the working year. Many analysts have attributed these numbers to the corporate attack upon labor unions and the declining number of rank-and-file union members nationwide. See Lawrence Mishel, Jared Bernstein, and John Schmitt, *The State of Working America*; Stanley Aronowitz and Jonathan Cutler, *Post-Work*; and Juliet Schor, *The Overworked American*.

musicians have been able to hold the ranks. The AFM today has 150,000 members, which is over half of all professional musicians in the US, and AFM members have a long tenure. Almost seventy-nine percent of AFM members stay in the union between ten and fifty years. Among the members of the AFM, 43.4 percent find work as casual or part-time workers at one-time events, primarily weddings. The second largest segment of AFM members, 32.8 percent, work in symphony orchestras. Musicians working in clubs and lounges make up 20.4 percent of membership, and musicians in theaters, on tour in traveling bands, and working as arrangers/copyists make up 7.8 percent, 9.0 percent, and 4.6 percent, respectively. AFM members who work in the recording industry are the fourth-largest group, consisting of 14.3 percent of the membership. The remaining 17 percent are categorized as "other" by the AFM. Women account for only 21.2 percent of AFM membership.

While the union density among musicians is relatively high, most union musicians work in places that do not fall under a collective-bargaining agreement. Fully seventy-seven percent of AFM members work for employers that do not have labor agreements (contracts) with the union. Thus, the majority of professional musicians in the US do not enjoy the protection and benefits that a union contract affords. The shift to a post-Fordist production system in the recording industry is one of the main reasons why many musicians, union and non-union alike, work under conditions that are not protected by union contracts.

High union density also suggests solidarity among musicians. However, due to the structure of the industry, two classes of recording artists have emerged that do not always act in unison. In a typical session, two types of musicians participate in making a record: royalty musicians, who consist of the name band (like the members of rock band R.E.M.), which is the principle act that signs with the label; and side or session musicians (the extras who might help R.E.M. by playing extra instruments during recording sessions), who are paid wages during the recording. Royalty musicians are given a share of the profit from the sale of their records, which is usually a small percentage. Big-name bands and individual artists who make hit records can enjoy huge incomes from their royalties, and because they are so popular, they don't generally need the protection of the union. Their popularity usually guarantees sweetheart contracts with relatively high royalty rates. Side musicians typically don't receive royalties and have to make a living off of the wages they earn playing "extra" instruments during recording sessions. Thus, the structure of the recording contract creates two classes of musicians who derive income from different places, even though both groups are likely to be members of the AFM. The development of two classes of musicians matured with the explosion of pop music after the Second World War, when teenage consumers first launched the record business into the stratosphere. Beginning in the 1950s, the rise in popularity of new music genres like rhythm & blues, rock and roll, and country music coincided with dispersed production, as the majors devised new relationships with independent labels in order to capture market shares in the new genres. There was a whole new set of musicians that needed to be organized, and more and more royalty artists were signing contracts with independents that were yet to be brought into the union. As we have seen, this problem still exists today. One of the best examples of the post-Fordist production arrangement in the music business is the relationship of Bertelsmann Music Group (BMG) and the Zomba Group of Companies, a case that will be examined in detail below.

The Music Industry's Shift from Production to Post-Production

While social scientists and media personalities have focused our attention on the negative effects of these new economic arrangements in the blue-collar, manufacturing sector—declining wages, loss of job security, shrinking union density, etc.—little attention has been given to the entertainment industry and the recording industry, in particular. Upon closer analysis, the mega-corporations that dominate the recording industry—AOL Time Warner, Bertelsmann AG, Universal (UMG), Sony, and EMI—have followed the lead of corporations in other industries like auto, steel, textile, aerospace, and electronics in a general pursuit of the post-industrial, anti-union economic agenda. Production in the new economy has become more and more dispersed even as the numbers of companies that dominate the economy become fewer and fewer. According to Bennett Harrison, author of *Lean and Mean: The Changing Landscape of Corporate Power in the Age of Flexibility,* "The empirical evidence seems overwhelming that the evolving global system of joint ventures, supply chains, and strategic alliances in no sense constitutes a reversal—let alone negation—of the two-hundred-year-old tendency toward concentrated *control* within industrial capitalism, even if the *productive* activity is increasingly being decentralized and dispersed" (p.171). In the new economy, concentration of corporate power and corporate hegemony over the economy is achieved through the monopolistic control of information systems, and through the manipulation of finance capital and the establishment of new ownership patterns via mergers and joint ventures. The direct control over the means of production is no longer the key element in corporate power as it was in the nineteenth- and twentieth-century industrial capitalist regimes of accumulation. In the post-Fordist regime, production is dispersed among smaller companies who serve as subcontractors as the mega-corporations lock up control over distribution—what Harrison calls "supply chains"—and over the flow of finance capital and information. What seems odd in this new arrangement is that the further the corporations move away from production, the more concentrated their power over the economy becomes. Another oddity in the new economy is the phenomenon of "going back to the future." As the mega-corporations gain power and become multinational entities, their power across the globe begins to eclipse that of the nation-state, taking us back to an arrangement of power that resembles feudalism. As the nation-state loses power, unions are left in an environment void of institutional support that was once provided by the federal government. In the industrial period, economic stability was achieved through the tripartite cooperation between labor, capital, and the government. In the post-industrial period, the captains of industry no longer seek the cooperation of unions—quite the opposite— and unions can no longer count on the government's support.

In the recording industry, the growing number of joint ventures, pressing and distributions deals, equity deals, production company contracts, and distribution deals between independent and major labels (and between independent and major *distributors*) is a good example of the increasing industry control and concentration of power among a small number of corporations at the top, coupled with dispersed production among many smaller labels at the bottom of the industry. The increasing market share of indies thereby translates into decreasing bargaining power of professional musicians and their organization.

The Changing Structure of the Recording Industry

In its earliest years, from 1901–1922, the industry was dominated by three firms: The Edison Phonograph Company, the Victor Talking Machine Company, and the Columbia Graphophone Company (later to become known simply as Columbia). These companies held a tight oligopoly on the industry until the Depression, when Edison went bankrupt. In the 1930s the names of the players changed, while the industry structure changed only slightly. The industry was still dominated by only three firms: Columbia, RCA Victor, and Decca Records. In 1929 the Radio Corporation of America (RCA)—a holding company controlled by General Electric, AT&T, Westinghouse, and the US government—bought the Victor Talking Machine Company and formed RCA Victor. RCA also formed a radio network, the National Broadcasting Company (NBC). CBS Radio was formed in 1928 when Arthur Judson left NBC to form a rival network, United Independent Broadcasters (which was subsequently reorganized as CBS). Eager to remain competitive with RCA, CBS purchased the American Record Company–Brunswick Record Company in 1938, which launched the Columbia label. Decca was formed in 1934 when the president of British Decca, E.R. Lewis, bought Brunswick from Warner Brothers.[11] Lewis used the catalogue from Brunswick to establish American Decca, later to be known solely as Decca. Decca put pressure on the other two majors by slashing record prices from seventy-five cents to thirty-five cents, and by becoming the first major to agree to terms set by the AFM, thereby ending a union strike. By signing with the union, Decca was able to outmaneuver RCA Victor and Columbia, who were still holding out against the AFM. These three firms enjoyed control over the record industry until the late 1940s, establishing the industry standard—not because they sold the most records, but because each one owned and operated their own production studios, manufacturing plants, and distribution outlets.

In the period between 1948–55, a fourth firm came to prominence in the industry. Capitol Records was formed in 1942 by two songwriters, Johnny Mercer and Buddy De Sylva, and a record retailer, Glenn Wallichs. But Capitol didn't hit it big until the early 1950s, when Frank Sinatra recorded thirteen top-five albums for the label. (Sinatra would later form his own label, Reprise Records, which also became part of Warner in the early seventies; in 1993 and 1994, he re-signed to Capitol for his two albums of duets.) In 1955 the British company EMI bought a controlling interest in Capitol that remains to this day. In this period, the major companies dominated the industry via a classical model of monopolistic vertical integration, controlling everything from artistic factors like songwriting and recording to business factors like publishing, manufacturing, marketing, merchandising, and distribution. Performers,

11. The Brunswick label in America was founded in 1916 by the piano-manufacturing company, Brunswick-Balke-Collender. It was purchased by Warner Brothers Pictures in 1930.

THE BIG

AOL Time Warner

Yr. 2000 Warner Music revenues: $4.2 billion.
Total corporate revenues: $36.2 billion.

4 AD
Antone's$~
Aquemini*$~
Asylum
Atlantic Records
Big Beat
Blackbird$~
Blitzz$~
Celtic Heartbeat~
Che~
Curb
Desert Storm*$~
Discovery
East West American
Elektra
Elementree$~
Fishkin$~
Flavor Unit*$~
Giant
Igloo~
John Dough
Kinetic$
Lava
Luaka Bop$
Mammoth$~
Maverick$
Nonesuch
Pyramid~
Qwest~
Reprise
Resound
Rhino$~
Sire
Slash
Sub Pop$~
The Music Label$~
Tommy Boy*$~
Top Dog*$~
Warner Brothers Records
Warner/Chappell Music Inc.

Vivendi/Universal

Yr. 2000 Universal Music Group revenues: $5 billion.
Total corporate revenues: $41.8 billion.

40 Acres and a Mule
A&M Records
Abkco Records
Aftermath*$
Almo
Antilles
Attic
Bloodline*$~
Blue
Capricorn
Cargo
CGI~
Cherry Entertainment$~
Chronicles
City of Angels$~
Decca
Def Jam*
Def Squad*$~
Deutsche Gramm.
DreamWorks
Eleven$~
Flawless*$~
Flip*~
Flyte Time$~
Fort Apache
Geffen Records
GTSP$~
H.O.L.A. Records$~
Hollywood Records
House of Blues
Imaginary Records~
Impact$
Interscope
Island Records
Kedar Entertainment$
L'Oiseau
Lil' Man*~
Load$~
Mammoth$~

Margaritaville Records
MCA
Mercury
Mercury Nashville
Mercury/Curb*
MoJazz
Mojo$
Motown
Murder Inc.*$~
Narada
Nothing Records
Outpost$
Pallas$~
Philips Classics
Point Music
Polygram Latino
Pure
Radio Active$
Rebound
Rising Tide Entertainment
River North
Roadrunner$~
Roc-a-fella*$
Scratchie~
SpunOut*$~
Step Sun
The Label*$~
Timbaland's Beat Club*$~
Track Factory~
Trauma
Triloka
True North
Twism
Twisted$~
Underworld*$~
Universal Music
Uptown
Verve Group
Wing

Following is a breakdown of some of the record labels partially or fully owned by the five international conglomerates that control ninety percent of the music industry. This chart is only a brief sketch; it does not include the many record companies distributed through the Big Five (but not necessarily owned by one of them).

Bertelsmann Music Group (BMG)
Yr. 2000 BMG Music revenues: $2.2 billion.
Total corporate revenues: $7.5 billion.

Arista Records
Bad Boy Records*$
BMG Classics/RCA Victor
BMG U.S. Latin
Flipmode*$~
J Records$
LaFace Records*$
Melisma Records$~
RCA Music Group
RLG Record Label Group Nashville
Time Bomb Records$
Wicklow Records$
Windham Hill Group$
Wyclef Records*$~
Zomba Group (eighteen labels)$~

EMI Distribution
Yr. 2000 EMI Music revenues: $3.3 billion.
Total corporate revenues: $3.9 billion.

Angel Records
Anise~
Blue Moon
Blue Note
Capitol Records
Doggystyle Records*$~
EMI Christian~
EMI Latin~
EMI Records
Ensign$~
Global Pacific
I.R.S. Records
Java~
Jobete Music$~
Manhattan~
Mesa
Netwerk
Pangaea
Priority*$~
Roswell$~
Virgin Records

Sony Music
Yr. 2000 Sony Music revenues: $6.4 billion.
Total corporate revenues: $63 billion.

550 Music
American Recordings*$~
Aware*
Big Cat~
C2
Caviant
Chaos~
Columbia B'way Masterworks
Columbia Nashville
Columbia Records
Crave$~
Creation~
Crescent Moon$~
Epic Records
Essential Classics
Facility
Flip$
Foodchain
Great Performances
Hall of Fame*$
Higher Ground
Hoppoh
Immortal$~
Independiente~
Jersey$~
Legacy
Lifestyle~
Loud*$~
Lucky Dog
Masterworks Heritage

MJJ~
Mosh~
Myrra~
New Deal~
Okeh
Ovum*$~
Roc-A-Block/Ruffhouse
Ruffhouse*$~
Ruthless*$~
SEON
Skint*$~
Slam Jamz
So So Def*$~
Sony Classical
Sony Discos
Sony Latin~
Sony Records
Sony Square~
Sony Tropical~
Sony Wonder
Soundtrax~
Stone Creek~
Trackmasters~
Tri-Star Music~
Undertainment*$~
Vivarte
Word*~
Work
Yab-Yum*$~

LEGEND

* Indicates a label focusing primarily on hip hop

$ Indicates a joint venture/equity deal

~ Indicates a non-union-signatory label

writers, producers, engineers, publishers, and the staff in charge of marketing and distribution often worked under the same roof.

In the 1950s, however, as radio stations began to target specialized markets, a growing number of independent labels started to challenge the power of the majors. The breakup of radio from one large national market into discrete local markets forced the majors to compete with independents that were producing two new genres of music: rhythm & blues and rock and roll. Labels in Los Angeles like Aladdin, Specialty, and Imperial recorded such artists as Fats Domino, Shirley and Lee, and Little Richard. Chicago's Chess Records signed Chuck Berry and Bo Diddley. Sun Records in Memphis introduced Elvis. As a genre, rock and roll jumped from 15.7 percent of the market in 1955 to 42.7 percent in 1959.[12] As a result of the popularity of rock and roll, sales industry-wide grew from $213 million in 1954 to $603 million by 1959. From 1948 to 1955, the number of firms (as opposed to labels, since many labels can be owned by single firm) that posted hits in the Top 10 ranged from four to seven. But from '56 to '59, this number rose to twenty-nine. For a brief time span, the majors lost half of their market share to independent labels.[13]

The majors responded to the competition by absorbing the successful independent labels in a wave of consolidation beginning in the 1960s. The number of firms recording singles in *Billboard*'s Top 100 dropped from a high of forty in 1960 to just twenty by 1971. Thus, while many different *label* names appeared on the charts, the number of *firms* was quite small. The period beginning in the mid-sixties was the first wave of consolidation and mergers, and led to mega-mergers, such as that of Warner Brothers, Elektra, and Atlantic into WEA Inc.; and PolyGram's acquisition of Mercury Records and Island Records. In 1979 RCA began distributing A&M Records, and United Artists merged with Capitol. RCA moved on independent labels again in 1983 when it acquired part of Arista from its competitor, Ariola. (By 1987, RCA/Ariola and Arista were under the BMG umbrella.) CBS and MCA were also busy in 1983; EMI bought an interest in Chrysalis Records, and PolyGram acquired the giant of indies, Motown Records.

The second wave of industry consolidation began in the late 1980s, as multinational conglomerates like Sony (Japan), the Seagram Company (Canada), Bertelsmann AG (Germany), and Time Warner took control. Sony acquired CBS

---

12. See Reebee Garofalo, *Rockin' Out: Popular Music in the U.S.A.* (Boston: Allyn and Bacon, 1997), p.152.
13. See Peterson and Berger, "Cycles in Symbol Production," in *On Record: Rock, Pop, and the Written Word,* edited by Simon Frith and Andrew Goodwin (New York and London: Routledge, 1990).

Records and its sublabels for $2 billion in 1988, Geffen was purchased by MCA for ten million shares of stock (worth $540 million) in 1990, and in 1992 Virgin was bought for $960 million by EMI and BMG acquired Arista and RCA.[14] The biggest merger to date occurred in 1998 when the Seagram Company acquired PolyGram and named the new label super-group UMG (Universal Music Group). The Seagram Company was later bought by Vivendi.

The Independent Labels' Role in the Post-Production of Music

Today, unlike a few decades ago when the majors competed directly with the independents, absorbing them when they became successful, the majors cooperate with the independents, pursuing "joint ventures," or equity deals, partial ownership, and distribution deals.[15] These arrangements indicate union avoidance; according to labor law, if an independent label is less than half-owned by a major, the major is not responsible for enforcing the terms of its labor agreements. Similarly, if a major label *distributes* a non-union, non-signatory label, it is not required to enforce the terms of the Phonograph Record Labor Agreement. In the past few decades, as the majors were absorbed into huge multinational corporations, they simultaneously developed novel production and distribution arrangements with independent labels that were garnering increasing shares of the market due to the popularity of rap/hip hop and alternative rock.

Outlined here are five types of arrangements between major labels and independents that to varying degrees threaten to undermine the leverage of union musicians. First, the major label will create a spin-off label and send it through both the major and independent distribution networks, with the new label referring to itself as an independent, even though it is entirely owned by the major. Sony's label 550 Music (Celine Dion) is an example. In most of these cases, the spin-off (or imprint) is a union label and remains true to guidelines established by the AFM. Second, a major label will buy part of an existing and successful indie label but will send the records exclusively through independent distribution networks. Warner Brothers' fifty-percent purchase of Tommy Boy (Coolio, De La Soul) is an example of this kind of arrangement, known as an "equity deal." The third arrangement is a different form of

14. See Krasilovsky and Shemel, *More About This Business of Music.*
15. See *The Global Jukebox* by Robert Burnett; Paul Lopes, "Innovation and Diversity in the Popular Music Industry, 1969–1990," *American Sociological Review*, p.57; and Richard A. Peterson and David G. Berger, "Cycles in Symbol Production: The Case of Popular Music," in *On Record*, edited by Simon Frith.

the equity deal, whereby a major will buy into an indie and send the records through the major distribution network. The relationship between BMG and Zomba (Backstreet Boys, 'NSync, Britney Spears, R. Kelly, A Tribe Called Quest, Mystikal, Too Short, KRS-ONE) fits this model, as we will show in detail below. Fourth, a major label will purchase all or half of an existing indie *distribution* company. This enables them to gain access to the indie marketplace through the smaller retail outlets. Sony's purchase of RED distribution, EMI's interest in Caroline Distribution, and Warner's partial purchase of ADA distribution serve as examples of this trend. Fifth, a major will merely launch its own "indie" distribution arm. Some of the deals listed above are considered "joint ventures," a growing trend in the industry.

In the last three cases, the majors end up distributing a significant number of non-signatory labels. It is a confusing landscape to map, because a label, by definition, is considered "independent" if it is *distributed* through independent networks rather than by the majors. A label can be partially owned by a major and access larger amounts of capital investment, but still be considered an indie. Tommy Boy is a good example: The successful hip hop label, though half-owned by Warner, is generally described as an independent. On the other hand, a label that is independently owned may not be considered an indie if it goes through a major distribution network. Such is the case with Zomba and its imprints. Add to this the fact that some "independent" distribution companies are now partially owned by the majors, and you get an extremely complicated arrangement.[16] The music industry is therefore dominated by entities that control distribution and are less focused on production.

Increasing Market Share for the Indies: Zomba Group of Companies

The year 1996 was significant, according to *Billboard*, because for the first time in almost five decades the independent labels, taken collectively, held the number-one spot for total market percentage of sales. In 1996, the indies held 21.2 percent of the market, while WEA held 21.1 percent, Sony 14.7 percent, PGD 13.1 percent, BMG 10.7 percent, UNI 19.6 percent, and EMI 8.7 percent. The indies had begun to garner significant percentages of the market in the early nineties; since 1996 they have held fourth, third, and second places, consistently taking over sixteen percent of the market. The rising popularity of hip hop/rap, alternative rock (derived largely from punk and metal), and

16. See *Billboard* (May 22, 1999 and March 26, 1994).

country music largely explains the explosive growth of the indies in the past two decades. Some of the most important indie labels were formed in the early eighties, including Jive (part of the Zomba label group), Priority, Profile, Tommy Boy, TVT, Roadrunner, Mammoth, Restless, Relativity, Sub-Pop, Rykodisc, and Big Beat. Although as a result of licensing deals and take-over bids by the majors none of these labels remained independent, there are reportedly three times as many indie labels today as compared to a few decades ago, but only one-third as many "successful" labels. Among the indies, most labels remain very small, typically selling between 20,000 to 35,000 CDs a year. Some indies, however, are much larger in scope, like Alligator and Rounder, two very successful companies that have been around for thirty years.

For the year 2000, independent labels accounted for 205,212 of the 288,591 albums that were released, or about seventy-one percent of titles. Yet the majors captured eighty-three percent of record sales. These numbers can be slightly misleading, given the way that the industry distinguishes between "independent" and "major." According to Billboard, a CD is considered indie if it is distributed independently. The industry focus on distribution may explain the collective anxiety regarding download-ing music over the Internet—a distribution system that can't be easily corralled. A notable giant among the indie labels is Jive, one of the many imprints that comprise the Zomba family. Almost all of the Zomba-owned labels are non-signatory, with Reunion Records being the sole exception. The Zomba Group of Companies is an example in which the major has only a partial ownership but virtually exclusive distribution rights. The signatory corporation, BMG, decentralizes its production by farming it out to the non-union company, Zomba. BMG sold Reunion Records to Zomba in 1996, then purchased a twenty-percent stake in Zomba's records division in the very same year.

The Zomba Group of Companies, founded as Zomba Enterprises Inc. in 1978 by Clive Calder (currently the CEO and Chairman), has grown into an interna-tional empire of more than fifty companies—encompassing record-label imprints, music publishing, recording studios, distribution companies, online licensing agreements, production music libraries, and equipment-rental companies—with annual sales that range between $50–$100 million.[17] Based in New York City, Zomba remains primarily an independently owned and privately held company, unlike Tommy Boy, which is half-owned by Warner and distributed independently. Even so, Zomba is no longer considered independent within the industry.

17. These sales figures are based upon information provided by the Wall Street Journal.

Zomba's imprint labels have been very successful in the past decade, with six albums among the top fifty best-selling albums in 1999. Zomba-owned Jive Records had the top two albums of 1999 with the Backstreet Boys' *Millennium* (6.4 million units sold) and Britney Spears's . . . *baby one more time* (5.7 million). Jive Records was so successful that year that it garnered fully 7.9 percent of the market share. Zomba, as a whole, was the second-best-selling label group in 1999, taking 8.75 percent of the market share. The Zomba family of imprints has albums of almost every genre occupying places in *Billboard*'s Top 200 charts. Tool, a rock band on the Volcano label, successful hip hop artists Too Short and A Tribe Called Quest on Jive, pop singer R. Kelly, also on Jive, Christian artist Michael Smith on Reunion, and Christian group Jars of Clay on Essential, have all been mainstays in the Top 200 for the past five years. Zomba has also managed to place albums in the top one hundred best-selling albums *of all time* with the Backstreet Boys, 'NSync, and Britney Spears. All the labels above, with the exception of Reunion, are non-signatory labels. The Zomba/BMG arrangement has the dubious distinction of being the leader in union avoidance, based upon the number of albums recorded by Zomba and manufactured and distributed by BMG. Other majors like WEA are following suit with similar deals.

Zomba Enterprises and Union Avoidance

Zomba Enterprises Inc. and the Zomba family of record labels are actually linked to another major as well, EMI. The ties to EMI, however, are much less significant than those with BMG. In 1996 Zomba signed a distribution deal with Virgin Records (owned by EMI) for Latin America, Europe, and Africa.

The connections go much deeper with BMG, a division of the German-based company Bertelsmann AG. BMG has become one of the most aggressive majors, recently signing a deal with Napster that would have BMG drop its lawsuit against the software company if Napster agrees to BMG's terms for online distribution (requiring users of the software to pay a fee for membership in order to download music). BMG's recent success accounted for thirty percent of Bertelsmann AG's total revenues for 1999,[18] and much of that success is a direct result of its partnership with Zomba.

In 1986 BMG and Zomba cut a manufacturing and distribution deal that gave BMG exclusive distribution rights to Zomba's US market. BMG handled most of

18. See *Business Week* (November 13, 2000).

Zomba's worldwide distribution until 1996, when Virgin became the label group's European and Latin American distributor. Zomba and BMG extended their manufacturing and distribution deal for a year in January 2000, after the two companies settled a lawsuit involving the boy band 'NSync, who had left BMG-owned RCA in October 1999 for Zomba-owned Jive.[19] BMG was eager to settle because at the time, the family of Zomba imprints accounted for nearly one-third of BMG's market share; BMG, in turn, was responsible for thirty percent of the total revenue for Bertelsmann AG.

The distribution agreement between BMG and Zomba has developed into other deals. In 1991, for example, BMG bought a twenty-five-percent interest in Zomba Publishing, Zomba Enterprise's most lucrative division. The publishing interests of Zomba include the catalogues of Def Leppard, Poison, Iron Maiden, Anthrax, Billy Ocean, Levert, Michael Jackson, Bryan Adams, Womack and Womack, Too Short, Boogie Down Productions, Kool Moe Dee, Digital Underground, A Tribe Called Quest, and DJ Jazzy Jeff and the Fresh Prince. Between 1996 and 1999 Zomba Music Publishing's catalogue grew from 100,000 to 200,000 copyrights. By 1999 Zomba Music had a song interest in sixteen of *Billboard*'s Top 200 albums.

In 1996 BMG extended its tentacles further into Zomba by purchasing a twenty-percent stake in Zomba's record division, which includes the following labels: Jive, Jive Electro, Volcano, Silvertone, Verity, Benson, Reunion, Brentwood Music, Music for Nations, and Essential. This deal, like the publishing deal, was understood as a joint venture rather than a merger. According to Strauss Zelnick, former CEO of BMG Entertainment North America, "Zomba is exactly the kind of entrepreneurial company we seek to partner with and the kind that really succeeds in our system. They maintain complete autonomy with our support, a balance not every major can make."[20]

This extensive involvement between BMG and Zomba has serious negative implications for the musicians' union. Estimates based on record sales for the year 2000 of Zomba artists Jars of Clay, Joe, 'NSync, Backstreet Boys, R. Kelly, and Britney Spears suggest that almost $2 million dollars ($1,944,481.12) has been lost to the union's Special Payments Fund (SPF) and almost $1 million dollars ($738,069.29) to the Music Performance Trust Fund (MPTF). BMG has post-industrial production arrangements with other companies as well: RCA—which is owned by BMG—has a

19. The lawsuit was filed in October 1999 by 'NSync's manager, Louis Pearlman (who also owns 'NSync's previous label, Trans Continental) and BMG. 'NSync was trying to get out of a bad contract with Pearlman by signing with Jive Records. The issue was eventually settled out of court as Zomba agreed to extend its manufacturing and distribution deal with BMG which was set to expire in June 2000. See *Billboard* (January 8, 2000).
20. Quoted in *Billboard* (November 9, 1996).

profit-sharing arrangement with Loud Records, a hip hop label, and BMG has an equity deal with Sparrow Records, a Christian-themed label.[21]

There is a myriad of other examples where arrangements between major and independent labels undermine the AFM. The following is merely a sampling: Warner's equity deal with Tommy Boy (mentioned above); Island/Def Jam's (owned by Universal/Vivendi) equity deal with Roadrunner Records (Sepultura, Slipknot); EMI's equity deal with Priority Records, another large hip hop label; and Atlantic Records' brief joint venture with Mammoth Records.[22]

The other arrangement that creates the conditions for a growing market share of non-union record labels is the equity deal between a major label and an independent *distribution* company. Sony's stake in RED distribution, the largest independent distributor in the US, is a prime example. RED Distribution is known mostly for its punk-rock labels like Epitaph (Rancid) and Roadrunner (Sepultura), but it also distributes rap powerhouse Loud Records.[23] EMI has a piece of the action, too, with a controlling interest in Caroline Distribution, a successful company that focused throughout the nineties on punk and alternative rock labels like Scratchie (a label owned by members of the Smashing Pumpkins) and Dischord (Minor Threat, Fugazi), and has more recently broken into electronic music. Thus, not only do the majors have equity and joint ventures with many of the best-selling independent labels, they also have similar deals with some of the biggest indie distributors.

Clearly, the structure of the music industry today has blurred the distinction between independent and major, but labor law remains stuck in the industrial era. If a label is less than half-owned by a major, then the major isn't responsible, legally, for any recording work that takes place at the smaller label. Therefore, neither the independent nor the major label is concerned with honoring the terms of the AFM's labor contract and recording contract. So, while the forces of production change the structure of the recording industry, labor law isn't able to protect the interests of musicians. As the indies take more of the market, and as they provide the majors with access to a steady stream of non-union musicians, the AFM loses money and members. The seventeen to twenty percent of the market controlled by the independents, combined with the nine percent of the market controlled by the Zomba labels—which are considered by *Billboard* to be majors—account for approximately thirty percent of the

21. *Billboard* (March 25, 1995).
22. *Billboard* (November 23, 1996, July 13,1996, and June 15, 1996).
23. *Billboard* (January 29, 2000).

total CD market. If you consider that many of the "non-indie"-distributed labels like Loud Records and Priority Records are non-union labels, then the market share for non-union-made CDs approaches forty percent. Many of these labels have albums that have reached "gold" status at the RIAA, selling over half a million copies. In all these examples, the indies are, more and more, becoming part of the establishment. Unlike a few decades ago when the indies were truly outside the "mainstream," today the indies are an integral part of the major labels' corporate plan to challenge the role of the AFM, a strategy that mimics the widespread corporate assault on union labor throughout the United States. It is largely a misnomer to say that the indies represent a challenge to the corporate control of the entertainment industry. On the contrary, we have shown that the indies are involved, sometimes unwittingly, in a process that aids and abets control of American music culture by a small handful of international conglomerates. As such, the indies find themselves in the ironic position of being the "anti-establishment" component of the establishment.

While the changing structure of the music recording industry has eroded the pay for professional musicians and undermined their union, there have been some encouraging developments as high-profile musicians like Courtney Love, Don Henley, and Ani DiFranco speak out about the structure of stealing prevalent in the industry. Popular royalty artists need to continue to raise awareness about the unfair nature of the industry among other musicians and the consumers of music. The AFM, for its part, needs to abandon the corporate/business unionism model and begin a new organizing campaign that can adjust to the new structure of the industry. The union can no longer view itself as junior partner to the major record companies, and only time will tell if professional musicians and their allies will be able to turn things around.

Michael Roberts is an adjunct lecturer in sociology and labor studies at Queens College and a doctoral candidate in sociology at the CUNY Graduate Center. He is currently a research fellow at the Center for Culture, Work, and Technology at the CUNY Graduate Center and Local 802 of the American Federation of Musicians. He would like to thank Stanley Aronowitz from the CUNY Graduate Center, Mark Ribot, Jay Schaffner, Joseph A. Eisman and David Sheldon from Local 802, and Riva Perry from Queens College for their inspiration and assistance in researching and editing this article. He would also like to extend a special thanks to Kathrina Suarez for her emotional support and intellectual companionship.

The Discordant Sound of Music:
A Report on the Record Industry
PREPARED BY THE ECONOMIC DEVELOPMENT DEPARTMENT OF THE NAACP

Editor's note: This was one of the first reports documenting widespread racial discrimination in the American recording industry. It was published by the NAACP on March 23, 1987; the statistics and information are reflective of that period, and differ at points from today's state of the music industry.

Foreword

In July 1985 the executive director of the NAACP appointed a task force to consider allegations of discrimination in the record industry brought to the Association's attention by present and former record-company employees, black entrepreneurs, and other individuals connected with the industry.

Subsequently, the NAACP's Economic Development Department, under the direction of Fred H. Rasheed, was given the responsibility of conducting an investigation into the record industry and developing a report. Representatives of that department met with the presidents of several major record companies—Capital/EMI, Warner, and MCA—attended a number of industry-related conferences to secure information on the industry, and conferred with representatives of four organizations identified as "industry watchdogs for blacks"—Black Radio Exclusive, Jack "The Rapper" Gibson, Black Music Association, and the Young Black Programmers Coalition.

In addition, scores of interviews were conducted with present and former employees of record companies, concert promoters, independent producers, entertainment lawyers, business agents, staff members of publications serving the industry, retailers, independent record producers, and business persons who sell products or services to the industry.

Statistical data, for reasons that will be explained in the report, were extremely difficult to obtain. However, through the scope of the investigation and the large number of persons interviewed, we believe we have fashioned an accurate document on the status of blacks in the record industry.

Report on the Record Industry

1. Introduction

The Recording Industry Association of America (RIAA) has reported that the industry accounted for $4.4 billion in sales in 1985. Recording-industry insiders, according to the respected music critic Clayton Riley, estimate that black artists are responsible for generating twenty-five to thirty percent of this revenue. The estimate includes recordings of such "crossover" artists as Prince, Michael Jackson, Lionel Richie, Sade, etc. Additionally, black consumers account for an estimated 11.4 percent of the annual sale of records, audio tapes, and video music cassettes.

With this major contribution to the economic health of the recording industry, it is relevant to examine the status of blacks therein. To arrive at this assessment, several questions need to be addressed:

1. Are blacks receiving a fair share of the economic opportunities generated by the industry?
2. Is there racial discrimination in the industry, and if so, to what degree is it present?
3. Are blacks equitably employed in behind-the-scene jobs?
4. Do black artists use their influence to promote and provide opportunities for other blacks?

Any examination of the industry needs to begin with an understanding that in many respects it is unique. Unlike other industries where the various parts form a well-integrated structure, the record industry is made up of a number of different autonomous entities, including major record companies, independent labels, recording artists, managers, agents, promoters, distributors, radio, television, and retailers. They cooperate with each other, but at the same time they retain their separate identities.

The task of finding hard answers is also complicated by the fact that the industry operates virtually free of federal regulations, government intervention, or public pressure. The largest organized group in the industry, the RIAA, represents eighty-five percent of the nation's record companies, but has no control or influence over the practices of its member companies, which dictate its own activities.

The industry is, therefore, a tightly knit and closed society that jealously guards information on its activities.

In order to reach an informed judgment on the questions raised above, it is helpful to first look at the separate entities that constitute the industry.

II. Major Record Companies

The nation's five major record companies are at the apex of the industry and account for roughly eighty-six percent of all record and prerecorded tape sales. They also derive power by their ability to sign artists to contracts and provide the initial money for production and promotion of the artist's records, tapes, and music videos against future sales.

Each of the major companies employs approximately three hundred people in management, professional, and technical positions. While each company is required to file an EEO 1 Report with the US Equal Employment Opportunity Commission, the agency combines their statistics with others garnered from the broad recording industry, so that those from the recording companies cannot be extracted. The companies themselves have refused to divulge their own statistics. However, one of the smaller companies has shared with the NAACP the information that four of its thirty-five management positions and two of its fifteen professional positions are held by blacks. If such figures are typical for the industry, then it is apparent that blacks are grossly under-represented at the professional and managerial levels.

It becomes somewhat easier to understand the status of blacks with the record companies by looking at the structure of a typical record company. There are several major departments—Artists and Repertoire (A&R), Business, Business Affairs, and Marketing. The last encompasses record promotions, publicity, merchandising, and product management. Under the A&R departments are the Black Music Division (Rhythm & Blues) and the Popular Music Division (Pop). Black artists enter through the black music division where there is normally less money available for promotional purposes than in the pop division, which handles white artists.

The treatment of the artists is different. For example, the records of most black artists are not promoted to white radio stations but are confined to black-oriented stations, where smaller audiences result in smaller sales. Of the more than nine thousand radio stations in the country, fewer than four hundred target their programming to black listeners so that the market for black artists is limited to less than thirty million people in a country of over 230 million.

Some black artists, however, do obtain a more enhanced position when their records achieve a "crossover" status. Simply defined, a "crossover" occurs when a recording by a black artist garners heavy play on "pop stations" and begins to appear on the "pop charts." Then it is moved out of the black music division and into the popular music division. The popular music division thus becomes the beneficiary of revenues generated by such crossover artists as Michael Jackson, Prince, and Lionel Richie, resulting in fewer dollars available to black music for artist development, promotion, and marketing.

The black managers with the record companies are primarily employed in the promotion of records by black artists at salaries that are somewhat less than those paid their white counterparts in the popular music division, according to interviews with present and past employees. Black executives with the record companies are tightly restricted in the exercise of authority. Their major function is to identify new black artists and to produce and promote their records. Only a few of the black executives are empowered to sign an artist to a contract and make decisions regarding expenditures for producing and promoting an artist. Most often, these decisions are made by white executives in the popular music division. Where black executives do control budgets, those budgets are significantly smaller than those in the popular music division. There are a few black executives who are not confined to black music divisions; however, they are most often assigned to staff positions such as personnel, as opposed to line positions.

Insiders report that there is a high turnover among black promotion managers, leading to the speculation that companies are engaged in "revolving door" practices of terminating blacks when they reach a certain level, replacing them with new black faces to do the same work at a lower level of compensation.

None of the major record companies has an affirmative-action program to recruit black employees or increase their representation in management and professional positions. The pattern of exclusion found in the top-echelon jobs also extends into other areas, with very few blacks being employed either on staff or under contract as photographers, promoters and sales representatives, make-up artists, art directors, sound engineers, and publicists (except for black media).

The companies spend a substantial amount of money on various goods and outside services, but minority purchasing policies and programs are nonexistent. This failure of the record companies to encourage the development of black businesses is especially striking in view of the vast amount of money these same companies derive from the black community. When asked why they did not utilize black businesses, the stock response of the companies was that they do not inquire or keep record of the ownership of the firms they do business with.

Another area where it becomes evident that record companies engage in racial differences is that of music videos. Videos are a fairly recent development in the business and have been credited with having a great deal to do with the financial upsurge of the record industry. However, from the very beginning of this development, black artists have been treated differently than whites. As an example, Music Television (MTV) was one of pioneers in the field, beginning around-the-clock broadcasting of videos in 1981 on cable television. For a period of time, MTV refused to play videos of black artists on the basis that rhythm & blues selections did not fit their rock format. The situation was brought to a head in 1983 when CBS/Epic Records threatened to pull all of its videos from MTV if Michael Jackson's "Billy Jean" video did not air. Columbia (CBS) did hold a trump card in that the "Billy Jean" video was taken from Jackson's tremendously popular album, *Thriller*. MTV relented, and subsequently three of Jackson's videos became MTV's biggest hits.

Nonetheless, there are still a significant number of black artists for whom the record companies will not produce videos, while they readily promote videos of white artists who generate substantially smaller revenues. In addition, in an effort to attract and appeal to white viewers, black artists have had to make concessions to white music-video programmers based on the perception of what white viewers will accept. Evidence is seen in the increasing presence of white personnel in the stage mix on black crossover videos.

III. Independent Record Companies and Producers

Nationally, there are some 350 independent record companies, but very few of them have the capacity to promote and distribute records on a large scale, making it necessary for them to sign contracts with the major record companies to distribute their records. This arrangement does not come without a price. In some instances it is a fee, and in others it is the risk of being taken over. As an example, during the 1970s CBS and Warner Communications gained control of a number of black-owned independents through distribution deals.

Faced with the difficulty of promoting and distributing records to a wide consumer market, independent producers are placed in an inferior bargaining position and become easy prey for exploitation by major record companies. Once a record achieves the status of a hit, it becomes important to get it to the retailers as quickly as possible in order to cash in financially. Without the extensive promotion and distribution systems of the major companies, independent record companies turn to independent distributors, who usually promote their records to a few markets at a time in order to concentrate their limited resources for maximum results. Independent distributors, numbering between thirty and forty nationally, distribute ninety-five percent of the records produced by independent labels. Independent labels currently represent approximately five percent of total record sales. They have been able to build on those music forms such as rap, jazz, blues, reggae, and gospel, which major labels have basically ignored.

Black-owned independent record companies remain a viable alternative to major labels for black entrepreneurs and artists, and are a potential source of employment for blacks who are denied the opportunity to apply their administrative, technical, and other skills with major labels.

IV. Radio and Promotion

Radio has traditionally been a critical factor in pushing the sale of records. Airplay can spell success or failure for a record, and therefore record companies are extremely anxious to secure as much exposure for their records as possible. This is accomplished primarily through record promoters.

Beginning in the 1980s, record companies cut back on their in-house promotion staffs and increased the use of independent promoters. This opened the door for black independent promoters, but, based on interviews with a number of them, they earned substantially less than their white counterparts. Record companies have attempted to justify this disparity by claiming that white promoters have larger territories and a greater number of radio stations to call on. What is not expressed, but what is true, is that for the most part black promoters are limited to black-music-format stations, while white promoters have been known to call on black-music-format stations as well as pop stations to promote records.

In March 1986 the industry was rocked by rumors that independent promoters were bribing radio programmers and disc jockeys to air new songs and help push them to the top of the charts. As a result, most major labels have terminated relationships with independent promoters, and although no black promoters were implicated, they suffered the same fate.

The question now is whether the major labels, in turning to in-house promotion staffs, will insure that blacks receive a fair share of those jobs at comparable salaries to their white counterparts, and end the practice of confining blacks to black-music-format stations. The evidence to date indicates that staffs are not being increased, and several of the major labels have actually reduced them.

Another aspect of radio to be considered has to do with advertising dollars, concert tickets, T-shirts, and other promotional material distributed by the companies. Black-music-format radio stations have charged that despite their having been instrumental in launching the careers of such crossover acts as Prince, Al Jarreau, and George Benson, the record companies give preferential treatment to pop and rock stations in the distribution of their promotional materials and treat black stations with "benign neglect."

This concern reached a boiling point in 1985 when a number of black-oriented stations in Los Angeles refused to air Warner Brothers records, charging that the company was guilty of discriminatory treatment in promotion and advertising support for crossover acts. The incident that prompted the boycott was a string of concerts by Prince where black stations claimed they had received little in the way of promotional aid for station giveaways when compared to the massive promotional freebies afforded the pop stations.

The boycott was called off when Warner agreed to make an effort to end such practices against the black stations. However, a recent survey of a number of black stations indicates that the discriminatory situation persists.

V. Distribution

The distribution network for records, similar to other distribution networks, tends to operate to the advantage of the large retailers, who benefit through volume buying, discounts, etc. Since black record retailers are relatively small operators, and many of them are single-store owners, they are at a disadvantage in the competitive marketplace.

Some sixty percent of all records are distributed through three major labels— CBS, Warner, and RCA. The distribution network is the backbone of the recording industry. The success or failure of an artist or label rests on the effectiveness of distributors in getting the product to retailers. It is in this area where independent labels experience the greatest difficulty. Distribution is a relatively unspecialized and low-capital-intensive side of the industry built on networking and informal relationships.

Distribution is accomplished through four major entities—major record audio retail chains, rack jobbers, one-stops, and direct mail.

The major record retail chains (such as Tower Records, Sam Goody, etc.) are responsible for approximately seventy percent of the gross dollar volume done by members of the National Association of Recording Manufacturers. This type of distribution is growing at a faster rate than other outlets, thus negatively affecting the long-term growth potential of other types of distributors. Unlike other record retailers, the large chains have in-house merchandisers and buyers who determine the mix, number, and shelving of record releases.

Rack jobbers and independent record brokerage companies select and buy in large volume for record stores, discount chains, and department stores. These jobbers have tremendous input into the record mix available in client stores and spend millions of dollars annually purchasing records directly from the manufacturers. The largest company, Handelman Co., accounts for approximately ten percent of the annual record sales, and some of its biggest clients are retailers such as Kmart, Sears, and Wal-Mart.

One-stops are retailers who stock and sell recordings of all labels, primarily to small, independent retailers who buy in low volumes and require specialized services and selections. Few of these one-stops can afford to stock all available recordings because of the large number of selections and labels, and due to their limited capital.

Though independent and one-stop distributors are technically separate, because of the well-established network between independent labels and independent distributors, distribution outlets often overlap. One-stops act as sub-distributors, often buying from independent distributors releases from the labels they command in order to service the needs of their customers. For this reason, independents and one-stops share similar problems and face similar obstacles. Though exact figures are not available, a significantly large percentage of one-stop customers are ethnic, especially black, independently operated retailers.

Because of the pricing policies on the part of manufacturers who offer more attractive terms to larger customers, one-stops are finding it increasingly difficult to supply independent retailers with records at a cost-effective rate. As a consequence, these retailers have to inflate their prices to their customers, forcing them into a non-competitive position and eventually out of the market.

Black retailers contend that since many of them are single-store owners, they cannot deal directly with the major distributors, thereby excluding them from taking advantage of advertising. Major distributors normally advertise their records and identify retail outlets where the records are available. In order to buy directly from distributors, one must own at least four retail outlets, have credit with two or more companies, and order a minimum dollar amount of records. This policy forces black retailers to deal with one-stop distributors at a higher cost.

VI. Recording Artists

The single most important figure in the recording industry is the recording artist. His or her talent is what drives the industry. There are a number of black superstars who command fantastic artist royalties and performance fees and exert enormous influence, but the question still remains as to whether once past the top level in the industry, blacks have equitable opportunities in the non-performing side of the business. To answer that question, some background is in order.

No other racial or ethnic group has had such a profound influence on American music as blacks. They created the uniquely American art forms of gospel, ragtime, jazz, the blues, rhythm & blues, bop, and progressive jazz. While they have been pioneers in blazing new musical trails, their music has often been copied by others who have gone on to gain greater wealth and prestige than the originators.

Dating back to the turn of the twentieth century and the emergence of ragtime and blues, black musicians such as Scott Joplin, Eubie Blake, W.C. Handy, Ma Rainey—and continuing with jazz musicians Louis Armstrong, Bennie Moten, Duke Ellington, and Count Basie—black influence on American music has been profound. In the thirties and forties, white musicians like Benny Goodman, Tommy Dorsey, and Artie Shaw took the black jazz idiom and created the swing era. In the fifties, as musical tastes began to change, Little Richard, Chuck Berry, Muddy Waters, Fats Domino, Otis Redding, James Brown, Ray Charles, and others ushered in the era of rock and roll that helped create white superstars such as Elvis Presley, Buddy Holly, and the Beatles. The appeal of black artists continued throughout the sixties and the seventies with Diana Ross and the Supremes, the Temptations, Gladys Knight and the Pips, Stevie Wonder, Barry White, the Jackson Five, and others. In 1984, albums by Michael Jackson, Prince, and Lionel Richie accounted for the sale of thirty-seven million copies in the United States alone.

Successful black artists today are multi-million-dollar corporations engaging the services of a multitude of people, including managers, business agents, publicists, attorneys, musicians, booking agents, sound and stage crews, graphic artists, and photographers. However, in the main, the top black artists employ very few blacks in these capacities, thereby increasing the difficulty of blacks making inroads into what are very attractive and well-paying positions.

There are notable exceptions. Major black artists who have been identified as having black managers include Stevie Wonder, Melba Moore, Freddie Jackson, SOS Band, Janet Jackson, Klymaxx, The Whispers, Shalamar, Sylvers, and Midnight Star. Most of these artists are produced by and record for independent black labels.

Historically, many black artists have had black managers during the early stages of their careers when they were attempting to break into the business. But once they achieved something approaching success, the artists usually replaced their black managers with white ones. This is an extremely important move since managers exert a significant influence on the career and business decisions of the artist. For example, managers influence the choice of attorneys, business agents, booking agents, concert promoters, publicists, etc., and they also serve as the liaison between the artist and third parties.

In most cases, if the manager of an artist is white, the independent professional and business people hired by the artist are white. As a result, many talented and skilled blacks are excluded from the tremendous economic opportunities generated by major black artists. One of the side effects of having white managers is that very few black artists make themselves available to support black institutions through endorsements and benefit performances. Attempts to persuade them to do so usually run into a dead-end at the manager's door.

Black artists maintain that the decision to use white managers, attorneys, agents, and promoters reflects a business and career move and has nothing to do with race. They contend that their opportunity to make money is short-lived and that they are therefore obligated to retain the best people available, regardless of color. The other side of the coin is that there are qualified blacks in all aspects of the industry, who, given the opportunity, can provide the professional services required by the artist. Sadly, they rarely receive that opportunity.

VII. Concert Promoters

An important source of additional income for recording artists, as well as a method of boosting their record sales, is through touring. Such tours are complicated and expensive undertakings involving managers, booking agents, and promoters, with expenses running anywhere from twenty thousand to several hundred thousand dollars a week. The key person is the booking agent, who works on behalf of the artist—through his or her manager—with concert promoters to set up local dates. The booking agent usually receives ten percent of the artist's proceeds from the tour as a fee. The artist is paid a flat fee plus a percentage of the gate. Out of this comes the cost for lighting and set-up crews, musicians, road managers, living accommodations, and travel costs.

Of the major booking agencies in the country, none is black, although a number of them have black account executives or junior agents. Norby Walters Agency in New York and Tri-Ad are two of the foremost agencies for booking black acts.

The local promoter is responsible for booking the facility and providing for insurance, security, production, advertising and promotion, limousine service, catering, and other miscellaneous costs associated with the concert. The promoter's compensation comes from ticket sales minus expenses. Blatant racial disparity is most pronounced at the level of these promoters; blacks contend they are precluded by the white booking agencies from promoting major black artists and for the most part have been limited to "share cropping" with white promoters who receive the bulk of the concert promotion business.

During the Jacksons' "Victory" tour in 1984, black promoters threatened to call for a boycott unless black promoters received a share of the tour's promotion. This effort was duplicated during Lionel Richie's tour in 1984, and again with Tina Turner's in 1985. These efforts were successful in that pressure was put on the corporate sponsor of the tour—in this instance, Pepsi-Cola—to intervene with the booking agents and the artists to ensure opportunities for black promoters.

A word of explanation is in order about corporate sponsors. Over the past several years, a number of major corporations have allocated a portion of their promotion budgets to sponsor concert tours. In addition to Pepsi, sponsors have included Coca-Cola (Julio Iglesias, Duran Duran, Lakeside, and Midnight Star), Coors (Jeffrey Osborne), Anheuser Busch (Lou Rawls and the "Bud Superfest" Tour), and Brown and Williamson, who began sponsoring the Cool Jazz Festival several years ago.

While some success has been achieved through the corporate sponsors, black promoters are still able to secure only a very small piece of the tour promotion business. With a tinge of irony, a number of the black promoters recall that they promoted the concerts of many of today's black artists before they reached superstar status, at which point they were dumped for white promoters. Since there are no opportunities for them to promote white artists, the black promoters see themselves in a Catch-22 situation.

Black artists defend themselves by saying that there are very few black promoters who can come up with the guarantees that assure an artist's fees and produce the necessary up-front money. The black promoters counter by saying that black superstars can be promoted by almost anyone because of their drawing power, and the reality is that the black artists lack any sense of loyalty to black promoters.

VIII. Conclusion

This report began by posing four questions. They are restated below with our conclusions:

1. Are blacks receiving a fair share of the economic opportunities generated by the industry?

By any objective measurement, they are not. Accounting for twenty-five to thirty percent of the revenue generated by the record industry, and returning some 11.4 percent to the industry in terms of its revenues, they receive only a minuscule proportion of its financial benefits. The industry is dominated by a handful of giant record companies who employ only a small number of blacks in creative and managerial positions and limit the power and authority of those they do employ. The companies do not have affirmative-action plans to increase their number of minority employees, nor do they make any effort to use minority entrepreneurs for the many products and services they require.

The principal benefits that do accrue to blacks accrue to performing artists. But even these artists, unless they have reached the status of "crossover," are handled differently than white artists, with smaller financial and other resources being devoted to the advancement of their careers. Many whites profit from the talent of black recording artists, but very few blacks are afforded this opportunity.

2. Is there racial discrimination in the industry, and if so, to what degree is it present?

The record industry is overwhelmingly segregated and discrimination is rampant. No other industry in America so openly classifies its operations on a racial basis. At every level of the industry, beginning with the separation of black artists into a special category, barriers exist that severely limit opportunities for blacks. The structure of the industry allows for total white control and domination. While the intent may not be to deliberately and consciously keep blacks out, the results are the same.

3. Are blacks employed equitably in behind-the-scene jobs?

Once again, the answer is in the negative. The record companies themselves have poor employment patterns and this spreads over into such ancillary activities as promotion, managing, and the staging of concert tours.

4. Do black artists use their influence to promote and provide opportunities for other blacks?

The answer is mixed, with some notable black artists making determined and commendable efforts to provide opportunities for other blacks. Several of these artists have been cited earlier. Still, there remains a sizeable percentage of black artists who do not use the services of other blacks to any appreciable degree, thereby decreasing the possibilities of blacks making significant headway in an industry to which they contribute so much. The reasoning of these artists is grounded in the belief that they are better served by whites. This attitude sends a devastating message to black professionals in the field and those who might be considering careers in the record industry. If black artists are not prepared to hire other black professionals, who will?

Leonard Pitts, editor of *Radioscope*, writing in *Billboard* in April 1985, summed up this paradox, which has not changed, with these words:

> It seems that once a black performer has achieved coveted crossover status, one of his (or management's) first acts is to sever or scale down ties to black roots . . . Black is no longer good enough. They (the artists) prettify it up with high-sounding euphemisms like "I don't see color" and "I make universal music," but the net results remain the same.

In summation, it is the view of the NAACP that if there are to be any changes within the record industry in terms of providing for the more equitable treatment of blacks, those changes will have to be induced by outside forces. There is no discernable mood in the record industry to do business any differently than it has always been done. Further, many of the major black artists are not inclined to challenge a system that has rewarded them so lavishly. Other blacks within the industry are fearful of becoming too outspoken because of the real possibility their employment could be terminated.

IX. Recommendations

1. Negotiations looking toward the signing of Fair Share Agreements with the major record companies should be undertaken immediately. These agreements should deal with not only employment and promotions, but also with the utilization of black professionals on a contract basis, the purchase of goods and services from minority vendors, and the placement of advertising in black media. The results of these efforts should be widely publicized in the black community.

2. A Commission for Equality in the Record Industry should be established to address the longstanding institutionalized barriers to equality for blacks in the industry. Membership should consist of representatives of major record companies, black artists, representatives of black trade associations connected with the industry, and representatives of the civil rights community.

3. Commitments should be sought from major black recording artists to use their influence in broadening opportunities for other blacks in the recording industry.

4. A non-profit clearinghouse should be established to expedite the increased involvement of blacks in the record industry by gathering and disseminating information on black technicians, professionals, and entrepreneurs seeking employment or economic opportunities in the industry; by monitoring the employment and entrepreneurial needs of the industry and sharing the information with the black community; and by encouraging young people to seek career opportunities in the industry.

This report has addressed at length the many contributions blacks have made to American music and how traditionally they have not shared equitably in its rewards. It is appropriate, therefore, to end with the observations of a famed and beloved black poet, Langston Hughes, as he spoke about the plundering of black music and the black cultural experience in the NAACP's *Crisis Magazine* in March 1940:

> *You've taken my blues and gone—*
> *You sing 'em on Broadway*
> *And you sing 'em in Hollywood Bowl,*
> *And you mixed 'em up with symphonies*
> *And you fixed 'em*
> *So they don't sound like me.*
> *Yep, you done taken my blues and gone.*
>
> *But someday somebody'll*
> *Stand up and talk about me,*
> *And write about me—*
> *Black and beautiful—*
> *And sing about me,*
> *And put on plays about me!*
> *I reckon it'll be*
> *Me myself!*
>
> *Yes, it'll be me.*

Tell Me Something I Don't Already Know:
The Harvard Report on Soul Music Revisited
BY DAVID SANJEK

It is difficult to examine the legacy of interaction between the mainstream music industry and African-Americans and not conclude that racism has driven the enterprise from the start. Even though any number of black individuals have risen to the top of the profession or released gold and platinum albums, the body of evidence overwhelmingly points to the subordination of victims to victors. African-Americans are rarely extended the credit as individuals that they receive as artists. At the same time, the general public knows only a handful of those artists. Tribute is paid to figures who have managed by fortune and by fortitude to maintain their presence as national icons. Aretha Franklin and Ray Charles come to mind in this regard, having received government medals of honor or induction into halls of fame. Other figures of considerable skill and achievement have managed by means of fate or a failure of will to become obscured from the historical record. Who but the most ardent fans can recall the achievements of either Esther Phillips or Little Willie John? Inequality seems as built into the structure of the entertainment business as it is into the fabric of our national consciousness. Little evidence exists to dissuade one from seriously considering Ellis Cashmore's claim in *The Black Culture Industry* that, "The most significant value of black culture may be in providing whites with proof of the end of racism while keeping the racial hierarchy essentially intact."[1]

Still, it is shortsighted to equate racial bias with institutional inequities as a matter of principle. The fact that the music industry treats its participants as so much fodder for exploitation should come as no surprise. Few industries, cultural or otherwise, act any differently. Also, music-business moguls endeavor to protect their own interests regardless of their race. Greed is an equal-opportunity instinct. Herman Lubinsky of Savoy Records and John Dolphin, owner of Los Angeles' Dolphin Records, one white and the other African-American, had similarly abysmal reputations. The only significant distinction between them is that Lubinsky lived to see retirement, whereas a disgruntled songwriter killed Dolphin. We are conditioned to conceive of those

1. Ellis Cashmore, *The Black Culture Industry* (New York: Routledge, 1997), p.2.

businesses that market and manufacture the forms of culture that sustain our lives as in conflict with the very materials we admire. In truth, the relationship between the individuals who create and those who merchandise popular music is neither symbiotic nor parasitic, but both. Individual achievements and the commodification process that transforms those efforts into merchandise are not antithetical enterprises. If we wish to examine the efforts of black creators, we then must pay attention to the people and institutions who enable those efforts to reach the mass public. As Simon Frith states in *Music for Pleasure*,

> The industrialization of music cannot be understood as something which happens to music, since it describes a process in which music itself is made—a process, that is, which fuses (and confuses) capital, technical, and musical arguments. Twentieth-century popular music means the twentieth-century popular record; not the record of something (a song? a singer? a performance?) which exists independently of the music industry, but a form of communication which determines what songs, singers, and performances are and can be.[2]

Unfortunately, our desire to understand how the industrialization of popular music takes place collides with the underwhelming amount of evidence about the history of that process. Recording technology may be nearly 125 years old, having been patented by Thomas A. Edison in 1877, yet we lack adequate documentation of the industry that his invention led to. By contrast, if we wish to study the film industry, detailed histories have been published about each of the major film companies and many of the most successful producers. With a few notable exceptions, a comparable body of information is not available about the record industry. Furthermore, if we focus upon the participation of African-Americans in that process, the evidence is even more paltry. A fair amount of research has been devoted to the small number of individuals or companies who have triumphed in the gladiatorial arena of popular entertainment.[3] One can read a handful of volumes, for example, on Motown Records and the achievements of its founder, Berry Gordy. However, we lack the most basic documentation about how black popular music was assimilated by the

2. Simon Frith, *Music For Pleasure* (New York: Routledge, 1988), p.12.
3. For more information on the participation of African-Americans in the record industry, see my essay "One Size Does Not Fit All: The Precarious Position of the African-American Entrepreneur in the Post-WWII Music Industry" (*American Music* 15:4 [Winter 1997]: pp.535–62). To be reprinted in *Always On My Mind: Music, Memory and Money* (Wesleyan University Press, 2002).

music business or how a small number of individuals took the initiative to succeed without the benefit of mainstream capital. Too few people realize the role of economic self-determination in the careers of such African-Americans as Don Robey (the owner of Duke-Peacock Records) and Vivian and James Bracken (owners of the Vee-Jay label), or examine how successful artists like Sam Cooke or Ray Charles used their own money to start independent labels and publishing companies. Until this is the case, the assumption that African-Americans are routinely crippled and contained by white businessmen will continue to pervade the popular imagination.

Also significant are those occasions when major record labels attempted to augment their roster with the acquisition of African-American performers by purchasing independent companies specializing in African-American music, making distribution deals with those organizations, or buying the contracts of artists whose records had mounted the charts. Examples range from RCA Victor's acquisition of Sam Cooke from Keen Records in 1960 to Atlantic Records' arrangement to distribute Stax Records in 1965. One of the most noteworthy of these interactions between the commercial mainstream and the domain of African-American self-initiative took place in 1972. CBS and their Columbia Records Group (CRG), the most successful such division in the music industry at the time, had made few if any inroads into black music in recent years. The only cutting-edge acts of color they possessed were Sly and the Family Stone and Santana. They endeavored to remedy that imbalance by establishing a black-music division in 1971, headed by the African-American executive Logan Westbrooks. His mandate was to "create a black marketing staff to penetrate the black market."[4] Soon thereafter, another executive, Larry Isaacson, commissioned his alma mater, the Harvard Business School, to conduct a study as to how the CRG might achieve such penetration. The result, "A Study of the Soul Music Environment Prepared for Columbia Records Group," was released on May 11, 1972.

The "Harvard Report," as this document is known, has achieved some degree of legendary status despite the fact that much of the executive staff at the Sony Corporation, the present owner of the Columbia catalogue, seem to be unaware of its existence. Costing five thousand dollars and researched by six Masters students over the course of six months, the document first came to public attention in Nelson George's *The Death of Rhythm & Blues*, published in 1988. George argues that assimilation by African-Americans into the commercial mainstream demands too many sac-

---

4. Rob Bowman, *Soulsville USA: The Story of Stax Records* (New York: Schirmer Books, 1997), p.280.

rifices, and that the Harvard Report is a notable example of how that perilous exchange takes place. More often than not, he believes, black individuals lose an unrecoverable portion of their identity in the process. "Pursuing an anglicized self-image," George writes, "these 'transformed' black people, with their belief that anything can be sacrificed to generate more capital, are one of the disturbing triumphs of assimilation."[5]

The Harvard Report made recommendations to the CRG that led to their investment in several black-music companies, specifically Philadelphia International Records, the label owned and operated by the producer-writers Kenny Gamble and Leon Huff, and Stax Records of Memphis, Tennessee. It also led to signing a significant number of black performers in following years such that in 1980, 125 new acts appeared on the CRG roster, including Earth, Wind & Fire, the Isley Brothers, and Weather Report. George raises the question of what benefits and loses resulted from this set of actions. He inquires to what degree a white-owned corporation's capital investment in a black business and the access to systems of distribution and promotion they possess compensate for the black company's loss of autonomy and racial self-definition. Does achieving economic goals necessitate a cheapening of cultural assumptions as well as an abandonment of racial imperatives?

Examining this document—what impact it had on black participation in the music industry and how that process has affected the present state of the business—is the purpose of this essay. As the Harvard Report has not been made available to the public, I will begin by pointing out the body of misconceptions that gathered in the wake of its implementation. Then I will summarize the report's recommendations, its underlying cultural and institutional assumptions, and explore their impact upon the major black businesses in which CBS became a participant, Philadelphia International and Stax. I will conclude by speculating about the long-term influence of the Report and how the investment of the major labels in black music has remained governed by a body of unexamined assumptions about audiences and performers. In the process, I intend to indicate how unusual it was that CBS felt the need to assemble such a document. For proof of the commercial value of rhythm & blues, all the company needed to do was consult the record charts of the day or spend time in the black neighborhoods of the country. They would then have discovered how much this form of music embodied the values, hopes, and needs of its consumers. Why did they feel the need to document that which they should have already known?

5. Nelson George, *The Death of Rhythm & Blues* (New York: Pantheon, 1988), p.xiv.

In that the Harvard Report was never made available to the public, various allegations spread in the aftermath of its release. It was assumed that the document suggested that in order to assure their supremacy in the music industry, CBS should purchase outright one of the major black labels, either Stax or Motown. If purchase were impossible, they should instead obtain rights to distribute the label. By so positioning themselves, CBS could potentially purchase the company when the opportunity arose. The paranoid dimension of these assumptions should come as no surprise, for the degree of interaction at the time of the Report's release between the CRG and the black record business was limited, to say the least. None of these options were raised in the document, however. Instead, it proposed the existence of a market for soul music valued at approximately $60 million. According to the Report, the CRG presence in that market had been hampered by "personnel oriented to the popular music field that differs fundamentally from soul music in the critical factors required for success."[6] To alleviate that discrepancy, the Report advised that the CRG "must establish an internal soul-music group and improve the quality of soul music released on recordings." CBS's failure to do so in the past occurred because of motives that the Report describes as racist, yet more likely were the result of total indifference. Consequently, the perception of the CRG in the black community was that of "an ultra-rich, ultra-white giant which has for the most part chosen to snub blacks in the business. Blacks in the trade feel that CRG has heaped upon them the ultimate insult: that of ignoring their existence." The body of the Report endeavors to indicate how these circumstances arose and how the CRG could eradicate them by creating a synergistic relationship with the black-music business.

Before indicating how that transformation might occur, the Report outlines the "soul market" as it existed in 1972. Defining this genre, the Report argues, is difficult except in terms of a "certain sound" characterized by its "raw, driving beat that is as much viscerally as aurally experienced"; its popularity among the black audience; and its production dominantly but not exclusively by black artists. This extremely general definition is accompanied by a "rough typology" that is rough indeed. It distinguishes between a series of artists on the basis of their "soul content," but argues that Miles Davis and Thelonious Monk possessed almost none whatsoever, a remark that many in the black community would find laughable. In fact, so vague is the document's description of this form of music that it finally defines the genre tautologically,

6. This and all subsequent quotations are drawn directly from a copy of the Harvard Report.

stating that soul music is what plays on black-listener-oriented stations or appears on *Billboard*'s soul chart. This section of the Report is more definitive about the size of the market despite the absence of relevant published data. It estimates its annual sales revenues to be $60 million, with approximate sales of twelve million albums and sixty million singles. The total market for recordings in 1970 is estimated at $1,660 million, and soul music is thought to account for around ten percent of that business.

The Report then offers a brief and unsatisfying history of soul music. It argues that the genre evolves on the basis of three trends. First, local-regional styles develop, which are then diluted and homogenized in an effort to achieve national popularity. In the process, the attachment of performers to a definable community of consumers is lost, replaced by a national constituency known on the basis of market research rather than face-to-face contact. Second, while that repertoire is initially defined by a largely race-specific audience, the production of "cover" records of soul music performed largely but not exclusively by white artists leads to a heterogeneous body of consumers. Third, companies with national scope broaden the market for soul outside the black community by either purchasing artists or entire record labels. The Report further alludes to an ongoing collision between undercapitalized independent companies with roots in the black community and large, well-endowed corporations that either buy out their small competitors or their best-selling artists. Historically, the treatment of black artists by those large companies has been quite racist, yet that ill treatment is overshadowed by the *indifference* toward black music on the part of major labels. RCA, Capitol, MGM, and Columbia are pointed out as particularly oblivious.

This characterization, like a number of other comments in the Report, is quite peculiar, as it illustrates a dubious acquaintance with the history of the record business. It fails to acknowledge limited but commercially successful efforts by RCA, particularly their acquisition of Sam Cooke from Keen Records, as well as the success of their 1950s sublabel Groove, and most notably Mickey and Sylvia's chart-topping "Love is Strange" (1957). More importantly, it fails to address the longstanding and prosperous interaction between black performers and Columbia Records. Despite having been commissioned by the very label, the writers of this document seem to have ignored their own sponsor's history. No mention is made of the fact that the company initiated the recording of blues in 1920 with Mamie Smith's "Crazy Blues" on the OKeh label, or the extensive involvement on the part of producer John Hammond with black performers. He signed Count Basie, Billie Holiday, and

Teddy Wilson, among many others, to Columbia and would have furthered the career of the blues legend Robert Johnson had the guitarist not died in 1938. In addition, the Report ignores the role Columbia played in the transformation of Miles Davis into an international icon. None of those omissions should obscure the general accuracy of the Report's findings on the music industry's poor treatment of black artists, but they do indicate a failure to conduct the kind of research one would expect from an institution like the Harvard Business School.

The principal means by which the public is made aware of black music, the Report continues, is through radio. Consumers were purchasing more singles than albums by black artists, although that was beginning to change as black performers began creating integral long-playing LPs rather than simply collecting groups of single releases. This practice was initiated by Isaac Hayes's first solo recording, *Hot Buttered Soul*, in 1969. Selling over a million copies, the album incorporated a number of extended tracks, most memorably an eighteen-minute version of Jimmy Webb's "By the Time I Get to Phoenix." It crossed over from the top of the R&B charts to the top of the jazz, pop, and easy listening charts, as well. The precedent led to Marvin Gaye's *What's Going On* (1971), Sly and the Family Stone's *There's a Riot Goin' On* (1971), and Stevie Wonder's *Innervisions* (1973). Nonetheless, the bulk of successful recordings at the time were singles, and the role of the black DJ in that process is underscored in the Report. Soul stations and their staff serve as critical gatekeepers in the process whereby black records cross over to Top 40 radio. Thirty percent of the Top 40 is estimated to be composed of songs that have achieved this transition. A major impediment to the DJ's role in this process is said to be the undocumented suspicion of payola, the exchange of assets for the playing of recordings.

The Report asserts that the CRG would be wise to create relationships with black broadcasters, yet it recognizes that payola will continue to be a formidable but not insurmountable obstacle. Once again, however, this section illustrates the Harvard Business School's failure to exhaustively research a subject. The fact that black DJs typically received lower salaries than white employees is not mentioned, nor that as a group they possessed little professional status. Neither is any attention drawn to the formation of the National Association of Television and Radio Announcers (NATRA) in 1965 or the failed efforts by black members of NATRA to press their case for a more substantial position in the industry. While those efforts may not have involved the exchange of payola, they did encompass the threat of physical harm, which resulted in an FCC investigation of the organization.[7] In the process, the focus of the group shifted from racially motivated self-determination back to a more mainstream position as a business advocacy group.

Clearly, the Report continues, in order to have viable product to offer to broadcasters, the CRG must compete with the existing soul record labels. Being late-comers to this market, the company is encouraged to pursue three goals: create a cadre of black staff at the CRG; recruit successful black personnel to fill the ranks of that cadre; and develop strong links with black radio. The aim of these efforts would be to shore up the CRG's relationship with the black community until they can implement the development of a Soul Product Group that exists as a semi-autonomous unit and acquires a strong roster of artists. In the meantime, the advocated approach will be effective as a tactic of "BUYING TIME WHILE THE REQUIRED INTERNAL SUPPORT ORGANIZATION IS STAFFED, AND DEVELOPED" [original emphases]. As that organization develops, the Report recommends as well that the CRG expand their current source of product by making custom label arrangements with existing "outside product resources" and thereby begin the process of establishing the company's presence and involvement in soul music.

An ambitious MBA student, Marnie Tattersall, who was later hired to work in the Black Music Division by Logan Westerbrooks, prepared an addendum to the Report. She advocated four goals, and believed they could lead to the CRG acquiring control over fifteen percent of the black market by 1978. None of them, however, were implemented by the CRG. First, she suggested that the CRG sponsor a conference that would include ten or fifteen of the top black program directors as a means of solidifying relations with broadcasters. Second, she encouraged tour support for black artists and the placement of those artists on bills that include top-drawer pop performers. Third, she called attention to the lack of black acts on television, alerted the company to the popularity of Don Cornelius's *Soul Train*, and promoted the possibility that CBS-TV show the program on affiliate stations. Last, she proposed that the CRG open retail record stores in black neighborhoods and initiate franchises to facilitate racially generated retail.

While the CRG abandoned all of Marnie Tattersall's recommendations, the Report did lead to the formation of the Soul Products Group. It also helped to initiate the company's engagement with African-American performers such that they

7. For further information on NATRA, see George pp.111–15.

could report the significant augmentation of their roster only a few years later. The other immediate consequence was that the CRG aggressively engaged in establishing relationships with a set of custom labels. CBS Records President Clive Davis reached out to Stax Records and Philadelphia International Records. Davis's public stance was that he had never read the Harvard Report and was acting upon his own initiative. Al Bell, the head of Stax, did not believe this to be the case, and assumed that Davis had in fact supplied Harvard with some of the vital statistics in the Report. Whatever the case, the company took action to involve itself in the distribution of both labels, despite the fact that Davis would leave CBS in May of 1973 following the accusation that he had spent $94,000 in violation of corporation expense-account procedures. (Nelson George believes that the cause was more likely drug payments to DJs in exchange for airplay.) The outcome of these arrangements was to the immediate advantage of both companies as well as the CRG, although the money invested could keep neither Stax nor Philadelphia International immune from the legal or economic pressures they encountered in the future.

Philadelphia International's Gamble and Huff had begun their professional collaboration in the mid-1960s. Their first successes resulted from either resuscitating the careers of veteran performers or working on a contract basis for other labels. In the first case, they enabled Jerry Butler's smooth baritone once again to rise to the top of the charts. He had not secured a hit record since the success of the Impressions' "For Your Precious Love" in 1960. While group member Curtis Mayfield had written the track, Butler commandingly delivered the lead vocal. Gamble and Huff re-launched his career with "Only the Strong Survive," a song with lyrics that reflected the duo's predilection for social uplift and homiletic appeals to the black community to pull itself up by its bootstraps. They achieved another success when Atlantic Records arranged for them to work with Wilson Pickett; the result was 1968's chart-topping "Don't Let the Green Grass Fool You." The duo formed Gamble Records in 1967 and released a set of hit records by the Intruders, including "Cowboys to Girls" (1968).

As is true of many independent labels, the company was unable on its own to secure successful distribution of their material and therefore entered into an arrangement with the legendary Chess Records of Chicago in 1968. That relationship, however, collapsed almost immediately in the wake of the death of one of the label's founders, Leonard Chess, in 1968, and the subsequent sale of the company's assets to the GRT Corporation. The access that Chess possessed to black radio and retail was lost, and Gamble and Huff suffered a period of retrenchment. Clive Davis's offer, therefore, was a welcome life buoy. It enabled the company, now called Philadelphia International, to attain financial security and begin expansion of its artist roster. The CRG in turn received the opportunity to help build a black label from the ground up and gave them access to a number of marketable black artists. This also set in place the administration by CBS of Mighty Three Music, Gamble and Huff's publishing firm, through the April-Blackwood catalogue.

Armed with capital and a dependable distribution system, Philadelphia International soon thereafter acquired the talents of the O'Jays, Harold Melvin, and the Blue Notes (featuring Teddy Pendergrass), among others. Their in-house band, collectively known as MFSB, began to assemble a unique market niche that was successfully promoted as "the sound of Philadelphia." Hits followed, including "Back Stabbers" (1972), "Love Train" (1973), and "For the Love of Money" (1974) by the O'Jays; and "The Love I Lost" (1973) and "Wake Up Everybody" (1975) by Harold Melvin and the Blue Notes; as well as MSFB's "Love is the Message" (1974) and such one-offs as Billy Paul's "Me and Mrs. Jones" (1972) and Joe Simon's "Drowning in the Sea of Love" (1972). Success permitted Gamble and Huff to create elaborate songs whose duration exceeded the customary three-minute single. The CRG appreciated this development, for it permitted them to market many of the label's releases as album sellers—just as they would a rock release—rather than pigeonholing the company as merely a creator of singles.

There was an inescapable irony at the core of the successful merger of interests between CBS and Gamble and Huff. Kenny Gamble perceived one aim of his label to be a platform for promoting not only his Islamic religious views but also his belief that strong family values and economic self-determination could assure a more solid future for African-Americans. That he was able to accomplish these ends through the corporate support of CBS did not erode the fact that the success of his company illustrated how capitalism and Black Nationalism might work hand in hand. Sadly, however, the label's string of successes was to collapse in the wake of a Newark, New Jersey–based grand jury investigation into the role of payola in black radio. The practices that the Harvard Report stated could potentially doom the status of black self-initiative in the record business proved to be fatal for Gamble and Huff. While he was not jailed, Kenny Gamble was fined $25,000 in 1976 for his role in kickbacks to black radio. Furthermore, Philadelphia International, like the rest of the record industry, was affected by the collapse of the entertainment economy in 1979. This also led to severe cutbacks at the black music division of CBS. Moreover, the focus upon labels like Philadelphia International waned as CBS's publicity machinery was devoted to the release of Michael Jackson's *Off The Wall* in 1979. Stars, not stables of singers, now reigned as the primary recipients of CBS's promotion. Also, the public's taste had taken a turn as a result of the focus upon rhythm and grooves that was gaining ascendance in the wake of dance music. Elaborate, issues-oriented lyrics seemed to expire in the disco inferno.

The relationship between CBS and Stax Records was more short-lived and traumatic than the predominantly harmonious interaction between the label and Philadelphia International. Dissention and disagreement governed the interaction between Stax and CBS virtually from the start. Stax had reached an institutional crossroads when its president, Al Bell, approached CBS president Clive Davis for assistance in the fall of 1972. A savvy, politically astute individual, Bell had substantially transformed the label since he came on board in 1965 as the company's first full-time promotion man. At that time, while most of the artists and many of the musicians and songwriters associated with Stax were black, the owners of the label were not. Established by a brother and sister, Jim Stewart and Estelle Axton—hence ST + AX—Stax became an overwhelmingly black-managed and community-focused organization under Bell's leadership. He was committed to the notion of black economic self-empowerment espoused by the Reverend Jesse Jackson, and believed the only hope for racial advancement in America was through control of the marketplace.

To that end, Bell instituted a strategic alignment with the Gulf + Western Corporation soon after Stax terminated their distribution affiliation with Atlantic Records in 1968. His hope was that the multimedia conglomerate would financially assist Stax in their expansion into new markets and genres, and give them access to more dependable national distribution. Also, since the company owned Paramount Pictures, Bell believed Stax might be able to enter the lucrative business of film soundtracks. Gulf + Western paid $4.3 million for the company, yet allowed them to retain control over all elements of Stax's operation except accounting and visual art. One of the complications of the label's relationship with Atlantic was that the agreement stipulated the master recordings created during the course of the contract belonged to Atlantic, not Stax. Therefore, once having aligned Stax with Gulf + Western, Stax needed to generate catalogue quickly.

Stax set about to create records with a vengeance, producing twenty-seven albums that could be issued simultaneously in May of 1969. The Herculean efforts sorely taxed the organization's resources, but it also led to the creation of Isaac Hayes's *Hot Buttered Soul* and the considerable success and acclaim that record accrued. In the first three years of the Gulf + Western agreement, Bell believed that Stax could generate 7.5 million sales. They surpassed that goal in the first year alone by moving ten million records. However, the relationship between Stax and Gulf + Western deteriorated rapidly, particularly over the issue of distribution. Bell assumed his product would not only reach major outlets but also continue to be serviced to the independently owned "mom-and-pop" establishments that were the bedrock of their customer base. This was not the case, and Stax set out to raise the necessary capital to buy back the label. They acquired the funds through the German PolyGram/Deutsche Gramophone Company, and in 1970 repurchased the label for $4.5 million. Soon thereafter, Stax arranged a loan of $2.5 million from the Memphis-based Union Planters National Bank to reacquire the forty-five percent of Stax stock that Deutsche Gramophone had obtained as part of the loan. At the same time, Jim Stewart informed Bell that the many changes in the organization had diminished his desire to remain in charge. He wished to sell his interest, and Bell therefore needed to obtain the capital to float the agreement.

Confronted with these administrative and fiscal dilemmas, Bell met with Clive Davis in the fall of 1972. He proposed that CBS buy out Jim Stewart's portion of Stax, but that idea met with resistance from the corporation's lawyers. As an alternative, CBS loaned Stax $6 million in return for which the company would distribute Stax's releases for a ten-year period. Another stipulation was that Stewart remain affiliated with the company for a five-year period to assure continuity. Bell assumed that Stax's arrangement with CBS would gain them access to "rack jobbers"—the individuals who maintained record inventories at major department stores, a portion of the market that Stax had heretofore failed to penetrate. These prospects, however, were dashed when Clive Davis was removed from CBS. Other elements of the CBS hierarchy failed to follow through on the verbal agreement that Davis had made. Paradoxically, the dissention that arose at CBS occurred despite the fact that Jim Tyrell, the first black executive placed in charge of marketing at the company, was assigned to administrate the accord. Tyrell came to realize that Bell had incorrectly assumed that the CBS agreement would permit Stax access to "co-op funds"—financial incentives set aside as a means of inducing rack jobbers and other distributors to take responsibility for moving a large volume of recordings in exchange for advertising support. Due to the massive creation of product on Stax's part, Tyrell feared that the company's merchandise would glut the market and result in excessive and expensive returns. The implicit verbal agreements under which Bell and Davis negotiated were no longer operative. As Rob Bowman explains in *Soulsville USA*, "Davis's and Bell's understanding was that Stax would not be distributed *by* CBS; rather, Stax's product would be distributed *through* CBS's branches."[8]

Consequently, Stax ended up making less on the sale of each LP operating through a major label than when they had been operating through independent distributors. The fact that Stax had to convince CBS of the viability of each of their releases led as well to the two companies often unwittingly competing with one another when Stax felt that the corporation was not sufficiently promoting one of its products. Also, CBS tended to determine their marketing decisions on a national basis, conceiving of the country as one incorporated territory. Stax, on the other hand, had always understood that the rhythm of its sales proceeded regionally, one portion of the country often picking up a record before another. They therefore targeted their marketing strategy on a region-by-region basis, gearing into action once an area indicated interest in a new release. In the end, Bell was convinced that the contract with CBS had been erected upon a mismatched set of expectations about how the market operated. As a longstanding independent label, Stax was committed to putting out as much product as possible and obligating their distributors to move it to customers. A major label like CBS purposefully kept their inventory smaller, for unsold records led to unrecouped capital.

While Stax quarreled with CBS over the terms of their agreement, the Memphis operation was coming apart at the seams. The causes of the dissolution of their association are labyrinthine in the extreme. In part, the miscalculations and chronic overextension of Al Bell's administration of Stax were to blame. Equally culpable were the executives at CBS, who appeared committed to repeatedly sandbagging the label. Whether or not they ever came out and publicly admitted it, CBS seemed intent on treating Stax's resources as a disposable commodity, stripping them of their worth at every turn. Oddly enough, while the Harvard Report advised against any attempt on the part of CBS to take over a soul label, this appeared to be their ultimate

8. Bowman, p.299.

goal with Stax. Rob Bowman's painstakingly detailed documentation of Stax's demise in *Soulsville USA* delineates the degree to which the two companies operated under antithetical assumptions about music and its audience. Little could dissuade the New York executives that Memphis, Tennessee was anything other than a cultural backwater and the local record industry a poor facsimile of the firms in New York City. They considered the mainstream R&B acts who sold the bulk of Stax's product to be run-of-the-mill performers, second-class citizens in the music business. The mom-and-pop stores at which most fans of Stax bought their records were anathema to CBS's marketing strategies. All of this antagonism climaxed in 1974 when CBS withheld forty percent of the money due Stax as a reserve fund against records paid for yet not sold. This further complicated Stax's ability to make loan payments to the local Union Planters Bank.

The result was, as Bowman argues, nothing less than "economic strangulation."[9] Stax endeavored to sever relations with the New York company, but was halted when CBS served the label with an injunction and restraining order that denied Stax any power to abrogate the CBS agreement. Stax responded with a $67-million counter-suit that only served to incur CBS's further wrath. It led as well to the revelation that CBS had withheld over $6 million for records they had sold. The legal wrangling between the two companies was finally settled in February 1975 when Stax agreed to repay its debt to CBS within a year, and CBS in turn would relinquish all rights to distribute the soul-music label. At this point, however, Stax was fiscally and administratively very much like a patient with one foot in the grave. The financial claims upon them by the Union Planters Bank and the various suits that followed brought on the demise of the company on December 19, 1975, when the doors to their offices were shut, and in November 1977, when the last of the label's assets were sold.

The collision between corporate culture and African-American self-initiative that doomed the interaction between Stax and CBS can also be witnessed on an individual basis. The careers of certain mainstream R&B artists became lost in CBS's commitment to crossover during the course of the 1970s. Executives, black and white alike, found themselves unable to sympathize with or to comprehend the interests and appetites of a mature black audience who would more likely encounter artists on the chitlin' circuit than at Madison Square Garden. This dynamic was starkly illustrated in a 1976 interview with LeBaron Taylor, head of CBS's black music division,

9. Bowman, p.320.

by Geoffrey Stokes of the *Village Voice*. He outlined the company's strategy for insti-
tutionalizing crossover to white consumers by choosing singles that would appeal to
both white and black audiences. Taylor also pointed out how CBS had reverted to
the practice of perceiving black artists as creators of singles, not albums. Gaps as long
as two months were allowed to elapse between the release of a single and that of the
album on which the song was featured. This was the case with the Manhattans after
their ballad "Kiss and Say Goodbye" sold 2.5 million copies in 1976.

Such actions flew in the face of the strategy outlined by the Harvard Report, which
advocated building audiences for R&B on black radio, achieving sales in that community of a half-million, and only then transferring attention to the white mainstream.
CBS's practices meant, according to the *Village Voice*, "that black radio listeners are
reduced to auditioning records geared for white audiences."[10] Consumers were to be
divided on the basis of race as well as class, and even age. This kind of market segmentation was parallel with the increasing segmentation of American society in general
into disparate constituencies based on race, gender, and class. In the mind of CBS
executives, music appeared to be a means of segregation, not integration.

Two artists whose careers suffered as a result of this strategy were Tyrone Davis and
the late R&B veteran Johnnie Taylor. Both entered into arrangements with CBS as a
means of securing a larger, more diverse audience only to find themselves ghettoized.
Taylor, a major star on Stax, recorded "Disco Lady" in 1975 to capitalize on the
emerging dance craze, and sold 2.5 million copies. While the song was targeted to a
young audience, Taylor's base constituency remained older. The success of "Disco
Lady" did not encourage CBS to build a strategy for Taylor's career at the label.

Tyrone Davis signed to Columbia in 1977. He had secured a string of R&B hits
on Brunswick Records, including a number-one single, "Turning Point." His first
release, "Get it Up, Turn it Loose," sold well to his established constituency, yet the
follow-up, "Get On Up, Disco," was a mismatched attempt to repeat Johnnie
Taylor's accomplishment. Davis's most successful release for Columbia, "In The
Mood" (1979), was an old-school ballad that sold 700,000 copies, yet would likely
have reached a higher number had the label been committed to his career. The fact
that it accomplished the sales figures that it did was largely due to the efforts of Paris
Eley, a black promotion head at the label. Regardless of their notable sales achievements, however, neither Taylor nor Davis ever received what Nelson George refers to

10. George, p.150.

as the "honorary pop pass" that would permit them to be treated by CBS as individuals with a broad appeal." The label apparently set and met limited expectations for their careers. Both men went on to record successfully for other labels until their recent deaths. The audience that CBS failed to reach and whose commitment to veteran performers the label seemed to disdain continued to purchase mainstream R&B. The depth of their devotion is most markedly illustrated by Z.Z. Hill's *Down Home Blues*, released by Malaco Records in 1982. It sold over a million copies and remained on *Billboard*'s black charts for more than a year. The title track has become a touchstone song in the black community in the deep South, a requisite for any band that wants to succeed among an audience of their peers.

* * *

Nearly thirty years have passed since the release of the Harvard Report. The effects of its recommendations upon the black-owned businesses that CBS wished to bring into its corporate orbit are mixed. Clearly, the access to capital and dependable systems of distribution assisted Gamble and Huff in their music's ascension to the pop charts during the 1970s. Their fall from commercial grace was not the result of entanglements with the corporate boardroom, but the consequence of their own miscalculations and unforeseen transformations in the public taste. Stax appeared to be on a collision course with fiscal and administrative upheaval when Al Bell turned to Clive Davis for assistance. The fact that their agreement was never consecrated on paper led to Stax's failure to receive the kind of financial assistance that might have assured its survival. It also seemed apparent that while CBS welcomed the prestige in the black community that they accrued as a result of associating with Stax, the two companies never shared a common understanding of their audience. A similar lack of appreciation occurred in the treatment of Johnnie Taylor and Tyrone Davis. CBS's failure to promote either man to a crossover audience and its conviction that their styles should match the times—not create an audience on the basis of musical excellence—reflects the reality that the Harvard Report is grounded in appeals to markets, not communities.

Both Philadelphia International and Stax had succeeded because they codified a sound that drew upon the needs and knowledge of their fans. The Harvard Business

11. George, p.169.

School defined those individuals as units, not human beings. For all CBS's fear that their actions might be perceived as racist, they made little effort to understand how race and culture intersect or why soul music had become the genre of choice for the black community (and a more racially diverse audience, as well). In their desire to remedy the "almost total indifference" on the part of the major record labels toward black music, CBS ignored virtually everything other than the profitability of music made and purchased by people of color.

The failure to understand any factors other than those governed by the market recur in the manner with which the Sony Corporation, as the company is now known, publicly documents its own institutional history. In 2000, the company released an ornate and extensive twenty-six-CD collection, *Soundtrack for a Century*, accompanied by a hardbound, three-hundred-plus-page commentary. The tracks selected represent all the key genres in which the corporation has participated, including rhythm & blues. Gerald Early, professor of English and Director of African and Afro-American Studies at Washington University, wrote the notes on the genre. He states, "When one looks back at the history of African-American popular dance music since 1945, its shape takes on the air of inevitability."[12] One entrepreneur after another, Early adds, has taken advantage of the right moment so that "somehow the story of this music has been the fulfillment of a certain national historic destiny."[13] One can believe such a trajectory of inevitability only if the collision between culture and commerce is left out of consideration. Very few things in life, cultural or otherwise, occur inevitably. The swift hand of circumstance is driven by a variety of factors. What is possible for us as consumers is the result of decisions made by a body of individuals, few of whom follow their whims or assume they are simply the agents of destiny.

The Harvard Report attempted to account for a narrow range of factors, and in the process enabled its sponsor to comprehend the gyrations of the record charts, but not what drew those customers to add one more commodity to their lives. The approach that the label took to their audience and their long-term goals were selective, to say the least. As stated earlier, there is an element to this document that illustrates a keen grasp of the obvious. All CBS needed to do to confirm the viability of R&B as a marketable genre was to look to their own company's past and be reminded of how

12. Gerald Early, "R&B: From Doo-Wop To Hip-Hop," from *Sony Music 100 Years* (Sony Corporation JXK 65750, 2000), p.253.
13. *Ibid.*

attractive black popular music had been to one generation after another. Instead, they chose to ignore their very own history. In that regard, an expression coined by the Stax studio musicians bears upon this issue. They labeled their tendency to remember arrangements during the course of a project and then forget them altogether once the session was over "slate memory."[14] The record industry possesses a comparable ability to dismiss what is no longer deemed of interest. While CRG executives could imagine in 1972 that they might acquire a fifteen-percent share of the soul-music audience, they were unable to conceive of why that body of individuals was attracted to the music in the first place. That set of interests and investments has been conveniently wiped away.

David Sanjek is the director of the BMI Archives. He is co-author, with his late father, Russell Sanjek, of *Pennies from Heaven: The American Popular Music Business in the 20th Century* (DaCapo Press, 1996), and is completing a collection, *Always On My Mind: Music, Memory and Money* (Wesleyan University Press, 2002). He has served as chairman of the US chapter of the International Association for the Study of Popular Music and has been a consultant to the Rock and Roll Hall of Fame, the Experience Music Project, and Songmasters: The American Road.

14. Bowman, p.116.

The Ballad of
the Mid-Level Artist

BY DANNY GOLDBERG

I used to run big record companies and now I run a small company, Artemis Records, which I also partially own. Universal and Warner Music Group, two of the current "Big Five" international music companies, have fired me. Artemis is distributed internationally by Sony and in the US by RED, which is predominantly owned by Edel, a European indie. I have a tangled web of friendships and feuds with executives and artists at every company. My wife, Rosemary Carroll, is an attorney who represents many artists. I am not objective, but I have opinions.

In the frenzy to identify exactly how the Internet will improve the music business, some Web executives and tech savants have claimed that digital distribution will lead to fairer and more generous contracts for artists. These claims are based on the oft-repeated assumption that major-label recording contracts are unfair to artists, allowing the labels to grab a disproportionate share of profits. Cathartic as it is to vent at record companies and carry the banner for artist empowerment, it seems to me that many of the attacks on the inequitable sharing of the pie have been overstated. The problems most artists have with record companies (and there are many legitimate problems, don't get me wrong) have nothing to do with how the money is divided up, so long as we are talking about acts that actually sell enough records.

It goes without saying that the blockbuster artists who sell millions of albums make lots of money. Not only do such sales levels generate millions of dollars in royalties (and goose important income streams such as publishing and performance fees), but they also provide these artists enormous leverage to renegotiate. Why, you ask, would a record company owed several albums by an artist improve her deal? Because record company executives are judged on their annual, sometimes even quarterly, performances.

When I was at Mercury Records, we agreed to give Shania Twain an increase in her royalty rate in the range of forty percent if she would deliver *Come On Over* in time for a fourth-quarter release in 1997. Shania had a weak deal despite having sold ten million copies of her previous album, *The Woman in Me*. The boost in royalty rate was conditional upon Shania finishing her work quickly; she did, and the Q4 (fourth-quarter) release of *Come On Over* significantly propped up the PolyGram numbers for 1997. And in the process, the renegotiated rate has earned Twain at least an extra $10 million. Every artist coming off a multimillion seller has similar leverage with the bosses of the big companies.

Conversely, artists who have a relatively small audience, say under 50,000 albums, clearly make no money for themselves or their record companies in the major-label game, so it really doesn't matter how their royalties are calculated or what their rate is.

But let's look at mid-level artists, many of whom—Aimee Mann, Chuck D, and Michelle Shocked, to name a few—have been outspoken critics of the major-label system. These are the artists who are most often plagued by the legitimate problems I alluded to above: insensitive executives who pressure them to copy current hit sounds; rapidly changing corporate cultures in which an artist can be romanced into signing in one season and virtually ignored by the time he delivers his album (often for reasons having nothing to do with the quality or even the commercial viability of the record); and the increasing demand on the soon-to-be-four remaining major record groups to act as efficiently managed profit centers for their multinational parent companies. This type of pressurized quarter-to-quarter accountability strikes many as antithetical to the spirit of the days when many labels stood loyally by their artists for year after year, building careers lovingly and patiently until sometimes the big payoff arrived, or if not, so what? Why can't all labels, goes the daydream, be like Warners in the 1970s?

That this image of art making nice with commerce is as much nostalgia-tinged fantasy as reality does little to diminish the hold it has on the collective unconscious, especially that of singer-songwriters. It should be noted, though, that this golden era of artist development was facilitated by a one-time-only, post-war baby boom that dramatically spiked the number of album-friendly record buyers. And any artist around then will tell you that the royalty rates back then were anything but golden. The profits generated by these factors provided the labels the ability to stick with artists for longer periods of time, also known as "artist development." The collapse of artist-development budgets was forestalled in the eighties when $9.98 cassettes were replaced by $16.98 CDs, a "conversion" which permitted continued double-digit annual growth despite the smaller Gen-X pool of buyers. When sales of catalogue CDs reached a saturation point in the early nineties and companies were still required to show the same growth, cutbacks in staff and a reduced commitment to artist development began in earnest.

Up until the 1970s, record companies unquestionably hoarded a disproportionate share of the profits, and many artists, especially black artists, didn't get paid at all. Over the last several decades, however, as the business grew, a class of lawyers emerged to take advantage of the record companies' needs for marketable product, and the deals themselves have vastly improved for the artists.

Some of the criticisms leveled at the labels hark back to earlier eras. For example, some PR-hungry artists and managers have claimed that there are still "breakage" clauses in contracts, remnants from the days of vinyl. In reality, most companies, including the one I ran, have long since eliminated them.

There are, however, still boilerplate formulas called "packaging deductions" (a twenty-five-percent reduction from the CD list price) and "free goods" (fifteen percent). Putting aside the murky origins of such clauses, the practical effect is straightforward: They reduce the value of a point on a $16.98 CD to between ten and eleven cents (a point is shorthand for a royalty percentage). For the purposes of this article, I am assuming a point equals ten cents, and that the royalty rate for our hypothetical mid-sized artist is fourteen points, or $1.40 per album.

So let's take our mid-level artist, and say that she managed to sell 200,000 copies of her latest CD. How does the artist make out? Based on a royalty rate of $1.40 per album, 200,000 CDs sold results in earned income of $280,000. However, before the artist buys her mom a car (or pays off her college loans), she first needs to deal with the dreaded recoupment. If our artist received a $25,000 advance and spent another $115,000 making the record, this $140,000 is deemed recoupable, which means that the label can collect that amount against royalties.

Also, let's assume the artist received $70,000 in tour support (recoupable) and another $70,000 in recoupable video and promotional support (this is usually split between the label and artist). That adds up to $280,000 in recoupable advances, thereby canceling out the $280,000 earned by the artist on points from her CD sales. Royalty-wise, it's a wash. (There's a holdback for returns of fifteen to twenty percent, but royalties for these "reserves" are usually paid out in eighteen months minus any actual returns.)

Album royalties, luckily, are not the only stream of income for an artist. Artists who write their own material enjoy a tremendous economic advantage over those who do not. If an artist writes her own songs, she earns additional monies known as *mechanical royalties*. Assuming a mediocre .75 percent mechanical rate per song, times eleven (a roundabout number of songs on an album), the hypothetical writer-artist would earn around sixty cents an album, or $120,000 on sales of 200,000 units. (Artists with a strong contract can get up to eighty-five cents in mechanicals per album—and these payments are all "from record one" and not subject to any kind of recoupment.) Solo artists like Mann or Shocked also don't have to divide royalties with other musicians, although they will have to pay managers, lawyers, and accountants (standard is approximately twenty-five percent of net income). They also can make extra money—facilitated, in our hypothetical, by the sale of 200,000 albums—from concert appearances, merchandise like T-shirts, and performance royalties, from radio airplay for example, which are collected and distributed by ASCAP and BMI. None of this is to suggest that an artist selling 200,000 albums is living large; she is, however, considerably ahead of ninety percent of Americans.

What would the label make on the sale of these 200,000 albums? Are labels making their parent companies' shareholders rich at the expense of these middle-class artists? Retailers pay around $10 an album, which amounts to a gross revenue for the label on those 200,000 CDs of $2 million.

No one knows exactly how much distribution and manufacturing costs. The big companies all have large overheads to provide these functions, often creating separate divisions to handle them. The record company presidents run their divisions with internal charges for manufacturing and distribution that add up to around $2.65 a unit. There's obviously profit built into that, but the per-unit figure varies, depending on the amount of overall record-group volume as well as unpredictable outside events such as retail bankruptcies. As a rule of thumb, I was always told to assume about $1-a-unit profit on these combined functions. For the purpose of this exercise, I'm assuming a "real" cost of $1.65 per unit for combined manufacturing and distribution.

Here are the record company's expenses:

- Recording and recoupable marketing costs: $300,000
- Mechanicals: $120,000
- Non-recoupable marketing: $600,000
- Manufacturing and distribution: $330,000
- Total label expenses: $1,350,000

This leaves $650,000 in profit, right? Not necessarily. Out of that comes all of the salaries of the people who work at the record company. These include the people who do the color separations for CD covers, who create websites for artists, and who make hundreds of calls to radio stations, journalists, and retailers. Struggling divisions spend more, but a healthy US record company with a decent catalogue allots around twenty percent of their gross revenues to overhead, or, in this instance, $400,000.

That still leaves the label with a profit of $250,000, right? Yes, and the middle-level artist has reason to gripe, but not without coming to terms with a fundamental fact: Big record companies weren't established to enable artists to sell 200,000 copies. Big record companies need big sales. Even the most astute A&R people are wrong two-thirds of the time. On average, even at a successful company the cost of promoting and marketing a label's "misses" eats up most of the profits, from not only the mid-level successes but even the gold-plus hits. Executives at major labels, then, are usually disappointed by sales of 200,000.

A major record company's profits come from the Shania Twains of the world, the very artists who have the least to complain about. Remember the $600,000 allocated to marketing on 200,000 albums? This represents thirty percent of the total revenue. On an album that goes on to sell millions, the share of income spent on advertising and promotion drops to ten percent, leaving an extra $2-an-album profit for the label. After a certain point, albums sell themselves through word of mouth.

Based solely on these numbers, you might wonder why Seagram spent all those billions to buy PolyGram in 1999. Those sky-high valuations take into account two other crucial factors: international profits and catalogue value.

Album prices are higher in Europe and Japan, and artist royalties are usually reduced to three-quarters of the US rate. Hence, labels clear more profit per unit sold. And once again, with rare exception, the artists who generate strong international numbers are those with big pop hits. Secondly there is the asset value of owning a catalogue, which is why master ownership is so jealously guarded. The Beatles's albums still sell millions each year. Bob Marley's *Legend* anthology sold five million copies in the nineties. Catalogues of hits make very high margins and generate money for decades through re-issues, compilations, licensing for soundtracks, etc. It is widely assumed that the widespread use of MP3 music files on the

Internet, like the introduction of any new format for music, will drive up the value of hit catalogues, but the key word here is "hit." No one ascribes much catalogue value to an album that sold 200,000 in its first release.

Mid-level artists are, in essence, valuable to labels only in terms of their future potential, or if they garner such great press that they help a particular executive burnish his or her reputation as a sensitive soul. Such repute, alas, is far less valuable in the marketplace than an expertise in marketing megabits or implementing cost-cutting.

One major label doing very well in the last year showed an aggregate profit margin (including a calculation for distribution and international) of a little over ten percent. Nonetheless, there was increasing pressure from the parent corporation and from Wall Street to raise the margin to over fifteen percent. Nine times out of ten, this is done by signing fewer new artists and by taking fewer marketing risks on the new artists under contract (staff cutbacks usually follow suit, as well).

If an album fails to create immediate excitement, word comes from on high to shift manpower and marketing dollars to a different project. This syndrome, far more than substandard royalty rates, is what devastates artists. After touring tirelessly and building a devoted fan base, after a year or two of pouring their hearts into writing and recording a record, after hearing cries of genius from friends and fans alike, artists naturally believe that with a little more advertising, one more video, and a real shot at radio play, they too could move millions. But the attention span of majors nowadays, with a few exceptions, resembles that of the thirteen-year-olds at the core of their audience.

Reduction of risk-taking by the major record groups means that cutting-edge musicians are driven to independent labels like mine, which have scarcer resources and lack the added profits from distribution or international sales. Indies have traditionally presented an alternative, both aesthetically and economically, to the blockbuster-driven mindset of the majors. In the 1980s several indie-rock labels such as Dischord and Touch & Go erected a payment system that gave artists fifty percent of the net profits.

This "partnership" may seem more artist-friendly, but the net amount of money made by artists on those labels is not demonstrably greater than it would have been with the same level of marketing in a royalty-based system. It's just that the major labels rarely find themselves spending so little in support of one of their albums. More recently the redoubtable Ani DiFranco has chosen to control her own infrastructure and forgo bids from majors and indies alike. I'd posit that in exchange for maintaining total business control, DiFranco has probably sacrificed income. (And in return for the greater per-unit margin, she's had to pay a year-round staff and be her own bank.)

This decade's version of the indie-label-as-salvation mantra is, of course, the Internet-based music company. There has been much talk about the bloat of the majors, and of how much more efficient the Internet will be. This is true up to a point, although bear in mind that the big companies (when they make the move to digital) will benefit from the same efficiencies that Internet companies are relying on, and they'll have the added clout of their catalogues. Undoubtedly the math will change with the advent of Net distribution. But Internet startups claiming the change will be seen in the next year or two are selling snake oil. Companies that have reaped positive PR by offering "artist-friendly" contracts and "new business models" have yet to mint a single real-life success story. One hundred percent of nothing is still nothing. If these companies start adding value to an artist via marketing and promotion, those costs will add up and inevitably be passed along.

Looking beyond the royalty mcguffin, there are some legitimate changes brought about by technology that could be especially advantageous to our mid-level artist. These include:

- *Lowering recording costs.* Remember the $115,000 recording budget? Home-studio systems like ProTools have dramatically reduced recording costs. This means that artists under contract can keep more of the money from an advance, and that unsigned artists can make a decent album much more cheaply, which increases their likelihood of getting a deal (funding and marketing) and making money sooner. If an artist makes an album for $45,000 instead of $115,000, with all other assumptions in the earlier model staying the same, they would begin earning their $1.40-per-unit royalty after 150,000 albums sold instead of 200,000.

- *Cutting out the middleman.* The biggest piece of the $16.98 pie still goes to retailers. For many years to come, retail is going to be very important to most artists. Some cult artists may make their music available exclusively on the Internet, thus permitting a much higher margin for them and/or lower prices for the consumer.

- *Retiring the CD.* Manufacturing and distribution costs are obviously going to decline as more and more music is delivered through the Internet. The savings from digital delivery can be divided among the artist, the label, and possibly the consumer. (Online and offline concert-ticket pricing has taught us that the price for music is determined not by the physical costs of delivery but by what consumers are willing to pay). In theory, in a pure digital marketplace, if an album costs $14, with half going to the artist, a royalty flow on the more cheaply produced album described above could commence at only ten thousand units sold, depending on the artist advance.

Before we celebrate the coming renaissance, recognize that it will take years before many of these costs are reduced, and that until labels figure out replacement revenue streams, they'll be loath to adapt to the new models.

Furthermore, there is no evidence that marketing costs, a major expense for labels, will decline. In a complex Internet environment, it will still take serious dollars to expose new music to potential fans, and top marketing and promotion staffs will never come cheap. Artists should be able to make a living at a lower sales level, but the vast majority of aspiring musicians, critical favorites, and local bar bands will still have a hard time supporting themselves and their families. The biggest obstacle to commercial fulfillment for all but the few genuine stars will not be the music business, but the wants of the people: the cruelest, most fickle, and most generous boss of all.

Danny Goldberg, president of Artemis Records and Sheridan Square Entertainment, has worked hands-on with more popular musical talent than any other recorded-music executive in the 1990s. He is also one of the very few who has worked with every major genre of popular music: rap, country, folk, classical, jazz, pop, rock, R&B, and jazz. This article first appeared online at Inside.com and is reprinted here with permission.

Part  2

The Politics of Race Music

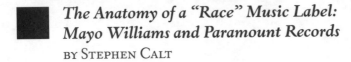

The Anatomy of a "Race" Music Label:
Mayo Williams and Paramount Records
BY STEPHEN CALT

"The big companies wouldn't touch it," Paramount's one-time employee Fred Boerner said of the "race" record, "so we got the jump on 'em." Indeed, when Paramount began its "race" recording program in the summer of 1922, only one record label—OKeh—had established a "race" series, and its catalogue ran to only fifty-odd items. The idea of recording blacks was still something of a novelty; less than three years had passed since OKeh had launched the recording vogue for black music by issuing Mamie Smith's *Crazy Blues*.

The general exclusion of blacks from the recording studio prior to Mamie Smith's appearance was partly due to their invisibility to Northern record executives as consumers. In the year of her debut, 85.2 percent of the nation's black population lived in the South, and 74.7 percent of them lived in rural areas. Before the advent of cheap portable phonographs, which first appeared in the First World War as a novelty intended for soldiers, blacks could not afford to buy Victrolas in appreciable numbers. To the extent that the industry was aware of black performers, it was no doubt hostile toward them. Cultural chauvinism and even imperialism pervaded the phonograph industry; in a speech delivered in June of 1919, OKeh president Otto Heineman had said:

> Thanks to American talent, it is possible for a music lover in Zanzibar to entertain his guests with "Yankee Doodle." Thanks to the progressive American record manufacturers, it is possible for the Eskimo mother to put her babe to sleep with "Mighty Lak A Rose" . . . The king of Zululand can learn the fox trot to the tune of Hindustan; and the caravan can step under the Pyramids for lunch and turn on the "Beautiful Ohio."

No one would extol the recording industry for making it possible for various ethnic groups to enjoy their own music, or for exposing whites to the music of alien cultures.

In June of 1922, when Paramount was on the verge of producing its first "race" record, the *Milwaukee Journal* smugly reported that the tastes of its readers ran to "high-class talent" rather than to "the decadent African rhythms" of jazz. Within record company circles, "race" records were viewed as a blot on the industry; as Ray Kornblum contemptuously said of the "race" records he wholesaled for OKeh in St. Louis in the 1920s: "It's a completely different world. The singing is terrible, the music is junk; it suits *their* tastes." No doubt his was a conventional industry opinion; in February 1924, the *Talking Machine Journal* bitterly noted:

> . . . hundreds of "race" singers have flooded the market with what is generally regarded as the worst contribution to the cause of good music ever inflicted on the public. The lyrics of a great many of these "blues" are worse than the lowest sort of doggerel and the melodies are lacking in originality, lilting rhythm, and any semblance to [*sic*] music worth.

It was only because recording policies of the 1920s were increasingly dictated by a new breed of salesmen who were willing to set aside their own musical tastes in the interests of commerce that "race" music became a fixture of the decade. Such was true of Paramount, a faltering label whose "race" recording orientation was decreed by its sales manager, M. A. Supper.

At the same time, Supper's decision to convert Paramount to a "race" label was boldly speculative, for he did so without offering trial balloons in the company's pop catalogue. "It is against our policy to manufacture a product before we know that there is both a dealer and a consumer demand," a Brunswick sales manager declared in February of 1924." That demand must be in evidence on both the part of the retail merchant and the public before there is a capital outlay for extensive production." The demand for "race" records that Supper perceived was largely gleaned from the pressing figures of Black Swan. Before its "race" program began in the summer of 1922, Paramount had dealt with only two black artists. Between February and July 1922, it featured six sides by New York's Lucille Hegamin, two of which were apparently leased from Black Swan, and two from Arto, a small West Orange company that had fallen into receivership the previous December. The company had also recorded W. C. Handy's daughter Katherine, whose records had not appeared on the market.

Paramount's initial investment in the "race" market was conservative: only twenty-odd such records appeared in the first year. As the company did not have a fixed budget for recording, its slow start can be laid to difficulties in lining up talent and developing distributors, and, perhaps, a wariness about encroaching upon Black Swan, whose failing business it continued to cultivate. Paramount's original catalogue relied heavily on Alberta Hunter, who had inexplicably vanished from Black Swan's recording ledgers after doing well for them in her debut in the spring of 1921. Fourteen of the company's first twenty releases featured Hunter, who then lived in Harlem and billed herself as "Brown Sugar." At the time of her debut record for Paramount, which was advertised in the August 19, 1922, issue of the *Chicago Defender*, she had established herself as the second-most-popular blues singer in the North and held a franchise at Chicago's fanciest black cabaret, the *Dreamland*. "She was a flea in Ethel Waters's collar," said her one-time accompanist Eubie Blake, who recalled she had the unusual ability to record a song in a single take.[1] Her "Down-Hearted Blues," the company's fifth "race" release, became a "race" hit. The company garnered its second hit with its thirty-fifth "race" record, the Norfolk Jubilee Quartet's "My Lord's Gonna Move This Wicked Race," which was announced in the June 30, 1923, issue of the *Defender*. Later, Paramount would puff up its "race" catalogue by reissuing most of the ninety-odd releases of Black Swan, which forfeited its masters to Paramount when it was unable to pay the latter's pressing bills.

"I don't think Pace was as dedicated to the record business as he was interested in insurance," Mayo Williams said, referring to its owner's main profession.[2] Lacking a sales force, Pace put his wife on the road as a traveling record salesperson. By the spring of 1924, Black Swan was defunct. Paramount, however, had moved into the black for the first time. "Race records put us over," Otto Moeser would recall. Afterwards, its executives never considered putting out a racially diversified product, and the company became the only label of consequence to specialize in black music.

If "race" records put Paramount over, it was J. Mayo (Ink) Williams who put "race" records over for Paramount. Williams, the first black to hold an executive

1. Alberta Hunter became the first black singer to use a white accompanist when she recorded with a Miff Mole group in February of 1923, and the first recorded blues singer to feature an unadorned piano accompaniment, drafting Blake in July of 1922, because, the latter thought, his rich bass compensated for a lack of orchestration. Blake rehearsed with her half-hour before recording two sides, for which he was paid $60–$70.
2. After leaving the record business, Pace would obtain a law degree from the University of Chicago.

position in a white recording company, was one of the most remarkable figures in the early recording industry, as well as the most successful producer of blues talent.

Williams's accomplishments were all the more remarkable because they went against the grain of his background, which was what would now be termed "upwardly mobile." In an age when indifference or even antipathy to blues was characteristic of educated blacks, Williams held the heretical belief that blues represented an important aspect of his racial heritage. When his friends sneeringly referred to him and his retinue of blues singers as "Mayo Williams and his dogs," he replied: "My dogs are thoroughbreds."

His appreciation of blues resulted from his strong attachment to his mother, an uneducated woman who relished the music, which he had first heard during his own childhood in Monmouth, Illinois. "Because of my mother I couldn't be what they used to call an 'uppity nigger,'" Williams recalled. It was to visit his mother (and a brother in prison) that he came to Chicago in 1921 after graduating from Brown University, where his chief interests had been football and philosophy, in that order. Though he had shared his enthusiasm for the early records of Mamie Smith with an older fraternity brother, Joe Bibb, a Yale student whose sister had married Harry Pace, music was not one of his early interests. "Nobody who had ever gone to school was interested in music then," he recalled.

Hoping to prolong his stay in Chicago, Williams played football with the all-black Hammond, Indiana Pros (then in the National Football League), sold bathtub gin to the Grand Terrace, a swanky jazz club on 35th and Calumet, and wrote sports articles for Joe Bibb's newly established *Chicago Whip*, a militant black weekly located at 34th and State Street. As Pace's brother-in-law, Bibb had obtained a position as Black Swan's executive treasurer. When Black Swan began faltering, Pace foisted a local distributorship on Bibb, who in turn appointed Williams as his collection agent. To add to the company's difficulties, he put most of the proceeds from Williams's collections into his own struggling newspaper.

None of Williams's various sidelines interested him so much as the prospect of becoming a banker in the fashion of his friend and mentor Fritz Pollard, the celebrated black athlete who had sponsored his admission to Brown after Williams (who met him at a track meet in 1912) had written him a letter asking for career advice. With starting bank salaries at twenty-five dollars a week, he looked about for a more lucrative line of employment. As an infant industry, "race" music gratified his organizational itch: "I wanted to go into something where I could be the organizer; show people how to do it." The collapse of Black Swan did not dampen Williams's interest in the industry, although he felt that it deterred moneyed blacks from afterwards investing in independent record companies.[3] "Black Swan was a variety company," he noted. "They weren't concentrating on blues. If they'd stuck with blues they would have been more successful."

Learning of Paramount's acquisition of Black Swan's masters, the twenty-eight-year-old Williams decided to pay company executives an unsolicited visit in Port Washington in hopes of securing a job. "I just jived my way into the whole situation," he recalled. He thought he was hired because of Paramount's ignorance of the "race" field: "They didn't know anything at all about this 'race' business until they got hold of Black Swan, and then they didn't know anything but what was selling—why it was selling, they didn't know . . ." In presenting himself to Paramount, he was undaunted by the fact that he knew nothing about music and next to nothing about "race" records. "I believed that a college man could sweep a floor better than anybody, and on the basis of thinkin' that I went on," he recalled. Although Williams inflated his credentials in order to better impress his would-be employers, he had to do a minimum amount of bluffing to talk himself into a job. "They knew that if I had any experience at all, I had more experience than they did."

Williams's visit to Port Washington probably occurred in the spring of 1923, shortly after the last Black Swan sessions were held in New York, by which time Paramount had placed about fifty items on the "race" market.[4] Luckily for him, it followed upon M. A. Supper's creation of a music publishing company, and it was this venture that provided him with an entrée into the organization. The impetus behind the new company arose from Supper's futile attempt to sell the rights to Alberta Hunter's "Down-Hearted Blues" (which had recently become an enormous hit by Bessie Smith) to the New York publishing firm of Bernstein and Shapiro. Dissatisfied with the money he received for its rights from another New York publisher, Jack Mills, Inc., Supper decided to form a publishing company that would automatically acquire the rights to all Paramount material. Thus was born Chicago Music, the earliest example of a record-company publishing satellite, a device that

3. In September of 1922, Pace's one-time partner W. C Handy announced the formation of The Handy Record Company, which was to be capitalized at $25,000. Nothing came of this venture.
4. It was not for another year, in the spring of 1924, that Paramount reissued Black Swan's catalogue under its own banner.

would (in the 1950s) ultimately deliver a death blow to Tin Pan Alley publishing. It was founded on a shoestring capital stock of $1200 on January 17, 1923, for the avowed purpose of "owning and dealing in copyrighted musical selections, and for isssuing licenses for their reproduction." Supper acted as its president and treasurer, his wife Viola as secretary, and his brother-in-law Frederick W. Boerner as "director."

Williams emerged from a meeting with Supper, Moeser, and Bostwick with a loose understanding that he was to supervise whatever recording sessions the company would hold in Chicago, which then represented new territory for it. He was formally offered only a position as "manager" of Chicago Music, in which capacity he was hired to administer copyrights of Paramount material. This basically clerical task consisted of arranging to have songs scored for publication and registering them with the copyright division of the Library of Congress. For his work he was to earn half of the two-cent fee per record sale that was allotted to music publishers. For his involvement in Paramount's blues recordings he would receive no salary, but a "talent" (as he put it) or sales royalty from those artists whose sessions he produced.

In extending Williams its offer of quasi-employment (he drew no salary from the company and held no position with it), Paramount was probably seeking someone who appeared to have contacts in the black entertainment world. It was a misguided article of faith among contemporary record executives that success in the "race" field depended on the use of "name" talent. As the Talking Machine Journal put it in 1926: "Selection of artists is one of the fundamental steps to succeeding in the race trade. The artists must be known to the Negroes and must be one of themselves." A few months after Williams went to Port Washington, OKeh enunciated the same policy in the Journal : "Every effort is made to release promptly the latest hits that have the greatest appeal to those who buy Negro records. These hits are recorded only by colored artists whose fame and popularity are unquestionably established." Yet even the best-known black entertainers of the period were obscure to white executives, who were not disposed to educate themselves by frequenting black entertainment circles.

Williams doubted that another company of the period would have taken on a black employee. At the same time, it is doubtful that any other black employee could have succeeded in Williams's position, which required consummate skill as a job politician. Where Perry Bradford (the songwriter who promoted Mamie Smith to OKeh) was confrontational and abrasive, Williams was tactful and circumspect. Although he was better-educated than his superiors at Paramount, "I never made any attempt to show it," he said. Nor did he attempt to advance his own hobby-horses at the expense of Paramount's interests. His own tastes in music ran to cultivated singers like his ex–fraternity mate Paul Robeson, whom he considered far greater than any blues singer.[5] Once, in the hopes of justifying company expenditures on operatic singers, Williams solicited public suggestions for talent in the *Chicago Defender*. When (to his dismay) ninety percent of the respondents recommended a blues singer, he discarded the notion of elevating Paramount's catalogue.

Like many gifted corporate opportunists, Williams translated his largely unspecified job into a mandate to create his own corporate niche and enlarge his role. Almost immediately upon being hired he silently undertook the responsibility of producing Paramount's "race" catalogue by finding and recording talent. His strategy succeeded because he was able to turn out best-selling records, to the amazement of his friend Fritz Pollard, who recommended Jelly Roll Morton and other musicians to Williams in an effort to assist him in his new career. "He didn't know a damn thing about music," Pollard (himself an amateur pianist and slide trombonist) said of Williams. Yet he quickly eclipsed Art Satherley, whose New York studio thereafter saw so little activity that it was finally closed in 1926. Although not formally an employee of the Paramount organization, Williams became, for all practical purposes, the director of its "race" recording program from mid-1923 through mid-1927. In this period he personally approved nearly all of the company's "race" talent, monitored all of its Chicago recording sessions, and designated the records Paramount released from the sessions.[6] Later he would be at a loss to explain his role with the company: For want of a better description, he likened himself to an "independent producer" for the label. Despite his lack of corporate credentials, he considered himself subordinate only to Moeser and Maurice Supper, who, unknown to Williams, held the actual title of Paramount "recording director" and drew a weekly salary as such.

Williams received no formal mandate from Supper to involve himself in scouting. His original motive for doing so was to fatten his publishing fees. Supper, who operated out of Port Washington and was preoccupied with both sales management and

5. As a college student, Williams introduced Robeson to sex at a brothel and continued his association with him during the years of Robeson's political activism, which sometimes caused the pair to be followed by FBI agents. His own political leanings, he declared, were left of Booker T. Washington's and right of W. E. B. DuBois's.
6. On occasion, Paramount dispatched Williams to New York to supervise "race" sessions. "I never could figure out why they had this studio in New York," he said, unaware of the fact that it had been the company's original recording site.

a private mail-order sideline in hair goods,[7] never even bothered to listen to Williams's finds. "Anything that sold was all right with him," Williams recalled, "and these blues were selling." Once Williams began turning up talent, Supper gave him carte blanche to record artists with a single qualification: Only the artist whose sales reached ten thousand copies would be eligible for a follow-up session.

Though sales ledgers dictated Paramount's recording policies, its sales and recording branches were completely divorced. For his part, Williams knew almost nothing about the company's sales markets. So complete was Williams's isolation from his employers that he did not even know that Paramount was primarily a "race" label, in which he was the principal player; he rather thought of the company's "race" division as but one of its successful branches.

Despite Williams's general feeling of independence as a record producer, he felt constrained to observe at least three disagreeable conventions he attributed to his employers. He never openly questioned the propriety of labelling black music as "race" music, although he considered the existence of such a separate retailing category to be demeaning to blacks. He made no attempt to ferret out white talent: "They didn't want me to be identified with the white records, or the white side of the situation at all." Mindful of an often-expressed industry assumption that blacks could not sing white material, he would not knowingly record non-blues compositions, even though he had a decided taste for ballad-style singing and considered it commercial. If an artist submitted a pop-styled ballad to him for consideration, he recalled, "I would very quickly say: 'Well, we can't use it. Write me a blues.' In doing it that way I'd save a lot of embarrassment for myself, the company, and the person."[8]

Williams's relations with both his superiors and subordinates would resemble the arm's-length stolidness with which Paramount's hierarchy treated him. In the interests of preserving his indispensability to the company, he never volunteered any information about his working methods to M. A. Supper. He kept similarly aloof from subordinates: "I didn't tell anybody all I knew—there are very few people you

---

7. Supper's product (probably a hair straightener) was called "Black Patti," a name suggested by Williams in honor of the black opera singer Sisseretta Jones. To obtain her permission to use her name in the venture, Williams called upon Jones in Providence, Rhode Island, on Supper's behalf.

8. This policy inhibited such singers as Alberta Hunter, of whom he said, "She could sing as many popular numbers as blues." The proscription against black crooners still existed in the 1930s, when Williams unsuccessfully championed ballad singers to Jack Kapp at Decca Records.

can trust in this business; very few. From the top to the bottom everybody's trying to screw everybody else; get in on the 'pie'."

After setting up Chicago Music in an office on the second floor of the Overton Bank Building at 36th and State Street (which rented at twenty-five dollars per month),[9] he drew his operational model from his wartime experience in officer's training school at Augusta, Georgia. "I knew that generals surrounded themselves with assistants and subordinates. I didn't know anything about music, so I used assistants, and I never relied on any one person too much for anything."

His chief subaltern was his enterprising secretary Aletha Dickerson, the pianist and booker for the Indiana Theatre at 43rd and Indiana, five blocks west of her apartment on St. Lawrence Avenue. "She was a pretty good hustler herself," Williams said of Dickerson, who was listed only as a stenographer in the local city directory. (Her sidelines included a record store at 31st and State Street.) It was Aletha who performed the actual clerical chores Williams had been hired to do. Occasionally she would recommend talent to Williams. She sometimes worked as a session pianist, but never recorded in her own right: "Aletha's touch was too light, and her voice was not good enough to record," he recalled. Although Williams considered her an excellent songwriter, he made a point of rejecting most of her compositions (as well as her attempts to have him record her husband, Alexander J. Robinson) as a calculated means of discouraging her from overestimating her importance. Because he neither wanted her to appeal to any higher-ups in the Paramount organization on any practical matter nor to become qualified to succeed him, Williams took pains to ensure that she would learn nothing about Paramount operations beyond what she could infer from his laconic correspondence with Supper and Moeser. He never discussed business matters with her.

The desire not to depend on a single employee necessitated Williams's hiring several arrangers to score songs for publication and to teach artists material. Although he chose them less for their musical facility than for their professional demeanor, the musical aptitude of his arrangers greatly impressed Paramount's traveling salesman Harry Charles, who recalled: "He had three or four in there, you know, was the best musicians you ever saw; to *write* (i.e., transcribe). But you'd have to make it (the song) up . . ." Most of the arrangers he used were not themselves recording

9. This building later became known as the Overton Hygenic Building.

prospects. Of Strathdene (Tiny) Parham, who sometimes did session work for Paramount, Williams noted: "He was a hell of a piano player, but he couldn't get 'down to earth' on blues."[10] Nevertheless, one of his arrangers, Tom Dorsey, eventually became a successful recording artist.

Unless a Paramount artist was given prepared material to record, the arrangers would transcribe songs from test-pressings of records Williams had already approved for release, earning three dollars per lead sheet. The varying ability of his arrangers to replicate the uncertainties of blues phrasing was another reason that Williams employed several of them, where one could have sufficed. He remembered that only a single transcriber, Kid Austin, had the ability to transcribe a song exactly as it had been performed by an artist. The demands of writing lead sheets, however, entailed no more than a rudimentary depiction of the melody line of the song, sufficient to make the work recognizable in the event of a copyright infringement.

Because Williams was absorbed with a variety of ventures, such as playing football (a sideline his employers were unaware of), bootlegging bathtub gin to waiters at the Grand Terrace, and furnishing local speakeasies and brothels with nickelodeons,[11] he did not attempt to create a publishing empire of Chicago Music. Unless a composition struck him as suitable material for a particular Paramount artist, he had no interest in purchasing it. Though Chicago Music lacked a single songwriter who was known to the record industry, it became the most successful black publishing house of the era. Thanks to its connection with a record company, Chicago Music prospered while black-owned publishing firms run by W. C. Handy, Clarence Williams, Maceo Pinkard, and Perry Bradford floundered in the early 1920s.[12]

At no time did Williams employ a songwriter or staff composer. Although he never advertised for material, he was deluged by compositions by amateurs who shared the old conceit that everyone has a song in his heart. "Some of them weren't worth the paper they were written on," he recalled. Like most Tin Pan Alley song publishers, he would not accept a so-called "song poem," or composition without accompanying melody. Most of his material thus came from working musicians,

---

10. Harry Charles said of Parham: "You could sing it [a blues] one time; he could play it back; he'd write it the next time."

11. "I went in two, three houses of prostitution, put my own jukeboxes in there, and spent my money right in the place," Williams recalled.

12. Clarence Williams, whose publishing company (Williams and Piron) stood on 31st and State, was his only local rival as a talent scout. "He would get just as many artists as I did," Williams said.

and not songwriters as such. Instead of buying merely the publication rights to songs, he bought every song he published outright, paying independent songwriters fifty or sixty dollars for material that was passed on to Paramount artists, and paying Paramount artists between five and twenty dollars for their material. The musicians and songwriters he worked with had no objection to selling their songs outright in this fashion; their credo, he said, was "Give me mine now Mister Williams; whatever you make beyond that, that's yours." On occasion he would give himself partial composer credits for a song he retouched (he was usually wont to correct the grammar of songs he published), sometimes using the pseudonym "Everett Murphy" (the name of a friend) because, as he put it, "I didn't wanna appear too much in the picture."

Artists who trafficked in sexual material, he recalled, did not know how to make their allusions implicit rather than explicit. If a song seemed too risqué to record, Williams would suggest euphemisms to convey the same meaning, thus creating a "double entendre" blues song. Considering them undignified, he placed a strict ban on the "coon songs" that were still in vogue among black entertainers.

Although Williams never shared his educated friends' contempt for musicians, he discovered that blues music was more appealing than the people who performed it. In time, he came to expect erratic behavior as the norm of blues singers. "Everyone's goofy in this business," Williams would say, without exempting himself from his axiom. "If you're not goofy when you get in it, you are by the time you come out of it." Unlike the ingratiating modern record executive who seeks "rapport" with musicians, Williams felt that any social contact—even to the extent of having dinner with an artist—would subvert the business relationship he sought to establish. His introverted personality and relatively exalted social status were further barriers to fellowship with blues singers. However, the artists he worked with were less guarded and deferential than they would have been with white executives. Often prospective artists who arrived at his office were openly incredulous to meet a black executive and would demand to see a white official. In 1927 the blues pianist Little Brother Montgomery actually refused to record for him in the belief that he could not be a bona fide record executive.

Unlike white executives of the period, Williams was forced to concoct social strategies for dealing with blues artists. Early on in his career he discovered that blues singers usually had ulterior motives for fraternizing with him. If a blues singer invited him to dinner, he discovered, he was expected to pay for the meal. If a blues singer invited him to a party, it was in the interests of borrowing money or persuading Williams to record a friend. After a few such experiences, Williams began shunning the company of blues singers altogether. "I trusted them about as far as I could throw an elephant," he said. As a practical business matter he felt that he would compromise himself unless he kept every artist at an equal distance. To fraternize with some musicians would be interpreted as favoritism and arouse resentment from less favored artists. "It's better to avoid the contact and avoid the conflict," he said. Sometimes artists with an imagined "in" with him would represent themselves as his personal talent scouts, and charge other musicians a fee for the privilege of auditioning for Paramount.

Female blues singers often tried to parlay their physical assets into recording contracts. "Some of them had more overtures than they had talent," he recalled. One Paramount reject tried to blackmail him with a threat to falsely tell Williams's wife that he had fathered her child unless he not only recorded her but bought her a fur coat in the bargain. When it became known that Williams was unreceptive to sexual propositions, some female blues singers took to calling at his office and asking for white Paramount executives by name in the (sometimes correct) belief that they would be more receptive to couch casting.[13] Other singers tried to ingratiate themselves with Aletha Dickerson in the hope that she would pressure Williams to record them.

Even when artists were not manipulative, Williams remained wary of them. Contact with blues singers meant exposure to their lifestyles, which invariably involved intemperate drinking and ungrammatical speech, two snares to which he felt personally susceptible. Blues singers frequently badgered Williams to drink with them, even during recording sessions: "I, like a damn fool, would," he said of his early days at Paramount. Having taken pains to shed his speech of colloquial mannerisms, Williams did not enjoy bantering with musicians who spoke in an uneducated idiom. He would ultimately marry a schoolteacher.

It was thanks partly to his aloofness that Williams would eventually acquire a reputation among artists for dishonesty. Such disgruntled Paramount properties as Alberta Hunter and Big Bill Broonzy created cameos of Williams as a crooked

13. It was not only blues singers who pressured Williams in this fashion. After he resisted the overtures of Aletha Dickerson in the 1930s, she reported him to the musician's union for using non-union talent at Decca.

conniver.[14] So did the propaganda of competitive music "purists" like Alan Lomax and the late John Hammond of Columbia, who aspired to be revered as the Great White Father of blues and jazz.[15] Although Williams's accomplishments in the blues field were doubtless more considerable than his larcenies, he had no desire to make others aware of them. He never sought favorable publicity for himself, even to the extent of not listing himself in the black *Who's Who* of the period. The criticism he received, he said, with genuine equanimity, "went in one ear and out the other." When interviewed in 1971 for a prospective biography, he made no attempt to exalt himself as a patron saint of blues singers. "I've got a good bit of Shylock in me," he said matter-of-factly. Without this quality, it is questionable that Williams would have been employable in a rapacious industry; as he recalled, an industry axiom of the period was: "Screw the artist before he screws you." The Paramount label institutionalized such cheating by writing a provision in its standard recording contract calling for a sales royalty computed as one cent for each "net" record sale. "That one cent 'net'," Williams said, "covered a multitude of sins." The "net" sale was computed after various expenses, most of them figments of bookkeeping, had been deducted. Nine out of ten Paramount artists, Williams recalled, received no royalty, regardless of their record sales.

Whereas bureaucracy enables modern record executives to insulate themselves from fraudulent bookkeeping, the brunt of dealing with artists (and thus becoming subject to their disaffection) fell directly on Williams's shoulders. It was Williams who paid them personally, deducting their fees from expense accounts he freely padded before passing them on to his superiors. It was Williams who ensured that the lowly Paramount "race" artist did not create trouble for the company; when an artist would ask for a copy of his Paramount contract, Williams would glibly promise to mail it. Most artists never received their requested contracts.

To his recollection, only Alberta Hunter was openly disaffected by his sharp busi-

14. Broonzy complained in his autobiography that he only received fifty dollars for recording two titles for Williams in 1927, "because they told me that I had broken one of the recording machines which cost five hundred dollars by putting my feet on it." This figure was the going rate Williams would have paid a performer of Broonzy's stature. His accompanist, Broonzy reported, "told a lie and got a hundred dollars. He told them his father had just died and that it would take a hundred dollars to bury him" (*Big Bill Blues* [New York: Oak Publications, 1964], p.46).

15. Lomax's 1950 biography of Jelly Roll Morton, *Mister Jelly Roll* (New York: Grosset and Dunlap), made scant mention of the fact that Williams had been the first person to record Morton. Instead, it dismissed him with a passing mention of his "catalogue of thousands of tunes that he composed . . ." (p.182), a criticism one could level at Lomax's father John Lomax, who copyrighted the "folk" songs of artists like Leadbelly as he collected them. Though Hammond made a minuscule contribution to the blues genre, he derived more publicity for having recorded Bessie Smith at the end of her career than did the recording director (Frank Walker) who had discovered her.

ness practices. "She said I screwed her out of publishing money," he recalled. The artists he was likely to short-change were the ones who borrowed money against future recordings: "You made up with one hand what you paid out with the other." One artist who got the upper hand in this low game of mutual chicanery was Ethel Waters, whose defection from Black Swan probably hastened the end of that label.[16] As a condition for recording four sides for Williams in April of 1924, she demanded that Williams buy a $700 Locomobile for her boyfriend. Soon afterwards Williams was contacted by Columbia Records, which had placed her under exclusive contract shortly before her Paramount session and threatened to sue in the event that Williams used her material.[17]

"I was better than fifty-percent honest, and in this business that's pretty good," Williams said of his dealings with blues singers. He noted that Gennett Records never paid its artists anything beyond a net sales royalty, which he doubted that most of its musicians actually received.

His unflattering self-portrait notwithstanding, it would be inaccurate to castigate Williams as a ruthless opportunist who routinely "cheated" talent. Because the terms of the "race" recording contract were inherently exploitative, there was little scope for outright cheating on the part of individual record executives. Most artists were paid according to the custom of the day, receiving a flat recording fee and waiving the rights to their compositions. In later years, following Williams's departure from the company, it dropped even the pretext of a sales royalty. The chief means by which dishonest recording officials of the era cheated artists was by filching composer credits for their songs in order to draw a publishing royalty. Of the seven hundred–odd titles Williams produced for Paramount, only fourteen bore his name as a composer. In eleven of these instances, he was listed as a co-composer. In no instance did he appropriate credit for a hit record. Owing to M. A. Supper's financial interest in Chicago Music, it would have been inadvisable for Williams to claim credit for Paramount hits, even had he been inclined to do so.

The ambitiousness of the average blues artist was such that Williams's success was not dependent on his ability to make a favorable impression on his artists. He felt that he could even afford to reject a recording prospect on social grounds. "There

16. In July of 1923 she signed an exclusive contract with Vocalion, but never recorded for them.
17. In her autobiography, *His Eye is on the Sparrow* (New York: Pyramid edition, 1967; pp.190–92), Waters angrily recounted the wreck of "my big beautiful Locomobile," with which her philandering boyfriend visited other women. She failed to mention the circumstances under which she obtained the car.

was more talent than any one company could handle," he recalled of the 1920s. "I could have missed a whole hell of a lot of good singers because there were more artists than there were places to put 'em." Artists were so plentiful that he only occasionally found reason to leave his South Side office, which was open from ten until five, to ferret out musicians. For the most part, he expected aspiring artists to visit him on the basis of his reputation as a record producer. This sedentary scouting system was practical because he was virtually the only "race" scout in Chicago, and because his office was situated in the heart of the black night-life district. Its surrounding neighborhood, ultimately displaced by the Illinois Institute of Technology and high-rise housing projects, was called the "Stroll": "Friday night to Monday morning that place was just like an Easter parade, or a promenade down the boardwalk in Atlantic City."[18] The denizens of the "Stroll" would become the subject of Ma Rainey's "Shave 'Em Dry":

> If it wasn't for the powder and the store-bought hair
> State Street women couldn't go nowhere.

On 34th and State, two blocks south of Williams's office, stood a celebrated three-story brothel known as Mecca Flats, which was commemorated on a 1924 Paramount recording by Priscilla Stewart:

> Mecca Flat woman, stings like a stingaree
> Mecca Flat woman, take your teeth outta me.

At 35th and State lay the Dreamland Cafe, a five-hundred-seat cabaret whose owner Billy Bottoms was a sporting colleague and fellow football player. The Deluxe Gardens, where Williams sometimes recruited jazz talent, stood on the same block.

Thanks partly to his proximity to such black entertainment meccas, Williams had no desire to acquaint himself with the scruffier blues culture that permeated the Black Belt, whose black population of 100,000 was exceeded only by that of New York, Philadelphia, and Washington, D.C. On countless street corners were to be

18. The black residential population was then wedged between 33rd Street and 39th Street, and was bounded to the east by Grand Boulevard. Williams himself lived at 4946 South Michigan, three blocks south of Jack Johnson's apartment. Although Johnson had appeared in vaudeville as a bass-fiddle player, it never occurred to Williams to record him or any other black celebrities. "We just weren't on the alert," he said.

found vagrant blues guitarists "playing for chickenfeed." Williams rarely gave them more than a passing glance. Although Williams heard talk of proficient blues musicians who played piano in South Side brothels (called "buffet flats") or lived in local "kitchenettes" (the subdivided single-bedroom apartments that housed recent Southern emigrés), he considered such places too dangerous to frequent in search of talent. Once he paid a visit to a "kitchenette" apartment to audition a blues singer: The unsettling sight of ten names on its mailbox deterred him from ringing the doorbell. He gave up attending the local house parties known as "chittlin' suppers" or "funky shakes" (then a disreputable phrase) after finding himself besieged at such affairs by would-be recording artists who wanted to cadge auditions, drinks, and handouts from him.

Despite his limited orbit, his inexperience, and his distrust of blues singers, Willliams became the most successful "race" producer of his time. It was through Williams's efforts that Chicago would loom as a center of blues recording, a position it retained until the music waned in the 1950s. By the venal standards of A&R work, he may have been the most successful recording scout of all time. Half of the forty-odd blues and gospel singers he recorded in three years at Paramount (at a clip of one new artist a month) sold well enough to justify at least one follow-up session. Four of his artists became company mainstays whose work sold consistently in the tens of thousands and who became blues legends.

Although Williams would have been satisfied had only a tenth of his finds produced hits, he expected all of his discoveries to become stars. He did not recall ever using a cut-and-dried musical yardstick to evaluate talent, and put no conscious premium on the theater singers who dominated Paramount's catalogue between 1922–26. Indeed, he did not even perceive them as a distinct category of blues performer: He considered each artist unique, and felt that labels (such as they existed in the 1920s) were of importance primarily to whites, who rarely purchased "race" records. He believed that the consumers whose tastes he tried to anticipate paid little attention to blues accompaniments. Rather, he believed that the impact of his artists depended primarily on their lyrics, with the quality of the singer's voice having secondary importance.

His inadvertent emphasis upon theater singers of the Mamie Smith mold would seem to have been largely a by-product of the kinds of places he patronized in search of talent, as well as his mild preference for established names. "The artist with a reputation in show business like the Theatre Owners Booking Associaton (T.O.B.A.) was always welcome at Paramount," he recalled. Although his early productions were imitative of the day's "race" recording trends, which favored female singers using band accompaniment, he doubted that he listened to as many as ten "race" records in the course of his scouting career. He was, in fact, generally scornful of singers whom he recognized as imitative, or who had previously recorded for other companies.

If he was impressed by a singer he heard in passing, Williams would request that he or she visit his office for a formal audition. Any singer who put in an unsolicited appearance would be granted an audition: "We never sent anybody away, though a lot of 'em could talk better blues than sing them." His auditions would usually entail a half an hour of evaluation. He would begin each audition by asking the aspirant to sing the piece that seemed most popular with his or her audience. About half the artists who auditioned for him were accepted.

The personal impression created by an artist was as important to Williams as his style of musical performance. His chief reasons for rejecting aspirants were that Paramount had more artists than it could handle, or that the artist in question struck him as unprofessional or unstable. If a prospective artist arrived at an appointed audition with friends, Williams would whisk him out of his office at the earliest convenient pretext and write him off as undesirable. In his early years at Paramount, he refused to record any singer who struck him as illiterate: "You didn't have a chance with me if you split a verb, even if you were one hell of a singer." A stickler for grammar, Williams never tired of correcting the speech of his artists. On the other hand, he had nothing against slang, which often figured in blues songs, remarking: "There were very few black slang expressions that I didn't understand."

In the course of evaluating talent, Williams developed an ideal physical image of a blues singer. For example, he believed that artists with wide mouths tended to have strong voices. "Those robusque (sic) stubby short artists could get more volume than those thin, willowy girls—you never could get a singer like Priscilla Stewart to do a song like Ma Rainey." Possibly owing to his own distaste for the "high yellows" of his race, who invariably scorned blues, Williams took pride in the fact that most of his best singers were black in hue. "I found that those deep contralto voices made the best blues singers . . . and ninety percent of the ones that were good were black; jet-black." He found that there was a racial backlash against singers who were extremely light-complexioned, such as Thelma LaVizzo, a New Orleans Creole he recorded in

1924. "She was very good," Williams said of her, "but her records never made it over the top: her complexion counted against her."

On tips from his arrangers or by following the theatrical columns of the *Chicago Defender* or *Whip*, Williams frequented local vaudeville houses in search of talent. Often he stood backstage to monitor the crowd reaction to an artist. One of his gimmicks was to attend blues-singing contests held in Chicago theaters and seek out the runner-up contestant in the belief that the singer in question would be less demanding and difficult to deal with than the winner. (Using the same strategy, his assistant Aletha Dickerson collared Priscilla Stewart and Jimmy Blythe in St. Louis.) Besides visiting theaters, he also sought out talent at the Columbia Hotel on 31st and State, where out-of-town T.O.B.A. artists boarded.

The black vaudeville theaters of the day were cluttered with performers whose stock in trade was their looks and costuming. "I never looked for any beauty in my blues singers," Williams said. "None of my blues singers were chosen because they were good-looking or made a beautiful stage appearance. I never found one of those stage artists who could do anything if she looked too good." From the outset of his scouting career, Williams recognized that theater singing was inimical to the kind of delivery he sought to capture on recordings. "In recording they had to sing from the soul, instead of just shaking and dancing," he said. "There was a great deal of difference between playing for a theater and playing for records, and I spent a great deal of time explaining this to the artists."[19] One popular theater singer who was never able to make the transition was May Alix, who was famed for her acrobatic splits while dancing. "May Alix appealed to theater-goers, but she just could not sing," Williams recalled. "In a lot of instances she kept jobs just by dancing. I never could do anything with her." Unable to coax a successful recording from her, Williams did the next-best thing: he used "May Alix" as a pseudonym for Alberta Hunter and Edmonia Henderson.

It was her lack of histrionics that most impressed him about Ida Cox (1896–1967), a Georgia-born, Knoxville-based vocalist who was one of his first and most successful discoveries. Her debut in 1923 marked the first recording of a theater singer with an understated vocal delivery. "Ida Cox was more queenly than you'd imagine,"

---

19. Harry Charles, who brought talent to Paramount in the late 1920s, encountered the same difficulty. "I recorded the best girl on a stage I ever saw," he recalled, "but she wouldn't 'go' on a record for nothin'. And I went to Port Washington . . . Old Moeser said: 'What the heck you recordin' that girl for?' I said: 'Why, she's good!' He says: 'Well, you musta went with her!—She ain't worth nothin'.'"

Williams said. "She stood flat-footed and sang; she didn't need any motion at all to put her song over." Her regal stage bearing led him to dub her "Queen of the Blues," a title he also concocted in the interests of stimulating racial pride. Williams discovered her at the Monogram theater, a seedy T.O.B.A. outlet located two blocks from his office at 3453 South State Street, near the old El. Throughout the early 1920s, the Monogram was Williams's best source of theater talent. In its rickety setting, it illustrated his conviction that blues was humble music. Ethel Waters wrote of it: "Of all those rinky-dink joints I played in, nothing was worse than the Monogram . . . the walls were so thin you stopped singing—or telling a joke—every time a train passed."[20] Williams, however, found it more suitable for his purposes than the elegant Grand Theatre on 31st and State, where he discovered Trixie Smith in 1924. "Nothin' but the lowlife people went to the Monogram," he recalled. "The upper crust went to the Grand." Williams was kept abreast of its acts by Lovie Austin, who played piano for the theater's three-piece pit band and worked as one of his arrangers.

His prize Monogram plum, Ma Rainey, became Paramount's best-selling blues singer of the early 1920s and the most successful theater singer besides Bessie Smith. Rainey had been scouring the South for some two decades before Williams discovered her in December 1923, and her popularity had probably long since peaked before its rejuvenation via record. On the eve of her discovery, the *Chicago Defender* only saw fit to mention the Monogram engagements of Ethel Waters and Edmonia Henderson (a Jackson, Tennessee native who made her debut around the same time as Rainey and probably headlined the bill on which Rainey was discovered). Williams's astuteness as a judge of talent is demonstrated by the fact that Rainey's debut session ran to eight sides, as against the two or four sides that his previous discoveries had been allotted on first sessions.

Rainey, Williams discovered, had an ample fund of recording material, most of which she worked up herself. It bothered him little that she was illiterate and unable to recite songs from a sheet, as did most of his discoveries. "What do you want, good grammar or good blues?" he later joked, in an apparent change of policy. In dubbing her "Mother of the Blues" he hoped to enhance her stage appeal, which would in turn, he thought, make her records sell better.

Rainey's studio debut marked the summit of the theater-blues vogue. For another

20. Waters, *His Eye is on the Sparrow*, p.77.

three years, theater-blues singers would retain their stranglehold on the "race" market, but none of its later exponents achieved stardom. The theater-blues genre was approaching exhaustion when Williams found Rainey: In all likelihood, record companies had tapped most of its limited talent by 1923.

It was Williams's flexibility and receptiveness to offbeat sounds that made him the pioneer of a new recording genre, that of the self-accompanied dance musician. In August of 1924, while walking through the market district of a racially mixed neighborhood called "Jew Town," he encountered a middle-aged New Orleans Creole named Papa Charlie Jackson singing on the corner of Maxwell and Halstead Streets. Jackson impressed Williams as a novelty act: "I was lookin' for somethin' like that," he recalled. "Somethin' different. He was a hell of a banjo player."[21] Jackson, a six-string banjoist, became the first male blues recording star in an industry that had been previously almost completely given over to female blues singers.

In retrospect, Williams's promotion of Jackson was a greater testament to his genius than his discovery of Ma Rainey, for nothing but his own intuition could have commended Jackson as a recording prospect. Although Jackson was a small-voiced baritone with only a street-corner reputation, Williams felt that his uniqueness would commend him to record-buyers. An avid tap dancer, he was particularly taken by Jackson's beat: "I could just see myself dancing to Papa Charlie, but not to those other artists," he said. "If you follow Papa Charlie, you find that he had good rhythm—you could dance by nearly every song Papa Charlie made. He was a one-man band." Jackson became the first black recording artist to perform dance music, which most city musicians and street singers did not play. On the strength of his fifth and most successful record, "Shake That Thing" (a quasi-blues that celebrated a dance of that name), Williams presented him to the Mardi Gras of 1926 and afterwards at a T.O.B.A. theater in New Orleans.[22]

Jackson was one of the first blues recording acts to rely primarily on his own material, and the first blues singer to record happy-go-lucky, uptempo music, instead of the ponderously slow, sorrowful blues that glutted the "race" market of the period.

21. Williams was probably the first recording executive to discover a blues street singer. In the later 1920s he frequently auditioned such artists: "I'd get in the crowd just like any other onlooker," he said. When the musician was finished with a set, Williams would ask him to visit his office. "A lot of them would think you're foolin' . . . they didn't believe you."
22. At the prompting of Jackson's sister, Williams then visited Algiers, Louisiana, "like a damn fool . . . In Algiers, they drink anything! I went over there and didn't know what was doin' for two or three days, and when I came to, I got myself outta Algiers and got myself outta New Orleans." In the late 1920s, Jackson lived a block from Williams, at 4847 South Michigan Street.

Nearly a third of his sixty-six recorded titles had echoes of vaudeville, minstrelsy, or pop music. Regardless of his metier, his approach was basically frivolous. "He did lean toward comedy," Williams said of him. The virtues of Papa Charlie Jackson were among his favorite song subjects. "Jackson's Blues" (1926) voiced the reaction of an imaginary listener of his music:

And he's wonderful, he's just as wonderful as he can be.
Say the reason I know the Paramount people was tellin' me.

But Jackson received no such accolades from Williams. Fearing that artists would either become complacent or get (as he put it) "the big head" if he displayed enthusiasm for them, Williams affected nonchalance toward their work. If musicians touted themselves to him (and, inevitably, he found they were braggarts), he would respond coldly: "We only know how good you are by what the sales figures tell us."

It was when drunk, which was often, that Jackson became most enamored of himself. "The more he drank, the more he showed off," Williams said of Jackson. "You couldn't tell when he was gonna 'tear his drawers' [make a fool of himself]." Although Jackson showed a remarkable ability to appear sober during his drinking bouts, alcohol made him erratic: "You might say to him: 'Why don't you come by and record?' and he might show up today or tomorrow or the next day; just disregard everything. He'd get out on a drunk, and wasn't physically able to make it." His alcoholism (which, Williams thought, led to his death in the late 1930s) also made him pleasantly pliable: "If you got a few drinks in him he'd do anything you wanted." In time, he would learn that Jackson was typical of the male blues singer: "I never had any male singers who didn't drink, and that was one thing you had to guard against."

The process of recording blues singers was difficult, regardless of their state of sobriety. Because singers were competitive and quarrelsome, Williams made a point of never scheduling two artists on the same date.[23] Prior to recording them, Williams rehearsed his artists in his office, which was equipped with a piano. Most of the singers drank freely during their rehearsals, and typically, Williams found, overestimated their ability to perform while intoxicated. Although Williams found it

23. The wisdom of this precaution was illustrated by a brawl that ten-odd blues singers waged in a Decca studio in the midst of a 1930s session. This incident so angered recording director Jack Kapp that he vowed never to record another blues singer, a ban he finally rescinded.

necessary to indulge blues singers' drinking, he refused to permit them to bring friends and family members to the recording studio, as most of his artists attempted to do.

Although Lovie Austin would sometimes act as an informal musical director, ensuring that musicians were in tune and singers on pitch, Williams did not concern himself with these niceties, which he felt were of no importance to the public. He himself could only detect gross deviations in pitch. He ordinarily spent the first half-hour of a session involving a new Paramount act explaining recording procedures, which he had learned from M.A. Supper. Before recording formally began, test waxes were cut to determine whether the music was being adequately recorded and to gauge the proper distance from the conical recording horn that was employed in the pre-microphone era (singers like Rainey typically stood a foot from the recording horn). Williams generally recorded three or four takes of each song, selecting the best one for issuing. The use of multiple takes also served as insurance, lest some accident befall the delicate wax that was used for recording masters.

The sessions Williams conducted generally ran for three hours with three or four songs constituting a complete day's recording. This low total was largely attributable to mistakes made by artists. Most of the artists Williams recorded had difficulty abiding by his routine cueing instructions. A system of lights would cue the artist to begin recording, and (at the approach of the three-minute limit of the 78rpm) to record the last verse of each song. The typical artist would either ignore the cue to complete the song or would overreact and stop playing altogether at the onset of the warning light. Often artists would leave out the title verse of their song, thus necessitating a retake. Except when Williams or his engineer became impatient, a proven talent like Rainey or Jackson would be indulged in as many takes as were necessary to satisfactorily complete a song. An untried singer, on the other hand, was allotted only about three bad takes before being dismissed.

Save for occasional sessions at its New York studio, Paramount did all of its "race" recording between 1923–26 in Chicago. Most of its Chicago sessions were held in a studio operated by Orlando R. Marsh (1883–1938), a native of Wilmette, Illinois, who had incorporated his Marsh Laboratories in 1922. Marsh was apparently first recruited by M. A. Supper and worked on a contract basis, charging a flat fee per master. His studio stood on the sixth floor of the Lyon and Healy Building (formerly the Kimball Building) on South Wabash Street, thirty-five blocks from Williams's office. "Marsh was a general recorder," Williams said. "You could go there, I could go there; anybody could go there." Originally he had been an employee of Essanay Pictures, a Chicago film company of the pre-Hollywood era that had featured such stars as Charlie Chaplin, Gloria Swanson, and Bronco Billy Anderson (its co-owners).[24] In addition to acting as Paramount's engineer, he recorded air shots for the original *Amos n' Andy Show* on WMAQ. His work was sufficiently novel to merit a contemporary feature by the weekly newsfilm Kinogram, which filmed one of his recording sessions. Within the recording industry at large he was best known for his claim to be able to reproduce a pipe organ (by a mysterious process that did not employ an acoustic recording horn), for which purpose he founded his own Autograph label in late 1923.[25]

"He had a (*sic*) old machine," Harry Charles said. "You couldn't hardly get a voice through it." Although Charles considered Marsh "good as there was then" in the recording field (his *Times* obituary hailed him as a "leader in the field of electrical recording"), his tendency to under-record artists gave his productions poor presence. Because of the studio's proximity to the El, recording had to stop whenever trains passed. Its lack of controlled room temperature caused recording wax to melt in hot weather, for which reason Paramount did little summer recording. Williams considered him a careless engineer; once studio mice ran amok in a box containing wax masters, scratching the discs and ruining a session involving six artists.

Sometimes Williams imported a Gennett engineer from Richmond, Indiana to record Paramount artists. "We used him to cross people up because many leaks would get out from Marsh about what we were doing . . ."[26] We had to be very careful about every move we made. If you got some advance information on an artist, you'd make an effort to get hold of him." These recordings were made in various other Loop studios: "In this one block on Wabash there, Jackson and Wabash right up to

---

24. In 1911 Essanay had produced an all-black film, *The Dark Romance of a Tobacco Can*, the plot of which the Negro Almanac summarizes thusly: "Man horrified to find girl he proposes to is Negro."
25. In the spring of 1924, Marsh began retailing his records on a nationwide basis; the label sold them for $1.50, or twice the prevailing price of records. In February of 1925 he garnished local publicity by recording a dance orchestra at the Trianon Ballroom before a live audience, offering each patron one free record. Soon, however, his record company went the way of its leading attraction, Jessie Crawford, who wandered off to Victor.
26. Williams blamed Marsh's leaks on his employees. The Gennett engineer, he recalled, had a real relish for blues and would party on the South Side after conducting sessions.

Adams and Wabash, there were about two or three other recording studios on each side of the street," Williams recalled. Williams also periodically favored rival studios in the interests of improving Paramount's sound: "It wasn't advancing as rapidly as others in the business," Williams said of Marsh's studio.

Williams, who kept informal ledgers of the sessions, paid his artists twenty-five or fifty dollars per side, a figure he arrived at without investigating the prevailing "race" rates. Featured accompanists were paid ten dollars per side; other sidemen received five dollars, and some, nothing at all. It was Williams's policy to issue all of the recordings he produced, because he considered it unfair to suppress the material of an artist bound by contract. Half of the material he recorded was intended as filler: "We didn't give a damn what the B-side of a record was—we would throw anything on the B-side. We didn't want two hits on the same record."

One of Williams's most ingenious methods of scouring up new material for Paramount artists was to take a blues singer to the studio to record his entire repertoire at random. If one of the songs that emerged from the session seemed more appropriate for another Paramount artist, Williams would then buy the song outright from the performer for ten or fifteen dollars and have an arranger teach it to the second artist. He used this method both with established Paramount attractions and singers who struck him as having promising material but no ability to execute it. Some of Paramount's most successful artists would acquire material in this fashion, which became widespread in the early days of rock and roll.

* * *

It was thanks largely to Mayo Williams that the Paramount label became a profitable enterprise, earning $100,000 in its most successful year. Trusting to Williams's judgement, M. A. Supper never attempted to interfere with him or question his decisions. "My word was final in anything that I wanted to do," Williams said. "[Paramount's hierarchy] didn't challenge it because they was makin' so much money . . . but I never asked for anything that was out of proportion to what I was earning for them." Although it indulged Williams's tastes, and provided him with such perks as a company automobile, the company did not greet him on an equal footing. Otto Moeser, for example, never set foot in Williams's South Side office; when he summoned Williams to business meetings at the Palmer House in Chicago's Loop, the latter was obliged to use the freight elevator to gain access to his hotel room. Although he considered himself a semi-welcome member of Paramount's wedding to "race music," Williams did not regard either Supper or Moeser as outright racists. To Williams, status was less important than the size of his royalty statements, and on this score he found nothing to complain about. "Supper was a slick one; as far as I know he was straight with me," he said. "If anybody was pitchin' a curve, I was pitching it in padding my expense accounts."

Despite such finagling, Williams became the consummate company man. He identified with Paramount to such an extent that he would buy his home furnishings from the Wisconsin Chair Company and his wedding ring from J. M. Bostwick's jewelry store. On the advice of Moeser, he would purchase stock in the Milwaukee Building and Loan Association with his record royalties, which accumulated too fast for him to spend. In turn, the Paramount product became so identified with Williams that the suffix of the trademark appearing on every record he produced read: "de Mayo 1923."

An outsider scrutinizing Paramount in the early 1920s would have beheld a bizarre series of charades. Its guiding genius was a man who was not even recognized as a company employee because of his race. While most of its products were recorded by freelance studios, each of its records bore a legend solemnly attesting to its production in "our own laboratories." With singular audacity in the recording business, the company feigned official nonexistence as soon as "race" records made it profitable. On its annual corporate statements, Moeser falsely reported that the New York Recording Laboratories had transacted no business during 1923 and 1924. For failing to file an annual report for 1926, the company formally forfeited its corporate status. By so doing, New York Recording Laboratories had no official existence except as a trade name (the exclusive rights to which it would automatically retain for the next twenty years). Apparently, Paramount resorted to this ruse to avoid paying taxes and to discourage lawsuits against it.

Mayo Williams, who considered himself a master of the sneak curve, was unaware of Paramount's fraudulent machinations and the fact that Supper had dissolved Chicago Music on July 1, 1924, in the apparent interests of making the company less accountable for its royalty statements. If it appeared that Paramount had taken the lowest ethical road available to it, its executives might have retorted that such was to be expected of a company that had already taken the lowest musical road available to it by specializing in a product that disgusted most record executives.

Stephen Calt is the author of three acclaimed musical biographies, *King of the Delta Blues: The Life and Music of Charlie Patton, I'd Rather Be the Devil: Skip James and the Blues,* and *Hellhound on My Trail: The Life and Legend of Robert Johnson* (Grove Press, 2002). He lives in New York City. This essay originally appeared in *78 Quarterly* (Volume 1, Number 4), and is reprinted with permission.

Crossing Over: From Black Rhythm & Blues to White Rock 'n' Roll

BY REEBEE GAROFALO

The history of popular music in this country—at least, in the twentieth century—can be described in terms of a pattern of black innovation and white popularization, which I have referred to elsewhere as "black roots, white fruits."[1] The pattern is built not only on the wellspring of creativity that black artists bring to popular music but also on the systematic exclusion of black personnel from positions of power within the industry and on the artificial separation of black and white audiences. Because of industry and audience racism, black music has been relegated to a separate and unequal marketing structure. As a result, it is only on rare occasions that black music "crosses over" into the mainstream market on its own terms. The specific practices and mechanisms that tend to institutionalize its exclusion and dilution change over time and, for the most part, remain unchallenged even to this day. In the last half century, the relative success of black artists has been determined by variables that range from individual preference and personal prejudice to organizational member-ships, population migrations, material shortages, technological advances, corporate configurations, informal networks, and government investigations. Inevitably, black popular music is affected by the prevailing economic and political climate. Still, black music (and the musicians who create it) continues on its creative course and also continues, against all odds, to exert a disproportionate influence on popular music in general. In this essay, we shall investigate the phenomenon of "crossover," beginning with an analysis of the social forces that gave rise to rhythm & blues in the 1940s.

The Rise of Rhythm & Blues

Prior to World War II, the popular music market was dominated by writers and publishers of the Broadway–Hollywood axis of popular music. They exercised their collective power through the American Society of Authors, Composers, and

---

1. Steve Chapple and Reebee Garofalo, *Rock n' Roll is Here to Pay: The History and Politics of the Music Industry* (Chicago: Nelson-Hall, 1977), Chapter 7.

Publishers (ASCAP), a "performance rights" organization that recovers royalty payments for the performance of copyrighted music. Until 1939, ASCAP was a closed society with a virtual monopoly on all copyrighted music. As proprietor of the compositions of its members, ASCAP could regulate the use of any selection in its catalogue. The organization exercised considerable power in the shaping of public taste. Membership in the society was generally skewed toward writers of show tunes and semi-serious works such as Richard Rodgers and Lorenz Hart, Cole Porter, George Gershwin, Irving Berlin, and George M. Cohan. Of the society's 170 charter members, six were black: Harry Burleigh, Will Marion Cook, J. Rosamond and James Weldon Johnson, Cecil Mack, and Will Tyers.[2] While other "literate" black writers and composers (W. C. Handy, Duke Ellington) would be able to gain entrance to ASCAP, the vast majority of "untutored" black artists were routinely excluded from the society and thereby systematically denied the full benefits of copyright protection. It was primarily artists in this latter group who would later create rhythm & blues.

Earlier in the century, after a hard-fought battle, ASCAP established in practice the principle, articulated in the 1909 copyright law, that writers are entitled to compensation for the public performance of their work. But it was not until the legal principle was extended to include radio that ASCAP began to realize its full economic potential. "ASCAP income from the radio, of which the networks paid about twenty percent, had risen from $757,450 in 1932 to $5.9 million in 1937, and had then dropped to $3.8 million the following year. It increased by twelve percent, to $4.3 million, in 1939."[3]

In 1940, after more than a year of rocky negotiations with radio, ASCAP announced its intention of doubling the fee for a license when the existing agreement expired on December 31. For broadcasters, who had always considered ASCAP's demands excessive, this was the last straw. The National Association of Broadcasters (NAB), representing some six hundred radio stations, formed their own performing rights organization, Broadcast Music Incorporated (BMI). "Taking advantage of ASCAP's stringent membership requirements, as well as its relative indifference to the popular and folk music being produced outside of New York and Hollywood, BMI sought out and acquired its support from the 'have not' publishers and writers in the grassroots areas."[4] When broadcasters decided to boycott ASCAP in 1941,

2. Eileen Southern, *The Music of Black Americans: A History* (New York: W.W. Norton, 1971), p.353.
3. Russell Sanjek, *American Popular Music and Its Business: The First Four Hundred Years: Vol. III, From 1900 to 1984* (New York: Oxford University Press, 1988), p.176.
4. Nat Shapiro, *Popular Music: An Annotated Index of American Popular Songs: Vol. 2, 1940–49* (New York: Adrian Press, 1965), p.6.

BMI was ready with a catalogue of its own. For the next ten months the United States was treated to an earful of its own root music. Authentic regional styles were broadcast to a mass public intact, not yet boiled down in the national pop melting pot. Though in its initial stages BMI came up with few songs of lasting significance, the Broadway-Hollywood monopoly on popular music was challenged publicly for the first time. Without this challenge, we might never have heard from composers like Huddie Ledbetter, Arthur (Big Boy) Crudup, Roy Brown, Ivory Joe Hunter, Johnny Otis, Fats Domino, and Wynonie Harris.

The success of these artists testifies to what critic Nelson George has referred to as "an aesthetic schism between high-brow, more assimilated black styles and working-class, grassroots sounds" that had existed in the black community for a long time.[5] A number of writers, notably Amiri Baraka (Leroi Jones), have written at length about class differences between jazz and the blues. While jazz was unquestionably an immensely popular and influential crossover music that introduced elements of the African-American tradition into the mainstream, it was also in some ways a product of the black middle class. Many of its most notable practitioners such as Duke Ellington, Coleman Hawkins, and Fletcher Henderson were college educated. By the thirties it was a music that had "moved away from the older *lowdown* forms of blues . . . a music that still relied on [an] older Afro-American musical tradition, but one that had begun to utilize still greater amounts of popular American music as well as certain formal European traditions."[6] The artists who pioneered rhythm & blues in the forties were much closer to their blues roots. While they often retained some semblance of the big-band sound, their initial popularity in the black community represented, in many ways, a resuscitation of the "race"-record market of the twenties and thirties. "While the term 'jazz' gave Whiteman equal weight with Ellington, and Bix Beiderbecke comparable standing with Louis Armstrong," writes Nelson George, "the term 'race' was applied to forms of black music—primarily blues—that whites and, again, the black elite disdained."[7] The race records of the twenties and thirties sold well, but primarily in regional markets.

The creation of a national audience for this regional music was aided significantly by the population migrations associated with World War II. Eastern and Midwestern GIs, who were stationed in Southern military bases, were exposed to

5. Nelson George, *The Death of Rhythm & Blues* (New York: Pantheon Books, 1988), p.176.
6. Leroi Jones, *Blues People* (New York: William Morrow, 1963), p.160.
7. George, *The Death of Rhythm & Blues*, p.9.

musical styles that had not yet become popular in the North. At the same time, large numbers of Southern African-Americans moved north and west to find work in defense plants, and they brought their music with them. In the forties, more than one million black people left the South, three times as many as the decade before. Newly emigrated African-Americans had enough money from wartime prosperity to establish themselves as an identifiable consumer group. In areas that received a high concentration of black immigrants, it was in the interest of radio stations to introduce some programming that would cater to this new audience. Gradually, some black-oriented programs, usually slotted late at night, began to appear on a few stations. It was this kind of "specialty" programming that would begin to tear down the walls of the race market at the end of the decade.

Having already alienated the music-publishing establishment of the day, the broadcasters—which is to say, radio—managed to arouse the anger of established musicians as well. The period before the end of World War II was the era of big bands, fancy ballrooms, and, most important for the musicians, live music on the radio. Radio was, in essence, their electronic ballroom; it provided very steady work. By and large, live music on radio meant live music performed by white musicians. As a rule, black musicians were barred from radio performances. Of course, there were exceptions, such as:

> live broadcasts of Duke Ellington at the Cotton Club and Chick Webb at the Savoy in Harlem, Earl [Fatha] Hines from Chicago's Grand Terrace, or maybe a late set from some California band from the West Coast Cotton Club. Significantly, these broadcasts weren't aimed at blacks. Broadcasters and advertisers were simply meeting America's demand for big-band music. These bands just happened to be black and popular.[8]

In the forties, radio began to experiment with programming recorded music. The musicians were not about to surrender their best gig to records without a fight. In 1942 the American Federation of Musicians (AFM) struck the major record labels and ordered a ban on recording. Months later, the musicians returned to the studios to find vocalists in charge. Vocalists belong to a different union—currently called the

8. *Ibid*, p.11.

American Federation of Television and Radio Artists (AFTRA)—and AFTRA did not join the strike. The AFM itself thus aided the rise of solo vocalists, who were now becoming the main attraction of the big bands, by allowing them free rein in the recording studios. With the rise of vocalists, the pop charts were gradually taken over by such figures as Bing Crosby, Perry Como, Dinah Shore, Vaughn Monroe, Frankie Laine, Doris Day, Jo Stafford, and, of course, Frank Sinatra. Throughout the post-war forties the only black vocal acts to make the year-end pop charts were the more pop-sounding artists like Nat "King" Cole ("For Sentimental Reasons"), Ella Fitzgerald ("My Happiness"), the Mills Brothers ("Across the Valley from the Alamo"), and the Ink Spots ("The Gypsy"). There were never more than two black vocalists on the year-end charts in a given year.

If the rise of the solo vocalist was a psychological blow to the big bands, it was the post-war economy that dealt the death blow. After the war, it was no longer feasible to support the elaborate production of twenty-piece orchestras as a regular attraction. Ballrooms disappeared and, unable to find steady work, the big bands gradually broke up. The black big bands, which had provided much of the impetus for the big-band sound, limped along for a while on one-nighters on the dying dance-hall circuit. The better-known black bands, like Count Basie's band and Duke Ellington's, could also count on an occasional hit record such as Basie's recording of "Open the Door, Richard" for Victor, which made the year-end pop charts in 1947. Still, it was clear by then that a musical era in the United States had come to an end, and it was reflected in record sales. Between 1947 and 1949 sales dropped off more than fifty million dollars, which at the time represented more than twenty percent of the dollar volume of the industry. The situation was worse for black artists. By the end of the decade not a single black performer could be found on the year-end pop charts.

The population migrations previously mentioned opened the possibility of a nationwide market for black music, which did not exist prior to World War II. The major companies never exploited this new market during the war because a shellac shortage caused significant cutbacks in the number of records that could be manufactured. Shellac was the principal ingredient used in making the old 78rpm records. During the Pacific blockade it became almost impossible to obtain the material from India where it is secreted by a tree-crawling insect. At the height of the shortage, in order to buy a new record it was often necessary to return an old one so that it could be recycled. Since the pop-music market alone was capable of absorbing virtually all the records that could be produced, the major labels concentrated their efforts there. The specialty fields, especially blues, jazz, and gospel, bore the brunt of the cutbacks, and were essentially abandoned by the major labels.

Whereas the shellac shortage had seriously limited the supply of specialty music, cross-cultural contact had, if anything, increased the demand. Thus, after the war ended, the major companies tried to regain control of the specialty markets. In the country & western field this proved to be relatively simple. According to pop historian Charlie Gillett:

> [T]he companies responded by heavily promoting various songs performed in versions of country & western styles. One tactic was to promote the strong Southern accent of most country & western singers as a "novelty," as Capitol did successfully with Tex Williams's "Smoke That Cigarette" in 1947, and as Columbia did for several years with various Gene Autrey songs, including "Rudolph, the Red-Nosed Reindeer" (1950). Alternatively, the country & western songs that were closest to the melodramatic or sentimental modes of conventional popular songs were promoted as popular songs—or, more frequently, recorded by popular singers in a style that was halfway between country and pop.[9]

Performers such as Frankie Laine and Guy Mitchell fit this latter category. Through these various manipulations, the country music field was soon firmly back in the hands of the major companies.

The black music market proved much more difficult to absorb. Having ignored black music for a number of years, the major companies had lost touch with recent developments in the rich and constantly evolving black culture. While these companies contented themselves with connections to the most prominent black innovators of the big-band sound, other black musicians were developing styles that were much closer to the blues. As the swing era declined, the music that was brought to the fore in working-class black communities came to be called rhythm & blues. If there was a transitional figure in this development, it was Louis Jordan. Signed to Decca, a major label, Jordan and his group, the Tympani Five (actually seven members), anticipated the decline of the big bands and helped to define the instrumentation for the black dance bands that followed. With a much smaller horn section, the rhythm became

9. Charlie Gillett, *The Sound of the City: The Rise of Rock and Roll* (New York: Outerbridge and Dienstfrey, 1970), p.9.

more pronounced. Jordan's material was composed and arranged, but selections like "Saturday Night Fishfry," "Honey Chile," and "Ain't Nobody Here But Us Chickens" evoked blues images not found in most black pop of the day.

While Jordan was said to have "jumped the blues," the rhythm & blues stars who followed in the late forties screeched, honked, and shouted. The raucous sounds of artists such as Wynonie Harris ("Good Rockin' Tonight"), John Lee Hooker ("Boogie Chillen"), saxophonist Big Jay McNeely ("Deacon's Hop"), and pianist Amos Milburn ("Chicken Shack Boogie") were something of a break from the recent musical past and a harbinger of sounds to come:

> Suddenly it was as if a great deal of the Euro-American humanist facade Afro-American music had taken on had been washed away by the war. Rhythm & blues singers literally had to shout to be heard above the clanging and strumming of the various electrified instruments and the churning rhythm sections. And somehow the louder the instrumental accompaniment and the more harshly screamed the singing, the more expressive the music was.[10]

Since this music did not readily lend itself to the production styles of the major labels, they continued to ignore the relatively smaller race market. This situation made it possible for a large number of independent labels to enter the business. It is estimated that by 1949 over four hundred new labels came into existence. Most important among these were Atlantic in New York; Savoy in Newark; King in Cincinnati; Chess in Chicago; Peacock in Houston; and Modern, Imperial, and Specialty in Los Angeles. The independents were generally hampered by a shortage of materials, lack of funds, and inadequate distribution. Yet, with a hit, profits could be substantial. Modern was able to sell its blues singles for $1.05 in the late forties, while the major companies were only getting seventy-eight cents for pop singles. Particularly with the increased affluence provided by the war, black people were willing to spend more for their music. The relatively small number of independents that survived the forties gained a foothold in the industry that would not be dislodged.

A number of technological advances set the stage for the growth and further expansion of rhythm & blues music and its eventual takeover of the pop market as rock and roll. The first of these was the introduction of magnetic tape, an invention stolen from

10. Jones, *Blues People*, p.171.

the Nazis during World War II.[11] Prior to this innovation, quality recording was tied to elaborate studios, cumbersome equipment, and a substantial capital investment. Recording facilities were located in a relatively few city centers and were firmly under the control of established corporate powers. Magnetic tape and its more versatile hardware changed that. Aside from bringing the obvious technical advantages of editing and better sound reproduction, magnetic tape made it possible for anyone to record anywhere. Operating from a small studio in Memphis, an enterprising young engineer named Sam Phillips could record B. B. King, Howlin' Wolf, Junior Parker, Rufus Thomas, and, later, Elvis Presley. The new technology clearly encouraged independent production and the formation of independent labels.

In 1948 Columbia's Dr. Peter Goldmark invented high fidelity. In what was to become known as the "battle of the speeds"—a contest that pitted Columbia's 33rpm record against RCA's 45rpm record—competition between the two giant firms yielded discs of excellent sound quality and maximum durability. These records were lighter and less breakable than the 78rpm records and were well suited to the rapidly changing pop market because they could be shipped faster and more cheaply. Again, independent production was encouraged.

Most audio and visual media—television, film, and, to a lesser extent, radio—are capital-intensive industries. They require huge sums of money for production. Records, on the other hand, do not depend on an elaborate transmission system as does television, and they are not affected by such government regulations as the assignment of frequencies on the electromagnetic spectrum. Particularly in the late forties, records emerged as a relatively inexpensive medium. It was in part for this reason that it was not easy for a few giant electronics firms to monopolize the business. Records soon became the staple of the music industry, surpassing sheet music as the major source of revenue in 1952. About the same time, radio overtook jukeboxes as the number-one hit-maker.

Another technological development strengthened local radio as the main vehicle for popularizing rhythm & blues; it involved a major media policy decision that had been made earlier in the century but which came to fruition in the early fifties. As early as 1935, RCA had announced plans to commit its research capabilities to the development of a then-unheard-of broadcast medium—television. In the late forties

---

11. See Erik Barnouw, *The Golden Web: Broadcasting in the United States: 1933–1952* (New York: Oxford University Press, 1968), p.204.

television became available as a consumer item. By 1951 RCA had already recovered from the cost of research and development and from the initial period of programming television stations at a loss. By 1957 there were thirty-nine million television sets in use, filling eighty percent of the homes in the United States. Because television quickly attracted most of the national advertising, network radio ad revenues fell off. Local radio grew as an effective medium for local advertisers. Experimenting successfully with new music, new programming, and new personalities, these independent stations eventually pushed aside the more staid network stations and in the process helped to revitalize the then-smaller record industry.

Local radio in the early fifties was very loosely structured. The independent deejays, or "personality jocks" as they were called, were in control. These men were not subject to the dictates of music directors, and there was nothing approaching the tightly structured programming and restrictive playlists that we see today. In the search for cheaper forms of programming, records provided the obvious answer. Record programming soon became the rule for radio, and the disc jockey replaced the live entertainment personalities who had dominated radio in the thirties and forties. Until the 1959 congressional payola hearings curtailed their power and "Top 40" programming rationalized the AM format, the independent deejays were the central figures in the record industry. They could and did make hits. Relying on their own inventiveness for popularity, they often experimented with "specialty" music as an antidote to the trivial popular fare of network radio. Rhythm & blues proved to be quite popular with white as well as black audiences. As early as 1952, Dolphin's Hollywood Record Shop, a black retail outlet, reported that its business suddenly consisted of forty percent white customers. They attributed it to independent deejays playing rhythm & blues records. Early rhythm & blues hits that were popular among both black and white audiences included Fats Domino's "The Fat Man" for Imperial (1950), Jackie Brenston's "Rocket 88" for Modern (1951), Lloyd Price's "Lawdy Miss Clawdy" for Specialty (1952), and Joe Turner's "Chains of Love" (1951), "Sweet Sixteen" (1952), and "Honey Hush" (1953) for Atlantic. All were recorded for independent labels.

As the market for black popular music expanded, so did the number of stations that played it. At first, the Deep South was the center for rhythm & blues radio. Gradually, white-oriented stations began programming some rhythm & blues shows to accommodate the potential audience for black music in Northern cities. As record sales indicated the surging popularity of rhythm & blues among white teenagers, white stations made a growing commitment to the music, and pioneering black dee-jays like "Jockey" Jack Gibson in Atlanta, "Professor Bop" in Shreveport, and "Sugar Daddy" in Birmingham were soon followed by white rhythm & blues deejays such as Alan Freed, who is remembered as the "Father of Rock 'n' Roll."

Rhythm & Blues Begets Rock and Roll

The rhythm & blues that these stations were playing, the forerunner of rock and roll, was itself a hybrid form. As a category, it had been adopted by the music business in 1949 as a more palatable catch-all phrase, replacing the designation "race" music. Still a code word for black music, it encompassed styles as diverse as gospel, blues, and jazz. In the nationwide musical market made possible by radio, a number of these traditions converged with some country influence to become rock and roll. Rhythm & blues artist Johnny Otis recalled the phenomenon from a West Coast per-spective:

> In the early forties a hybrid form of music developed on the West Coast. What was happening in Chicago was another kind of thing altogether. It was all rhythm & blues later, but the Chicago bands, the people that came up from the Delta, came up with harmonicas and guitars—the Muddy Waters and the rest of them. They had a certain thing, and we loved it, and we were influenced by it to a certain degree. But on the Coast, the people who were there, like myself and Roy Milton, T-Bone Walker, and Joe Liggins and the Honeydrippers, we all had big-band experience. We all thought in terms of big bands, but when it became impossible to maintain a big band and work and make a living we all had to break down, and when we broke down, we didn't break down to just a guitar and a rhythm & blues section. We still tried to maintain some of that sound of the jazz bands. We kept maybe a trumpet, a trombone, and saxes—this was a semblance of brass and reeds, and they continued to play the bop and swing riffs. And this superimposed on the country blues and boogie structure began to become rhythm & blues. And out of rhythm & blues grew rock and roll.[12]

12. Johnny Otis interviewed by the author, Cambridge, Massachusetts, 1974.

By the time rock and roll established itself as an independent style, the horn section described by Otis had been reduced even further, first to a single saxophone, and then to no horns at all. The rhythmic base of the boogie structure had become even more dominant. And the music was hardly limited to California.

Although its roots were in the Deep South, the music that became rock and roll issued from just about every region in the country. Most of its formative influences, as well as virtually all of its early innovators, were black. T-Bone Walker's pioneering work with the electric guitar on the West Coast had an obvious effect on the Memphis-based B. B. King ("Three O'Clock Blues," "The Thrill is Gone"), whose single-string runs influenced dozens of rock guitarists to follow. Delta-born Muddy Waters ("Got My Mojo Working") "electrified" the blues in Chicago; shortly thereafter Bo Diddley ("Bo Diddley") crossed over into the pop market as a rock and roll star with his distinctive variant of the style. The New Orleans boogie piano of Professor Longhair influenced Fats Domino, whose successful rhythm & blues career was transformed into rock and roll legend with hits such as "Ain't That a Shame," "I'm in Love Again," and "Blueberry Hill." The jazz/gospel fusions of Ray Charles ("I Got a Woman," "What'd I Say") and the more pop-oriented gospel stylings of vocalists like Clyde McPhatter ("Treasure of Love," "A Lover's Question") and Sam Cooke ("You Send Me," "For Sentimental Reasons") brought the traditions of the black church into the secular world of rock and roll. The assertiveness of Joe Turner, veteran blues shouter from Kansas City, was taken up by female vocalists such as Ruth Brown ("5-10-15 Hours," "Mamma, He Treats Your Daughter Mean") and Lavern Baker ("Tweedle Dee," "Jim Dandy"), and carried to an extreme in the outrageous rock and roll performances of Little Richard ("Tutti-Frutti," "Long Tall Sally," "Rip It Up"). The elegant harmonies of urban vocal groups like the Orioles ("Crying in the Chapel"), the Crows ("Gee"), the Chords ("Sh-Boom"), and the Penguins ("Earth Angel") ushered in a whole genre of rock and roll known as doo wop. Even with the new name, however, there was no mistaking where this music came from. As late as 1956 *Billboard* referred to the music as "a popularized form of rhythm & blues." What made the mainstream popularity of this music that much more incredible was the vast array of social forces that stood in its way.

In the fifties one of the factors that kept rhythm & blues from expanding in popularity in its original form was the rapid turnover of artists working in the field.

Billboard reported the following in a retrospective article on the year 1952: "On the whole, the older more established artists held their own throughout the year, less than a handful of new names established themselves in the pop field, and less than that in the country & western division. The rhythm & blues department where artists turn over like leaves in the fall followed its usual pattern this year."[13]

The "usual pattern" of rhythm & blues turnover continued throughout the 1950s. Groups like the Chords, the Charms, the Spiders, the Spaniels, the Crows, and the Four Tunes, all of whom had pop hits in 1954, could not be found on the year-end pop charts one year later. Often catapulted to success from a neighborhood street corner or, like Little Richard, from a bus terminal kitchen where he was washing dishes, black musicians seldom had access to good advice about record contracts, royalty payments, marketing, promotion, or career development. As a result, they were routinely swindled out of their publishing rights and underpaid for record sales.

Rhythm & blues artist Jimmy Witherspoon recorded "Ain't Nobody's Business" on the Supreme label owned by a dentist named Al Patrick. "But I didn't get one penny royalty," complained Witherspoon. "Patrick paid me a flat fee for the session. I was supposed to get so much on each record sold, which he never paid me."[14] In some cases black artists were not paid for recording at all. Said Saul Bihari, founder of Modern, an independent label that included on its roster Lightnin' Hopkins, John Lee Hooker, Etta James, and B. B. King:

> We used to bring 'em in, give 'em a little bottle of booze and say, "Sing me a song about your girl." Or, "Sing me a song about Christmas." They'd pluck around a little on their guitars, then say "OK" and make up a song as they went along. We'd give them a subject and off they'd go. When it came time to quit, we'd give them a wave that they had ten seconds to finish.[15]

The major companies were no more principled in their treatment of black musicians. Ahmet Ertegun, the president of Atlantic, tells an interesting story about a Columbia representative who came to see him in the early years of Atlantic:

13. *Billboard* (January 3, 1953): p.3.
14. Arnold Shaw, *Honkers and Shouters: The Golden Years of Rhythm and Blues* (New York: Collier Books, 1978), p.213.
15. Saul Bihari quoted in "World of Soul," *Billboard* (June 23, 1967): p.26.

He wanted to make a deal whereby Columbia would distribute for Atlantic records because we seemed to be very good at what he called "race" records. So I said, "Well, what would you offer us?" He said, "Three percent." "Three percent!" I said, "We're paying our artists more than that!" And he said, "You're paying those people royalties? You must be out of your mind!" Of course he didn't call them "people." He called them something else.[16]

Another practice that served to limit the crossover potential of black artists was the widespread use of "cover versions" of rhythm & blues hits. Strictly speaking, a cover record is a copy of an original recording performed by another artist in a style thought to be more appropriate for the mainstream market. Table 2.1 lists some of the better-known cover records. In the vast majority of cases, black artists recording for independent labels were covered by white artists signed to one of the majors. In the 1950s covers were commonly used by the major companies to capitalize on the growing popularity of rhythm & blues among white listeners. Cover records were often released within the expected chart life of the original and, owing to the superior distribution channels and promotional power of the majors, often outsold the originals. But most of them lacked the feeling and sense of excitement that the originals conveyed.

Several dozen songs were successfully covered by the majors in the early years of rock and roll. RCA began by covering Gene and Eunice's "Kokomo" with a version by Perry Como. Columbia covered the same song using Tony Bennett. Columbia and Victor were so reluctant to have anything to do with rock and roll that they were less aggressive with cover versions than other majors. Mercury and Decca had the most luck of the major companies. Mercury's Crew Cuts, aptly named for the fifties teenage audience, recorded a cover version of the Chords' "Sh-Boom" (originally on Atlantic's Cat label) that became the fifth-best-selling popular song of 1954.

Following the success of "Sh-Boom," the Crew Cuts systematically pillaged the rhythm & blues charts, covering hits like Nappy Brown's "Don't Be Angry" (Savoy), the Charms' "Gum Drop" (Deluxe), and the Penguins' "Earth Angel" (DooTone). Georgia Gibbs, also signed to Mercury, covered Etta James's "Wallflower" with a cleaned-up version called "Dance with Me, Henry." The original version sold 400,000 copies for Modern while the Gibbs cover sold one million records for Mercury. Decca

16. Ahmet Ertegun interviewed by Steve Chapple, New York, NY, July 1974.

used the McGuire Sisters (on their Coral subsidiary) to cover the Moonglows' "Sincerely" (Chess) and made it the seventh-best-selling pop single in 1955.

Cover Records and Original Artists

Song	Original Artist	Cover Artist
"Crying in the Chapel"	Sonny Til and the Orioles	June Valli
"Sh-Boom"	Chords	Crew Cuts
"Earth Angel"	Penguins	Crew Cuts
"Don't Be Angry"	Nappy Brown	Crew Cuts
"Gum Drop"	Charms	Crew Cuts
"Goodnight, Well It's Time to Go"	Spaniels	McGuire Sisters
"Sincerely"	Moonglows	McGuire Sisters
"Dance with Me, Henry" ["Wallflower"]	Etta James	Georgia Gibbs
"Tweedle Dee"	LaVern Baker	Georgia Gibbs
"Kokomo"	Gene and Eunice	Perry Como
"Shake, Rattle and Roll"	Joe Turner	Bill Haley
"Hound Dog"	Big Mama Thornton	Elvis Presley
"Money Honey"	The Drifters	Elvis Presley
"Lawdy Miss Clawdy"	Lloyd Price	Elvis Presley
"Ain't That a Shame"	Fats Domino	Pat Boone
"I Almost Lost My Mind"	Ivory Joe Hunter	Pat Boone
"Tutti Frutti"	Little Richard	Pat Boone
"Long Tall Sally"	Little Richard	Pat Boone
"I'll Be Home"	Flamingos	Pat Boone
"Hearts of Stone"	Charms	Fontaine Sisters
"Little Darlin'"	Gladiolas	Diamonds
"I'm Walkin'"	Fats Domino	Ricky Nelson
"Party Doll"	Buddy Knox	Steve Lawrence
"Butterfly"	Charlie Gracie	Andy Williams
"I Hear You Knocking"	Smiley Lewis	Gale Storm

Pat Boone, more than any other artist, built his reputation as a rock and roll singer by covering black rhythm & blues tunes. His label, Dot, was the most successful company at the practice. In 1955, Dot got fifteen percent of the popular singles on the charts and shortly after achieved the status of a major company by setting up its own distribution system. Boone recorded "Ain't That a Shame" (Fats Domino), "I Almost Lost My Mind" (Ivory Joe Hunter), and "Tutti Frutti" (Little Richard), among others.

In order to obtain the far larger royalties from performances, record sales, and sheet-music sales available in the white-audience market, small record companies that consigned publishing and copyrights to themselves sometimes took their rhythm & blues songs to the big companies to be covered. Such practices kept the black version of the song out of the popular market and denied the original singer the royalties that would have come if the record company/publisher had pushed the first version as a potential crossover hit. By 1956, however, this initial suppression of black music was less generally successful. Rhythm & blues had merged with and changed into rock and roll, which was becoming a dominant popular style, and the original versions of songs were in demand by a more sophisticated white audience.

The profitable practice of covering records was greatly aided by the copyright laws. The appropriate law under which artists worked in the fifties had been written in 1909, and thus did not include recorded material. Under the 1909 copyright law, it was impossible to copyright a particular recording of a song; one could only copyright the original sheet music. Thus, while a publisher received a royalty payment for the use of his publication and a composer received a royalty payment for the performance of his music, no royalty was derived from the actual recording. The performer was paid only for the sales of his records. In this period of heavy cover activity it was the performer who suffered. Most of the performers whose songs were covered were black.

The wording of the 1909 copyright law often led to other abuses. Even though the royalty payments on any piece of music were supposed to be divided by the writer and the publisher (usually fifty percent each), many performers who wrote their own material never got their royalties. According to Lee Berk, lawyer and founder of the Berklee School of Music in Boston:

> The US Copyright Act speaks of a situation in which, in the case of an "employee for
> hire," it is the employer and not the composer who will have the right to be consid-
> ered author or composer of the work. In such a case, then, the employer would also
> be the proprietor of the work by the fact of the employment relationship, and would

have not only the right to copyright the work and name himself as copyright proprietor, but also the right to name himself composer.[17]

The name that appeared on the record might not have been the actual author of the song. More important, even if the real author were credited on the record, his name might not have been registered with the publishing rights organizations (ASCAP and BMI) that collected the royalty payments for artists.

Fred Parris, for example, wrote "In the Still of the Night" and recorded it with his own group, The Five Satins. The record is a rock and roll classic. Re-released in a number of oldies anthologies, the record has probably sold millions of copies. With proper credits, "In the Still of the Night" should have been worth tens of thousands of dollars for Parris in mechanical royalties alone (one cent for every record sold), not to mention performance royalties of 2.5 cents for every radio play. Had Parris also owned the publishing, the record would have been worth more than twice that figure. As to what really happened with the recording, Parris claimed:

> I don't know about BMI. Okay, I used to see BMI on every label, but I never knew what it meant. I didn't become a BMI writer—and this is very sad—until after the bulk of the plays on "In the Still of the Night." So what was happening was my name was on the label, I'm the writer, I'm getting a fair shake . . . I'm not going to try and incriminate anyone, but somebody else's name was in at BMI as the writer, and that was where the money came from. When I got out of the service and went to them with my problem, they said "Okay, we feel sorry for you." And again, I still didn't have enough knowledge of the business, and I didn't have enough patience, you know, to say, "Well, I'll see my attorney about this. I'll wait." Instead I wanted the money right then. They said, "Okay, we'll make it retroactive from such and such a date." But that "such and such a date" was nowhere near where the bulk of the sales were. So I came up with a figure of something like $783.[18]

A final factor that helped to suppress black music and musicians was the technological innovations in the industry that required equipment changeover in the record-buying public. The late 1940s saw the development of unbreakable 45rpm

17. Lee Eliot Berk, *Legal Protection for the Creative Musician* (Boston: Berklee Press, 1970), p.177.
18. Fred Parris interviewed by the author, Cambridge, Massachusetts, 1974.

and 33rpm records that required different playback equipment than had been used for the 78rpm records. Because of a simple lack of money, the black record audience was slower to make this switch than the white. Victor and Columbia were marketing three-speed record changers by 1952, but as late as 1956, rhythm & blues records were still sold in the black community as shellac-based 78s. Independent distributors evolved formulas for predicting when a song would cross over into the white market on the basis of the demand for the disc in the 45rpm configuration. Of course, to go into a separate 45rpm pressing, a rhythm & blues record would have to show evidence of very strong sales potential. The dual technology had the effect of delaying mainstream exposure for many rhythm & blues artists. While not a conspiracy of the major record companies, the lock-and-key relationship of new and better records and the new record changers tended to isolate black music.

Even with such obstacles to overcome, the mainstream acceptance of rhythm & blues surpassed all expectations. A *Billboard* headline announced: "1955—The Year R&B Took Over Pop Field." The dramatic numerical increase of black artists in the popular market was second only to their influence in shaping public taste. Reviewing the year 1956, *Billboard* offered the following assessment:

> Looking closely at the twenty-five rhythm & blues platters that made the pop charts, it is interesting to note the great variety of rhythm & blues artists and styles that found pop acceptance. It was not only the slicker, pop-oriented singers like Clyde McPhatter and Otis Williams who hit in the pop market, but also those working in the traditional style like Shirley and Lee, Little Richard, and Fats Domino. Their impact, in fact, has virtually changed the conception of what a pop record is.[19]

By the mid-1950s this music, now called rock and roll, had become "perhaps the most profound and enduring reshaping of a dominant musical style to have taken place since the Renaissance."[20]

---

19. *Billboard* (December 22, 1956): p.10.
20. Christopher Small, *Music of the Common Tongue: Survival and Celebration in Afro-American Music* (New York: Riverrun Press, 1987), p.371.

Rock and Roll: Black or White?

Were it not for the dynamics of racism in our society, the man who would most likely have been crowned the "King of Rock 'n' Roll" was the son of a carpenter from St. Louis—Chuck Berry. When Berry walked into the offices of Chess Records on the recommendation of Muddy Waters, his demo of "Ida Red" (backed with a blues number, "Wee Wee Hours") had already been turned down at both Capitol and Mercury because it sounded "too country" for a black man. On the advice of Leonard Chess, Berry gave the tune a "bigger beat" and changed the title to "Maybellene," taking the name from a hair-cream bottle. Said Chess a few weeks before he died:

> I liked it, thought it was something new. I was going to New York anyway, and I took a dub to Alan [Freed] and said, "Play this." The dub didn't have Chuck's name on it or nothing. By the time I got back to Chicago, Freed had called a dozen times, saying it was his biggest record ever. History, the rest, y' know? Sure, "Wee Wee Hour," [sic] that was on the back side of the release, was a good tune too, but the kids wanted the big beat, cars, and young love.[21]

For his part, Freed and another deejay named Russ Fratto were credited as co-writers of the song. The country-tinged "Maybellene" went to number five on the pop charts in 1955.

> But his next four singles, performed in a blues style and presenting in their themes some strong criticisms of aspects of American life, showed his interests much more obviously. Judges and courts in "Thirty Days," credit and car salesmen in "No Money Down," high culture in "Roll Over Beethoven," and all these and more in "Too Much Monkey Business" were cause for complaint. Since these records were performed in a strong "blues" voice, the songs . . . received relatively little attention from disc jockeys.[22]

The songs Berry is best remembered for are the simpler, teen-directed, but still socially relevant recordings he turned out later, such as "School Days" and "Rock

21. Leonard Chess quoted in *Rolling Stone* (January 18, 1973): p.38.
22. Gillett, *The Sound of the City*, pp.96–97.

and Roll Music" in 1957, and "Sweet Little Sixteen" and "Johnny B. Goode" in 1958, all of which reached the Top 10 on the pop charts.

Other rock and roll artists may have had more and bigger hits than Chuck Berry, but none matched his influence in defining the style. "As rock and roll's first guitar hero, Berry, along with various rockabilly musicians, made that instrument the genre's dominant musical element, supplanting the sax of previous black stars."[23] In his writing and performing, he had the uncanny ability to relate rhythm & blues to white teenage culture without disowning his blackness. He was a true storyteller in the folkloric sense of the term, but he was also a man for his time. As he recently told his fans: "I said: 'Why can't I do as Pat Boone does and play good music for the white people and sell as well there as I could in the neighborhood?' And that's what I shot for writing 'School Day'."[24]

Berry's career was interrupted in 1962 when he was convicted of a violation of the Mann Act and sent to prison. He had done no more than bring a girl back with him from a tour in Mexico, but because she was underage, he was convicted. It took two trials. The first was vacated because of the prejudice shown by the judge, who referred to Berry as "this Negro." The underlying meaning of the conviction was shown in a headline of the time, cited by Michael Lydon. It read "Rock 'n' Roll Singer Lured Me to St. Louis, Says Fourteen-Year-Old."[25] Berry's songs continued to be recorded, and he staged a comeback in 1972 with a song as commercially successful as it was puerile: "My Ding-a-Ling."

The second wave of rock and roll performers to hit the charts were white. These were the rockabilly artists Elvis Presley, Carl Perkins, Gene Vincent, Jerry Lee Lewis, and Johnny Cash, and their country cousins, the Everly Brothers and Buddy Holly. Their music was widely regarded as an amalgam of rhythm & blues and country & western, the first tradition being upheld by black artists, and the second by predominantly white ones. Both rhythm & blues and country & western exhibited a spontaneity that differentiated them from the Tin Pan Alley pop of their day. But the relative contribution of each to the equally authentic rockabilly strain is more difficult to pinpoint. Johnny Cash's "I Walk the Line," for example, was closer to traditional country material, with country phrasing and the bass line providing a steady country rhythm. The Everly Brothers' close harmonies were also characteristic of the country

23. George, *The Death of Rhythm & Blues*, p.68
24. Chuck Berry interviewed in the Taylor Hackford documentary, *Hail! Hail! Rock 'n' Roll*, 1987.
25. Michael Lydon, *Rock Folk: Portraits from the Rock 'n' Roll Pantheon* (New York: Dell, 1968), p.20.

genre, but their unorthodox, syncopated guitar riffs clearly established them as a rock and roll act. Similarly, Presley, Perkins, and Lewis often sang with a traditional country drawl, but in their up-tempo tunes the lyric phrasing and driving rhythms clearly came from the rhythm & blues tradition.

The phenomenon of country-flavored rock and roll had its origins in the rather unlikely figure of Bill Haley ("Rock Around the Clock"), a middle-aged, slightly balding guitarist who was signed to a major label. His heroes were Bob Wills and his Texas Playboys, who played a culturally mixed brand of music known as Western swing, but his sound came closer to Louis Jordan. His producer, Milt Gabler (who had also been Jordan's producer in the forties), told chronicler Arnold Shaw that he consciously modeled Haley's sound on Jordan's jump beat. "We'd begin with Jordan's shuffle rhythm," said Gabler. "You know, dotted eighth notes and sixteenths, and we'd build on it. I'd sing Jordan riffs to the group that would be picked up by the electric guitars and tenor sax . . . They got a sound that had the drive of the Tympani Five and the color of country & western."[26]

Country music is usually seen as having developed from the Anglo-Celtic folk tradition. Among those immigrants from the British Isles who settled in the valleys of the Appalachian Mountains, this music retained much of its original character. In the slave-owning South, however, where most of the rockabilly artists came from, there was a continuing interaction between the European and African cultures, despite the legally enforced separation of the races. While there is no question that cultural crossover was a two-way process, there is considerable controversy over which musical elements can legitimately be considered Africanisms—and, therefore, the contribution of black artists—and to what extent they influenced styles generally performed by whites—in this case, rockabilly. The debate usually includes a discussion of variables such as tonal inflection, instrumentation, "blue notes" and musical scales, the call-and-response style, and rhythmic patterns.

According to African music scholar John Storm Roberts, there is an "intimate connection between speech and melody in African music, which arises partly from the fact that so many African languages are tonal."[27] As Hettie Jones commented, "The song you sing is what you mean to say."[28] This heightened sense of music-as-language

26. Milt Gabler quoted in Shaw, *Honkers and Shouters*, p.64.
27. John Storm Roberts, *Black Music of Two Worlds* (New York: William Morrow, 1974), p.189.
28. Hettie Jones, *Big Star Fallin' Mama* (New York: Dell Publishing Co., 1974), p.41.

extends to African concepts of musical instrumentation as well. In traditional African music, instruments are often used to approximate human speech. They are not simply external devices used to produce notes and "melody," as in European music. African talking drums, for example, did not send messages by using an abstract Morse code–like system of tapping. They replicated the pitch and rhythmic patterns of the language; they really talked. In addition to this "'talking' function that goes far beyond the well-known use of talking drums, or even talking flutes, xylophones, and so forth," Roberts notes that there is also a "semi-personification of instruments, which are considered to have some form of soul."[29] Centuries later Ray Charles said that it was this human quality that attracted him to country music instrumentation: "I really thought that it was somethin' about country music, even as a youngster. I couldn't figure out what it was then, but I know what it was now . . . Although I was bred in and around the blues, I always did have interest in other music, and I felt the closest music, really, to the blues [was country & western]. They'd make them steel guitars cry and whine, and it really attracted me."[30]

At first the blues was a largely improvisational music, with no standard form or rhythmic pattern. Interacting with the European diatonic scale, the blues eventually became standardized into two or three common forms, the best known of which is called the "classic" blues. The notation of the diatonic scale, however, did not accommodate the way the bluesmen really sang. Their deviations from European melodic regularity came to be known as "blue notes." A blue note sounds a little flat, but not flat enough to be the next note down on the scale. There is some controversy not over whether such tones exist but whether they constitute an Africanism. While "an ambiguous third," to use John Storm Roberts's term, appears in the music of more than one continent, the flatted seventh is more of a defining characteristic of the blues. According to noted African scholar Kwabena Nketia, "The flatted seventh is frequent and well-established in Akan vocal music."[31] Such tones are also common in rockabilly songs such as Elvis Presley's recording of "Hound Dog," and Jerry Lee Lewis's "Whole Lotta Shakin'," both of which also follow a classic twelve-bar blues structure.

Another Africanism that found its way into rock and roll was the call-and-response style. In African culture this style is used in religious ceremonies as well as

29. Roberts, *Black Music of Two Worlds*, p.190.
30. Ray Charles quoted in *Rolling Stone* (January 18, 1972): p.18.
31. Kwabena Nketia quoted in Roberts, *Black Music of Two Worlds*, p.190.

collective work. Most commonly identified with gospel music, the style was probably introduced to America in the work songs of the slaves. In traditional African music the call-and-response style exists primarily as a vocal form where a lead singer is answered by a chorus, but in America instrumental variations of this device also developed in blues and jazz. Both forms of call-and-response were evident in blues-based rock and roll. It is also possible, however, to establish a link to the more country-oriented rockabilly strain, which at times employed instrumental fills in a way that suggested an African influence.

"European and Anglo-American folk music sometimes has instrumental bridges between the verses," says Roberts. "It must be said that this is rare, however, and most Anglo-American singing was unaccompanied until so late that a black influence could be postulated," especially in those cases where the "instrumental sections were clearly used not as a bridge to lead to the next vocal line, as a European musician might use them, but as an answer to the previous one."[32] One can hear these instrumental responses in rockabilly songs such as Bill Haley's "See You Later, Alligator" and in "Wake Up Little Susie" by the Everly Brothers. In these instances, to use the words of musicologist Christopher Small, "the instrument is too much like a second voice to allow us to call it merely accompaniment; this second voice seems to work in a way which reminds us more of African call-and-response procedures than of European concepts of melody and accompaniment."[33]

The most significant contribution black music made to rock and roll, of course, was its rhythmic base. Says Small, "Rhythm is to the African musician what harmony is to the European—the central organizing principle of the art."[34] Not surprisingly, African music is polyrhythmic. In America, where slaves were generally denied the use of drums (thought to be politically dangerous, since they could be used to signal an uprising), other percussive practices such as finger popping, hand clapping, and foot stomping were developed. Polyrhythms were not found in European folk forms or their American country derivatives, which invariably accented the so-called strong beats and reinforced a single unsyncopated sustaining rhythm. The "Big Beat" that was rock and roll, which accents the second and fourth beats of each measure, was African-derived. It is found in virtually every up-tempo rock and roll tune, including the rockabilly style. In 1954 *Billboard* described Elvis Presley as "the youngster with

32. *Ibid*, pp.182–83.
33. Small, *Music of the Common Tongue*, p.201.
34. *Ibid*, p.25.

the hillbilly blues beat."[35] Bill Haley stated the issue most clearly when he told his audience, "I felt that if I could take a Dixieland tune and drop the first and third beats and accentuate the second and fourth, and add a beat the listeners could clap to as well as dance, this would be what we were after."[36]

In addition to the musical Africanisms that pervade rock and roll, including the rockabilly strain, the influence of black music and musicians can be seen in the personal lives and styles of the memorable rockabilly performers. Prior to the emergence of rockabilly, Sam Phillips, founder of the archetypal rockabilly label, Sun, had been almost exclusively a blues producer, having recorded blues giants like B. B. King, Bobby Bland, Howlin' Wolf, and James Cotton very early in their careers. According to his secretary, Marion Keisker, Phillips used to say: "If only I could find a white man who had the Negro sound and the Negro feel, I could make a billion dollars."[37] With Elvis Presley, his dream of a white man who could sing black came true, and it transformed Sun Records into an overwhelming commercial success.

Each of Phillips's white singers had grown up in an environment that mixed black and white cultures to a degree unknown in the North. This crossover of cultures created the conditions that gave rise to rockabilly, and through it to the dominant strain of rock and roll itself. Presley was reared in Mississippi until his late teens when his family moved to Memphis, Tennessee, in search of work. Later he described growing up:

> I'd play along with the radio or phonograph, and taught myself the chord positions. We were a religious family, going 'round together to sing at camp meetings and revivals, and I'd take my guitar with us when I could. I also dug the real low-down Mississippi singers, mostly Big Bill Broonzy and Big Boy Crudup, although they would scold me at home for listening to them. "Sinful music," the townsfolk in Memphis said it was. Which never bothered me, I guess.[38]

Margaret McKee and Fred Chisenhall described "Elvis Presley watching Old Charlie Burse, 'Ukulele Ike,' twitching his knee, rocking his pelvis, and rolling his

35. *Billboard* (December 11, 1954). Cited in Nick Tosches, *Country: Living Legends and Dying Metaphors in America's Biggest Music* (New York: Charles Scribner's Sons, 1985), p.52.
36. *New Musical Express* (September 21, 1956). Quoted in Gillett, The Sound of the City, pp.328–29.
37. Sam Phillips quoted in Peter Guralnick, *Feel Like Going Home: Portraits in Blues and Rock 'n' Roll* (New York: Outerbridge and Dienstfrey, 1971), p.140.
38. Elvis Presley quoted in Gillett, *The Sound of the City*, p.36.

syllables during a show at a Beale Street honky-tonk (the style Elvis copied to launch the blue-suede blues)."[39] Similarly, Jerry Lee Lewis explained how he

> used to hang around Haney's Big House, that was a colored establishment where they had dances and such . . . We was just kids, we wasn't allowed in. So we'd slip around to the back and sneak in whenever we could. I saw a lot of 'em there, all those blues players. No, it wasn't anything about us being white, we was just too young. See, it wasn't no big thing just because it was a colored place. Of course we was about the only ones down there.[40]

Carl Perkins, the son of a sharecropper, said,

> I was raised on a plantation in the flatlands of Lake Country, Tennessee, and we were about the only white people on it. I played with colored kids, played football with socks stuffed with sand. Working in the cotton fields in the sun, music was the only escape. The colored people would sing, and I'd join in, just a little kid, and that was colored rhythm & blues, got named rock and roll, got named that in 1956, but the same music was there years before, and it was my music.[41]

Although it borrowed heavily from black culture, rockabilly was still a legitimate musical movement that integrated black-based blues with country & western styles. It had its own identity and, obviously, in singers like Presley, Perkins, and Lewis, performers of real originality and talent. Unfortunately, it is impossible to separate the popularity of white rock and roll from a racist pattern that exists in American music whereby a style that is pioneered by black artists eventually comes to be popularized, dominated, and even defined by whites as if it were their own. That has been the history of black music in America from ragtime, to jazz, to swing—and rock and roll was no exception. Johnny Otis commented that

> black artists have always been the ones in America to innovate and create and breathe life into new forms. Jazz grew out of black America and there's no question about that. However, Paul Whiteman became the king of jazz. Swing music grew

39. Margaret McKee and Fred Chisenhall, *Beale Black and Blue: Life and Music on Black America's Main Street* (Baton Rouge, Louisiana: LSU Press, 1981), p.9.
40. Jerry Lee Lewis quoted in Guralnick, *Feel Like Going Home*, pp.150–91.
41. Carl Perkins quoted in Lydon, *Rock Folk*, p.32.

out of black America, created by black artists Count Basie, Duke Ellington. Benny Goodman was crowned king of swing. In the case of rock and roll, Elvis Presley—and in this case, not without some justification because he brought a lot of originality with him—became king. Not the true kings of rock and roll—Fats Domino, Little Richard, Chuck Berry . . . What happens is black people—the artists—continue to develop these things and create them and get ripped off, and the glory and the money goes to white artists. This pressure is constantly on them, to find something that whitey can't rip off.[42]

This skewed racial pattern makes the task of unearthing an accurate history of American popular music that much more difficult, and it seriously underestimates the degree of cross-cultural collaboration that has taken place. Styles are described (and defended) in terms that are clearly racial rather than musical. "[R]ockabilly is hillbilly rock and roll," insists Nick Tosches. "It was not a usurpation of black music by whites because its soul, its pneuma, was white, full of the redneck ethos."[43] "[I]t was that to a degree," acknowledges Arnold Shaw, "though it would probably be more accurate to describe it as the sound of young, white Southerners imitating black bluesmen."[44]

Were it not for the artificial separation of the races, popular-music history might read surprisingly differently. According to Jimmy Witherspoon, "Chuck Berry is a country singer. People put everybody in categories, black, white, this. Now if Chuck Berry was white, with the lyrics he writes, he would be the top country star in the world."[45] Just as an artist need not be limited to a single performance style, so pieces of music do not automatically have a genre; they can be performed in many idioms. There have been any number of country & western covers of Chuck Berry songs, including Hoyt Axton's "Maybelline," Freddy Weller's "Too Much Monkey Business" and "Promised Land," Waylon Jennings's "Brown-Eyed Handsome Man," Buck Owens's "Johnny B. Goode," Linda Rondstadt's "Back in the USA," Emmy Lou Harris's "You Never Can Tell," and Johnny Rivers's "Memphis."[46]

42. Johnny Otis interviewed by author, Cambridge, Massachusetts, 1974.
43. Tosches, *Country*, p.55.
44. Shaw, *Honkers and Shouters*, p.497.
45. *Ibid*, p.215.
46. George Lipsitz, *Class and Culture in Cold War America: A Rainbow at Midnight* (South Hadley, Mass.: J. F. Bergin Publishers, 1982), p.224.

Even with these contradictions, however, the vintage rock and roll years were generally good for black musicians. From a low point of three percent in 1954, the percentage of black artists on the year-end pop charts rose to an unprecedented twenty-nine percent in 1957. In addition to Chuck Berry, black artists like the Platters ("Only You," "My Prayer," "Great Pretender," "Magic Touch"), Bill Doggett ("Honky Tonk"), Fats Domino ("I'm in Love Again," "Blueberry Hill," "I'm Walkin'," "Blue Monday"), Frankie Lymon and the Teenagers ("Why Do Fools Fall in Love"), Little Richard ("Long Tall Sally"), Sam Cooke ("You Send Me"), the Coasters ("Searchin"), Johnny Mathis ("Chances Are," "It's Not for Me to Say"), the Bobbettes ("Mr. Lee"), and Larry Williams ("Short Fat Fanny"), all made the year-end Top 50 during this period. These and other black performers also scored with lesser hits on the weekly pop charts as well.

Reebee Garofalo has taught at the University of Massachusetts, Boston, since 1978. He is the co-author of *Rock n' Roll is Here to Pay* (1977) and the editor of *Rockin' the Boat* (1992). As a fan, musician, and educator, he is immersed in music, particularly its use as a community resource and an educational tool. This article originally appeared in *Split Image: African-Americans in the Mass Media*, edited by Jannette L. Dates and William Barlow (Howard University Press, Washington, D.C., 1990), and is reprinted here with permission.

"All for One, and One for All": Black Enterprise, Racial Politics and the Business Of Soul
BY BRIAN WARD

There's nothing wrong with singing and dancing or running track . . .
the only thing that's wrong is that we don't own it. —HAROLD BATTISTE[1]

The AFO experiment

As soul music matured during the early- to mid-1960s, the racial pattern of record label and radio station ownership changed very little. Whites continued to own all but a handful of black-oriented stations and to control most of the companies producing and distributing black music. There were, however, a number of important black initiatives and enterprises during the first half of the 1960s which appeared to augur well for black economic opportunity within the industry. They also revealed that most successful black entrepreneurs behaved suspicuously like their white counterparts when pursuing and protecting their own economic interests.

One partial exception to this generalization was Harold Battiste's All For One Records (AFO), which represented the most self-consciously politicized and imaginative bid for black economic and artistic power within the rhythm & blues field in the early sixties. Born in New Orleans in 1932, Harold Battiste came of musical age around the end of World War II listening to an eclectic range of secular and sacred, black and white, musical forms. "It was just music that you either liked or you didn't. It was not separated into categories," he recalled. On radio he heard big-band jazz, much of it white swing played on the *Mid-day Serenade* show, and was fascinated by the stirring, but unidentified, theme tunes to programs like *The Lone Ranger.* Closer to home, he heard blues and even a little gospel, admired and emulated the jump sounds of Eddie "Cleanhead" Vinson and Louis Jordan, and flipped over the dazzling artistry of bebop. After showing early flair as a drummer, he dabbled in clarinet, played occasional alto sax with the Joe

---

1. Harold Battiste interviewed by Brian Ward, University of Newcastle upon Tyne Oral History Collection (UNOHC) November 8, 1995.

Jones Band, and more regularly contributed baritone sax to local favorites the Johnson Brothers.[2]

In the late 1940s and early 1950s, Battiste also attended Dillard University, where he earned a degree in Music Education, finally got to put names to all those anonymous classical theme tunes, and received an invaluable grounding in musical theory that would later serve him well as a writer-arranger. After graduation he worked for several years as an itinerant teacher in Louisiana's black public schools. In 1956 he resigned rather than succumb to the racist expectations of a segregated system. Battiste felt that while white kids were being taught music properly, learning the fundamentals that would enable them to understand, appreciate, and play in any style, it was considered more than enough if black children could learn tunes by rote. No great believer in theories of innate, or at least untutored, black musical excellence, Battiste tried to offer his pupils the same thorough grounding in the rudiments of music that white children enjoyed. He was duly censured by the school superintendent for such "uppity" ideas. "I felt that they expected less coming out of the black schools . . . and when I was challenging it, they felt threatened or something by me being aware that there was a discrepancy between black and white."[3]

Disillusioned with teaching in this environment, Battiste headed out to the West Coast hoping to pursue a jazz career. He hooked up with Ornette Coleman and cut a demo, "Janie," which he tried to hawk around various companies before ending up at Specialty and running into Bumps Blackwell. Blackwell was not particularly interested in the Coleman side, but asked Battiste to sit in on a session he was doing with a newly secularized Sam Cooke. Battiste helped write the vocal arrangements and played on "You Send Me." Shortly thereafter, he was back in New Orleans working as pointman for Specialty in the Crescent City, rather like Dave Bartholomew did for Imperial.

Battiste's broad remit for Specialty gave him an insight into every aspect of the recording business. He was responsible for distribution and promotion—although his attempts to get Specialty's discs in shops and on the radio were impeded by owner Art Rupe's steadfast refusal to use payola. He also served as talent scout and

2. This account of Harold Battiste's career draws on AFO Notes File, Harold Battiste papers (hereinafter "HB"). H. Battiste, *Hal Who? Selections from the Scriptures of Harold Who?* (Los Angeles: At Last, 1989); J. Broven, "Harold Battiste: All for One," *Blues Unlimited* 46 (1984), pp.4–15; J. Berry, J. Foose, & T. Jones, *Up from the Cradle of Jazz: New Orleans Music Since World War II* (Athens, Ga.: University of Georgia Press, 1986), pp.143–53. Battiste interview.
3. *Ibid.*

writer-producer, cutting big hits with local white rocker Jerry Byrne ("Lights Out"), Little Richard, and his clone, Larry Williams. Battiste was even expected to place the orders for everything from stationery to recording tape, and to keep on top of the office's accounts.

When his formal relationship with Specialty ended in 1959, Battiste rejoined the revitalized Joe Jones's band, which was then riding high on the success of its Battiste-produced hit "You Talk Too Much" on Joe Ruffino's Ric Records. Battiste began to work for Ruffino as an A&R man/arranger/producer, both in New Orleans and in New York. It was around this time that his welling frustrations with the workings of the record industry came to a head. Battiste later described Joe Ruffino as "a scoundrel of a man . . . he didn't pay people and that's why he was my jumping board to AFO." Ruffino's reluctance to pay what was due was hardly uncommon among either white or black record executives, but Battiste now saw it as "an extension of what was bothering me in the school system." More precisely, what was bothering Harold Battiste was the rampant exploitation of black musicians in the industry and a woeful lack of black power to correct such abuses.[4]

Since the mid-fifties, Battiste had been interested in the teachings of Elijah Muhammad and the Nation of Islam. Under the influence of local trumpeter Emory Thompson, Battiste—like Lynn Hope, Chuck Willis, and Screamin' Jay Hawkins—had joined the Black Muslims. In particular, Battiste was drawn to Muhammad's economic program, which called for blacks to secure ownership of the businesses that served their community and thereby create black-controlled wealth and opportunity. "I began to go over in my mind what he was saying . . . one of the fundamental problems we are having: We don't own anything." While the mainstream civil rights movement prioritized the ballot and the desegregation of public facilities, Battiste "felt that to have economic independence was more important than to be able to go to the same hotel, or sit-in, or go to a movie, or whatever they wanted, whatever they were fighting for. Y'know, I was with them, but I just thought that we needed to have economic independence first." He felt that the experience of other successful ethnic groups in America proved that "once you've got economic independence, then you can *demand* [political and civil rights], you don't have to ask for that, you can buy it."[5]

4. Harold Battiste quoted in "All for One," p.10. Battiste interview.
5. *Ibid*.

In November 1959, Battiste drafted a manifesto for a "musician's cooperative," to be "founded on the principle that today's record industry is realizing tremendous success which is largely due to the participation of MUSICIANS." Those musicians, he argued, "have performed millions of dollars worth of music on record," but "rarely shared in the profits that they have contributed their talents to earning." This, Battiste reasoned, was "because they have performed as *laborers*, thus earning a salary . . . and thereby eliminating any possibility of becoming eligible to share in the profits of the very lucrative record industry." To emphasize his point, Battiste calculated that if saxophonist Lee Allen (suggestively disguised as "Musician X" in the original document) played on one recording date a week, with each session yielding three songs, he would earn an annual income of $2,522 for his contribution to 156 sides, or 78 record releases. If, however, Allen had a two-percent royalty deal and just one of those records sold 500,000 copies, he would earn over $10,000 from that disc alone.[6]

As Battiste saw it, blacks were being hired because they were such good and profitable musicians, and they needed to capitalize on their special talents. "We sing and dance. We ought to own that. There's nothing wrong with singing and dancing or running track . . . the only thing that's wrong is that we don't own it." On May 29, 1961, in conjunction with five like-minded black New Orleans musicians collectively known as the Executives, Battiste successfully incorporated AFO (All For One) Records and At Last Publishing, both designed "to demonstrate to musicians that they could own the product of their creativity and enjoy greater independence."[7]

Much as envisioned in Battiste's 1959 blueprint, AFO was run as a sort of cooperative enterprise in which the musicians who played on the label's sessions waived any payment for their work, but became co-owners of those recordings. They then took an agreed percentage of any money their recordings earned and thus escaped the tyranny of the existing system, where they were usually paid a flat-rate union session fee—around forty-five dollars in the early 1960s—regardless of the extent of their creative input, or how many millions of copies of their work were later sold.

The biggest problem AFO faced was circumventing the rules of the American

6. Battiste, "Statement: Musicians Cooperative Records Inc.," AFO Notes File, HB (November 19, 1959).
7. Battiste interview. Battiste, "Diary: 29 May 1961," *Hal Who?* The executives at AFO were Mel Lastie (executive secretary and cornet), Alvin Tyler (treasurer and sax), Roy Montrell (A&R and guitar), Peter Badie (bass), John Boubreaux (drums), Battiste (president, piano, and sax). See H. Battiste, "Letter to Whom It May Concern", n.d., box 1, folder: Outgoing Mail, AFO, HB.

Federation of Musicians (AFM), which insisted on designating all musicians as laborers, to be paid no more and no less than the standard fee per session. This lack of cooperation from the union was not unusual in New Orleans, or elsewhere for that matter. In 1960, the AFM had more segregated locals than any other union except the railway clerks. Moreover, while some black AFM officials campaigned vigorously to overthrow a Jim Crow structure which was by no means unique to the South, many others actually supported continued segregation. In 1957, the leaders of forty out of forty-seven all-black locals voted against mergers with their white colleagues. The most sincere of these leaders did so out of concern that black demands would go unheeded in integrated locals where there were simply more white members than black. Others more selfishly feared the loss of the personal prestige and power which they had established in their own little black fiefdoms.[8]

Tommy Ridgely, who spent a good part of his career in and out of trouble with the segregated black New Orleans AFM local 496, felt the whole thing had "always been a racket," and told tales of greed, corruption, and two sets of account books kept by a self-perpetuating black elite. Battiste felt much the same. Local 496 was "more a hinderance than anything else. We had a lot of run-ins with the union. It seemed as though those guys, that was their private club and they ran it the way they wanted, they manipulated the rules to suit them." It was not the last time Battiste was to be disappointed by the attitude of blacks in positions of relative power in the industry.[9]

While AFO was a very self-consciously black enterprise—from its black business cards to its use of black lawyers—it also harbored ambitions to shift as many units as possible to as many buyers as possible, irrespective of race. Consequently, Battiste arranged for the national distribution of AFO product through the New York–based Sue label, which had already enjoyed major success with Ike and Tina Turner ("A Fool In Love," "I Idolize You"). When the deal was first mooted, Battiste was blissfully unaware of the race of Sue's owner, Henry "Juggy" Murray, and was simply looking for effective, affordable distribution. However, "When I met him at the airport and he turned out to be black, I said, 'wow, man, this is better than I thought!'" Battiste saw his relationship with Murray as another step toward his dream of building a black "conglomerate entertainment enterprise" that would incorporate record-

8. Battiste interviewed by W.B. Gould, in Black Workers in White Unions: Job Discrimination in the United States (Ithaca, N.Y.: Cornell University Press, 1977), pp.126–7, 416–19.
9. Tommy Ridgley interviewed by Tad Jones, Hogan Jazz Archive, April 23, 1986 and June 26, 1986. Battiste interview.

ing, theater bookings, management: "all the facets of entertainment that basically they say niggers can't do."[10]

In its first year of business, AFO produced a number of fine nascent soul records, all with a highly distinctive polyrhythmic echo of New Orleans marching-band and jazz music. The most successful of these were Barbara George's black chart–topping "I Know" and Prince La La's vaguely voodun "She Put the Hurt On Me." Unfortunately, however, Battiste's bold experiment began to flounder as narrow economic self-interest began to eclipse any broader sense of racial unity and cooperation. The connection with Sue ended acrimoniously when Juggy Murray, who had begun to describe and treat the fiercely independent AFO as nothing more than a subsidiary of Sue, lured away Battiste's biggest star, Barbara George, with a fur coat and a Cadillac. It was, Battiste noted bitterly, "the same thing we expected some white folks would do."[11]

At the time Battiste was deeply aggrieved that another black man could have treated him this way. "That disillusioned me completely," he recalled. In retrospect, however, he recognized his own naïveté in assuming that racial solidarity, rather than economic and status considerations, would automatically dominate the agendas of black capitalists like Murray. "I was operating on an ideal; Juggy was operating on the real . . . The blindness I had, of feeling that because he was a black cat he would understand what I was trying to do, made me very vulnerable." Murray, on the other hand, had pursued a perfectly consistent and predictable course in seeking to maximize his economic rewards and leverage. It was Battiste, with his heroic, but perhaps intrinsically flawed, vision of a more cooperative, communalist form of black capitalism who was the exception to the black entrepreneurial rule, not Juggy Murray.

Before the falling out with Murray, AFO "wasn't work, it was a mission," Battiste recalled. After the "bubble had been burst," however, he rapidly lost interest. In August 1963 Battiste and most of the AFO Executives moved to Los Angeles to work for steady pay at Sar and Derby, the labels cofounded by his old associate Sam Cooke. After Cooke's death, Battiste spent a lengthy period as musical director for Sonny and Cher, and as a producer for Sonny Bono's Progress Records. In 1967 he produced the critically acclaimed *Gris Gris* album for Dr. John, a persona he helped

---

10. Battiste quoted in "All for One," p.12.
11. Battiste interview. "AFO Diary Notes: March 27, 1962 and March 29,1962," in Battiste, *Hal Who?*; Broven, "All for One," pp.12–13.

to create for Mac Rebbeneck, the gifted, if dissolute, white New Orleans musician who had been playing black clubs and sessions since before anyone could remember—and who was so thoroughly integrated into the black R&B scene that he even joined the black local 496, for all the good it did him.

Battiste's appetite for black economic and educational empowerment diminished little over the years. As well as keeping AFO and At Last Publishing just about alive—and relaunching them in the 1990s—he founded Marzique Music. In tandem with AFO's cornetist and executive secretary, Mel Lastie, he also ran Adormel Music and the Hal-Mel production company responsible for 1970s hits by Tami Lynn, King Floyd, and Alvin "Shine" Robinson. In the eighties, Battiste fused his educational and musical concerns by founding the National Association of New Orleans Musicians, from which emerged a jazz outfit called Novia and a wild rhythm & blues/funk ensemble called the New Orleans Natives. Undaunted by a minor heart attack and stroke, the indomitable Battiste returned from Los Angeles in the late 1980s to take up a teaching position at the University of New Orleans, where he joined a remarkable jazz studies department chaired by Ellis Marsalis, an old jazz buddy from the days when they had chased Ornette Coleman and their dreams over to the West Coast.[12]

The Motown Miracle

Harold Battiste was always a musician first; then a writer, an arranger, a producer and, finally, almost by default, a record-label owner and music publisher. He deeply resented the fact that racism and corruption in the industry meant that he had to devote so much of his time and energies to playing entrepreneur instead of playing music. Nevertheless, when he started AFO and At Last Publishing in the early 1960s, Battiste had high hopes that it would serve as a model for other blacks to move into ownership of the means of rhythm & blues production and dissemination. Ever the educator, he saw what he was "doing as more of an experiment or demonstration" for others to follow.[13]

It was, of course, pure coincidence that a few years after Battiste founded AFO, Smokey Robinson won Berry Gordy's in-house competition to write a company

12. Battiste interview. "Diary: August–September 1967," in Battiste, *Hal Who?*. For Hal-Mel holdings, see Harold Battiste, Letter to L. Grundeis, December 1, 1969, in *ibid*.
13. Battiste interview.

song for Motown with an anthem called "Hitsville, USA"—sung in unison once a week at Motown's plenary studio meetings—which included the line "we're all for one and one for all." Yet Motown and Gordy's triumph, so redolent of broader black aspirations, struggles, and achievements in the sixties, did represent an ambiguous and partial realization of Battiste's dream "that someone like him would surface." Sometimes, however, Motown also evoked memories of Juggy Murray and the mercurial nature of racial loyalties in the face of economic self-interest.[14]

The basic history of the Motown Corporation has been recounted many times, by insiders, outsiders, mud-slingers, and tribute-bringers. Yet, that remarkable story warrants brief rehearsal here since it illuminates both the nature and dilemmas of black entrepreneurial capitalism and the routine misrepresentation of the label's achievements and racial credentials in much of the existing literature.[15]

In 1929 Berry Gordy was born into an ambitious middle-class black family with roots in Georgia farming and retail, which had relocated to Detroit during the 1920s. There, in addition to running a painting and construction firm, his father, Berry Sr., opened the aptly named Booker T. Washington Grocery Store, and instilled in his children the virtues of frugality, discipline, family unity, and hard work so dear to the "Wizard of Tuskegee." Less committed than some of his siblings to the formal education that Booker T. Washington had also advocated, Gordy left school at the eleventh grade to become a professional boxer. In 1953 he indulged his love of modern jazz by opening the 3-D Record Mart. Unfortunately, the masses of black Detroit cared little for the music and in 1955 the venture failed, forcing Gordy into a much-vaunted, but relatively brief, sojourn on the production line at Ford. 3-D's failure had a profound impact on Gordy: Rarely again would he put aesthetic, artistic, or, for that matter, racial considerations ahead of a simple concern for whether and how widely his products would sell.

Gordy's breakthrough in the music business came as a songwriter when he co-authored "To Be Loved" and "Reet Petite" for Jackie Wilson. In early 1958 he pro-

---

14. B. Gordy, *To Be Loved: The Music, the Magic, the Memories of Motown: An Autobiography* (New York: Warner, 1994), p.169. Battiste interview.

15. This account of Motown draws from the following sources: P. Benjaminson, *The Story of Motown* (New York: Grove, 1978); D. Bianco, *Heatwave: The Motown Fact Book* (Ann Arbor: Pierian,1988); G. Early, *One Nation Under a Groove: Motown and American Culture* (New York: Ecco, 1995); S. Frith, "You Can Make It If You Try," in I. Hoare (ed.), *The Soul Book* (London: Eyre Methuen, 1975), pp.32–59; N. George, *Where Did Our Love Go?* (New York: St Martin's, 1986); Gordy, *To Be Loved*; G. Hirshey, *Nowhere to Run* (New York: Macmillan, 1984), pp.184–92; D. Morse, *Motown and the Arrival of Black Music* (London: November, 1971); J. Ryan, *Recollections—The Detroit Years: The Motown Sound By the People Who Made It* (Detroit: the author, 1982); J.R. Taraborelli, *Motown: Hot Wax, City Soul and Solid Gold* (New York: Doubleday, 1986).

duced "Get a Job" for the Miracles, with whom he also had a management deal. As the Miracles' career took off, Gordy apparently managed to retain control over their contract only by persuading black deejays to threaten a boycott of several white labels who were trying to poach the group with more generous terms. Apocryphal though this story may be, it illustrates a recurring pattern in Gordy's business dealings whereby he appealed to black solidarity and pride to secure whatever protection and preferential treatment the few blacks with power in the industry could offer. Throughout the 1960s, Gordy would shrewdly use race, so often an impediment to black economic advance, as one of the tools of his entreprenerial ambitions.[16]

Using family money, Gordy had formed Tamla—his first label—in January 1959, releasing a blues-tinged black pop number called "Come To Me" by husky-voiced Marv Johnson. When that disc began to pick up extensive regional airplay on WJLB-Detroit and the black-owned WCHB-Inkster, Tamla simply could not cope with the demands of mass production and national distribution and leased the master to United Artists. UA had both the financial resources to pay for the pressing of tens of thousands of copies before it had recouped any monies from sales, and the distribution network to place those discs on record racks and radio playlists around the nation. Gordy learned more about distribution in 1960 when Tamla acted in that capacity for Barrett Strong's highly successful and aptly titled "Money," a song co-written and produced by Gordy and released on the eponymous Anna label run by his sister and her husband, the ex-Moonglow Harvey Fuqua.

By this time, Gordy had established various fiefdoms within the Motown empire: the Motown Record Corporation, Hitsville USA, and Berry Gordy Jr. Enterprises. He also set up his own publishing firm, Jobete Music, and a management agency, International Talent Management Inc. (ITMI). Around the turn of the decade he supplemented Tamla with a host of subsidiary labels like Motown itself, Miracle (renamed "Gordy" in 1962), Mel-O-Dy, VIP, and a gospel experiment, Divinity. This strategy was primarily designed to protect against the possible failure of individual labels, but it proved unnecessary as Gordy began to rack up an impressive run of crossover hits with artists like the Marvelettes, the Contours, Marvin Gaye, and Mary Wells.

Aside from the astonishing quality of so much of Motown's music, what differentiated the label from most of its black- and white-owned rivals was Gordy's extraor-

---

16. George, *Where Did Our Love Go?*, p.25.

dinary business acumen, ingenuity, and the single-mindedness—many would later claim ruthlessness—with which he set about realizing his dreams. At the heart of Motown's economics were the classic business strategies of vertical integration and cross-collateralization. Gordy controlled and profited from every aspect of the careers of his artists, writers, and musicians, and every dimension of record production and promotion. Put simply, Gordy developed a structure that enabled Motown to offset losses on any unprofitable projects with income from another branch of the total operation. For example, all Motown performer-writers were required to sign with Gordy's Jobete Publishing Company, which not only claimed its own share of the songwriter's income, but also ensured that Gordy could recoup any costs incurred in the preparation of recordings by making deductions from the relevant artist's songwriting royalties.[17]

Similarly, all Motown acts and creative personnel were managed by ITMI, which did relatively little to protect their financial or artistic interests, but made money for the corporation by arranging notoriously mean and restrictive contracts for the young black hopefuls who joined the label. ITMI routinely took a cut of the weekly salaries paid to all the corporation's creative staff, whether they had been productive that week or not. Gordy considered paying non-productive staff a gesture of great generosity, but it has to be measured against the fact that all weekly payments were later reclaimed by the company against the artist's royalties from any recordings. ITMI also controlled the income from live performances, organizing gruelling Motown tours on which the artists were given a daily allowance, again deductible from any future royalties. In return, artists and writers were permitted only periodic access to Motown's accounts, which Gordy refused to allow the Recording Industry Association of America to audit until the seventies, and had few rights concerning when, what, and with whom they recorded.

Motown royalties were usually fixed at a meager rate of eight percent of ninety percent of the wholesale price of albums and singles. By 1968 bitter disputes over those royalties led the brilliant songwriting and production team of Lamont Dozier and the brothers Eddie and Brian Holland to leave the label, eventually winning a court settlement worth several hundred thousand dollars. Others, like Eddie Kendricks of the Temptations, also began to question if Motown's much-vaunted

17. For the economics of Motown, see *ibid.*, esp.pp.25–86, 139–54; Taraborelli, *Motown*, pp.9–12.

family ethos was really just a front for an exploitative mode of black paternalism, not very different from exploitative white paternalism. Martha Reeves was torn between gratitude and disillusionment with the way Motown treated its artists. "Motown had signed us to ironclad contracts and turned us into international stars. Yet after several years of million-selling records and sold-out concerts, in 1969 I realized that my personal income was but a fraction of what it should have been." When Reeves began to ask questions about her earnings, she "suddenly experienced a lack of personal and professional attention."[18]

There is some evidence that Motown's studio musicians were treated more generously than its name artists and writers, but this was all relative. The going rate for a Motown session in 1962 was $7.50 a side, and until 1965 the label routinely paid musicians below union scale. Although by the second half of the decade musicians like pianist Earl Van Dyke, leader of the Funk Brothers studio band, could earn five-figure sums annually, there was still resentment about the lack of artistic credit and adequate financial recompense for musicians who had virtually co-written songs that went on to earn millions of dollars. Although Gordy later protested that Motown writers and musicians were paid exactly what they were owed according to the letter of their contracts, Motown was in fact perpetrating precisely the kind of exploitation of its artists that had prompted Harold Battiste to form AFO. James Jamerson, one of Motown's finest bassists, recalled, "There is sometimes a tear because I see how I was treated and cheated. We were doing more than we thought and we didn't get any songwriting credit."[19]

The Motown Sound and the Myth of Authenticity

Consummate musicians like James Jamerson, Earl Van Dyke, Benny Benjamin (drums), and James Messina (guitar) were crucial in the development of what has become instantly recognizable, if analytically elusive, as the "Motown Sound." Yet, given the oceans of print devoted to this "sound," one of the most striking features of Motown's early output was not its homogeneity, but its diversity.[20]

18. See O. Williams (with P. Romanowski), *Temptations* (New York: G.P. Putnam, 1988), pp.136–7; M. Reeves & M. Bego, *Dancing in the Street: Confessions of a Motown Diva* (New York: Hyperion, 1994): p.8.
19. James Jamerson quoted in I. Stambler, *Encyclopaedia of Pop, Rock and Soul* (New York: St Martin's, 1974), p.149. See also George, *Where Did Our Love Go?*, pp.86, 107; Hirshey, *Nowhere to Run*, pp.186–9. For Gordy's own account of these matters, see *To Be Loved*, pp.267–72.
20. The most accessible and sensible musicological analysis of the Motown Sound is J. Fitzgerald, "Motown Crossover Hits 1963–1966 and the Creative Process," *Popular Music* 14 (1995): pp.1–11.

Bluesy performers like Mabel Johns, Barrett Strong, and Marv Johnson were initially balanced by coy girl groups like the Marvelettes and soloists like Mary Wells. Long-forgotten white acts like the Valadiers co-existed with the Four Tops, who at first found themselves on Gordy's Jazz Workshop subsidiary, where they experimented with big-band arrangements of Tin Pan Alley standards. The Supremes recorded everything from Rodgers and Hart tunes to country & western, and from a Sam Cooke tribute album to a collection of Beatles songs, hoping to find a winning formula. Meanwhile, Marvin Gaye was encouraged to indulge his considerable talent for crooning on albums like *Hello Broadway* and *A Tribute to the Great Nat King Cole*. With such an eclectic mixture of styles, and Gordy's keen eye for any potentially lucrative market niche, it was easy to credit the 1962 *Detroit Free Press* article that announced that Motown was about to launch a line of polka records.[21]

Eventually, however, Motown did more than just produce a diverse range of records, any one of which might appeal predominantly to a different market. It forged a flexible house style which appealed across regional, racial, and even generational boundaries. "We were a general-market company. Whether you were black, white, green, or blue, you could relate to our music," Gordy rightly boasted. From the maelstrom of early experimentation, it was Martha Reeves who blazed the gospel-paved, string-lined trail to the label's mid-1960s crossover triumph. In the summer of 1963, Holland-Dozier-Holland furnished Reeves with "Heatwave" and then "Quicksand," on which they enlivened the slightly mannered basics of the girl-group sound with a driving gospel beat, tambourine frenzy, and soaring strings. Above it all, Reeves—who was comfortably the finest female vocalist on Motown's books until Gladys Knight joined and ran her close in the late 1960s—unleashed her rapt soul vocals.[22]

Following the Top-10 pop success of these recordings, this basic formula was refined and adapted to fit the peculiar talents of individual Motown acts. The leonine roar of lead singer Levi Stubbs meant that the Four Tops retained the melodrama of the Vandellas' recordings on songs like "Reach Out, I'll Be There" and "Bernadette." By contrast, the Temptations harked back to their doo-wopping origins as the Primes to feature rich harmonies and a generally sweeter sound on Smokey Robinson—penned

21. *Detroit Free Press*, cited by George, *Where Did Our Love Go?*, p.49.
22. Berry Gordy quoted in *Rolling Stone* (August 23, 1990): p.71.

and produced songs like "It's Growing" and "My Girl." The most successful of all the Motown acts to work within this basic framework was the Supremes, for whom Holland-Dozier-Holland softened the hard-driving gospel beat with more prominent strings and muted brass. The mix was topped with vocals by Diana Ross, which were much lighter and breathier than Martha's, on chart-topping songs like "Where Did Our Love Go?" and "Baby Love." The Supremes proved to be the perfect black crossover act. Between 1964 and Ross's departure from the group in 1969, they secured twenty-five pop hits, including twelve number ones; only the Beatles could claim more.

If there was a classic "Motown Sound," neither its ubiquity nor its rigidity should be exaggerated; not even for the period between 1964 and 1967, when it was at its zenith. In 1965 Motown released the Miracles' soulful post–doo wop lament "Ooo Baby Baby," Jr. Walker's saxophone-led blues stomp "Shotgun," Stevie Wonder's grinding rock 'n' soul remake of Tommy Tucker's "Hi Heel Sneakers," and Marvin Gaye's gospel shout, "Ain't That Peculiar." All were highly successful, yet all somehow circumvented, or greatly extended, the basic formula.

Even those artists who stuck tight as a Benny Benjamin backbeat to the classic Motown Sound could, just like that precocious skinsman, actually produce a broad range of moods and shadings within its confines. Thus 1965 also saw the release of the Temptations' melancholic "Since I Lost My Baby," the Contours' barnstorming "Can You Jerk Like Me," the Four Tops' distraught "Ask The Lonely," and the Vandellas' disturbing, claustrophobic masterpiece "Nowhere to Run."

Despite this constrained diversity, however, the idea of a single Motown Sound, clinically designed by a team of songwriters and producers led by Gordy, Robinson, Holland-Dozier-Holland, William Stevenson, and Ivy Hunter, and mechanically riveted onto the label's recordings by musical artisans, pervades the literature. Not only is this view inaccurate and informed by an insidious mode of racial stereotyping, it has become, in Jon Fitzgerald's phrase, a "major impediment to general acknowledgement of Motown's role as a major *innovative* force in 1960s popular music."[23]

The signs adorning the offices of Motown and Stax respectively—"Hitsville, USA" and "Soulsville, USA"—have frequently been taken to symbolize a com-

---

23. See Fitzgerald, "Motown Crossover Hits," pp.4–9, on the creativity of Motown, even at its most "formulaic."

pletely different musical ethos, commercial agenda, and even a different degree of artistic and racial integrity between the two labels. Critics have regularly made unfavourable comparisons between the slick Motown soul production line and the more relaxed, spontaneous atmosphere of Southern labels like Stax, with their rootsier feel and country-fried licks. Paradoxically, Southern soul, largely recorded on white-owned labels by integrated groups of musicians who drew on black and white musical influences, has been reified as more authentically black than the secularized gospel recordings of black musicians on a black-owned label with virtually no white creative input—at least not until Englishwoman Pam Sawyer made a name for herself as a staff writer in the late sixties with songs like the Supremes' "Love Child."

Even the usually sensible Arnold Shaw fell headlong into this trap, describing Motown in terms which made it sound like a pale imitation of something blacker, something more real, more substantial, lurking in the southlands. Motown songs, Shaw claimed, "are light and fluffy. It is hardly soul food, but rather a dish for which white listeners have acquired a taste . . ." In a similar vein, Mike Jahn derided Motown as "a black-owned version of popular schmaltz," thereby recycling conventional stereotypes about the nature of "real" black music, much as Tony Cummings did when he casually dismissed Marvin Gaye's crooning as "appalling . . . ill-conceived mush-mallow." Cummings was apparently unable to countenance even the possibility that a black American singer could be a magnificent interpreter of Tin Pan Alley Americana.[24]

Critics have tended to privilege the recordings of Stax, Fame, and their Southern brethren over those of Motown, largely because the musicians who played on those Southern sessions have been viewed as genuine artists, not artisans. Southern players, so the legend goes, improvised amazing riffs and spontaneously wove together sublime rhythmic and harmonic patterns from the very warp and weft of their souls. Those protean moments were then instantly committed to tape and transfered, unsullied, onto vinyl.

Contrary to this popular myth, however, Southern soul records—with some exceptions—were rarely produced in single, improvised live takes. Overdubbing

24. A. Shaw, *The World of Soul* (New York: Cowles, 1970), p.169; M. Jahn, *The Story of Rock from Elvis to the Rolling Stones* (New York: Quadrangle, 1975), p.11; T. Cummings, "An English Way to Marvin Gaye," *Black Music* (December 1976): p.14. Michael Bane reduced Motown to "white music produced by blacks." M. Bane, *White Boy Singing the Blues* (London: Penguin, 1982), p.170. For the sign metaphor see, for example, A. Shaw, *Black Popular Music in America* (New York: Schirmer, 1986), p.218; Hirshey, *Nowhere to Run*, p.304.

was common—even at Stax, where Otis Redding's oft-quoted statement that "we cut everything together, horns, rhythms, and vocals . . . we didn't even have a four-track tape recorder. You can't over-dub on a one-track machine," has been accepted as chapter and verse for all 1960s Southern soul. In fact even at Stax, vocals were frequently added after the instrumental tracks were laid down, and many records were assembled from carefully splicing together the best moments from many alternate takes.[25]

This is not to deny that Southern studios had marvellously talented musicians whose long hours of practice and laid-back jamming generated moments of great musical invention and almost uncanny understanding. Rather it is to suggest that, just like at Motown, arrangers, producers, and engineers were also vital in shaping the recorded, or more accurately, the released sound of Southern soul records. A good example was Joe Tex's magnificent soul jeremiad "Hold What You Got," which was an unusable mess until Buddy Killen took the tapes from Muscle Shoals to Nashville for remixing and overdubs. The point is that while purists have tended to see post-recording technologies as, by definition, a corrupting influence on rhythm & blues, such interventions have often helped to realize the musical vision of the artist or writer more fully.[26]

An even more telling example of this creative use of studio technology involved James Brown's "Papa's Got a Brand New Bag," which was originally an extended slow-groove jam, recorded in February 1965 in Charlotte, North Carolina by a dog-tired band dragging its weary way to a gig. In post-production, however, Brown decided to remaster and slightly speed up the recording to create the familiar dance cut. With its volcanic bass lines erupting in surprisingly on-beat places, stabbing brass riffs, and the percussive chiming of Jimmy Nolen's guitar, "Papa's Got a Brand New Bag" was a truly seminal moment in the development of soul and funk. It did not, however, emerge fully formed in a single impromptu session, but from a potent combination of inspiration, contemplation, and technological manipulation.[27]

And yet a crude reification of black spontaneity has continued, linked to the enduring belief that all *real* black music must be visceral rather than cerebral in

25. Otis Redding quoted in *Rolling Stone* (January 20, 1968): p.13. For a good contemporary description of a Stax session, see P. Garland, *The Sound of Soul* (Chicago: Regnery, 1969), pp.147–52.
26. For "Hold What You Got," see B. Hoskyns, *Say It One Time for the Broken Hearted* (Glasgow: Fontana, 1987), pp.113–14.
27. See C. White and H. Weinger, "Are You Ready for Star Time?" in C. White et al. *Star Time*, (n.p.: PolyGram Records, 1991), p.27.

chararacter, springing from the instinctual needs of the body rather than the intellectual or meditative workings of the mind. Certainly when Rickey Vincent wanted to
validate the brilliance of the Godfather's 1973 hit, "The Payback," he automatically
turned to Brown's superfine trombonist Fred Wesley and his recollection that the
session had been "a rush job," with James delivering a "completely spontaneous"
vocal and rejecting the engineer's offer to remix with an imperious "don't *touch* this."
For Vincent this represented the quintessence of Brown's black art and creativity. Yet
the fact remains that a month later the basic track was remixed and garnished with
the brass overdubs and eerie female vocal embellishments that transformed a fasci-
nating funk fragment into a classic record.[28]

Indeed, it is worth remembering that much of Brown's music, live and in the studio, was actually heavily orchestrated. In some ways Sammy Lowe and Alfred "Pee
Wee" Ellis, who wrote many of the charts for Brown's bands, were heirs to jazz
arrangers like Duke Ellington and Charles Mingus, who tailored their compositions
to the specific talents of their musicians. Lowe and Ellis translated Brown's musical
ideas and sketches into flexible, but highly structured arrangements. These allowed
his musicians to stretch out and express themselves, but demanded that they maintain the discipline and cohesion necessary to keep the whole thing together. Post-
production technology was then applied to turn these slabs of raw funk into a series
of sharp, utterly compelling dance records.

Part of the problem in all of this has been a confusion between what it takes to be
a great, creative, innovative musician, and what it takes to make great records. Of
course, the two are not mutually exclusive, but they are certainly not synonymous.
Rock and pop are full of wonderful records made by players of sorely limited musical
ability who have barely known which end of a piano to blow, but who have been
blessed with a fine ear for the combinations of words, rhythms, and sounds that can
move minds, bodies, and souls. Even in rhythm & blues, where the caliber of musicians has been generally high, neither technical proficiency nor simple sincerity were
necessarily enough to guarantee a great record.

Given, then, that there was considerably more to making Southern soul records
than simply opening the mikes to pick up the sounds of innate black and/or white
musical genius, the differences between the Stax and the Motown studios were

---

28. R. Vincent, *Funk—The Music, the People, and the Rhythm of the One* (New York: St. Martin's, 1996), p.84.

rather less marked than the similarities. Motown's Funk Brothers mostly comprised gifted Southern jazz exiles and, much like its integrated Southern counterparts, was a tight unit consisting of musicians who were simultaneously skilled craftsmen and trusty production workers, with a maverick streak of inventive genius bubbling to the surface every once in a glorious while. "They'd let me go on and ad-lib," explained James Jamerson, using precisely the term Jerry Wexler applied to the atmosphere in Southern studios ("extremely ad-lib"). "I created, man," Jamerson insisted. "It was repetitious, but had to be funky and have emotion."[29]

Bidding for the Mainstream

While there is no evidence that any black-oriented label or rhythm & blues artist ever sought anything less than the widest possible commercial success, it is nonetheless true that Berry Gordy went to extraordinary, often hugely creative lengths to give his performers the opportunity to make it with white audiences. This was a matter of presentation as well as sound. Motown acts were formally schooled by Maxine Powell, the owner of a Detroit finishing and modeling school, in matters of etiquette, deportment, cosmetics, and elocution. Gordy felt this might make them more acceptable to white America and an expanding black middle class for whom mainstream notions of respectability remained important.

Veteran dancer Cholly Atkins was hired to supervise the sophisticated stagecraft and slick choreography that was designed to equip Motown acts for the "transition from the chitlin' circuit to Vegas." Touring London in the autumn of 1964, Mary Wilson made no secret of Gordy's, and the Supremes', crossover ambitions and their willingness to adjust to white expectations to achieve them. "We want to get into the night-club field and we know we're going to have to change our style a good bit to get there. We're working on that kind of singing now . . . I know there's a lot of work ahead of us but we really hope to play the Copa some day." The following July, the Supremes became the first of many Motown acts to play that New York shrine of middle-American wealth and respectability; in 1967 they were the first Motown artists to play the even ritzier Las Vegas Copa.[30]

29. James Jamerson quoted in N. George, Buppies, B-Boys, Baps & Bohos (New York: HarperPerennial, 1994), p.171. See also Fitzgerald, "Motown Crossover Hits," p.9; Jerry Wexler quoted in Hirshey, Nowhere to Run, p.299.
30. Cholly Atkins quoted in George, Where Did Our Love Go?; Mary Wilson quoted in Melody Maker (September 19, 1964), p.7.

Music critics, far more than fans, have frequently struggled with the idea that showmanship, artifice, and spectacle can sometimes be the vehicles, as well as adornments—or worse, replacements—for genuine creativity, expression, and artistic endeavor. Certainly, most accounts that focus on Motown's unapologetic pursuit of the mainstream market assume that it was simply impossible to produce music that was artistically potent, truly expressive of aspects of contemporary mass black consciousness, and at the same time an ambitious show-biz phenomenon hugely popular with a bi-racial audience. For example, in a particularly pompous and insensitive 1967 article, rock critic Ralph Gleason used the fact that the Supremes and Four Tops were choreographed to support his claim that black soul performers were "almost totally style with very little substance." Gleason denounced them for being "on an Ed Sullivan trip, striving as hard as they can to get on that stage and become part of the American success story." In fact, as Simon Frith has recognized, "If some of Motown's marketing strategies have touched depths of cynicism, that just makes its continued musical inspiration even more humbling."[31]

Motown's unparalleled popularity among black consumers suggests that the black masses shared little of the critics' sense of fakery and fraud. The corporation enjoyed 174 black Top 10 entries during the 1960s. Apparently unable to recognize *real* black music without the guidance of critics like Gleason, blacks even bought huge numbers of records by the Supremes, the be-wigged flagship of Gordy's race treachery and integrationist aspirations, giving them twenty-three black hits and five number-ones before the restoration of a separate black chart in 1965 and 1969. These black consumers were not unthinking, malleable sponges, who, racial loyalties notwithstanding, bought Motown products they did not really much like simply because Berry Gordy told them to, or because they were force-fed them on the radio. They bought Motown records because they could dance to them and relate to their timeless, often witty, erudite, and passionate messages of love, loss, loneliness, joy, and belonging.

Moreover, black acts at Motown and elsewhere had always worn their sharp mohair suits and silk gowns with, as Marvin Gaye might have said, much pride and joy, seeing them as symbols of how far they had come from humble beginnings.

31. R. Gleason, "Like a Rolling Stone" (1967), repr. in J. Eisen (ed.), *The Age of Rock Sounds of the American Cultural Revolution* (New York: Random House, 1969), p.67, Frith, "You Can Make It," p.59.

Certainly, the spangled pursuit of success carried no stigma among black fans who had routinely been denied equal opportunity to compete for the financial rewards and recognition of the mainstream, but who in the 1960s glimpsed the prospect for a real change in their fortunes. While Gleason and other critics may have preferred their black artists poor and marginalized, Motown made the earnest bid for mainstream success and respect a matter of black pride.

Singer Kim Weston believed that it was the voracious black appetite for such conspicuous images of material success that explained much of Motown's extra-musical appeal and cultural resonance. "When I was coming up in Detroit I had no one to look up to who had made it. Through Motown's help and guidance, today's kids have all the Motown stars to emulate. We were from all sorts of backgrounds and we found success right here in our hometown." Fortunately, this fit perfectly with Gordy's personal ambitions and his own conception of the role and responsibilities of black capitalists. For Gordy, the creation of personal wealth and the spirited pursuit of mainstream success was in itself a form of racial politics, and black economic and cultural leadership.[32]

What Motown offered in its sixties pomp, then, was less a dilution of some authentic black soul than a brash new urbane synthesis of pop, R&B, and gospel, derived from, and perfectly fitted for, a particular moment in black and American history. Stylistically, Motown resolved some of the earlier musical and personal dilemmas of the black pop era, when a Jackie Wilson or even a Sam Cooke had sometimes struggled to reconcile roused black pride with the enduring dream of making it—the bigger the better—in the mainstream of American entertainment.

Realizing that dream was a large part of what the "Movement" was all about in the 1960s, Berry Gordy succeeded better than any black man of his day in fulfilling it. Between 1960 and 1969, Motown released 535 singles, of which 357 made either the rhythm & blues and/or pop charts. Twenty-one of those records reached number one on both the pop and rhythm & blues listings; six made the top slot in the pop charts alone; twenty-nine reached number one in the rhythm & blues charts only. By 1965 Motown had a gross income of around eight million dollars and was the nation's leading seller of singles. Five years later it was the richest enterprise in African-American history. All this with a music fueled by gospel and much closer to the

32. Kim Weston quoted in Ryan, *Recollections*, profile 40.

"black" end of a national black–white musical spectrum than any popular style that had previously enjoyed such sustained and massive white appeal.[33]

Brian Ward is a lecturer in American history at the University of Newcastle upon Tyne in England. He is the co-editor of *The Making of Martin Luther and the Civil Rights Movement* (NYU Press, 1996) and author of *Just My Soul Responding: Rhythm & Blues, Black Consciousness, and Race Relations* (University of California Press, 1998), in which this essay was first published.

33. For statistics, see George, *Where Did Our Love Go?*, p.139; Shaw, *Black Popular Music*, p.224; Bianco, *Heatwave*; and Taraborelli, *Motown*, pp.i–ii.

Soul for Sale: The Marketing of Black Musical Expression

By Mark Anthony Neal

Black political agency seems embedded in cultural performance with the performing revolutionary. The selling of black political culture suggests a race discourse abstracted from material struggles and radical agency. Where performance reigns, vacuous renditions of black revolutionary struggles take center stage. Performing blackness reworks the history of radicalism to market "Black Power" as a commodity. —Joy James[*]

Forever emblematic of stark class divisions within the African-American diaspora, the Stax/Volt and Motown recording companies began the 1970s with divergent notions of progress. Despite its multiracial ownership, the Stax/Volt recording company had always maintained a privileged relationship with its black constituency, particularly those still based in the American South. Motown, on the other hand, made no secret about its investment in the mainstream consumer public as a vehicle for black middle-class mobility—a mobility that would remain largely symbolic for Motown's core black constituency. As Stax/Volt set its corporate vision inward to the complexities of black urban life, Motown set its visions upward into the higher realms of corporate diversity and development. In the aftermath of these developments, Stax/Volt faced bankruptcy as Motown fell prey to the very marketing and production strategies it helped to develop, as soul, both the music and its cultural icons, became mass-market fodder for corporate America's entertainment and marketing devices.

The corporate ideologies of Stax/Volt and Motown were parlayed through their investment in two singular cultural and social events in 1972. Although WattStax, an all-day outdoor concert featuring the Stax/Volt roster of artists, and the Motown-produced cinematic biography of Billie Holiday were worthwhile social and cultural endeavors, both revealed a lack of attention to the quality music production that had grounded each company's success. Major corporate entities, perhaps sensing an ide-

---

* Joy James, *Transcending the Talented Tenth: Black Leaders an American Intellectuals* (New York: Routledge, 1997).

ological shift on the part of black-music producers and distributors, began to appropriate the music and the iconography of soul for use in the highly combative arena of cultural commodities. Within such a context, the black popular music tradition would be divorced from many of its organic sources, sources that often sought to invest the tradition with a highly politicized and critical consciousness. By the mid-1970s both Motown and Stax/Volt would be largely marginalized from the dominant positions in black popular music production, though for entirely different reasons, while the last great artist produced under the tutelage of Berry Gordy, Michael Jackson, would be poised to become the most popular recording artist ever, albeit while under contract with a major entertainment conglomerate.

Soul in the 'Hood: WattStax and Black Corporate Responsibility

Buoyed by their abruptly severed distribution deal with Gulf + Western and the popular and widely circulated expressions of black capitalism—personified in part by Jesse Jackson, his Operation Push organization, and the National Black Political Assembly—Stax/Volt began the seventies captivated by notions of black corporate responsibility. In March 1972 the largest black political caucus in United States history was held in Gary, Indiana. The Gary convention stood on the two major pillars of black capitalism and black political empowerment. As Manning Marable explains:

> The National Black Political Assembly was a marriage of convenience between the aspiring and somewhat radicalized black petty bourgeoisie and the black nationalist movement . . . The collective vision of the convention represented a desire to seize electoral control of America's major cities, to move the black masses from the politics of desegregation to the politics of real empowerment, ultimately to create their own independent black political party.[1]

The National Black Political Assembly represented the pinnacle of the grassroots and national political movements of the 1960s and early 1970s. The assembly remained a dominant influence on post–civil rights black political thought throughout the decade of the seventies, particularly among those shaped by the modern

1. Manning Marable, *Race, Reform and Rebellion: The Second Reconstruction in Black America,*(University Press of Mississippi), p.123.

black nationalist tradition. The Stax/Volt corporation was, perhaps, also impacted by these narratives of black empowerment, as witnessed by the many great changes the company underwent in the early seventies.

The immediate impetus for change was the emergence of Al Bell as the label's sole proprietor, in effect turning a highly successful integrated recording label into a highly visible black-owned one. Jim Stewart's exit from Stax/Volt coincided with the company's efforts to end its distribution deal with the Gulf + Western conglomerate.[2] In some ways, these events underscore Stax/Volt's fixation with the overwhelming shadow cast by the larger and more visible Motown, particularly in the eyes of a core audience base who took pride in Motown's "black-owned" status. Stax/Volt could, of course, boast that its new "black-owned" status was not earned by cultivating a mainstream audience at the expense of the core constituency both companies claimed to represent. In an era when visions of black corporate development abounded, Al Bell's Stax/Volt cast itself as the more responsible corporate "big brother." The full weight of such responsibility would be realized with the ambitious WattStax project of 1972.

The Watts district of Los Angeles had been etched in the minds of the mainstream American public since violent upheavals in the summer of 1965. Those riots, along with similar exhibitions of urban unrest in Newark and Detroit, were emblematic, at least among mainstream white sensibilities, of the deteriorating conditions of urban life. In this regard, the racial component of many of the urban riots of the 1960s were further examples of the black urban "horde" that threatened to undermine the sophistication of American urban life. Many critics identify these upheavals as a primary impetus for the white middle-class flight from cities during the 1960s that stimulated the deterioration of American urban life in the 1970s.[3] Stax/Volt's relationship with the neighborhood underscored the need for responsible corporate intervention within inner cities, even if such support was limited to underwriting summer festivals.

Implicit in the notion of responsible corporate intervention are examples of savvy business acumen. Stax/Volt's core consumer constituency of Southern blacks had begun to migrate from the American South into industrial Los Angeles during the post–World War II period as part of the second phase of black mass migration from the South. Since the end of World War II the black population in Los Angeles had

2. Nelson George, *The Death of Rhythm & Blues* (Obelisk, 1991), pp.138-139.
3. Marable, *Race, Reform and Rebellion*, pp.123-124.

grown by four hundred percent by the end of the sixties.[4] Given the potential constituency that Stax/Volt could cultivate through a relationship with the community, social responsibility could easily be equated with quality business decisions. With the exception of some support from the Schlitz beer company, the WattStax effort was entirely underwritten by Stax/Volt. The moment still remains an apex in black corporate community relations, and probably informed the civic responsibility expressed by contemporary "gangsta rap" entrepreneurs like Suge Knight and Dr. Dre.[5]

The WattStax recordings (a second festival was recorded in 1973 under the banner of WattStax II) at once highlight the possibilities of corporate-based community activism and the significance of listeners whom black popular music had begun to distance itself from. In an era when popular music events were increasingly held in large municipal stadiums, Stax/Volt dared present such a concert as a gift to urban black America. *Essence* magazine staff writer Vernon Gibbs wrote of WattStax II:

> The concert, which was the climactic event in the Seventh Annual Watts Summer Festival, was sponsored by Stax records and featured members of the Stax lineup exclusively . . . In a very handy way, all good interests were served as we see a clear example of black helping black. If there is a nation united by something like a common ideology, these are the kinds of channels that constructive effort must take.[6]

Like the live recordings of Julian "Cannonball" Adderley and Donny Hathaway, the WattStax recordings presented black popular music in an organic context that highlighted massive audience interaction with the music. Such efforts by Stax/Volt were laudable given the physical demise—a development that portended a national trend in black urban spaces during the 1970s—of valuable institutions within the Watts community. The singular presence of the Reverend Jesse Jackson—again harking back to Adderley and the *Country Preacher* recording session at Jackson's Operation Breadbasket—suggested that the triad of black corporate responsibility, political activism, and quality aesthetics could serve as a paradigm for African-American empowerment beyond the limitations of grassroots and organic movements. The ultimate failure of this paradigm in any sustained or significant manner

4. Brian Cross, *It's Not About a Salary . . . Rap, Race and Resistance in Los Angeles* (Haymarket Series), p.8.
5. Knight and Dr. Dre, who were the administrative and creative pillars of the highly controversial Death Row recording company have been known to furnish Mother's Day dinners for Compton and Watts area mothers as well as donating turkey dinners for poor and working-class individuals in these neighborhoods.
6. Quoted from the liner notes of the WattStax II recording.

underscores not only the limited vision of many black corporate entities, but, more notably, the overwhelming presence of mainstream corporate interests in the production of black popular music.

Motown Goes Hollywood: Diana Ross and Black Middle-Class Desire

Unlike his contemporary Al Bell, Berry Gordy saw black progress in terms of the integration of mainstream and elite American institutions by blacks with highly textured middle-class sensibilities. As Al Bell followed his black working-class constituency to Los Angeles, Gordy consciously abandoned his working-class constituency in Detroit in favor of the fast-paced and highly competitive culture industry of Los Angeles. While Gordy's decisions during this era spoke to a legitimate need to diversify the corporate interests of Motown, the company's relocation to Los Angeles and subsequent dislocation from black urban life served as an ironic and prophetic symbol of black middle-class development. If Motown was founded firmly on black middle-class aspiration, the post–civil rights Motown was premised on black middle-class mobility.

Given Motown's investment in mainstream middle-class interests, the urban riots of 1967 in Detroit made moving to the West Coast a logical transition. In this regard, Motown's move mirrored mainstream middle-class movement, while portending black middle-class movement during the 1970s. Never driven by the communal responsibility that undergirded the civil rights movement or the later Gary convention, Gordy's abandonment of Motown's working class following in Detroit did not seem problematic, particularly given the view that the company represented a valuable symbol for black communal aspiration. Unfortunately, during the 1970s Motown would come to better represent the rather tenuous status of the black middle class—and its relationship to sustained economic power.

Gordy's corporate desires manifested themselves under various guises, not the least of which was in the area of songwriting and production credit.

Embroiled in a bitter legal battle with former Motown songwriters and producers Lamont Dozier, Eddie Holland, and Brian Holland (H-D-H), Gordy would recruit a second trio of staff writers and producers to usher Motown's sound into the 1970s. While the names Holland, Dozier, and Holland were nationally renowned, most would know the trio of Deke Richards, Fonso Mizell, and Freddie Perren only as "The

Corporation."[7] They were named as such to circumvent the type of popularity and, ultimately, power within the Motown corporation that Holland, Dozier, and Holland had held during their prime. Clearly an effort on Gordy's part to maintain the strict hierarchy at Motown, the name also underscored Gordy's quest for corporate maturity, as no "real" corporation should be beholden to the individual whims of its employees.[8]

The subtle elevation of Diana Ross within the Motown hierarchy personified Gordy's own quest for corporate/social mobility. Ross's calculated break with the Supremes to pursue a solo career was wholly supported, if not inspired, by Gordy. Diana Ross served as the commercial icon who would deliver Motown into the next phase of its development. By chance, Ross's emergence as a solo artist coincided with the development of the first major body of black feminist work. Devoid of any particular political or racial agenda, Ross nevertheless came to represent the full articulation of black "divahood" for a generation of young stars in the making. Motown's development of a cinematic treatment of Billie Holiday's life would serve as the vehicle for Ross's superstardom and Gordy's own middle-class aspirations. According to Nelson George, the screenplay for *Lady Sings the Blues*, partially written and fictionalized by Motown executives Suzanne DePasse and Christine Clark, "transformed Holiday's story into a parable of Motown's rise: a strong black man, played charmingly by Billy Dee Williams, battles to harness a female singer's headstrong energy and ambition."[9]

A critical and commercial success, *Lady Sings the Blues* helped Ross draw an Oscar nomination. Given the paucity of balanced portrayals of black women within the film industry—an industry notorious for positing Aunt Jemima–like figures Hattie McDaniel and Butterfly McQueen as dominant black female icons—Ross's Oscar nomination was well received within an African-American diaspora starved for positive representations. In this context, Ross's success at once highlighted a black woman's independence and mainstream acceptance for a black CEO from Detroit. Commenting on the film, Gerald Early writes:

> When Gordy financed the film . . . he insisted on so distorting the life of the famed jazz singer Billie Holiday, upon whose autobiography the film is supposedly based, that in effect he simply swallows the life of Holiday into an ocean of pop-culture

7. Fonce Mizell would later team with brother Larry and introduce the Motown production line technique to jazz trumpeter and innovator Donald Byrd. Black Byrd, the initial product of this collaboration, would go on to become the best-selling record ever for the Blue Note recording label.
8. Nelson George, *Where Did Our Love Go?: The Rise & Fall of the Motown Sound* (St. Martin's Press, 1987), pp.185-186.
9. *Ibid.*, pp.191-192.

kitsch for the benefit of Ross . . . What interested Gordy most about the life of Holiday as a vehicle for Ross was precisely what interested Ross herself: that Holiday was the only sufficiently gigantic bitch-goddess of popular culture whose art could legitimate Ross's own standing as the reigning black bitch-goddess of her own day.[10]

Gordy always believed that black women were the logical channel for a sustained mainstream commercial acceptance, in part, according to Early, because Gordy felt that "black women were less threatening and, in some ways, more comforting to the white public than a black man would be, especially with the intense sexuality and sensuality that the 'new' popular music of rhythm & blues and rock and roll suggested."[11]

Despite Ross's high visibility, her success, like the commercial success of *Lady Sings the Blues*, betrayed many of the sentiments expressed by a burgeoning black feminist movement, premised in part on the idea that black women would be the dominant agents within their lives and experiences. Ultimately, Gordy's calculated control over Ross for much of her career represented little change from the standard uses of black women within popular culture. Ross's image as an independent black woman was as saccharine as her singing voice, while Gordy parlayed this imagery into a limited victory for black capitalist patriarchy. Gordy's distortion of Holiday's life is even more disturbing in that it mirrors mass consumer culture's proclivity to divorce African-American expressive culture from its political and social roots, solely for the purpose of mass-market acceptance. In this regard, Gordy became the very corporate animal he had aspired to become. Ross and Gordy revisited their contradictory narratives of middle-class mobility and pseudo–black feminist imagery with the production of *Mahogany* in 1974. A commercial and critical failure, the film represented the problematic aspirations of Gordy and Ross. In *Mahogany*, the classic theme of "poor girl gets lucky, makes it big, and must choose between the bright lights and her high-school boyfriend" is weaved along the sensibilities of a burgeoning black middle class, lacking both identity and a sense of rootedness. Early writes of *Mahogany*:

A brilliant film, mythifying in concise symbolic terms the middle-brow black struggle for identity. Ross, whose acting is much better here because the role is much

10. Gerald Early, *One Nation Under a Groove: Motown and American Culture*, p.119.
11. *Ibid.*, pp.117-118.

closer to her own experience, plays a ghetto-dwelling, struggling, department-store clerk who wishes to be a high-fashion designer . . . In the meanwhile, she is torn between her love for Billy Dee Williams's character, a committed activist in the ghetto running for public office, and her love of success and the artsy European life which she has grown accustomed to. Gordy here has superbly conflated the old Hollywood formula of a woman torn between her career and her man with the identity struggle of the successful middle-class black.[12]

Within this context, Gordy cast his lot with the well-intentioned activities of Williams's character, who is constructed in the vein of a "blaxploitation" staple: the committed, though inadequately empowered "brotherman." In this narrative, the quest for black love is set firmly against the overwhelming "whiteness" of mainstream success. This narrative is perhaps buoyed by Gordy's tacit acknowledgment that Motown was outclassed and outfinanced by the larger corporate entities in the entertainment industry; a notion further enhanced by the fact that Gordy himself took over main directorial duties midway through the film.

Unfortunately, Ross, who must be seen as a metaphor for the black popular music tradition, is caught between the patriarchal struggles of two opposing corporate entities: the diversified corporate conglomerate and the independently owned black business. The periods in which *Mahogany* and *Lady Sings the Blues* were produced were in fact dismal for Ross's promising solo recording career, in that much of the sass and energy that her image suggested were stifled by Gordy's crossover fixation. Ross's solo career really did not reach its potential until the late 1970s and early 1980s, with songs fittingly entitled "It's My House" and "I'm Coming Out." Ross left the company during the early 1980s.

Ironically, a non-Motown-produced film mined the Motown catalogue—often brilliantly—to give rootedness and substance to the music's role in the lives of the black urban poor and working class of the Midwest. Directed by black director Michael Schultz and based on an autobiographical script by Eric Monte, *Cooley High* is the definitive cinematic portrait of black city life during the 1960s. Released in 1975, the film documents the middle-class aspirations of a cadre of black males living on the boundaries of poverty in Chicago. The music of Motown is woven in and out of the daily experiences of the film's protagonists, suggesting the pervasiveness of the company's

12. *Ibid.*, p.121.

sound in the lives of the black masses. Further irony is realized in the fact that the main character, played by Glynn Turman, aspired to become a Hollywood screenwriter.[13]

Ultimately, Gordy's quest for massive crossover appeal was expressed not with a woman, but with a little black boy from the same Gary, Indiana that housed the 1972 National Black Political Assembly. The sudden emergence of Michael Jackson and the Jackson Five underscored several trends in the development of Motown and the marketing and distribution of black musical expression.

Soul for Sale: Blackness, Blaxploitation, and the Commodification of Soul

The Jackson Five was the last major act produced by Motown prior to its relocation to Los Angeles and, arguably, the most popular ever produced by the company. Had Gordy completed his move before the end of the sixties, the group might never have signed with the label; Gary, Indiana was part of the Midwestern scene that Gordy felt so compelled to leave. To a certain extent, the Jacksons would never know the familial atmosphere of Motown/Detroit—they were the last act on the label who could bear witness to Gordy's guiding hand—and Motown/Los Angeles held no special place for them. Critic David Ritz writes:

> A transitional group merging with a transitional company, moving from factories to dreamland, from working class dreams to Hollywood reality, the J5 and their mentor discovered themselves at the start of a new cycle fueled by old drives and well-worn patterns . . . Gordy worked the boys harder than these hard-working children had ever been worked before. In contrast to Gary, L.A. looked like paradise, but the assembly-line sensibility of Detroit prevailed.[14]

While the Jackson Five was groomed exclusively in the early years by Motown staffer Bobby Taylor, Gordy made the conscious decision to base the group in Los Angeles, recording more than seventy tunes with the quintet during their first year on the West Coast. With Taylor's subsequent dismissal—representative of Gordy's own post-Detroit worldview, Taylor was accused of saddling the Jackson Five with an outdated sound: the group was firmly in the hands of "The Corporation."[15]

13. Nelson George, *Blackface: Reflections on African-Americans and the Movies*, pp.60-61.
14. Liner notes, *Soulsation: 25th Anniversary Collection*, p.34.
15. *Ibid.*, pp.37-39.

Aside from the group's first three releases, Gordy's fascination with Diana Ross and producing films increasingly kept him out of the very artistic loop that helped distinguish Motown's sound from other companies during the sixties. As evidenced in Gordy's own belief that the Jackson Five was little more than a novelty act, the group's record sales dropped with their growing maturity. But their earlier success sent ripples through the recording industry, spawning a whole generation of copycat artists and producers trying to reproduce the doo-wop sound that foregrounded the Jackson Five sound. According to Nelson George, one Motown staffer and "Corporation" member was wooed away from the label explicitly to re-create the Jackson Five sound in other acts, most notably the Sylvers family group.[16]

While the popular success of Michael Jackson can arguably be construed as a novelty or fad, the Jackson Five appealed to a market segment that had never been exclusively targeted by black popular music producers, namely those in their early teens and younger. Michael Jackson's stature as a popular icon during the early seventies was contingent on commercial support from eight- to fifteen-year-olds. When Michael Jackson reemerged in the late 1970s and the early 1980s as the dominant popular music artist of his generation, he did so at the instigation of the Epic/Columbia recording company. The often surreal marketing of Michael Jackson is foregrounded on corporate America's appropriation and improvement upon the very strategies that Gordy developed during the 1960s. What is significant here is that the corporate annexation of black popular music began precisely at the moment that Motown was witnessing its greatest success marketing and selling black popular music in the form of Michael Jackson and the Jackson Five. It was only natural for corporate entities to attempt to reproduce marketing strategies that helped build a black popular music industry directed largely toward American youth culture. Stuart Ewen and Elizabeth Ewen write:

> Youth, embroiled in the "free market" courting practices of modernity, was perceived as a market whose most absorbing problem is that of personal adornment . . . Such a definition of "youth" cast the young as ideal consumers, unconcerned with questions of profligacy or waste; committed to an understanding of needs that placed them within the confines of a continually changing marketplace.[17]

16. George, *Where Did Our Love Go*, pp.185-186.
17. Stewart Ewen and Elizabeth Ewen, *Channels of Desire: Mass Images and the Shaping of American Consciousness* (University of Minnesota Press, 1992), p.223.

Thus, the musical taste of American youth culture, mercurial in its own right, was partly driven by the very volatility that Paul Gilroy argues is a structural component of black popular music due to the tradition's own attempts to resist intense commodification. This volatility would hurt the quality of music, because it hindered the successful development of lasting traditions both within and beyond the marketplace.

Ironically, it would be the Jackson Five and Michael Jackson in particular who would attain the mainstream acceptance that Berry Gordy craved. After the Jackson Five, Motown never, with the exception of Lionel Richie, produced artists of the same caliber as during the 1960s. In addition, Motown lost many of its artists and producers—including Marvin Gaye, Diana Ross, the Jackson Five, the Spinners, Ashford and Simpson, and Gladys Knight and the Pips—to corporate entities. In the case of the Spinners, Ashford and Simpson, and Gladys Knight and the Pips, this split occurred before the artists reached their artistic and commercial maturity. While the subsequent demise of Motown as a major player could be blamed on Berry Gordy's decreasing involvement in the aesthetic process at Motown, the fact remains that with corporate entities increasingly dominating the production and marketing of black popular music, neither Motown nor any other independent black label would ever again be the singular conduit for new black talent.

* * *

In an influential essay originally published in *Esquire* magazine, author Claude Brown writes, "The language of soul—or, as it might be called, "spoken soul" or "colored English"—is simply an honest portrayal of black America. The roots of it are more than one hundred years old."[18] Brown's commentary bespeaks the larger social and cultural connotations of the word "soul." Generally associated with the genre of music that bore its name, throughout the 1960s soul became primarily linked to evocations of black communal pride. In this regard, soul came to represent an authentic, though obviously essentialized blackness that undergirded the Black Power and civil rights movements with which soul music has come to be associated.

With the subsequent annexation of black popular music, in which the soul genre was then the dominant form, the larger meaning of soul was also deconstructed for

18. Brown, "The Language of Soul," *Rappin' and Stylin' Out*, p.135.

use within mass culture. Divorced from its politicized and organic connotations, "soul" became a malleable market resource merchandised to black and white consumers alike in the form of music, television shows, and hair-care products. This process underscores a major facet of contemporary consumer culture, which has often sought to separate the iconography of political struggle from the organic sources and intentions of such struggles. William L. Van Deburg writes:

> Soul was closely related to black America's need for individual and group self-definition . . . In this sometimes crazy quilt world of the cool, the hip, and the hustle, stylized forms of personal expression were developed which not only conveyed necessary social information, but also could promote a revitalized sense of self. At its most fundamental, soul style was a type of in-group cultural cachet whose creators utilized clothing design, popular hair treatments, and even body language (stance, gait, method of greeting) as preferred mechanisms of authentication.[19]

The commodification of "soul" had a particularly strong impact on African-American popular expression, as political resistance was often parlayed as an element of style. This is not to suggest that the Afro hairdo or the dashiki were as politically meaningful as sit-ins or mass rallies, but that many of the icons of black social movements were invested with some vestige of oppositional expression. Nevertheless, the marketing of soul reduced blackness to a commodity that could be bought and sold without the cultural and social markers that have defined blackness.

For instance, within the maelstrom of commodities exchange, the cultural meaning of the Afro hairstyle was subordinated to consumer products that supposedly enhanced the ability to grow an Afro. Most importantly, these products could be accessed by a mainstream public simply as an element of contemporary style, which in the case of Afro wigs could be easily removed when they proved socially problematic. Once emblematic of the increased militancy of the youth wings of the civil rights and Black Power movements, the Afro simply represented a stylistic choice, although as the decade wore on, the Afro again became demonized, along with a black youth underclass, as an element of a deviant criminal subculture of African-American men.

19. William L. Van Deburg, *New Day in Babylon: The Black Power Movement and American Culture, 1965-1975* (University of Chicago Press, 1992), p.195.

These earlier developments had serious implications for black social life because blackness—loosely defined as a broad-based and diverse black identity, largely grounded in the black communal experience—was also displaced from its organic sources. Paul Gilroy writes that black identity

> is not simply a social and political category to be used or abandoned according to the extent to which the rhetoric that supports and legitimizes it is persuasive or institutionally powerful . . . It is lived as a coherent (if not always stable) experiential sense of self. Though it is often felt to be natural and spontaneous, it remains the outcome of practical activity language, gesture, bodily significations, desires.[20]

As the 1970s progressed and black public life began to exhibit signs of deterioration predicated on black middle-class flight, the demise of central cities, and the destruction of community institutions dating before the riots, black identity—in other words, blackness—was largely mediated and thus determined by the mechanisms of mass consumer culture. Yes, Berry Gordy's attempts at Hollywood filmmaking were efforts to broaden the scope and visibility of blackness, particularly as such efforts were related to black middle-class concerns about self-identity; but Motown was incapable of competing with the larger, more established corporations, who unfortunately often viewed black identity, and the notions of blackness so integral to it, solely as a medium with which to expand their market shares.

During the 1970s Sherman Hemsley's George Jefferson, Esther Rolle's Florida Evans, Ron O'Neal's Superfly, Pam Grier's Foxy Brown, and Antonio Fargas's Huggy Bear emerged as the dominant representations of blackness on the television and movie screens, in effect erasing political icons like Malcolm X, Fannie Lou Hamer, Eldridge Cleaver, and Angela Davis. Though images of the black buffoon, black maid, black superstud, oversexed black woman, and black pimp broke no new ground in black stereotypes among white Americans—the major political and cultural icons of the 1960s made distinct efforts to revise such stereotypes—these images represent the first that would be wholly consumed by African-American audiences as emblematic of black identity.

The desire for identity that foregrounds much of black expressive culture forced corporate entertainment industries to walk a fine line between diversifying their

20. Paul Gilroy, *The Black Atlantic: Modernity and Double Consciousness* (Harvard University Press, 1995), p.102.

market activities and acknowledging a black middle-class and working-class buying public. In their efforts to sell soul to the masses, through the short-lived but prolific era of blaxploitation, corporate America's uncompromising revisioning of the meanings and icons of blackness introduced both cartoonish and surreal constructions to the general public. Steven Haymes writes that these processes transform black culture "into signifiers, absent of historical references to black life and absent of signification other than making luxury consumer goods pleasurable to middle-class whites. This stripping of history and signification from black culture has reduced it to a simulacrum."[21]

The prevalence of absurd imagery like that of *Shaft* and *The Mack* suggested that the social crises of the sixties and early seventies could be solved by Hollywood during the course of ninety-minute voyages into hyper-black fantasies that often featured groundbreaking and award-winning musical soundtracks by performers like Isaac Hayes, Donny Hathaway, Marvin Gaye, and Curtis Mayfield; recordings that satiated both mainstream curiosities about blackness and African-American desire to consume their own images. Hayes's *Shaft* soundtrack and Curtis Mayfield's *Superfly* soundtrack were not only among the first generation of blaxploitation soundtracks, but were definitive examples of soul music in that era. The conflation of black musical expression with black imagery in the form of blaxploitation cinema and network television afforded mainstream consumers unprecedented access to black popular expression.

Just as Hollywood and the Ziegfeld Follies quelled the resistance of America's poor and working classes in the 1930s, so mass consumer culture in the 1970s offered narratives of blaxploitation to the restless and unsatisfied masses of the African-American "nation." Furthermore, this strategy was aimed at the most uncritical segment of the black community, namely black urban youth, who did not have the benefit of the presence of a black middle class capable of presenting counternarratives of black struggle. Perhaps even more enlightening is an examination of how commodified soul translated blackness, in audience-friendly ways, to a mainstream and burgeoning television-viewing public that was in part African-American. Two fairly popular, though short-lived television shows from the mid-1970s illustrate both the problems and possibilities of soul's commercial uses.

21. Stephen Nathan Haymes, *Race, Culture, and the City: A Pedagogy for Black Urban Struggle* (State University of New York, 1995), p.51.

That's My Mama debuted in the fall of 1974. The sitcom was largely a vehicle for actor Clifton Davis; it also featured Theresa Merritt, in the role of Mama, and Ted Lange, better known to television viewers as bartender Isaac from the *Love Boat* series. Introduced the same year as Norman Lear's more successful *Good Times*, *That's My Mama* was perhaps the first television sitcom to use expressions of soul as a primary thematic device. The show was a caricature of itself, boldly pronouncing its pastiched blackness, especially in Lange's character, who served as a sounding board and prop for overly animated and decontextualized examples of black dress, black speech, and black style. The centrality of Merritt's three-hundred-pound character to the storyline reconstructed and conflated centuries-old caricatures of black women with contemporary black iconography. Primarily set in the barbershop owned by Davis's character, the sitcom missed a valuable opportunity to capture the multi-discursive and highly critical exchanges that have marked such spaces within the traditional black public sphere. The barbershop exchanges, like the soul aesthetic that the show attempted to parlay, were often reduced to banal clichés of the black experience—clichés that were ultimately rejected by the show's primarily black audience.

Using many of the same clichés as *That's My Mama*, including a three-hundred-pound Mabel King as the contentious mother figure, *What's Happening* was introduced to television viewers in the autumn of 1976. The sitcom proved more popular than its predecessor, in part because of its conscious playing to teenage sensibilities via its largely teenaged cast. The half-hour show scarcely missed an opportunity to validate mainstream America's perceptions of single-parent households, frivolous black youth, and the overstated tensions associated with black male–female relations. More important than what it confirmed to mainstream audiences were the issues that *What's Happening* failed to address, issues integrally linked to mass culture's proclivity to de-emphasize black reality.

The show, set in the Watts district a decade after the riots of 1965, offered an ample opportunity for mainstream America to glimpse the everyday conditions of perhaps this country's most visible icon of racial tension. While the show succeeded, however humorously, in capturing the depressed economic state of Watts, it also offered a glimpse of a highly depoliticized Watts. This is ironic given the show's link to Watts's radical political past. The show's title was borrowed from the name of a real coffee shop that served as a focal point for the district's burgeoning activist class. The Watts Happening Coffee House, which was emblematic of both the formal and informal spaces of the black public sphere in Los Angeles, was a meeting place for the Black Panthers, Maulama Karenga's United Slaves organization, and other local writers and activists. *What's Happening*, which was largely set in "Rob's Coffee Shop," totally ignored the vibrant political culture that was central to its namesake's legacy.[22]

Nevertheless, *What's Happening* and *That's My Mama* remain two of the few examples of television programming that at least attempted to capture the realities of black public spaces, however truncated. Ironically, such television programming occurred at the same time real institutions within the black public sphere were under siege. Nowhere is this more evident than in the demise of affordable public venues for live music. In the early 1970s Don Cornelius introduced a television concept that helped address the problems of affordable performances and in the process created one of the great commercial institutions within the African-American diaspora.

Soul Train was one of the more successful venues to access black popular music. It was also one of the only venues available to black urban centers, which, with specific exceptions—cities like Atlanta, New Orleans, and Memphis—had lost the very commercial venues that were integral to the chitlin' circuit dynamics that dominated the production, reproduction, and distribution of black popular expression before the civil rights era. The longest-running black television show in television history, *Soul Train* was born in 1971 and partly influenced by Dick Clark's successful *American Bandstand*. Cornelius attempted to use television as an apparatus to promote and distribute black popular music. Amazingly in tune with organic developments in the black community, the show's success was partly generated from the immediate exposure afforded to many of the newer dance styles within the black community. Sensitive to the various regional articulations of soul, the show in effect gave national exposure to the "local" within the African-American diaspora. Given the role of dance within traditional black social experiences, *Soul Train* was a visual affirmation of the black communal ethic. In this regard—and ultimately the thing that separated the show from *American Bandstand*—*Soul Train* served as an electronically derived audiovisual extension of the chitlin' circuit, privileging organic developments within black expressive culture.

22. Cross, *It's Not About a Salary*, p.10.

Produced explicitly for syndication and remaining relatively untouched by a disinterested white corporate structure, the program gained a national following among segments of the African-American diaspora and mainstream consumers. Though the show did nothing to familiarize its young audiences with jazz and blues—*Soul Train* never broadened its scope beyond soul music—it nevertheless remains one of the great examples of a black presence within the post–civil rights mass-consumer marketplace. The success of *Soul Train* would presage the emergence a full decade later of venerable black and urban institutions like Black Entertainment Television and Video Music Box, particularly as an inexpensive and accessible conduit for audiovisual representations of African-American music.

The developments of the early 1970s had radical implications for the nature, production, distribution, and meanings of black expressive culture in the post-soul era. Several genres and entities emerged as the decade progressed that addressed both the realities of African-American communal life and the mass commodification of black popular expression; others, however, affirmed and validated the new spatial and commercial terrain of that expression.

Mark Anthony Neal is assistant professor of Africana Studies at the State University of New York at Albany. He is the author of *Soul Babies: Black Popular Culture and the Post-Soul Aesthetic* (forthcoming from Routlege, 2002); and *What the Music Said: Black Popular Music and Black Public Culture* (Routledge, 1998), in which this essay was first published.

Part 3

Do Plantains Go with Collard Greens? The Political Economy of Jazz and Salsa

If You're Black Get Back:
Double Standards in the Recording Industry
BY FRANK KOFSKY

How do recording company executives decide what kinds of music will (and will not) be recorded, in what quantities, and with what amounts budgeted for promotion? This is a pivotal question in any analysis of the political economy of jazz because, when all is said and done, the fate of entire genres of music—not to mention that of the artists who create them—rests on the outcome of such decisions. And although estimates of potential profits and losses, to be sure, influence the decisions, those estimates are not, in and of themselves, what determine the final outcome.

For our purposes it suffices to investigate the way in which the topmost stratum of executives at a single firm, Columbia Records, has approached jazz. Nothing is lost by way of universality in restricting ourselves to this one corporation, because Columbia's immense size and wealth make it the bellwether of the industry. When Columbia executives choose to expand the scale of their jazz-recording activities, heads of other companies feel secure in doing likewise, confident in the knowledge that the massive outlays Columbia can expend on advertising will have spillover effects that benefit them as well. Conversely, when Columbia sees fit to retrench on its production of jazz albums, other companies will be quick to do the same. It is hardly surprising, therefore, that those periods in which Columbia issued jazz recordings in quantity—the years 1957 to 1965, for instance—were ones of comparative prosperity for jazz musicians, while those in which its involvement with jazz was reduced (1967–1976, say) were far more lean by comparison.

No sooner do we begin our inquiry into the attitudes of Columbia executives regarding jazz than we confront the figure of John Hammond. Hammond spent several decades with Columbia, retiring in 1975 as the director of talent acquisition, a position he had held since the close of the 1950s. In June of 1969, he attended a three-day conference on Black Music in College and University Curricula at Indiana University, the proceedings of which were captured on tape, transcribed, and later published as part of a book, *Black Music in Our Culture*.[1] Hammond's comments there, it will soon be clear, are invaluable for understanding how senior recording company executives view jazz and other forms of black music.

The participants at the conference lost little time in getting to the heart of the matter with Hammond. The first question put to him directly after his typically self-aggrandizing summary of his career was, "What avant garde jazz is Columbia Records engaged in recording now?"[2] Hammond's answer, a characteristically skillful blend of evasions, distortions, and quarter-truths, is virtually impossible to paraphrase. To convey the full flavor, therefore, I will quote the bulk of it then subject it to scrutiny bit by bit.

With his two opening sentences, Hammond immediately sought to position himself on the side of the angels: "I'm recording [saxophonist] Archie Shepp and [drummer] Sonny [*sic*] Murray on Monday. We ought to have a lot of fun." Assuming that Hammond's recording session with Shepp and Sunny Murray actually took place—which is by no means certain—surely after nearly thirty years have elapsed it is not impermissible to ask: When are the results going to be made available? But, of course, it is well within the bounds of possibility that no such recording session was ever planned, much less held. For one thing, neither Shepp's name nor Murray's appears in the index to Hammond's autobiography, nor is there any mention of a recording session with these artists in the "selective discography" included in that volume.[3] For another, Hammond, as I will show momentarily, was himself implacably hostile to the type of music Shepp and Murray then played. Accordingly, we probably should view Hammond's statement about a recording session with Shepp and Murray as a ploy—analogous to observing that some of one's best friends are colored—intended to get him off the hook by showing that where the jazz revolution of the 1960s was concerned, his heart was in the right place. Thus, the executive continued in a similar vein:

> Although I'm director of talent acquisitions and an executive producer at Columbia,
> I do not make the final decisions . . . [I]n this specialized field of pure jazz the possi-

---

1. Dominique-René de Lerma, ed., *Black Music in Our Culture: Curricular Ideas on the Subjects, Materials and Problems* (Kent, Ohio: Kent State University Press, 1970).
2. *Ibid.*, p.54.
3. See John Hammond and Irving Townsend, *John Hammond on Record* (New York: Ridge Press/Summit Books, 1977), pp.412, 415, 416.

bility of an enormous profit is minimal, even with the biggest artists like Miles Davis and Thelonious Monk. The records may only break even. I've been recording with Sonny [*sic*] Murray,[4] and you know the business will hesitate to make concessions when numbers might last eighteen minutes and might not even get much airplay, even in the underground. I'm sorry we've never recorded Cecil Taylor. He is a genius, but he is being recorded. Archie Shepp is under contract to Impulse. Albert Ayler and a lot of those guys are being recorded. One of the problems is that Columbia is a huge operation. We need to sell about 15,000 copies a year of a recording with the accounting system we have, the money it costs to package the thing [and so on].[5]

Following that deluge of exculpations, equivocations, and outright falsehoods, a few factual corrections may come as a breath of fresh air.

Item 1: No doubt Cecil Taylor is "a genius," but, Hammond's assertion notwithstanding, he was not "being recorded" in 1969, had not been recorded for three years—his entire output for the 1960s numbered fewer than half a dozen discs—and would not have a new album issued by an American company of even moderate size until the middle of the 1970s. As was also the case in his fictionalized account of the death of Bessie Smith, Hammond either knew the truth about Taylor's recording activity or could have learned it in a matter of minutes with one or two well-placed telephone calls. As was again the case with the circumstances of Bessie Smith's death, any ignorance on Hammond's part was hardly inadvertent. If nothing else, it enabled him to parry a potentially embarrassing question in front of an audience of educators evidently anxious about the reception being afforded the newest innovations in jazz by the country's largest producer of phonograph records.

Item 2: No one with whom I have spoken or corresponded and no analysis I have read supports Hammond's contention that Columbia or any other record company "need[s] to sell about 15,000 copies *a year* of a recording" [my italics] in order to show a profit. On the contrary, the evidence suggests that most jazz albums begin to earn profits as soon as they reach sales on the order of two thousand copies for a medium-sized firm, five to seven thousand copies for a larger one. But regardless of

4. Note the second reference to Sunny Murray—again, however, with no specific information about titles, albums to be released, or anything else.
5. *Ibid.*

whether a jazz recording starts to become profitable after two, five, or seven thousand copies have been sold, even the largest of these amounts is still a far cry from the 15,000 copies that Hammond claimed was the minimal *annual* sales figure acceptable to Columbia's executives.[6]

Item 3: What is more, conclusive evidence that Hammond was deliberately misleading his audience can be obtained from an unimpeachable source—Columbia Records itself. In 1951, that firm brought out four long-playing albums of performances by Bessie Smith. According to Chris Albertson, "This fine series was a slow but steady seller which the company kept in its catalogue for nineteen years," until it was deleted to make way for the new Bessie Smith reissue recordings Columbia released in the 1970s. During the nineteen years they were in print (roughly the same years that Hammond worked at Columbia), Albertson informs us, these four albums sold a *total* of about 20,000 copies—or, on the average, slightly fewer than three hundred copies per album per year.[7] If Hammond were still alive, it would be most enlightening to have him explain what ever became of the sales figure of "15,000 copies a year of a recording" with which he attempted to mystify his listeners at the Indiana University conference on black music. Even he would have to agree, would he not, that three hundred copies per annum is a considerable distance from 15,000?

Item 4: But perhaps the 15,000 copies is merely an *average* that applies to Columbia's overall operations but not to each and every recording released on that label. Hammond, naturally, isn't notably lucid on this point—when your aim is to befuddle your hearers, clarity is not the most probable outcome. Still, inasmuch as Columbia's most popular albums sell hundreds of thousands (and in some

6. A detailed calculation of the "break-even point" at which the sales of a jazz album just suffice to recover the costs of production is incuded in my 1973 doctoral dissertation in history at the University of Pittsburgh, "Black Nationalism and the Revolution of Music: Social Forces and Stylistic Change in the Music of John Coltrane and Others, 1954–1967," pp.385–89. The sources I employed for that calculation are: Richard Nicholls, "Where Your $5.98 Goes," *Rock* (December 14, 1970): p.21; Bob Koester, "The Record Producer: A Dollars and Cents Analysis," *Coda* (March 1967): pp.2–5; a letter from Koester to the author, May 13, 1971; a telephone interview with Koester, April 25, 1973; Francis Newton [E. J. Hobsbawm], *The Jazz Scene* (Harmondsworth, Middlesex: Penguin Books, 1961), pp.172–3, notes A, B. In his letter to me of May 13, 1971, for instance, Bob Koester, himself the owner of a recording company (Delmark Records), states: "I don't think they [Columbia Records] require 15K [15,000 sales per annum], tho[ugh]. I guess that 5K would keep an album in print until they ran out of paper (covers and liners)." Koester likewise estimates the initial pressing of a Columbia jazz record at 10,000 copies. In a telephone interview on September 21, 1978, Pat Britt, who produced the majority of jazz recordings released on the Catalyst label, supplied a figure of eighty-five cents as the unit cost to the company of an album. Using the numbers given by Koester and Britt and bearing in mind that records are usually sold to the distributor by the manufacturer at twice the cost of production, it follows that Columbia would realize a profit on an initial pressing of 10,000 copies after 8,500 had been sold. If the original run were smaller, of course, the break-even point would be correspondingly lower. A first pressing of 5,000 copies, for example, would need sales of only 4,250 copies to recoup production expenditures.
7. See Chris Albertson, *Bessie* (New York: Stein and Day, 1972), p.232.

instances, even millions) of copies apiece, if the 15,000 copies a year is an average, as opposed to an individual criterion, there is no reason it cannot be attained by allowing the greater sales of popular records to compensate for the lesser sales of jazz records. For that matter, if the 15,000 copies is interpreted in this sense, it should even be possible for Columbia to release jazz albums that do not even recover their full costs of production.

Such a line of reasoning was in fact endorsed by Hammond's boss, Clive Davis, who was the head of Columbia Records from 1967 until he was discharged in the spring of 1973 and "served with the company's civil complaint against me, alleging $94,000 worth of expense-account violations during my six years as president."[8] Davis's words on this score are completely unambiguous: "Everything doesn't have to pay for itself. But if you are willing to release albums that lose money, you should either balance them with profitable ones or believe that the loss was worth taking for the sake of the music."[9]

Given the testimony of Columbia's former president that "everything *doesn't* have to pay for itself," there should be no obstacle to that company's issuing jazz albums that sell fewer than 15,000 copies a year. The only problem is that such an enlightened policy of corporate noblesse oblige was not devised to benefit art music created in the African-American tradition, but to support music composed in the European symphonic ("classical") idiom. What is more, such a flagrant double standard—subsidies for European concert music, pay-your-own-way for jazz—was enthusiastically defended by that great patron of black music, John Hammond. At the same Indiana University conference on black music in 1969 from which I have already quoted some of his remarks, Hammond declared his allegiance to this double standard in terms that leave no room for misunderstanding. "Once in a while," he explained,

> Columbia will undertake something like the recording of all of [Anton von] Webern's works. This may have sold three or four thousand copies, and the company may have lost up to $30,000 on the venture, *yet they make up for it with the popular hits that come out* [my italics].[10]

8. Clive Davis and James Willwerth, *Clive: Inside the Record Business* (New York: Ballantine Books, 1976), p.235.
9. *Ibid.*, p.282.
10. Quoted in *Black Music in Our Culture*, p.115.

Though Hammond on this occasion claimed that such losses are sustained only "once in a while," another of his statements at the Indiana University conference makes it unmistakably plain that *deficits incurred in the production of recordings of European symphonic music are a regular and predictable aspect of Columbia's operation.* In his own words:

> Now you know if we sell 20,000 copies at retail of, say, a [Gustav] Mahler symphony conducted by [Leonard] Bernstein, we think we're doing pretty well, *even though 20,000 sales doesn't pay a quarter of the cost* [my italics].[11]

A pity that none of Hammond's listeners thought to demand to know how he and Columbia Records could react with such equanimity to losses of tens of thousands of dollars on symphonic works by Webern and Mahler while still insisting that every single jazz recording sell 15,000 copies a year. It would have been most edifying, one may be sure, to hear his attempts to contrive a plausible answer to *that* query.

To give the devil his due, the double standard articulated so plainly by Hammond—hundreds of thousands of dollars to subsidize the recording of European symphonies, not one cent for jazz—is not original with him. On the contrary, in defending it, he was, one supposes, merely "doing his job" as an upper-level executive of, and prominent spokesman for, Columbia Records. That much emerges from the remarks of former Columbia president Clive Davis:

> Obviously, not every decision was determined by profit-and-loss consideration. We willingly lost money on Vladimir Horowitz. Each of his albums cost Columbia in guarantee, recording, and advertising expenses about a hundred thousand dollars; they generally recouped half that amount. But it *was* Horowitz . . . We decided that the business loss was more than offset by the musical contribution and the accompanying prestige.[12]

And again:

> Now it costs from twenty-five to fifty thousand dollars to record a classical album. The losses on this can range from minor to substantial, especially if you add in adver-

11. *Ibid.*, p.113.
12. *Clive*, p.272.

tising outlays. [Recordings by certain symphony orchestras] generally sold well over a long period of time; so you couldn't compute your profit-loss ratio in the first or second year . . . Yet, even if sales were calculated over a five- to ten-year period, most classical recordings failed to recoup their recording costs.[13]

If only corporate executives at the rank of Clive Davis and John Hammond were so graciously resigned to accepting financial losses from the production, promotion, and distribution of jazz recordings![14]

But, of course, they are not. Nor does it take a great deal of abstruse thought to discover why. For businessmen of the Davis and Hammond variety, the symphonic music of Europe is, as Davis's comments about Vladimir Horowitz quoted above explicitly acknowledge, a matter of infinite prestige. Only a philistine, therefore, would be so gauche as to soil something that sublime by mentioning fiscal considerations in the same breath.

Jazz, in contrast, as we have been informed all too many times, is nigger music. Oh, to be sure, it isn't played in whorehouses any more, and now there are some white misfits who also are involved in it. But when push comes to shove, it is still nigger music, and nevermind if some of the niggers happen to be white. Subsidize nigger music? What an absurd notion!

Also related to the question of subsidies is a different aspect of the double standard for symphonic versus jazz artists that comes into play when sales of recordings begin to decline. In the case of the symphonic artist, the unprofitability has more or less been anticipated all along—witness the remarks by Clive Davis on Vladimir Horowitz—and thus can be greeted with a philosophical shrug of the shoulders and some offhand comments about art, culture, the cosmos, and the like, should it actually materialize. But if the sales of a *jazz musician's* albums begin to show signs of slipping, then, my friends, it is time to storm heaven and earth. Only by keeping this fact in mind can we understand the unrelenting pressure that former Columbia president Clive Davis applied to Columbia jazz artist Miles Davis in striving to convince the latter to play jazz-rock, appear at the Fillmore East and "other rock halls around

---

13. Ibid., p.267.
14. To make my position unambiguously clear, I have no objection to subsidizing the recording of works by Gustav Mahler—indeed, it is not uncommon for me to make a 120-mile round trip for the pleasure of seeing one of his symphonies performed. All I ask is that the same largesse be showered on African-American music of comparable weight and quality.

the country," go on tour with the popular music group Santana, and so forth.[15] To the degree that the morass into which jazz sank during much of the seventies and eighties was an outgrowth of Miles Davis's earliest steps in this direction at the end of the sixties, a considerable share of the responsibility for this lovely state of affairs, too, can be laid at the door of the executive Mr. Davis.[16]

What needs underscoring in this connection is that the head of Columbia Records would have reacted in a drastically different fashion had it been Vladimir Horowitz rather than Miles Davis whose record sales were dwindling. Can you imagine him urging Horowitz to perform at the Fillmore East, play on the same bill as Santana, and the like, in order to boost the sales of his recordings? If that suggestion would be regarded as obscene when tendered to the pianist, why should it be thought any more appropriate when made to an influential and creative jazz musician? Could the answer be, because European symphonic music is Art-with-a-capital-A, whereas jazz is . . . you-know-what?

In light of such attitudes toward black music, no wonder that the leading innovators in jazz during the 1960s found conditions at Columbia Records anything but hospitable. The hostility to the new developments of that decade, moreover, was as fully shared by John Hammond as by any of his colleagues at Columbia, his carefully crafted image as the altruistic benefactor of black music and musicians notwithstanding. Thus, when he was safely out of earshot of the participants at the 1969 Indiana University conference on black music, he permitted himself the indulgence of expressing his actual feelings about the kind of music performed by Archie Shepp, Cecil Taylor, Albert Ayler, et alia:

15. See Clive, pp.299–303; the quotation is from p.301.

16. As is evident from his exultation over the decision of pianist Herbie Hancock to align himself with the camp of jazz fusion; Davis's ecstatic account of Hancock's conversion is in Clive Davis and James Willwerth, *Clive: Inside the Record Business* (New York: Ballantine Books, 1976), p.165. Note further that drummer Max Roach's experience with Atlantic Records is very similar in this regard to that of Miles Davis at Columbia. "During the early seventies," Roach has related,

> I was called into Atlantic and it was suggested to me that I do some material that was familiar to the world, *for sales* [my italics]. It was suggested in such a subtle way. Nesuhi Ertegun [Atlantic vice president] said, "Max, we've been knowing each other for years and you should really be rich" . . . So I said, "Yeah, I couldn't agree more, but how do I go about it, Nesuhi?" And he proceeds to tell me that you piggyback, coattail on different songs, basically you do familiar material. So I went home and called him and said, "Well, I'll do Negro spirituals, which is familiar material." Of course, I missed the boat. That was the last record I did for them.
>
> During that time was the beginning of fusion and crossover, the styles that prevail today. When I read Clive Davis's book, Miles [Davis] was asked to do the same thing.

Roach's testimony demonstrates that efforts at pushing jazz musicians into playing fusion and crossover styles were an industry-wide phenomenon, not merely the idiosyncratic whim of one or another recording company executive. See Bert Primack, "Max Roach: There's No Stoppin' the Professor from Boppin'," *down beat* (November 2, 1978): p.21.

What they're putting down really doesn't make that much sense to me. When you throw out tonality and certain disciplines, you're left with not enough. A record supervisor is not really in control of a session like that . . . You just have to give the musicians their heads.[17]

And if there is one thing on which John Hammond insists where black musicians are concerned, it is that he must be "really in control." But if nothing else, this statement should suffice to explain why the recording session with Archie Shepp and Sunny Murray that Hammond claimed to be producing in 1969 has never yet seen the light of day.

Frank Kofsky (1935–97) was a frequent lecturer on the history of jazz. He is the author of several books about music, including *John Coltrane and the Jazz Revolution of the 1960s* (Pathfinder, 1998) and *Black Music, White Business: Illuminating the History and Political Economy of Jazz* (Pathfinder, 1988), in which this essay was first published.

17. Hammond's remarks are quoted in John McDonough, "John Hammond: Man for All Seasons," down beat (March 4, 1971): p.13. Both this typically laudatory title and the equally flattering portrait that follows are the inevitable result of taking the executive's lavish self-praise at face value. Interestingly enough, though, Hammond's position on the new forms of jazz in the 1960s was essentially a reiteration of his response to the bebop revolution of the 1940s: "To me, bebop is a collection of nauseating clichés, repeated *ad infinitum*"; Hammond is quoted in Ron Russell, Bird Lives!: The High Life and Hard Times of Charlie (Yardbird) Parker (New York: Charterhouse, 1973), p.173.

Kind of Blue: Jazz Competes with Its Past, Settles for the Hard Sell
BY RICHARD B. WOODWARD

For two decades now the high-minded phrase "Jazz is America's Classical Music" has served as a kind of marketing jingle for the music during the culture wars. As popularized by Billy Taylor, Grover Sales, and others, the slogan became a patriotic rallying cry in the eighties—and the perfect topic sentence for a challenge-grant application— by those seeking to bring intellectual respect and institutional focus to jazz.

That the campaign succeeded beyond anyone's dreams is evident all over the academic map, most notably at Lincoln Center, where America's classical music is now an endowed program of study and performance, right up there with drama, ballet, opera, and Europe's classical music. But be careful what you wish for.

What nationalist boosters of jazz never expected when they struck gold with their classical allusion is that both veins of music would end up suffering similar fates. For many of the same reasons, jazz and classical music find themselves limping into the millennium under the burden of a glorious but sclerotic sense of tradition, and supported by an aging audience base that shows no sign of rejuvenating any time soon.

Throughout the nineties, record sales in both genres have shared the same dire statistical profile: a low, flat, and at times sinking line. The Recording Industry Association of America (RIAA), which gauges the popularity of different music genres, has classical and jazz running neck-and-neck at the back of the pack, each with about three percent of the business, just ahead of oldies and New Age. In 1998 jazz fell to 1.9 percent, two-tenths of a percent ahead of soundtracks and far behind religious at 6.3 percent.

Even if the RIAA's numbers are debatable (based as they are on a telephone sample of 3,051 record buyers, with a 2.2 percent margin of error), the worry among executives at the major jazz labels is not. "When you look around, things are extremely tough," says Matt Pierson, who heads the jazz department at Warner Brothers. "It gets harder to sell jazz every day," admits Tom Evered, general manager at Blue Note, and this view is seconded elsewhere. "Why isn't jazz selling?" asks Ron Goldstein, president of the Verve Music Group. "That's a question we discuss every day." The best that can be said about the situation for new jazz artists, according to producer Michael Cuscuna, is that "it's not quite as bleak as it was in the seventies."

The attention deficit in the general-interest media to the crisis in the jazz record business is itself telling. The shrinking market for symphony orchestras has been widely reported and received extensive coverage in the *Times*. But despite the money flowing through Lincoln Center, jazz remains very much a stepchild of American culture. You would think that the decision by BMG and Sony to dissolve or fire the contemporary jazz departments at RCA and Columbia respectively—two of the most storied labels in the history of American music—might be a big story somewhere. But not even *Billboard* took note.

One explanation for the puzzling silence may be that in recent years several singers, notably Diane Krall and Cassandra Wilson, have reached far beyond hardcore jazz listeners. But the main reason is probably that the reissue programs at these labels are thriving. Like classical music, jazz now boasts a set of canonical giants— Armstrong, Ellington, Bird, Monk—familiar to record-buyers young and old. Twenty years ago a Coltrane record in a rock collection betokened a taste for the esoteric. But when any style is up for grabs and eclectic sampling is the name of the game, everything is equally exotic. With *Kind of Blue* selling five thousand copies *a week*, Miles Davis has never been more a la mode.

The repackaging of dead jazz giants and the profit surge that the CD explosion brought to record companies has led to an unprecedented supply of jazz available in stores and online. "The market is flooded with great music," says Pierson. Fantasy, for example, which pioneered reissues with its Jazz Classics series in 1983, now has 1,200 titles in its catalogue. The ten-part Ken Burns documentary series, narrated by Wynton Marsalis, which first aired on PBS in January 2001, can only accentuate this positive trend.

It's the plight of living instrumental artists in this venerable tradition that signals trouble for jazz. Virtually any young critical favorite you can name—James Carter, Joe Lovano, Joshua Redman, Maria Schneider, Danilo Perez, Jackie Terrasson, Greg Osby, Kenny Garrett, David Sanchez, Dave Douglas, Geri Allen, Roy Hargrove, Brad Mehldau—is lucky to sell 15,000 records domestically in a CD's eighteen-month shelf life. Usually they fail to do even that. Ditto for legends Sonny Rollins, Tommy Flanagan, Joe Henderson, or Oscar Peterson. And as well-publicized and richly rewarded as Wynton and Branford Marsalis have been, their recent sales figures are no better than anyone else's, which may be one reason their future at Columbia is cloudy.

"Seven years ago Joshua and Roy and Marcus were selling 75,000 units," says Goldstein. "But in the last few years the bottom has fallen out."

"Any jazz artist who looks at CDs as a way to make money is being unrealistic," as Evered bluntly puts it. "A lot of artists just don't understand that's the way it is now." It takes nerve for a media conglomerate to invest in new jazz today when rap and teen-pop seem to offer much steeper upside potential. The ratio of cost to return for living artists is one reason the music's dead heroes are so prominent. Why risk 25K touring a quintet who haven't a prayer of airing on MTV when you can mine your catalogue of Miles and Coltrane for nothing?

"It's expensive to break a new act," says Pierson, who has labored to establish Redman, Mehldau, and Garrett among others at Warner Brothers. "It costs between $15–60,000 to make a record, depending on how much you pay the sidemen. But with touring, advertising, and promotion, you're talking about at least another $30–50,000 to market a record you hope will sell 10,000 units. You have to place your bets very carefully and believe that in the long run it will pay off in someone becoming a major artist."

Jazz still has a few advocates like Bruce Lundvall, who has directed Blue Note within the Capitol group for fifteen years—continuity unique in the recent corporate history of the music. But BMG's folding RCA jazz into pop, releasing all artists from their contracts (except Dave Douglas), may be the new corporate paradigm.

"When major labels are recording jazz that is important but doesn't necessarily sell in large numbers, you need someone at the top who cares about it," says Cuscuna. "And there just wasn't anyone at RCA who cared about jazz anymore."

The case of Sony/Columbia, where a commitment to jazz had always emanated from on high, has been a variation on this theme since George Butler's departure in 1996. Jeff Levinson, head of the division for the last three years, worked in tandem with Branford Marsalis, who doubled as artist under contract and creative consultant. During their tenure they issued some superb records, including David Sanchez's sensational *Melaza* and David Ware's *Surrendered*, a brave—if perhaps foolhardy— attempt to make the saxophonist less of a cult figure. Marsalis's own *Requiem*, released in 1999, is maybe the most stirring record anyone in his family has ever made. But none of these cracked the 10–15,000-unit ceiling, and neither has any of the twelve—count 'em, twelve—discs Wynton released on Columbia in 1998 and 1999. Levinson was forced to walk the plank in July 2000. The rest of his department jumped ship soon after.

That Columbia has reconstituted the division under Jeff Jones, director of their reissue imprint Legacy for the last five years, says a great deal about the priorities of jazz at the major labels these days. Jones has no experience producing new records, but neither has he been losing Sony's money. He makes all the right noises about "our commitment to stay in the jazz business." He is negotiating with Branford's agent so that he remains an artist with the label. And although Columbia has no formal ties with Branford's brother anymore, Jones avers that when "the American public sees Wynton Marsalis on the Ken Burns series they will fall in love with him."

At the same time, Jones talks about finding the "most commercial and credible artists we can" and making jazz "fun, so that it's not just for the critics. The trend everywhere is more urban and teen-oriented. I don't think it's just jazz." Every major jazz label to survive must embrace artists who fit a "smooth" format or who create hybrids of pop, fusion, New Age, techno, and rap—trends that Wynton abhors and Burns largely ignores. Jones sounds as perplexed as other executives about the future of straight-ahead jazz within this market. "Over the last couple of years it's been very difficult to sell jazz," he admits. "And I don't really know why."

In fact, why this has happened is actually easier to explain than what to do about it. Jazz may have found a home in academia, but the older infrastructure that supported new talent for much of its history has crumbled over the last twenty years in the US. The music can't be heard anymore on either commercial radio or television; critical writing about jazz on a regular basis in mass-circulation magazines has all but vanished; and the club circuit outside New York has shrunk dramatically. "West of the Hudson things drop off pretty quickly," says Evered. "Where musicians used to make money touring and playing, and using CDs as calling cards, that's disappearing."

"Younger jazz artists are not going to have careers the way that the older ones once did," predicts Cuscuna. "Wynton realized early on that you can't survive for long with recordings or on the road anymore. Building his career at Lincoln Center was a very smart move."

The tradition that Marsalis so ardently touts, in conjunction with technology that gives everyone access to any kind of jazz at the click of a mouse twenty-four hours a day, has created a far more crowded field than existed twenty years ago.

"When Joe Lovano puts out a new record, he's not only competing with his contemporaries for sales," says Cuscuna. "He's also up against Gene Ammons and Coltrane and every record ever made. The whole history of the music is now available on CD, and that's a problem for anyone who hopes to break through."

Of course, it's sales of old records that allow companies to record new ones. Not everyone thinks the ubiquity of the jazz giants is a bad thing either. "The re-releases are setting the bar very high for new players," says Evered. "That should be a challenge." Jones says he loves the new David Sanchez record. But when someone walks into a store with twenty dollars and has to choose between a fresh face and a classic, "it's hard to argue against Miles Davis."

It makes no more sense to blame stifling tradition, as interpreted by Wynton Marsalis, than it does corporate greed or the CD for the sad state of jazz. Every cultural enterprise—from books to movies to other music genres—now competes with its own past, more readily and cheaply available than ever before. There is more of everything now except time. But while books and movies have held their own in this new psycho-economic climate, jazz and classical music have ossified. The painful truth is that if jazz were more popular, its infrastructure would still be strong. Its core constituency, however, has hollowed out.

"The audience for straight jazz is made up of aging white males," says Pierson, with only slight exaggeration. "In ten years, after they've all had heart attacks, it'll be left with no audience."

Younger players have awakened to this rude reality as well. "They come out of school to find out they're playing for an older crowd," says Evered. "The audience they thought would be there when they got out has moved on to other kinds of music."

The dexterity of these musicians is not in question. With Latin timbres and polyrhythms invigorating mainstream practice, the instrumental expertise required to keep with one's peers is higher than ever. Sanchez's *Melaza* makes demands on musicians and listeners alike that exist in no other popular music. Twisty-daredevil compositions and an adrenalized septet, with three percussionists driving the tempo, could in less assured hands spin out in a violent musical wreck. Instead the band burns rubber and hugs every hairpin turn, and within the intricate rhythmic machinery beats a large melodic heart. Sanchez is as hot and cool a player as jazz can put forward at the moment.

"Artistically, the music's in good shape," says Evered. "And let's face it: Jazz is not for beginners. Much of the best is, for want of a better word, cerebral. It will never find a mass audience, and it never did."

But along with Ornette, jazz once upon a time also had Cannonball Adderley and Herbie Hancock with hit records. Before he was a Lincoln Center museum piece, Louis Armstrong made the pop charts. But jazz has no big stars anymore, not with any critical credibility. Classical music is actually healthier when you consider the frenzy over Cecilia Bartoli or Andrea Bocelli, who have posted numbers that jazz best-sellers like Diane Krall and Cassandra Wilson can't touch. The RIAA figures are especially grim when you consider that it defines jazz to include Kenny G.

Smaller record labels will continue to document the most adventurous jazz, as they always have, and the larger ones can stay in the game if they bet smart, stay lean, and don't expect too much. Blue Note has made money every year for fifteen years with a roster of artists in the classic tradition as well as plenty of nontraditional acts like Medeski, Martin & Wood. Even so, eighty to eighty-five percent of the records the company has released during that time are out-of-print.

"I think there's a responsibility that the five major labels remain in the jazz business," says Matt Pierson. "But the mentality of the executives in charge of corporations is different these days. Soon they may no longer see it that way." The loss of RCA leaves only four major labels—Columbia, Blue Note, the now Universal-controlled Verve, and Warner Brothers—still in the business.

Jazz had a fleeting chance to crossover to a mass audience in the early nineties when Branford fronted the *Tonight Show* band. The effort failed for several reasons, mainly chemistry with the host. When Jay Leno re-tooled his show to overtake Letterman's in the ratings, as if to underline how friendless the music identified with Marsalis had become, the new producers added near the top of their list of things to fix: No more jazz players sitting in.

The Ken Burns series may be the last, best hope for jazz to connect with the American public again. No doubt the canonized figures will get another boost. Columbia/Legacy and Verve have released twenty-three CDs keyed to the series, and there's a five-CD Columbia box as well. But jazz of the last forty years is crammed into the last show, with Herbie Hancock, Weather Report, and John McLaughlin receiving short shrift, and Keith Jarrett and Pat Metheny, certainly the best-selling jazz instrumentalists of the last five years, not even mentioned. The record industry and working musicians can only hope that the series, which documents as never before how vital the music has been to twentieth-century American life, doesn't also inadvertently suggest that the greatest players of jazz lived ages ago, in the classical past.

Richard B. Woodward has written about jazz for more than twenty-five years in numerous magazines, newspapers, and books. Currently editor-at-large for *DoubleTake* magazine, he lives in New York City. This article originally appeared in the *Village Voice*, January 16, 2001.

Crossover Schemes: New York Salsa
as Politics, Culture and Commerce
BY KARL HAGSTROM MILLER

Salsa is a powerful cultural force with two sharp edges: one, the objectively progressive effect of representing both national and international expressions, acting as an instrument of cohesion for oppressed people; the second, dominant side, the reactionary role of serving as a medium of bourgeois ideology and carrying all the corrosive features of a bourgeois cultural commodity.

—FELIX CORTES, ANGEL FALCON, AND JUAN FLORES, 1976[1]

World music is popularly believed to be a "roots" phenomenon, an expression of national and ethnic identities and multicultural diversity. Yet, as the analysis of recent examples reveals, world music could also be more properly considered as a typical product of consumer society.

—VEIT ERLMANN, 1996[2]

Twenty years separate the above statements. Despite the changing fashion of word choice within the academy, the authors come to very similar conclusions. Each finds the music under question to express cultural and political values and to be an important site of both national and international identity formation. Yet each goes to great pains to distinguish these attributes from the music's function as a commodity within a capitalist economy. The arguments assume that cultural and political messages are irretrievably altered by the process used for their circulation—McLuhan's "the medium is the message" under a different guise. They also assume that the authentic "roots" of ethnic identity are so fundamentally opposed to capitalism that contact between the two results in the virtual destruction of the former: The music is either one or the other; it cannot be both.

The history of New York salsa music belies such neat distinctions. Between 1965 and 1976, New York City was the center of the creation of this new brand of Latin music. The history of the music can be told as three distinct stories. First, it is a story

1. Cortes, Falcon, and Flores, "The Cultural Expression of Puerto Ricans in New York: A Theoretical Perspective and Critical Review," *Latin American Perspectives*, 3:3 (Summer 1976): p.127.
2. Erlmann, "The Aesthetics of the Global Imagination: Reflections on World Music in the 1990s," *Public Culture* (Summer 1996): p.467.

of the formation of a hybrid musical style. The music was deeply rooted in Afro-Cuban rhythms and forms, yet it was developed primarily by Puerto Rican musicians from East Harlem and the Lower East Side. It often featured strident brass arrangements influenced by big-band jazz and a theatrical performance style not unlike much of the rock music of the period. Second, the story of salsa can be told as the creation of a unique discursive space in which Puerto Ricans in New York found a way to combine their shared cultural heritage with their present concerns and experiences in East Harlem. Through the music, as well as in other spaces, some Newyoricans developed a political stance that combined local politics with a sense of solidarity with all Latinos. Finally, salsa's history can be told as a business success story. The music became a national and international commercial success due to the coordinated work and strategic planning of a number of record labels and the mass media. Its spread throughout the US and the world was due in part to its promotion as both a medium for pan-Latino politics and an infecting dance groove.[3]

These aspects of the music were intimately related. The music's role in galvanizing a grassroots social movement among New York Puerto Ricans was instrumental in the sale of salsa records. Both musicians' political allegiances and their desire to sell records to larger audiences affected the sound of the music. Similarly, the formation of a pan-Latino identity around salsa music rested partially on the national and international distribution of albums by independent and major record companies.[4] This is not to say that the relationships among Puerto Rican nationalism, individual musicians, and commercialism were without conflict. There were indeed struggles between those advocating different relationships to the market or to grassroots polit-

3. A few key examinations of salsa and Latin music in the U. S. include: Cesar Miguel Rondon, *El Libro de la Salsa: Crónica de la Música del Caribe Urbano* (Caracas: Editorial Arte, 1980); Peter Manuel, "Salsa and the Music Industry: Corporate Control or Grassroots Expression?," in Manuel (ed.), *Essays on Cuban Music: North American and Cuban Perspectives* (Lanham: University Press of America, 1991), pp.159–180; and Peter Manuel, "Latin Music in the New World Order: Salsa and Beyond," in Ron Sakolsky and Fred Wei-han Ho (eds.), *Sounding Off!: Music as Subversion/Resistance/Revolution* (New York: Autonomedia, 1995), pp.277–284. See also Ruth Glasser, *My Music is My Flag: Puerto Rican Musicians and Their New York Communities, 1917–1940* (Berkeley: University of California Press, 1995).

4. Overcoming the divide between culture and commerce identified by Cortes et al. and Ehrmann is complicated by a methodological divide within the academic study of popular culture. Chandra Mukerji and Michael Schudson argue that scholars have divided the study of popular culture into what they call the "production-of-culture approach" and the "subjective-experience approach." The first is characterized by a focus on the internal logic of large capitalist organizations. Adherents argue that the agency of either consumers or individual corporate decision-makers plays less a role in the development of commercial cultural products than do the more abstract market structures or organizational environments of particular industries. In contrast, the "subjective-experience approach" focuses on the uses to which popular culture is put by individuals or social groups. Taking its theory less from sociology than from anthropology and linguistics, this approach is concerned with cultural products as discursive texts in which signs and signifiers acquire meaning at the point of consumption rather than production. See Chandra Mukerji and Michael Schudson (eds.), *Rethinking Popular*

ical organizations. Yet the occurrence of such struggles suggests all the more that the political and commercial aspects of the music were deeply intertwined.

Salsa as a Local Music Culture

[T]here is little doubt that salsa, as far as Puerto Rican New Yorkers are concerned, is a musical vehicle for making a political statement to the world, but especially to the broad Anglo community in the New York metropolitan area. The statement, in fact, can be verbalized as follows: We will not be amalgamated.
—DAVID MEDINA, BILLBOARD, 1976[5]

At one point in 1964, the only place one could buy Johnny Pacheco's new album was from the trunk of his car. The percussionist and flutist had spent almost a decade performing and recording with some of the biggest Latin musicians in New York. He had backed Tito Puente in the fifties and had ushered in the 1960 *charanga* craze with Charlie Palmieri and his Dubonéy Orchestra. He had also racked up experience with several record labels including industry heavyweight United Artists and Alegre Records, the largest independent Latin label in the country. Yet by 1964 Pacheco was disillusioned with the existing labels and what he saw as their uneven treatment of Latino musicians. Since the 1920s, major labels such as RCA Victor and CBS had maintained Latin catalogues under their "ethnic" division, tossing low-quality products onto the shelves with little incentive to reinvest their profits in a market they believed lacked ongoing growth potential. The majors, however, hoped that each new genre, from the tango to the *pachanga*, could be successfully marketed to non-Latino consumers. Each time, the labels lost interest once the latest dance craze had past, and the musicians and their Latino supporters dropped from the labels' sights. To avoid again falling prey to such "rip-off" techniques, Pacheco founded Fania

Culture: Contemporary Perspectives in Cultural Studies (Berkeley: University of California Press, 1991), pp.26–32. The scholarship that falls into these two camps is too numerous to detail, so I will limit myself to mentioning two recent studies. The first, an example of the production approach, is Richard Burnett's *The Global Jukebox: The International Music Industry* (New York: Routledge, 1996). Burnett does the very important task of exploring the corporate consolidation and integration that has taken place within the music industry over the past thirty years, yet he remains unable or unwilling to say anything about the effects this process has had on either the music that is produced or the ways in which consumers use popular music in their daily lives. A recent example of the subjective approach is George Lipsitz's latest book, *Dangerous Crossroads: Popular Music, Postmodernism and the Poetics of Place* (London: Verso, 1994). Lipsitz traces the complex intermingling of musical cultures within contemporary diasporic populations, yet he utterly fails to examine the active role played by transnational entertainment corporations in making this possible and profitable. In the history of salsa, the cultural and political meanings of the music were intimately linked to the ways in which record companies promoted and distributed their products, so the scholarly divide identified by Mukerji and Schudson must be overcome.
5. David Medina, "Salsa is also a Political Force," *Billboard* (June 12, 1976): p.6.

Records with lawyer Jerry Massucci and began driving around to local New York Latin retailers with the label's products. Over the next decade Fania grew exponentially, and by 1976 the label controlled the lion's share of a multi-million-dollar local salsa industry.[6]

The salsa industry in New York during the late sixties and early seventies was part and parcel of a larger movement for Puerto Rican political and cultural nationalism. One cannot be understood without the other. Pacheco and Massucci had designs to create a label by and for the local Latino community. Early Fania recordings by such artists as Willie Colon, Ray Barretto, and the Fania All Stars spoke directly to the lives and concerns of much of the East Harlem Puerto Rican population. Fania and its expanding roster of artists developed direct links with members of the Young Lords and with Izzy Sanabria, founder of the magazine *Latin NY*. These three organizations shared resources, ideas, and personnel in order to achieve two explicit goals. First was the development of a base of commercial and political support for Latino-controlled institutions within the Newyorican community. Toward this goal the small-scale, local distribution of Fania, *Latin NY*, and *Palante*, the Lords' weekly newspaper, was an asset for growth rather than a liability. Each was able to address the specific issues and experiences of the community rather than cover the more general concerns of a larger readership. Second, the three organizations worked separately and together to promote the "recognition" of Puerto Ricans and Latinos by non-Latino political and commercial organizations. Yet they demanded that such recognition be on their own terms.

When Pacheco started Fania, he was by no means the only one dissatisfied with the Latin music being released by major record companies. The music industry that had discouraged Pacheco had also failed to hold on to the young generation of working-class Puerto Rican music fans in New York. The majors were pushing a style of music devoid of any local content. Pablo "Yoruba" Guzman later described the music of the period as an "'international' Latin that was really a bleached upper-class 'hispanic' equivalent of Caterina Valente and Connie Francis."[7] In the late sixties, young Newyoricans began dancing to artists like Willie Colon who came from and spoke to their community. Colon, whose first album, *El Malo*, was released by Fania in 1967 when the trombonist was still a teenager, did not play music that endeared him to the

6. Rondon, *Salsa*, pp.49–50; Manuel, *Salsa*, pp.164–167; Manuel, "Latin Music," pp.277–279; Ray Terrace, "Fania's First Ten: N.Y. Label is Broadening the Base for its Music," *Billboard* (October 25, 1975): p.57.
7. Pablo "Yoruba" Guzman, "Siempre Salsa!," *Village Voice* (June 25, 1979): p.92.

established Latin music industry. Yet his songs about daily life in *El Barrio*, set to a beat that combined Latin percussion with African-American R&B grooves, were an instant success with his peers.[8]

Colon's hybrid music can be partially understood in terms of the historical role of Puerto Rican musicians in both the predominantly African-American neighborhood of East Harlem and New York City as a whole. Ruth Glasser has examined and identified the unique position held by many Puerto Rican musicians within the New York scene between the world wars. She suggests Puerto Rican musicians often created alliances with their African-American counterparts based on shared musical roots and an understanding of their common marginalization and oppression within US society. At the same time, many Puerto Rican musicians were able to work as important contributors to white swing bands, accessing dance halls and other jobs unavailable to many equally skilled African-American musicians. Thus, Glasser argues, many Puerto Ricans were able to elide the strict racial segregation that characterized the swing era and provide specific human links between white and black bands. Similarly, skilled Puerto Rican musicians were able to cross ethnic barriers within the Latin music industry, playing integral roles in the development of a pan-Latino style by combining their experiences with both Cuban and Mexican music in the city. This "paradoxical ethnicity," as Glasser dubs it, operated in two ways. On the one hand, it granted many Puerto Ricans access to a large variety of musical situations. They enjoyed relative economic security, as well as opportunities for creative innovation that were denied many African-American and white musicians unable to cross racial barriers within the music industry. On the other hand, such fluid racial and ethnic identity often hindered the articulation of a specifically New York–Puerto Rican identity.[9]

By the late sixties this was beginning to change. Musicians such as Colon, Pacheco, and conga player Ray Barretto began incorporating more "traditional" Puerto Rican elements into their music. Colon and Barretto fostered a resurgence of the *plena*, a musical form indigenous to the island that had been practically ignored by US Latin musicians since the 1930s. The *plena* held particular importance to

8. Tito Puente derided the young Colon for playing "kiddie music." See Vernon Boggs, "Visions and Views of Salsa Promoter Izzy 'Mr. Salsa' Sanabria: Popularizing Music," in Boggs, *Salsiology: Afro-Cuban Music and the Evolution of Salsa in New York City* (New York: Excelsior, 1992), p.191. For background on Colon, see Cesar Miguel Rondon, *El Libro de la Salsa: Crónica de la Música del Caribe Urbano* (Caracas: Editorial Arte, 1980), pp.49–50.

9. See Glasser, *My Music*; see also Ruth Glasser, "Paradoxical Ethnicity: Puerto Rican Musicians in Post World War II New York City," *Latin American Music Review*, 11:1 (June, 1990): pp.63–72.

Puerto Rican nationalists. Since it was one of the few Puerto Rican styles that did not have direct roots in Cuba, many argued that the *plena* should be considered the national music of Puerto Rico. Colon also hired Yomo Toro, a virtuoso of the guitar-like Puerto Rican *cuatro*, thereby bringing the instrument increased exposure. For Barretto, these moves were accompanied by a reinterpretation of the music that was being made throughout the US. In the 1960s, he later explained, "the whole basis of American rhythm . . . changed from the old dotted-note jazz shuffle rhythm to a straight-ahead straight-eighth approach, which is Latin."[10] These artists were but part of an exploding Newyorican salsa scene that gave rise to neighborhood retail stores, clubs like El Cheetah, and Fania, the label that was in the position to profit most from the artistic shift toward Puerto Rican traditionalism.

Similar changes were afoot outside of the Latin music scene. The year 1969 marked the formation of the Young Lords Organization (later the Young Lords Party) in East Harlem. The grassroots, pan-ethnic group maintained a dual commitment to community-based action and support programs and the promotion of Puerto Rican pride and nationalism. Influenced by both the Black Power movement and the historical struggle for Puerto Rican independence, the Lords offered a "Thirteen-Point Program and Platform" demanding a socialist society, Latino community control of its own institutions, education about Afro-Indio culture, and self-determination for all Latinos. The platform also stated an opposition to "capitalists and other traitors" who "are paid by the system to lead our people down blind alleys."[11] The value the Lords placed on Latino culture hinted at the possibilities of alliances with salsa musicians such as Colon and Barretto, yet the Party's opposition to capitalism meant that their relationship to the local salsa "industry" was less than perfect.

In a number of articles, writers for *Palante* insisted that all music was inherently political and that a music's politics were often connected to the economic motives of the musicians. Deriding certain unnamed salsa bands that refused to donate their services for a Lords benefit, one writer claimed, "These bands have our people, mostly young, dancing while they reap in all the profits. This music pacifies us and keeps our minds away from the realities of life—poor housing, poor health care, bru-

10. Roberts, *Latin Tinge*, p.160–164; On the discussion of the *plena* as a national music of Puerto Rico, see Jorge Duany, "Popular Music in Puerto Rico: Toward an Anthropology of Salsa," *Latin American Music Review*, 5:2 (Fall/Winter 1984): pp.192–194; Peter Manuel, "Puerto Rican Music and Cultural Identity: Creative Appropriation of Cuban Sources from Danza to Salsa," *Ethnomusicology*, 38:2 (1994): pp.249–280.
11. The "Young Lords Party Thirteen-Point Program and Platform" was printed, among other places, on the last pages of every issue of the party newspaper *Palante*.

tality from the police, poor jobs, etc." In contrast, the writer praised Ray Barretto for both his continued support of the Lords and the content of his music: "Music should be revolutionary. It should reflect the culture, the history, and the experiences of the people . . . Bands like Ray Barretto give these messages to our people. These bands comprehend the necessity of change. They do not need to play for money because they have love and respect for our people, which will help them to survive."[12] It is important to note that the writer praised Barretto for both the content of his music and his economic support of the Young Lords; a number of participants in the salsa scene would continue to conflate these two in coming years.

Barretto took his support for the Lords beyond just playing benefit concerts. He also employed leaders of the Party to write the liner notes for several of his Fania albums. Lords spokesman Felipe Luciano, for example, wrote the notes for Barretto's 1972 *Que Viva la Musica*, and the former Young Lords Minister of Information, Pablo "Yoruba" Guzman, wrote the notes for Barretto's self-titled 1975 Fania album. The presence of Young Lords on Ray Barretto's albums suggests that Barretto shared their political concerns and goals. It also indicates that he and others at Fania believed that a market for the albums existed among those either directly involved in the organization or those sympathetic to its goals. Historically, record companies have understood liner notes primarily as a form of advertising. It is therefore unlikely that Fania would repeatedly employ Lords to write notes unless they believed that the authors' identities as activists would prompt sales.[13]

One complication of this theory is that Guzman was not identified as a Young Lord on *Barretto* but as the associate editor of *Latin NY* magazine. One year prior to the album's release, Guzman (depending on who is telling the story) had quit or had been kicked out of a Lords organization that was crumbling under the pressure of both internal disagreements and infiltration by a number of government counter-intelligence organizations. The activist was moving away from the strictly anti-capitalist philosophy of the official Young Lords platform, leaning instead toward the pursuit of Puerto Rican political goals through the promotion of Newyorican culture. Toward this end he worked at *Latin NY* and later as public relations director for

12. "Music Belongs to the People," *Palante*, 3:2 (January 1971): p.7.
13. For an interpretation of the historical role of liner notes, see Frank Kofsky, *Black Nationalism and the Revolution in Music* (New York: Pathfinder Press, 1970). For a confirmation of the role of nationalist movements in the sale of Latin music, see Earl Paige, "Midwest Sparkles with Hot Sales," *Billboard* (November 25, 1972): p.13. When Paige asked Harry Frenkel, owner of Chicago's Pan-American Records, to explain the recent rise in Latin sales, Frenkel responded, "Everyone has heard of black power, but now we have brown power."

Fania.[14] Guzman's ambiguous presence on the album is symbolic of the changes that were occurring within both the salsa industry and the Puerto Rican political movement. Each was struggling to achieve a new balance between politics and commerce. In 1975, when the album was released, Guzman's public identity within the Puerto Rican community may still have been as a Lord. For consumers who were not aware or supportive of the Young Lords, however, the album's liner notes were provided not by a Puerto Rican nationalist, but by the associate editor of a magazine identified by the mainstream press as an insider's guide to the latest dance craze.

Newyorican graphic artists Izzy Sanabria and Walter Velez started *Latin NY* in 1973. The magazine began as a small, English-language flyer that listed where and when salsa music could be found in New York. It presented a cohesive image of the local salsa community by establishing links between radio programs, record stores, live concerts, and dances. Sanabria quickly became the voice of the magazine. The young entrepreneur shared several views with the Young Lords. First, he believed that only Latino-owned media could properly represent the Newyorican community. Second, like *Palante*, *Latin NY* became an important venue for internal debates regarding the relationship between Newyoricans and dominant cultural and political powers, as Sanabria dedicated increasing amounts of his editorial space to such discussions. Again echoing some writers in *Palante*, Sanabria believed that mainstream visibility and recognition of Puerto Ricans' culture were central to their political and economic advancement. Yet the conclusions reached by Sanabria and the Lords regarding how to achieve such recognition and what it would look like were decidedly different.[15]

While the Lords focused on Puerto Rican culture as a tool for the development of power, unity, and strength within the Latino population, *Latin NY* emphasized the power of Puerto Rican culture to teach non-Latinos about the living conditions in *El Barrio*. Writers for the magazine also saw salsa as a possible ticket to visibility and

---

14. It is unclear what instigated this shift. Guzman himself claims that the Lords were "kids" that could not overcome the factionalism and dogma that plagued many organizations on the left. He had to move on to other things. See Pablo Guzman, "La Vida Pura: A Lord of the Barrio," *Village Voice* (March 21, 1995): pp.24–31. Marina Roseman, however, claims that political repression forced several within the Puerto Rican nationalist movement to turn away from direct action toward the media and the arts. Even this transition is rather ambiguous. One former Lord she interviewed saw it less as a break than as a shift in the type of art that they were producing: "When we were in the party, I realized that this was nothing but theater, and we had to be theatrical about what we did." See Marina Roseman, "The New Rican Village: Taking Control of the Image-Making Machinery," *New York Folklore*, 6:1–2 (1980): p.46. Perhaps more to the point, neither Guzman nor Roseman identify the change from direct action to cultural production as contradictory. They instead see it as a practical response to the political environment in which Puerto Rican activists found themselves in the mid-seventies. Also see Guzman, "Siempre Salsa!," *Village Voice* (June 25, 1979): p.92; for more background on the Young Lords, see the video by Iris Morales, *Palante, Siempre, Palante, The Young Lords* (1996).
15. "The Story of Latin NY," *Latin NY* (May 1977): pp.29–40.

power within the American mainstream. Sanabria repeatedly described the importance of positive representations of Puerto Ricans in the non-Latino media as a means of gaining entrance to the corridors of political power. Salsa, he hoped, would provide the elusive key.

The English content of *Latin NY* thus served two purposes for Sanabria. First, it catered to a demographic that he claimed had been overlooked by existing English- and Spanish-language media: second- and third-generation working-class Puerto Rican immigrants to New York whose primary language was English yet who still maintained a strong cultural identification with Puerto Rico. Their working-class identity, strengthened by several years of Young Lords activity, alienated them from much of the Spanish media, which instead courted the middle-class Latino population. At the same time, they found little coverage of Puerto Rican culture and politics in the English press. *Latin NY*, Sanabria proudly maintained, filled this void. Second, his English-language magazine provided an important vehicle to spread information about Newyoricans to the non-Latino population and consumers. He succeeded, and dominant media soon seized on the magazine as an important window into the burgeoning New York salsa scene. It is again important to understand how these two goals were mutually reinforcing and made possible by the local character of the magazine and the community it represented. Sanabria took full advantage of his role as industry spokesman, often reprinting mainstream coverage of his magazine and using the ways in which he was represented as a springboard for his editorials. He criticized the racism of the mainstream media and the ways in which writers denigrated or characterized Newyorican culture. He then theorized about how Newyoricans could better represent themselves to the non-Latino press in order to more effectively achieve their political goals. Sanabria thus effected a continuous redefinition of Newyorican culture in dialectical engagement with the dominant media. He, like the Lords, pursued "recognition" by white America, yet demanded that the recognition be on Newyoricans' terms.[16]

Latin NY pursued recognition for Latinos, but it was also a consumer magazine. The publication was perhaps the most important place in which new salsa albums were advertised, reviewed, and otherwise brought to the attention of record buyers.

16. *Ibid*, pp.6–7; Izzy Sanabria, "Publisher's Page: Why Salsa & Latin New Yorkers Aren't Recognized (Part 2)," *Latin NY* (June-July 1977): pp.6–7, 65. Regarding the mainstream media's use of Sanabria as a spokesperson for the local salsa community, see Boggs, "Sanabria," pp.187–89. For specific examples, see Ray Terrace, "Latin Music Ignored by Academy," *Billboard* (March 22, 1975): p.33; and Stewart Alter, "Are Second Generation Hispanics Seeking New Media Experiences?," *Advertising News from New York* (May 21, 1976): p.8.

The magazine's relationship to the music industry can best be illustrated by examining its connections to Fania; *Latin NY* and the record label were integrated in a number of important ways. First, graphic artist Izzy Sanabria was the chief album-cover designer for the label. Sanabria first became recognized as an important member of the salsa community as the designer of early albums by Johnny Pacheco. He believed that Latin albums needed professional artwork in order to both become commercial successes and promote positive images of Latino culture. "Growing up in New York City as a Latin Artist," he recalled, "I was always concerned about the negative images that were projected about Latins in all the media. Latin covers was just one of them and one which I thought might be within my reach."[17] Pacheco and Fania gave him the opportunity. Second, Fania gave important financial support to the magazine through a key loan and extensive ongoing advertising.[18] Third, *Latin NY* offered important coverage to Fania artists. In the second annual *"Latin NY* Music Awards," for example, Fania artists received twenty out of the thirty prizes awarded.[19] Fourth, both were intimately involved in lobbying the National Association of Recording Arts and Sciences to include a Latin category in its annual Grammy Awards. This campaign both pressured industry leaders to recognize the power of Latin consumers and called for "unity" within the Latin-American population as an important precursor to change.[20] Finally, as mentioned, the two shared the services of Guzman.

Salsa "Crossover": Major Labels, Independents, and Musicians

We think Columbia Records is particularly well-suited to maintain its leadership of the recorded music industry. Because of the versatility of our catalogue—which covers literally every point of the music spectrum—we can and do capitalize on the rapidly changing public tastes.

—ARTHUR TAYLOR, PRESIDENT OF CBS, 1973[21]

Since the inception of the record industry near the turn of the century, a few major companies have dominated sales, and those companies have also produced "ethnic"

---

17. Izzy Sanabria, "Latin Album Covers Reflect Music's Sophistication," *Billboard* (July 27, 1974): p.30.
18. "The Story of Latin NY," p.31.
19. See Fania advertisement in *Latin NY* (June–July 1976): p.39. This incredible success may seem like nepotism (and perhaps it was), yet Fania was reportedly having equal economic success. See Rudy Garcia, "Salsa is Exploding," *Billboard* (June 12, 1976). Garcia reports that Fania controlled seventy percent of the entire salsa market.
20. "The Story of Latin NY," p.39; "Latin Scene," *Billboard* (February 23, 1974): p.26; Terrace, "Latin Music Ignored," p.33.
21. Richard A. Peterson and David G. Berger, "Cycles in Production: The Case of Popular Music" [1975], reprinted in Simon Frith and Andrew Goodwin (eds.), *On Record: Rock, Pop & the Written Word* (New York: Pantheon, 1990), p.155.

recordings for US immigrant markets. Between 1900 and 1920, Victor and RCA issued thousands of recordings to cater to the diverse range of immigrants that were entering the US. Columbia similarly developed a large "ethnic" division—between 1908 and 1923 the company produced six thousand "foreign" records as opposed to five thousand "domestic" releases during the same period. Often the recordings were made and marketed by the companies' foreign subsidiaries and then reproduced for domestic consumption. The pressings were usually limited to a few thousand copies, and industry executives saw the records primarily as incentives for immigrants to purchase phonographs. The labels' commitment to their "ethnic" divisions waned as the market for phonographs became saturated in the 1920s, yet it was periodically rejuvenated as various "ethnic" genres gained wider popularity among American consumers.[22]

Latin music in the United States has experienced a number of such waves of popularity. The tango craze of the 1910s and 1920s found Latin rhythms appearing in dancehalls and theater shows throughout New York City. For a brief time Cuban and Puerto Rican musicians in the city found their skills in demand both within their own neighborhoods and among the predominantly white audiences in downtown nightclubs. Throughout much of the 1930s *rumbas* sold well with white audiences and a minor industry developed to produce English-language versions of Cuban songs. Many non-Latino composers and musicians got in on the act and began including Latin elements in their performances. The forties, John Storm Roberts argues, were a high point for the popularity of Latin music in the US. Hollywood produced numerous Latin musicals and promoted a number of Latino stars to national fame. The seedbed was also planted for the flowering of Cubop and Latin big-band jazz in the early fifties as African-American and Latino musicians increasingly played together and sought ways to integrate their music. Fania star Ray Barretto was, in fact, an important part of this scene, playing with Charlie Parker and Max Roach, among others. The fifties also saw the growth of a *mambo* scene among white dancers as well as a developing non-Latino audience for Tejano and Mexican *conjunto* music from the Southwest.[23]

22. Pekka Gronow, "Ethnic Recordings: An Introduction," *Ethnic Recordings in America: A Neglected Heritage* (Washington, D.C.: American Folklife Center, 1982), pp.1–10.
23. Roberts, *Latin Tinge*; Glasser, *My Music*; Lise Waxer, "Of Mambo Kings and Songs of Love: Dance Music in Havana and New York from the 1930s to the 1950s," *Latin American Music Review*, 15:2 (Fall/Winter 1994): pp.139–176; Peter Narváez, "The Influences of Hispanic Music Cultures on African-American Blues Musicians," *Black Music Research Journal*, 14:2 (Spring, 1994): pp.203–24.

Each of these "crossover" successes must be understood in terms of the coming together of three groups with three different concerns: the major companies in the music industry searching within their "ethnic" divisions for music with "crossover" potential; the independent labels, who, as we have seen in the case of Fania, may have displayed some combination of economic and political understandings of "crossover"; and, certainly not least important, the musicians themselves, who in many cases discussed crossover in terms of both advancing their careers and exercising their artistic freedom to perform and compose with a diverse array of other musicians.

The major record labels attempted to gain from each of the successive waves of Latin music popularity, yet the artists that brought each genre to the ears of non-Latinos were often signed to small, independent labels. The major Cuban-influenced output of Dizzy Gillespie, for example, was recorded for minor labels such as Vogue and Verve. Similarly, Tito Puente and Tito Rodriguez recorded many of their hit records for Tico and West Side Latino respectively.[24] By the time the New York salsa scene was developing, several of the majors, especially RCA and CBS, had dedicated themselves to the incorporation of the new music into their companies.[25]

Columbia Records' attempts to integrate itself into the soul-music market offer a hint about how the majors approached the Latin market. Painfully aware of the profits that were being made by independent soul labels in the late sixties, Columbia hired the Harvard University Business School to conduct an industry survey and develop a "plan of action" for the record company. The report, titled "A Study of the Soul Music Environment Prepared for Columbia Records Group," was submitted in mid-1972. It detailed how the soul labels, black retail stores, and especially black radio were important to fostering both soul and Top 40 hits. One section of the report concluded:

---

24. Roberts, *Latin Tinge*, pp.234–238. Sergio Santana, *¿Que es la Salsa?: Buscando la Melodia . . .* (Medellín: Ediciones Salsa y Cultura, 1992), pp.154–169.

25. Peterson and Berger, "Cycles," pp.140–59. Sociologists Peterson and Berger suggest that the repeated success of independents in breaking new popular musical trends is no accident. Their survey of the corporate composition of the American Top 40 between 1948 and 1973 maintains that there has been an inverse relationship between industry consolidation and musical heterogeneity. In other words, they find that as more independents were able to get into the Top 40, the musical style and lyrical content of the songs became more diverse, and vice versa. In order to explain their findings, Peterson and Berger suggest a cyclical model of the recording industry that looks something like this: Corporate consolidation and the attempts to repeat past commercial successes lead record companies to produce very similar music; as audiences become bored with listening to the same music over and over, they begin to turn toward different sounds produced by small independents; when such independents begin to have commercial successes the majors establish a business relationship with them and begin to pressure them to repeat their initial successes.

In sum, soul radio is of strategic importance to the record companies for two principal reasons: First, it provides access to a large and growing record-buying public, namely, the black consumer. Second, and for some of the record companies more important, it is perhaps the most effective way of getting a record to a Top 40 playlist.

The report insisted that soul stations remained underutilized routes to Top 40 radio. Disc jockeys at black radio stations, the report explained, maintained a larger control over the songs that they played than did their Top 40 counterparts. "The discretionary part of the Top 40 playlists, on the other hand, is more often selected from among those new releases which have gotten on and stayed on other playlists, such as soul." Black radio thus served as a launching ground for Top 40 material, with about thirty percent of the songs on the national pop charts originating on the soul charts.[26]

The report also suggested that CBS acquire market share through three methods: a long-term program of market integration to outflank the other majors such as RCA and Capitol, and talent raids and distribution deals with the independents in order to access profits without incurring the costs of artistic development. As Nelson George reports, Columbia at least took the latter advice and the number of major black artists on the label rose dramatically from two in 1971 to 125 by the end of the decade.[27] CBS, Columbia Records' parent company, also appears to have used the lessons of the Harvard Report in its approach to the Latin music market.

The US Latin market was smaller than the market for soul, but similarly controlled by a few independent companies. The majors began to show interest in Latin music around 1969 after virtually ignoring it for over a decade. The increasing industry attention to Latin music can be charted through its coverage in *Billboard*. The coverage between 1968 and 1977 can be broken down into three basic periods. From 1968 to 1972 coverage of Latin music in the magazine was almost nonexistent. The few articles that were written focused on the increased demand for the music among Latinos.[28] In late 1972, Latin coverage increased notably (at least partial evidence that the campaigns for Latino "recognition" by *Latin NY* and others within the salsa community were having an effect on the dominant industry). On November 25, 1972,

26. Harvard University Graduate School of Business Administration, "A Study of the Soul Music Environment Prepared for Columbia Records Group" (May 11, 1972): pp.8–9. The author would like to thank Norman Kelley for supplying a copy of the report.

27. Nelson George, *The Death of Rhythm & Blues* (New York: E.P. Dutton, 1988), pp.135–138.

28. See, for example, Claude Hall, "Latins in US Are Starving for Latin Music: Roulette's Levy," *Billboard* (April 27, 1968): p.6; and "Latin American Beat on Upswing Globally: Garcia," *Billboard* (December 27, 1969): p.39.

Billboard published a supplement titled "Latin Explosion," which highlighted the exponential growth of a number of regional Latin scenes, including New York salsa. The magazine then began featuring a weekly Latin column and included Latin sales charts broken down by city. The supplement maintained a careful balance between Latino markets already flourishing on independent labels and the potential for the music among non-Latinos, possibly because it was unclear which way future sales would develop. Very quickly thereafter, however, the magazine's focus began a decided shift toward assessing the potential for crossover. This trend would slowly continue over the next several years. When *Billboard* published its next major supplement regarding the music in 1976, "Salsa Explosion," little was said about salsa as a local music phenomenon. The focus was almost exclusively on marketing the music nationally to pop and disco fans.[29]

CBS, in accordance with the Harvard Report and the industry-wide appreciation of Latin music displayed in *Billboard*, integrated itself into the salsa industry. By 1972 CBS had signed the label Caytronics to distribute its Latin catalogue, giving itself a foot in the door if ever a Caytronics artist was to need the wider distribution. More substantially, in 1975 Columbia signed the Fania All Stars, the independent's best-selling group, to produce a number of disco-based albums in order to pick up on the biggest national dance craze of that fall, the Latin Hustle.[30]

Jerry Massucci was not sitting around his Fania office oblivious to the growing attention major labels were paying to regional Latin artists. He, like executives at other independent Latin labels, had actively been pursuing a crossover success since at least 1971. A number of people within the salsa scene took very explicit steps to promote the music to non-Latino consumers, advancing many of the specific political concerns of Newyoricans in the process.

In 1971 Massucci produced and nationally distributed a full-length film titled *Our Latin Thing (Nuestra Cosa)*. The film featured the Fania All Stars and alternated between scenes of the group playing to a sold-out audience at the Cheetah nightclub and portrayals of street life in the Newyorican neighborhoods of East Harlem and the Lower East Side. It implied a direct relationship between the Newyoricans' everyday lives and the brand of salsa music and dancing evidenced at the concert. The film

29. "Salsa Explosion," *Billboard* (June 12, 1976): pp.1–23.
30. Caytronics advertisement, *Billboard* (November 25, 1972): p.1–3; "Fania All Stars Cut Album in L.A.," *Billboard* (November 1, 1975): p.65.

itself became something of a crossover, reaching more viewers than any Fania album had and eventually grossing over $700,000. It gave many white consumers their first exposure to salsa, either by directly seeing the movie or through reading some of the numerous reviews of the film that appeared in media with a predominantly white readership such as *Rolling Stone*, *Time*, and *Newsweek*. Such national exposure in the mainstream media might have been an important cause for the increased attention *Billboard* began giving salsa soon after.[31]

Massucci also began attempting to get Fania records onto black radio. He claimed black radio was a logical first step in creating a larger audience for the music, due to the similarities between salsa and the R&B of the period. "An increase in airplay," he told *Billboard*, "will do a lot to educate the non-Latin to Latin sounds and to eventually strengthen the overall market." His view of black radio as an entry into the US charts and the importance he placed on developing a knowledgeable promotion team echoed several of the suggestions that Harvard had made to Columbia Records. This implies that a salsa crossover was being equally pursued by the majors and the independents, albeit from different positions of power within the industry.[32]

Massucci and others also attempted to create a salsa crossover by bringing the sound and recording of the music more in line with that of the Top 40 of the period. Like Sanabria regarding Latin album covers, Massucci suggested that professional production of salsa albums was necessary before the music would be able to compete with that produced by the major labels. Most Latin albums were still being hastily recorded virtually live in the studio using two-track or four-track equipment. This was in part due to budget constraints of the Latin labels. In another sense it was a result of the lack of Latino-controlled recording studios. Sound engineers who had access to more advanced multi-track equipment rarely had experience recording the complex Afro-Cuban rhythms and arrangements played by salsa bands, and vice versa. Fania alleviated the problem by developing a relationship with Good

---

31. Rondon, *Salsa*, pp.51–52; Jim Melanson, "Salsa Gets Television Network Promotion," *Billboard* (March 8, 1975): p.35. Pablo Guzman gave *Our Latin Thing* a mixed review in *Palante*. His concerns indicate the compromises that Massucci had made in order to promote salsa to a national audience. First, Guzman praised the film for being one of the first commercial movies to show the reality of Puerto Ricans' lives in *El Barrio*, including the poverty, the housing conditions, and the routine police harassment. It provided positive and diverse representations of Newyoricans, and simply by doing that, Guzman argued, it was better than any major film that preceded it. Judged against other locally produced art, however, it failed, for it did not explicitly endorse political change or struggle. As discussed here, the relationship between national recognition and the local political meanings of salsa were again in tension. See Pablo Guzman, "Film Review: *Our Latin Thing?*," *Palante* (August 4, 1972): p.9.
32. Jim Melanson, "Fania to Romance Black Radio," *Billboard* (January 6, 1973): pp.1, 11.

Vibrations, a state-of-the-art sixteen-track recording studio, in early 1972. This gave Fania artists access to the overdubbing, multi-tracking, and rich stereo separation already evident on many pop records, thus overcoming another obstacle to crossover. By the end of the year, Good Vibrations was getting enough work from the label that it acquired the nickname "The Fania Studio."[33]

The advanced equipment at Good Vibrations not only served Fania's dreams of commercial success, it also provided a new level of artistic freedom to the musicians, who often viewed crossover in terms of both profits and the ability to record what, and with whom, they wanted. From the perspective of the musicians involved, the process of crossover was quite complex. It was not, as Veit Erhmann suggests in the statement that started this essay, simply a capitulation of roots music to market forces. Rather, it was at times a denial of the false marketing categories imposed upon music by the record industry.

The example of Ray Barretto illustrates this point particularly well, for his relationship to Newyorican politics has already been established. Born in Brooklyn, yet raised in the Puerto Rican community of East Harlem, Barretto had maintained a profitable musical presence in New York for over twenty years. His success was based on a virtuosity and versatility that enabled him to find work playing in a vast array of styles and situations. In the early fifties, Barretto played with bebop musicians such as Charlie Parker, Max Roach, and Nat Adderley in both Harlem and the midtown clubs around 52nd Street. Later in the decade he performed on a number of influential rhythm & blues dates. As a band-leader he had a minor hit in 1961 with "El Watusi," a precursor to the boogaloo style of Latin-influenced R&B that would create a sensation in the second half of the decade. Finally, his impassioned playing garnered him gigs with mainstream rock heavyweights such as the Rolling Stones.[34]

Such genre-hopping and collaboration with African-American and white musicians placed Barretto squarely within the long tradition of Puerto Rican music-making in New York identified by Ruth Glasser. Barretto did not view the crossover of salsa into the pop-music market as a betrayal or denial of the music's roots within the Puerto Rican community but as a continuation of the type of musical combinations he had long been pursuing. He actively supported Puerto Rican nationalism

33. Sam Sutherland, "N.Y. Studio Scene: Sessions Get More Sophisticated, Experimental," *Billboard* (November 25, 1972): p.1–12.
34. John Storm Roberts, *Latin Tinge: The Impact of Latin American Music on the United States* (Originally printed in 1979; Reprinted in *Trivoli: Original Music*, 1985), pp.137, 161–63; J. L. Torres, "The Essential Flight of Ray Barretto," *Latin NY* (March 1977): p.26–29.

and "traditional" music, yet refused to allow the industry to pigeonhole him within one genre and market him only to Latino listeners. Barretto viewed artistic creativity, financial security, and crossover as equal parts of the same issue. "If we keep doing what we have been doing," he explained in 1976, "we are not going to get out of the 'cuchfrito circuit' and we'll still be playing the small clubs on weekend dates for a few hundred dollars a week. We have got to expand our musical consciousness and develop our talents to the fullest."[35]

The brand of salsa that started in the late sixties within the Puerto Rican neighborhoods of New York became something of a national phenomenon by 1975. Its success was the result of concerted efforts by major record companies such as CBS, independent labels, and salsa musicians to promote the music beyond Latino consumers. For some, such crossover was pursued in the hopes of increasing their profits. Others, however, saw the promotion of salsa as part of a larger program to gain recognition for Newyorican and Latino concerns both throughout the nation and across the globe.

Salsa As a Transnational Music Culture

Salsa is like an international urban folklore. Salsa is the folklore of the city—not of one city, but of all cities in Latin America. —RUBEN BLADES (MUSICIAN)[36]

In the 1976 *Billboard* supplement, "Salsa Explosion," David Medina identified salsa's roots in the Puerto Rican nationalism movement in New York as a potential obstacle to crossover. However, he assured his readers that once the music was picked up by Latinos in other countries it "will cease to be a New York phenomenon and a political statement and will become [a] truly representative genre of Latin music."[37] Medina was only half right. From about 1971, the New York salsa sound began to spread throughout much of Latin America due in part to the concerted marketing campaigns of Latin record labels and distributors. Salsa did lose much of its local content as performers and fans in other Latin American countries picked it up. Similarly, as salsa was increasingly marketed internationally by companies like Fania, New York musicians began to incorporate song forms and lyrics that would hold spe-

35. Rudy Garcia, "Salsa is Exploding!!!," *Billboard* (June 12, 1976): p.1–2;.
36. *Salsa: New York and Puerto Rico*, video produced by Shanachie (1985).
37. Medina, "Political Force," p.1–10.

cific meanings in other regions. Yet the diminution of salsa's local content did not also imply its forfeiture of political content. From the early 1970s, several proponents described salsa as a potential source of pan-Latino solidarity. The international dissemination of the music by record companies helped the music play a role in the formation of such an identity by providing music fans throughout Latin America with shared experiences and cultural texts. Salsa was a transnational style in at least three important ways: its relationship to Cuban music, its role within a pan-ethnic and internationalist political movement in New York, and its promotion by Latin labels that were increasingly transnational themselves.

Salsa was an outgrowth of Afro-Cuban rhythms and forms that had a long history of transnational movement and influence. Early Cuban music was the result of intermingling between first peoples on the island, Spanish colonists, and Africans forcibly brought as slaves. Island inhabitants created a hybrid style that retained aspects of its three dominant influences: Spanish ten-line verses and harmonic structures; West African styles of melodic drumming, bits of the Yoruba language, and a version of the three-two timeline now known as *clave*; and instruments native to the Caribbean such as the *güiro*. Due to Cuba's central location within the transatlantic slave trade, the music of the island had a substantial eighteenth- and nineteenth-century influence throughout much of Latin America and the Southern United States.[38]

In the twentieth century, Cuban music continued its international sway. Puerto Rico was heavily influenced by the musical traditions of the larger island. Its national styles were often rearticulations of Cuban popular song forms, and by the 1930s the professionalization and industrialization of Puerto Rican folk traditions such as the *plena* and *jíbaro* music often meant performing the genres with Cuban rhythms and instrumentation. What is less commonly cited is the incredible influence Cuban music had throughout much of the globe. Musicologist Peter Manuel maintains that, not unlike American rock from the 1950s to the 1980s, the Cuban *son* was the biggest international commercial genre during the first half of the century. The *son* provided the basis for the US mambo craze mentioned above, and it maintained a similar influence throughout the Spanish Caribbean and even in much of Africa. In the latter two cases, as in Puerto Rico, people often turned to Cuban styles as an alternative

---

38. Roberts, *Latin Tinge*; Juan Duany, "Popular Music in Puerto Rico: Toward an Anthropology of Salsa," in Boggs, *Salsiology*, pp. 69–85; Narváez, "Hispanic Music Cultures."

209

to what they may have considered a more insidious form of cultural imperialism coming from Europe and the United States. Yet Cuban styles were not always readily accepted. Even in Tanzania, where the *son* represented a partial re-Africanization of dancehall music, president Julius Nyerere complained, "Many of us have learnt to dance the *rumba*, or the *cha cha cha*, to rock and roll and to twist and even to dance the waltz and fox trot. But how many of us can dance, or have even heard of, the *gombe sugu*, the *mangala*, *nyang'umumi*, *kidou*, or *lele mama* [Tanzanian genres]?"[39] The history and politics of how Cuban music became so internationally influential is beyond the scope of this article. What is important, however, is that salsa's global spread was preceded by that of Cuban music.

Salsa thus had claims to an international status because it was rooted heavily in Cuban music that had been an international genre for quite some time. As record companies began marketing the New York style of salsa throughout Latin America, listeners in most countries were well prepared, for their national musics often shared some level of Cuban influence. Salsa musicians thus did not help foster a pan-Latino identity by importing a new musical sensibility throughout the region as much as by effectively marketing a music throughout Latin America that brought to the fore what many of the local music cultures already shared.

It must be noted that salsa's international success was due not only to its incorporation of Cuban elements but to the fact that Cuban musicians were politically and economically unable to market their music on the same scope that New York salsa players were. The US embargo against Cuba following the Cuban revolution in 1959 created a number of circumstances that effected the international spread of the Cuban sound. Travel between New York and Cuba became much more difficult; thus, the developments of Latin music in Cuba and New York became more distinct than they had been before. Several older New York Latin musicians, including Tito Puente and Mongo Santamaria, have argued that New York salsa is simply Cuban music circa 1959. There is some truth to the view, for direct Cuban influence diminished at about that time. In addition, Cuban musicians were (and continue to be) denied equal access to international markets because the embargo limited the ability of US–based labels and distributors to handle their products. While foreign subsidiaries might have marketed Cuban music to other countries, this was done less often than one might imagine due to transnational labels' increasing desire to integrate domestic US and

39. Manuel, "Puerto Rican Music," pp.250–51, 277; Glasser, *My Music*, pp.18–34.

international marketing and distribution plans. It became much more profitable for a company to handle only artists that it could sell in all of its territories.

Fania took particular advantage of the US embargo. The label often recorded songs by Cuban composers without crediting them on the record. Fania maintained a policy of writing "D.R." for *derechos reservados* or reserved rights in the place of composer credits for its Cuban material, and a large percentage of the label's output was so designated.[40]

Another way in which salsa operated as a transnational music involved its role within the local New York movement for Puerto Rican nationalism—a movement that was explicitly internationalist in focus. The Young Lords' "Thirteen-Point Program and Platform" voiced the importance of a pan-Latino worldview. The lives of all Latinos and third-world peoples, they argued, were intimately linked through both common histories of colonialism and, in many cases, a shared African heritage. Change required concerted action and social, political, and economic alliances that disregarded national borders. It also required a pan-ethnic movement within the United States. Young Lord activist Felipe Luciano explicitly linked salsa culture and politics when he identified the multicultural identity fostered on the salsa dance floor in his liner notes for a 1972 Barretto album:

> Our common denominator with the oppressed all over the world is rhythm. The most common sight is to see bloods black, brown, yellow, and red, dancing to Ray. And to tell you the truth, it gets very difficult to tell in dim lights and smoke haze who is who 'cause they all be stepping fast or slow-dancing and breathing hard.[41]

A similar focus on the international freedom struggle was evident in the lyrics of many salsa songs. Ray Barretto's 1975 *"Testigo Fui"* is but one example. The song tells the story of Africans, brought to Puerto Rico as slaves, laying claim to the island and defying the oppression of their masters. *"Testigo Fui"* makes Africa central to the

40. Charley Gerard with Marty Sheller, *Salsa!: The Rhythm of Latin Music* (Crown Point, Indiana: White Cliffs Media Company, 1989), pp.6–9. Also see Roberta Singer, "Tradition and Innovation in Contemporary Latin Popular Music in New York City," *Latin American Music Review*, 4:2 (Summer 1983): pp.183–202. Singer identifies the important role that has been played by record collectors within the salsa community. Separated from current Cuban music due to the embargo, many musicians turn to those who have extensive collections of older Latin music in order to learn the history and traditions of the style. Records are thus important material holders of memory. Singer's finding might also suggest why salsa sounds to some like older Cuban music.
41. Felipe Luciano, liner notes for Ray Barretto, *Que Viva la Musica* (New York: Fania SLP00427, 1972).

history of Puerto Rico and the rest of Latin America. In this it echoes the emphasis on African heritage as a foundation of international solidarity that Young Lords such as Guzman maintained throughout their writings in *Palante*.[42]

Fania worked hard to make salsa an international genre and, in the process, became transnational itself. In 1971 Massucci created a new subsidiary of the label, Fania International. Originally designed as a Puerto Rico–based distributor for the label's cadre of New York artists, Fania International soon grew to include its own diverse roster of musicians culled from throughout Latin America. The label featured salsa musician Roberto Roena, romantic balladeer Roberto Yanes, and the Chilean folk group Los Angeles Negros. In 1973 Fania opened a major sales and distribution center in Panama to improve access to South American markets. Similarly, 1974 saw the label sign licensing agreements in Holland and Spain. Finally, the label created a presence in Africa with their 1976 sponsorship of a Muhammad Ali fight in Zaire. These international operations better allowed Fania to coordinate international tours and product distribution and put the label in the position to further foster a certain type of transnational community.[43]

Billboard inadvertently found evidence of such a community in its 1973 coverage of the music's reception in Puerto Rico. *Billboard* first reported that New York salsa's arrival in Puerto Rico had caused a significant drop in the sales of American rock artists among island consumers. About a month later it reported that the "Americanization" of some salsa recordings had hurt Puerto Rican sales of the genre. Puerto Rican salsa fans, *Billboard* suggested, shared with many New York fans a desire for music in *clave*, the three-two pulse that is at the heart of Afro-Cuban rhythms. The magazine argued that Puerto Ricans rejected rock and "Americanized" Latin music because the styles were off *clave* and thus not "pure" or "authentic" Latino culture. Many older Latin musicians had similarly rejected the fusions of Cuban-based forms with African-American R&B during the 1960s because they were off *clave*. Tito Puente may have expressed a common view when he derided the young Willie Colon for his "inability" to play in *clave*, thus linking the rhythm not only to cultural "authenticity" but also to musical competence and quality. However, Puerto Rican record distributor Charles Tarrab gave a different explanation for the sales trends. "Puerto Rican youth is into music on all levels," he

42. "Testigo Fui" on Ray Barretto, *Barretto* (New York: Fania SLP00486, 1975).
43. "Fania Operation Set in Panama," *Billboard* (October 13, 1973): p.13; Agustin Gurza, "Fania Tries a Non-Salsa Label," *Billboard* (October 2, 1976): p.90.

told *Billboard*. "But also present is a strong sense of nationalism—something which is evident now with salsa product outselling American pop and rock discs on the local market."[44]

What is missing from the *Billboard* coverage but can perhaps be inferred is the position that Puerto Rican music fans also found in the *clave* rhythms of New York salsa evidence of a shared social reality and the potential for political solidarity with Latino communities outside of Puerto Rico. Musical signifiers such as *clave* may have been integral to the formation of an imagined counterpublic among Latinos separated by geography. Clapping the *clave* rhythm along with a salsa performance, for example, was a way for audience members to participate actively in a salsa concert. It displayed a certain proficiency with the music that was shared by performers and an audience—a proficiency born not out of committed musical study as much as through exposure to Latino culture.[45] Clapping *clave* was also identified as a means of creating unity or community out of an audience, as when journalist Vinnie Puentes described the pride in hearing "36,000 hands clapp[ing] '*clave*' in unison" during a Fania All Stars show at Madison Square Garden.[46] Fania played a significant role in the expansion of this imagined community by sending groups such as the All Stars on tour throughout Latin America. They thus provided one more opportunity for the formation of a pan-Latino community around shared experiences of spectatorship and participation in the concerts.

This point is nicely symbolized by the group's 1975 two-volume album, *Fania All Stars Live at Yankee Stadium*. Half of the album was actually recorded at the Roberto Clemente Stadium in San Juan, yet the two audiences are indistinguishable—each cheer and clap in synchronized *clave*. Live All Stars recordings from Africa (1974) and Havana (1976) show similar effects. The Fania All Stars helped create a transnational listening community by providing a common link between many local communities. They garnered international attention for artists such as Ray Barretto and Ruben Blades, whose songs spoke of the pan-Latino identity formed out of a common struggle and history, and in the process they helped turn what began as a small, local music culture into an international phenomenon.

44. Jim Melanson, "Sales Bow in P.R. Cuts Into US Sales," *Billboard* (March 3, 1973): p.100; "Americanization of Latin Product 'Weakens Mart,'" *Billboard* (April 7, 1973): p.16. On Puente, see Boggs, "Sanabria," p.191.
45. Gerard, *Salsa!*, p.13–15.
46. Puentes, "Fania All Stars Kick off World Tour at Garden," *Latin NY* (September 1977): p.19.

Salsa and the Global Music Industry

CBS recognizes that [Latin America] is economically, politically, geographically, and demographically difficult, but at the same time, through years of experience it understands that it is impossible to wipe from the map the whole territory and its more than two million inhabitants. Therefore, we know for a fact that there will always be a market for records, and that there will always be buyers.
—MANUEL VILLARREAL, CBS RECORDS INTERNATIONAL, 1975[47]

We help make local artists international artists. We help make international artists local artists.
—CBS RECORDS INTERNATIONAL, 1977[48]

The story of salsa provides a unique opportunity to re-evaluate a number of the scholarly interpretations of the "world music" phenomenon of the early 1980s. Several scholars have recently begun to explore the consolidation and globalization of the music industry in that decade. The merger frenzy affected the industry greatly. It has been credited with the homogenization of music cultures throughout the world: As international superstars such as Michael Jackson were pushed into country after country, local music cultures were damaged. Similarly, some have argued that the rise of giant entertainment conglomerates resulted in an obliteration of difference and a devaluation of politics as local, politically charged genres were taken out of their specific contexts and marketed as "world music" to unknowing or unsympathetic audiences seeking novelty.[49]

Such analyses must be reconsidered on two counts. First, the supposed loss of political meaning as music is marketed internationally must be re-examined in light of the previous discussion regarding the growth of a transnational political and cultural community around salsa music. The mass-marketing of local music can often result in its consumption by people who do not know or care about the political meanings the music holds within its original locale, yet it also holds the possibility of

47. Enrique Ortiz, "Latin America: A Point of Pride in the CBS World of Music," Special CBS Records International advertising supplement, *Billboard* (January 25, 1975): p.56.
48. CBS Records International advertisement, *Billboard* (August 6, 1977): p.34.
49. On corporate consolidation, see Burnett, *The Global Jukebox*. Regarding world music, see Will Straw, "Systems of Articulation, Logics of Change: Communities and Scenes in Popular Music," *Cultural Studies*, 5:3, pp.368–88; Steven Feld, "Notes on World Beat," *Public Culture Bulletin*, 1:1 (Fall 1988): pp.31–37; and Erlmann, "Global Imagination."

bringing the music to the attention of other communities that might share the musicians' political positions. Many of the criticisms of world music are based on its consumption by a white middle-class audience within the US. The salsa example suggests that this group is not the only demographic that may be buying internationally marketed music.[50] Furthermore, the timeline of recent corporate consolidation must be understood to extend back to at least the mid-sixties. Once this is established, the history of entertainment transnationals' relationship to local music cultures, salsa included, appears more complex than recent scholars have allowed. The world music phenomenon of the 1980s—basically, the production of international artists able to crossover into the mainstream US charts—was in fact partially the result of local communities demanding access to the improved marketing mechanisms that were being developed by entertainment transnationals.

CBS, for example, began its international enterprises not in the eighties but the mid-sixties. In 1965, the same year Fania released its first album by Johnny Pacheco, CBS consolidated its foreign operations under a new subsidiary called CBS Records International. The new company set up headquarters in Mexico City, where CBS had established its first Latin-American presence in 1946. The company published a seventy-page advertising supplement in *Billboard* to celebrate its tenth anniversary, in which CBS presented its philosophy behind the formation of the company and its plans for the future. Goddard Lieberson, president of Columbia Records in 1965, stated the purpose of the company as twofold: "To contribute significantly to the musical culture of each country by recording native artists and furthering the international recognition of each nation's creative talent; and to increase worldwide distribution of repertoire produced by American artists and Columbia Records, USA." In order to accomplish these goals, CBS International pursued strategies of corporate consolidation and control similar to those that were helping them integrate themselves into the domestic soul and Latin markets: acquisition of existing companies, joint ventures, and distribution deals. It was in fact the potential profits from distribution that most concerned CBS

---

50. While salsa provides one such example of mass-marketed music providing important links between regionally distinct subcultures, there are certainly other examples. See Louis Meintjes, "Paul Simon's *Graceland*, South Africa and the Mediation of Musical Meaning," *Ethnomusicology* (Winter 1990): pp.37–73; and Neil J. Savishinsky, "Transnational Popular Culture and the Global Spread of the Jamaican Rastafarian Movement," *New West Indian Guide*, 68:3, pp.259–81. Each argues that while white US consumers may not identify with the politics of the musics, their international marketing resulted in a number of alliances between specific oppressed populations throughout the world.

International. As Walter Yetnikoff, president of CBS International in 1975, recalled, "Licensing program[s] would have been the more usual [strategy] and would have assured immediate return, but it would have eliminated the move toward today's massive distribution profits."[51]

The international operation allowed CBS to access various local music markets and to profit from the traffic between them, and, perhaps more importantly, gave them the opportunity to organize their production and marketing operations on a global scale. The umbrella corporation enabled them to coordinate the release of albums and promotional films, artist tours, and publicity campaigns across national borders. As marketing service director Bunny Freidus explained,

> CBS International within the past two years is making sure that success in one territory is translated throughout Europe. If an artist has a record breaking in the UK and goes to Europe for promotion, the European marketing office moves quickly to tie in TV, radio, and press in Germany and Spain, Holland and Belgium, France and Scandinavia. No other American record company can offer its artists such total coordination.[52]

While CBS may have been at the forefront of such corporate consolidation within the Latin-American music industry, several other transnationals were creating similar infrastructures during the same period. Polydor, for example, established a Mexican division in 1965 and declared a similar goal of increasing the sale of American artists in Mexico while searching local markets for crossover artists. These two goals were often in tension with one another. While these companies entered countries under the declared agreement that they would promote native artists both within the country and internationally, they often devoted most of their energies to promoting local consumption of US artists. Local populations often combated the majors, characterizing their attempts to impose US music on them as blatant cultural imperialism and demanding that they remain true to their promise of promoting local talent. Polydor faced such a predicament in 1975 in Mexico. Local retailers stigmatized the company as simply an importer of US product. In fact it was: Only thirty

---

51. Mort Goode, "CBS International: A Decade Dedicated to 'Total Service' Worldwide," Special CBS Records International advertising supplement, *Billboard* (January 25, 1975): p.5.
52. "Creative Strategy Seen as Key to CBS Global Marketing Plans," CBS Supplement, p.66.

percent of the label's output was from Mexican artists. Luis Baston, general director of the label, vowed to bring the two categories into balance in accordance with the wishes of local retailers and the company's original declarations. CBS had a similar story to tell regarding its operations in Jamaica.[53]

These incidents, as well as the New York salsa story, suggest that those involved in local music cultures may have actively pursued the international exposure and distribution that transnationals made possible. The world music phenomenon of the 1980s thus must be considered in terms of such local demands for music conglomerates to use their new integrated operations to promote local talent to international markets in the 1970s. The US distribution of music from other nations potentially allowed local musicians increased profits and the international exposure of their political concerns. In the case of salsa, such distribution involved compromising the specific local content of the music, but, as we have seen, this was a concession that many in the New York salsa industry had long been willing to make.

Karl Hagstrom Miller is a historian and musician living in Austin, Texas. He has written about Tejano music, tourism, advertising, and Charles Mingus's demands to get paid. He is currently completing a doctoral dissertation at New York University examining the racial segregation of culture in the early recording industry and social sciences. The author would like to thank Ellen Noonan and Rachel Mattson for reading early drafts of this article and offering helpful suggestions and support; Lizabeth Cohen, Toby Miller, and Robin D.G. Kelley for their close analysis and insights; and Norman Kelley for his kind yet pointed editorial hand.

---

53. Marv Fisher, "Mexican Polydor: Luis Baston Attempting to Balance Domestic & International Releases," *Billboard* (July 19, 1975): p.29; Roger Wallis and Krister Malm, *Big Sounds from Small Peoples: The Music Industry in Small Countries* (London: Constable, 1984), pp.97–100.

Part 4

The Politics of the Noise

Money, Power, and Respect:
A Critique of the Business of Rap Music
BY YVONNE BYNOE

How do you count the influence of the art and culture? It is not only Black people that are doing Black music and are being influenced by Black music. The entire culture is being exported.
—DICK GRIFFEY, CHAIRMAN, SOLAR RECORDS
(FROM THE HARVARD REPORT ON URBAN MUSIC, 1994)

Back in the day, a rap artist may have secured a recording contract by simply telling the A&R guy, "Listen to my demo"; however, the road to rap stardom has changed dramatically. Today, rap music is a hierarchical, $1.8 billion-a-year industry,[1] where decisions about artists and their audiences are made in boardrooms, supported by reports and projections—just like any other business. From its humble beginnings in the Bronx as a form of community entertainment for Black and Latino youth, rap music and its accompanying Hip Hop culture have become international phenomena. Rap enthusiasts and artists can now be found in every continent on the planet. Aside from rock music, which dominated the market with a twenty-five-percent share, rap/Hip Hop outsold all other genres (country, jazz, classical) with 12.9 percent of the music market in 2000. As a cultural idiom, it has greatly influenced fashion, film, advertising, publishing, theater, and even professional sports. According to year-end reports from Soundscan (a consumer tracking system founded in 1991), sales of rap albums jumped twenty percent in 2000, the largest increase for any musical genre, with total music sales for the year only increasing four percent over 1999.

Despite the wealth that is being generated by rap music, it is concentrated in the hands of relatively few corporations that own radio conglomerates and have national record distribution capabilities. Black Americans, while still driving the artistic engine of rap music, are not necessarily the chief beneficiaries of Hip Hop's economic boom. Cultural activist April Silver, in her essay "Hip Hop: Cultural to Corporate Entertainment,"[2] states that, notwithstanding a list of Black and Latino Hip Hop–generated millionaires,

1. See RIAA's 2000 Consumer Profile and March 3, 2001, News Brief.
2. April Silver, "Hip Hop: Cultural to Corporate Entertainment," *Doula: The Journal of Rap Music and Hip Hop Culture*, Volume 1, Issue 1 (2000): p.6.

[H]ip hop's expansion into the global marketplace, coupled with its phenomenal profitability, is tantamount to a ripple effect in a disturbed pond. Although our voice has been signaled across the world and our presence has been announced, our conditions remain virtually unchanged. Black and Latino people are still disenfranchised politically, economically disadvantaged, and socially marginalized.

Any critical thinker acknowledges that America, regardless of its attempts to promote itself as a classless meritocracy, is in reality a stratified society in which *who* one knows is often more important than *what* one knows (or how talented one is). Similarly, rap music's "anti-social" labeling in the media distorts the fact that is has become part of the established system of US-styled capitalism whereby those with access to education and/or capital rule and exploit those who do not. Each entertainment genre wrestles with the balance between commerce and art, with artistic puritans disdaining commercialization and business interests seeking mass appeal. Rap music, however, adds the dimensions of race and socioeconomic status to this already complicated discourse. There is an expectation that, since the vast majority of money being generated by the Hip Hop industry comes from "Black" stories, Blacks should be reaping a larger share of the profits than they are currently receiving.

There are two recurring, intertwining dialogues in the area of rap music and Hip Hop culture. The first involves the financial control that is wielded by White-run entities in a genre that creatively remains beholden to Black Americans. The second is concerned with whom the music actually represents, since rap music and Hip Hop culture are still primarily identified with Black youth—while being chiefly marketed to White audiences around the globe.

Who Controls the Money?

Any discourse that focuses on the business of rap music must first distinguish between the "Hip Hop industry" and the "Hip Hop community." Essentially, the Hip Hop industry is comprised of entities that seek to profit from the marketing and sales of rap music and its ancillary products. The Hip Hop industry includes record companies, music publishers, radio stations, record stores, music-video shows, recording studios, talent bookers, performance venues, promoters, managers, disc jockeys, lawyers, accountants, music publications, and music/entertainment websites. There is also an entire service sector that is primarily dependent on Hip Hop–industry clientele for its survival, including restaurants, florists, hotels, travel agents, limousine services, party planners, publicists, rental agents, fashion designers, stylists, barbers, hairstylists, make-up artists, and photographers. By contrast, the Hip Hop *community* is comprised of adherents to Hip Hop culture and mere consumers of rap music and its accoutrements—the fans. The Hip Hop community includes males and females of all races and ethnicities, generally in the age range of twelve to forty.

Understanding the importance of record distribution is crucial to comprehending the power structure of the music industry, since practically anyone can have a record pressed up or a CD burned. Distribution is one of the two crucial elements needed to successfully launch a national musical talent; the other is radio play. Radio provides a medium for a record company to "advertise" its artists' records. Once a demand for the records has been created, a record company, through its distribution network, must ensure that the desired records are delivered quickly to retailers in order to meet consumer demand. In this equation, the entities that own the means of distributing records and control the airwaves in effect rule the industry. With a few exceptions, this means that White-owned corporations are reaping the lion's share of the profits from rap music and its ancillary products. In today's marketplace, five conglomerates control ninety percent of US music distribution: AOL Time Warner, Vivendi/Universal, Bertelsmann Distribution Group, Sony Music, and EMI Distribution; the only American company among these is Warner. These multinational companies are the primary channels by which rap music (via subsidiary rap record labels) is distributed both domestically and internationally.

The Telecommunications Act of 1996 facilitated the control of radio by a few conglomerates. This legislation allowed one radio company to increase its ownership to eight stations in a given market, thereby squeezing out many independent radio-station owners. For example, in 1998 New York City had twenty-three FM stations, and three companies—Chancellor Broadcasting, CBS, and Emmis Broadcasting—controlled eleven of them. Moreover, the Telecommunications Act abetted the loss of thirty-nine Black-owned stations nationwide. In the area of rap music media, which supports the efforts of radio and the record companies, *Source* magazine,[3] headed by

3. The Source Entertainment, Inc., publishes *Source* magazine, *Source Sports* magazine, and TheSource.com. It also produces compilation CDs, *The Source All Access* television show, and the annual Source Awards.

David Mays, with 449,000 subscribers per month, easily outpaces its main competitor, *XXL* magazine, which is published by Harris Publications. Smaller, independent regional and nationally distributed rap magazines, like *Stress* or *Murder Dog*, are no match for these corporate-backed publications. MTV and Black Entertainment Television (B.E.T.), national cable television stations, remain the chief broadcast outlets for rap videos.

How Did We Get Here? CBS and the Harvard Report

The systematic colonization of Black music began in 1971 when Columbia Records Group (CRG)[4] commissioned the Harvard University Business School to conduct an investigation about how they should better situate themselves to benefit from "soul" music.[5] Although historically some major record companies were involved in Black music, the majority shunned the genre and its audience. CRG was weak in the area of soul music, although Sly and the Family Stone recorded for Epic Records; Columbia had recently lost Aretha Franklin, whose talents they had not known how to cultivate, to Atlantic Records. Moreover, CRG head Clive Davis realized that R&B records, such as those coming from Motown groups like the Supremes and the Temptations, were crossing over to the pop charts. CRG was missing out on a lucrative business opportunity and wanted to increase its market share in this genre. The resulting report, submitted on May 11, 1972, titled "A Study of the Soul Music Environment" (also called "The Harvard Report"; discussed earlier in this volume), analyzed the American soul-music market as well as CRG's prior attempts at participation in that market, and then issued recommendations about how CRG could catch up with the times. The Harvard Report became the blueprint by which CRG increased its market position; subsequently, other major record companies replicated CRG's tactics.

The Harvard Report determined that the soul market constituted at least $60 million in annual sales. The Report also indicated that soul music "has a broad appeal that extends far beyond Black customers."[6] Cultivating Black radio, according to the report, was important for CRG in order to solidify its position on the Top 40 charts; White radio stations would only add to their playlists soul records that had been

---

4. Columbia Records Group is currently known as Columbia Records and is a division of Sony Music Entertainment. Sony Entertainment purchased parent company CBS Records in January 1988.
5. Rhythm & blues and soul are often considered two separate but related genres. The Harvard Report, however, uses the term "soul" to encompass both.
6. This and all subsequent Harvard Report quotes are drawn from a copy of the 1972 document.

already popularized on Black radio. It was clear that Black music and radio were needed as part of a larger plan by CRG to dominate the recorded music market. The report stated, "The Negro audience thus serves as a test market for many of the selections that reach the Top 40 stations. Records having strong sales in the ghetto record stores as a result of air-play over R&B stations will soon be heard by Top 40 listeners." The report concluded that CRG had been hampered because it was an organization staffed by White personnel versed in the area of pop music but with no knowledge of soul music. The Harvard Report recommended that CRG establish an internal, semi-autonomous soul music group and improve the soul music that they were producing.

CRG saw a three-tiered competitive challenge that included established labels with historical connections to soul music, other major labels, and smaller independent companies. The most formidable competition would come from nationally distributed companies, like Motown, Stax, and Atlantic, that already had dominant positions in Black music as well as financial and management resources. In the second position were other major record companies such as RCA, Capitol, and MCA, which were deemed to have no more expertise in Black music than CRG. The report concluded that CRG would be battling these companies for the "limited available Black professional and management personnel." Moreover, the Report indicated that CRG could outmaneuver these competitors by initiating a long-term strategy for soul music rather than seeking short-term profits from an "opportunistic 'creaming' program." Another key component of CRG's strategy was the smaller independent record companies. The Report indicated that the independents could be a source for product (i.e., "hot masters"), talent, and experienced personnel for CRG's promotion and production staff. Small, independent labels could also serve as a source for "captive" independent producers. The Report's recommendations resulted in the virtual dismantling of Black independent record companies, which were all too often under-capitalized endeavors that could not obtain conventional bank or vendor credit and were reliant on a patchwork of regional distribution arrangements. CRG and other major record companies soon began to lure away key personnel and talent from the Black independents with offers of more money and a national distribution apparatus. Motown, the last major Black independent record company, held out until 1988, when it became part of MCA.

Most importantly, the report indicated that CRG, through "[a] broadened distribution in the Black community, which an expanded soul program would bring, could serve as a distribution arm for their proprietary product under a custom label program." This recommendation was the precursor to successful Black producers, with no particular business skills, drawing deals with major record companies.

One example of this strategy, however, was evident prior to the submission of the Harvard Report to CRG. Producers Kenny Gamble and Leon Huff, who became famous for their "Philadelphia Sound," joined the CRG family in 1971 with the inception of their Philadelphia International Records label. Gamble and Huff, formerly associated with Motown Records, signed a production and distribution deal that provided the producers with a small budget of $5,000 per single and $25,000 per album, according to the record-industry exposé, *Hit Men.*[7] For their meager investment, CRG soon realized major successes. Within nine months of executing the production and distribution agreement, Philadelphia International Records had hits with Billy Paul, the O'Jays, and Harold Melvin and the Blue Notes; and later with former Blue Note lead singer Teddy Pendergrass. Gamble and Huff provided CRG with nine gold singles in 1972, and the O'Jays' first two albums sold a combined 750,000 copies, an impressive figure at the time. Based on the success of Philadelphia International Records, CRG signed another distribution deal with Stax Records, home of the Staple Singers and Isaac Hayes. CRG invested $7 million in the deal, but overspending on the part of Stax ultimately resulted in a financial loss for CRG.

The Harvard Report's final rationale for CRG wholeheartedly expanding into the soul market is prophetic, and crucial to an understanding of rap music and the Hip Hop industry:

> Soul music is one of the very few basic art forms which is indigenous to America, although its own roots may be traced to Africa. It has been and probably will continue to be a vital and influential force on contemporary popular music. And soul is by no means a static music form. It too will continue to change. Companies able to work successfully in this art form will be in a position to relate more dynamically to its impact on other forms of popular music, such as pop and rock. This will be especially important as these three music styles converge upon one another.

---

7. Frederic Dannen, *Hit Men* (New York: Vintage Books, 1990).

Rap Independents

The very first record companies to enter the rap game were Black-owned, including Sugar Hill Records, Winley Records, and Enjoy Records. These small companies were operated by Black music veterans who had enjoyed previous success. Joe Robinson and his wife, Sylvia Robinson, for example, owned Sugar Hill Records; Sylvia was formerly a member of the singing duo Mickey and Sylvia, whose one hit was "Love is Strange." The Robinsons' previous company, All-Platinum Records, had gone bankrupt in the mid-seventies during a Newark, New Jersey federal grand jury investigation into payola practices. Joe Robinson was eventually convicted for tax evasion and hit with a fine.[8]

Despite Sugar Hill Records' success in the early eighties with "Rapper's Delight" by the Sugar Hill Gang and "Funk You Up" by Sequence, its sales were only about $2 million annually and its independent distributors alleged that the company owed them more than $500,000 in advances. In order to stay afloat, Sugar Hill Records subsequently signed an onerous "pressing and distribution" deal with MCA records that called for MCA to receive twenty-five percent of gross sales. The structure of the deal spelled failure for Sugar Hill from the onset. As part of the arrangement, MCA would not advance Sugar Hill any money to sign artists or produce records, and it would not accept any returns on previously manufactured Sugar Hill Records. The deal was collateralized by Sugar Hill Records' ownership rights to Checker Records and Chess Records master recordings of such legends as Muddy Waters, Howlin' Wolf, and Chuck Berry. This meant that if Sugar Hill could not meet its financial obligations to MCA under the terms of the agreement, MCA would take ownership of the Checker and Chess masters. On November 20, 1984, Sugar Hill Records filed an $80-million lawsuit against MCA, charging that it had been defrauded and was on the verge of bankruptcy because of a racketeering scheme engineered by MCA executives. Sugar Hill alleged that MCA had prepared "fraudulent accounting reports" and had made unauthorized "secret sales" of Sugar Hill's inventory as cutouts. Sugar Hill also charged that because of the resulting financial instability, it had been forced to sell MCA its principal asset, the Checker Records and Chess catalogue, for a mere $481,000. The case was settled out of court in 1991, but the Robinsons received no money.

8. William Knoedelseder, *Stiffed.* (New York: Harper Collins, 1993), p.26.

While it is clear that the original Black independents were edged out of rap music by the major record companies' consolidation of record distribution, and by their own bad management and poor financial planning, better-educated and better-financed Black entrepreneurs did not immediately follow them into the rap business. Middle-class Black Americans, generally speaking, were not interested in rap music. Most saw rap as ghetto music that was beneath them, and Black record-industry executives thought that "multi-racial" disco would have more longevity than "Black" rap. Historically, the Black bourgeoisie has been loathe to associate itself with the cultural products of the lower classes, whether it was the blues, jazz, or rap. Many middle-class Blacks embraced disco and the trappings of exclusivity and wealth that accompanied Studio 54 and its local imitators. After the decline of the Black Power movement, radio began rejecting the soul and funk sounds of artists like James Brown, Curtis Mayfield, the Funkadelics, and the Ohio Players, in favor of non-racial, techno mantras. In 1977 New York City's WBLS-FM, then recognized as the nation's preeminent Black radio station, changed its tag line from "the total Black experience in sound" to "the total experience in sound," demonstrating its programming shift. The station's program director, Frankie Crocker, who epitomized the disco era with his tony Sutton Place address and his Rolls Royce, made no secret that he was a proponent of disco and not the emerging rap.

The failure of the Black middle class to enter the rap music business left the field open for White executives. The next wave of independent rap record owners would overwhelmingly be young White men. In 1981 Baskin-Robbins ice-cream heir Corey Robbins started Profile Records. With an investment of $750, Profile Records produced the legendary "Genius of Rap" by Dr. Jekyll (Andre Harrell) and Mr. Hyde (Alonzo Brown). The fledgling record company sold 150,000 units of the twelve-inch single. Profile would also be the first home of Run-D.M.C., producing "It's Like That" (1983), "Sucker MCs" (1983), and "You Talk Too Much" (1985), as well as Rob Base's hit, "It Takes Two" (1988). In the same year former college DJ Tommy Silverman founded Tommy Boy Records and hired former exotic dancer Monica Lynch as his girl Friday. Tommy Boy Records would go on to produce artists such as Afrika Bambaataa, Force MDs, Stetsasonic, Queen Latifah, House of Pain, De La Soul, and Capone-N-Noreaga.

Despite the commercial success of "Rapper's Delight" and other rap records, the genre was still not one in which major record companies or commercial radio were willing to invest their resources. This shortsightedness allowed the second wave of independent rap record companies to operate below the radar of corporate America. These small companies could react quickly to the rap market's demand by pressing and manufacturing relatively inexpensive twelve-inch singles. Furthermore, these independents utilized "underground" vehicles like local DJ battles, "mom-and-pop" record stores, street promotion, and club DJs to advertise and sell their records. Independent radio shows like Mr. Magic's Rap Attack, which began in 1980 on New York's WHBI (airing on Saturdays from 2–5 a.m.), would play a crucial part in developing a hardcore rap audience. Similarly, in 1984 Los Angeles' KDAY, the nation's first all-rap format, broke new artists and helped to spread the music to the West Coast.

The Rise of Black Rap Moguls

Although the new independents were predominately White entrepreneurs, the most enduring and influential name in rap music and Hip Hop culture is Russell Simmons, a Black American. In 1977 Simmons, along with his partner, Rick Rubin, a New York University student, began to lay the foundation for the Def Jam empire. In 1979, as managers, they orchestrated the signing of Kurtis Blow to Mercury Records, which made him the first rap artist signed to a major record company. By 1985 Def Jam Recordings had sold 500,000 records and had entered into a $600,000 record deal with CBS records. The Def Jam Recordings roster now boasts an impressive list of rap music stars, including LL Cool J, Run-D.M.C., Slick Rick, EPMD[9], the Beastie Boys, Public Enemy, Method Man, Foxy Brown, Redman, and DMX. Additionally, Def Jam created a joint venture with Roc-a-Fella Records, home to rap superstar Jay-Z. Simmons' ventures also include Rush Management and RSTV, which produces Russell Simmons' Def Comedy Jam, launched on HBO in 1991. Def Jam Pictures, which produced the movies *Krush Groove, Tougher than Leather, Gridlock'd, The Show* documentary, and *How to Be a Player*, also co-produced the Eddie Murphy vehicle *The Nutty Professor*. Additionally there is Phat Farm, an apparel concern; Rush Media, an advertising agency; and the website 360 Hip Hop, a joint venture with Black Entertainment Television (B.E.T.).

Russell Simmons is also important to Hip Hop history because Def Jam Recordings eventually became the model for rap music executives. Former artist Andre Harrell joined Def Jam Recordings in 1983 as a $200-per-week Vice President

---

9. EPMD's first album, Strictly Business, was released in 1988 on Priority Records.

of A&R and went on to run Uptown Entertainment, founded in 1986 as a joint venture with MCA. Harrell would later be tapped to take over Motown Records in 1995. The seven-year, $50-million Uptown Entertainment deal with MCA was intended to cross Black artists into films and movies. Harrell and his Uptown artists created the ghetto-fabulous style and popularized rap tinged R&B called "New Jack Swing." Its roster of artists included Mary J. Blige, Jodeci, Heavy D and Boyz,[10] Father MC, Christopher Williams, Al B Sure!, and Guy. Uptown became the co-producer of the popular weekly cop show, *New York Undercover*, which regularly featured rap and R&B artists as well as the latest street fashions. The company also produced the movie *Strictly Business* in 1991. Before joining Motown Records, Harrell reportedly sold his stake in Uptown Entertainment for $40 million.

Howard University student Sean "P-Diddy" Combs (formerly known as "Puffy") would start out at Uptown Entertainment as an intern; under the mentorship of Harrell, Combs would go on to found Bad Boy Entertainment, a 50/50 venture with Arista Records, in 1995. Artists associated with Bad Boy Entertainment include rap artists Craig Mack, the Notorious BIG (now deceased), The Lox, Mase, Black Rob, and P-Diddy himself, as well as singers 112, Total, Faith Evans, and Carl Thomas. Combs also runs Daddy's House recording studio and has made a substantial amount of money from his Hitmen production team. Aside from music-related ventures, Combs owns Justin's, a restaurant named after his first son, with locations in New York City and Atlanta. Lastly, there is the Sean John clothing line, which includes luxury items like fur coats. Sean John racked up $100 million in sales last year, up from $25 million in 1999. Russell Simmons, Andre Harrell, and Sean "P-Diddy" Combs are quite possibly the most influential figures in the development of modern Hip Hop culture.

The Relevance of Race and Money in Hip Hop

One of the primary critiques of rap music and Hip Hop culture is that it promotes an updated version of the minstrel show for the benefit of White consumers. Minister Conrad Muhammad, founder of A Movement for CHHANGE (Conscious Hip Hop Activism Necessary for Global Empowerment), has been engaged in a public scrimmage with Russell Simmons over the acceptance within the Hip Hop industry of the use of derogatory terms such as *bitch*, *nigger*, and *'ho*. In the May 1, 2001

10. Dwight Meyers, p.k.a. Heavy D, would later be asked to take over the presidency of Uptown Entertainment after Harrell's departure.

Village Voice Simmons painted Muhammad as a rap music censor and asked fans not to "support the open and aggressive critics of the Hip Hop community (i.e., C. DeLores Tucker, Bob Dole, or Conrad Muhammad.)" Muhammad responded by stating, "Whites have accepted Russell Simmons as the guru of Black youth culture. He has sold them a bill of goods—that we are penny-chasing, champagne-drinking, gold-teeth-wearing, modern-day Sambos."

In 1994 the Harvard University Consultation Project produced the "Harvard Report on Urban Music," a revision of the 1972 study. In it Russell Simmons states, "Black culture is for everyone, not just for Black people. I want to be positioned to get a piece of the entire marketplace, not just the Black community's marketplace."[11] Just as the first Harvard Report indicated thirty years ago, Black Americans remain the arbiters of American popular culture; however, as a consumer base, they are often jettisoned in favor of White consumers. Soundscan generates the reports by which the record industry analyzes the success or failure of music releases. Since Soundscan is a costly system to implement, the sales of smaller independent retailers, who often service Black communities, are largely excluded. With 1997 Soundscan reports indicating that approximately seventy-one percent of rap music buyers in America are White, they, rather than Black buyers, have become the targeted audience for rap music.[12]

A serious schism has developed around who and what Hip Hop culture should represent. In light of sustained racial discrimination and economic inequities, it is still evident that the concerns of Black and White youth are not the same. Since the public face of rap music is still black, Blacks perceive themselves as constituting the genre, while Whites like Tiffany Fuhant say that the twenty-percent increase in rap sales last year suggests that "[h]ip hop music has moved beyond Black culture and Black people and has become more mainstream."[13] This gap within the Hip Hop community indicates that the vision of the genre will be directed to serve its most important sector, which according to Soundscan is White youth. The Hip Hop industry's decision to intentionally target White rap consumers means that overtly socially conscious and/or pro-Black[14] messages have

11. "Harvard Report on Urban Music," Section V, Personnel, Exhibit 3, p.9.
12. Soundscan figures from the article "Black Like Them" by Charles Aaron, which was published in the November 1998 issue of *Spin* magazine.
13. See http://www.Tuduhant.tripod.com/entries/010301-011101.htm.
14. "Pro-Black" in this text is defined as celebrating Black beauty, life, and culture, as opposed to an interpretation that relates either to Black Nationalism or anti-White commentary.

been substantially sacrificed in rap music to accommodate a "we-are-the-world" ethos based on hedonistic consumerism and general youth rebellion.

Critics like activist Conrad Muhammad and filmmaker Spike Lee, who lampooned rap in his movie *Bamboozled*, are not looking to censor rap music, but to encourage the industry to be more sensitive to how lyrics and music videos influence young people, Black and White. Whereas in the past there was a wide array of rap music styles and messages, today the Hip Hop industry markets ghettocentric and lascivious rap content globally as the singular Black experience. Unfortunately for many people around the world, their first and only knowledge of Black Americans will come from these music videos and CDs. While this material, produced and promoted by Black rap artists and Black executives, may indeed be entertaining to Whites, it is often offensive to Blacks within the Hip Hop community. Moreover, the perpetuation of stereotypical images of Black youth begs the question: Would White consumers be so interested in rap if more of the music and videos depicted Black Americans as multi-faceted human beings rather than as ghetto primitives?

Classism Among Blacks in Hip Hop

While it is generally true that middle-class Black adults tend to be repulsed by rap music and Hip Hop culture, their children, by contrast, have often embraced it. In analyzing the business of rap music, it is necessary to point out that despite the media hype, Blacks in positions of power in the industry are rarely illiterate men from the lower class—most are middle class and/or have attended college. Russell Simmons grew up in the middle-class section of Hollis, New York, a Black community; his father was a professor, and Simmons attended City College/C.U.N.Y. Sean "P-Diddy" Combs, who grew up in Mount Vernon, New York, graduated from the private Mount St. Michael's Academy and attended Howard University. Andre Harrell is the only member from the Def Jam trio who actually grew up in the 'hood. Harrell was raised in the Bronxdale Projects, attended Lehman College for three years, and was a radio account executive before joining Def Jam Recordings. Ironically, unlike Simmons, who wanted to sell raw rap music, Harrell, who experienced street life first-hand, wanted to produce a music and a culture that spoke to the good life.

Aside from Simmons, Harrell, and Combs, there are other notable Hip-Hopreneurs. Even most of the moguls who came from gritty urban environments attended college.

No Limit Records CEO Master P, born Percy Miller, grew up in the infamous Calliope Apartments in New Orleans, now known as the B. Cooper Apartments. Master P, however, won a basketball scholarship to the University of Houston; after moving to California, he studied business at Merritt Junior College in Oakland. Marion "Suge" Knight, the formerly imprisoned head of Death Row Records, grew up in Compton, California, but attended the University of Nevada at Las Vegas. Although So So Def CEO Jermaine Dupri did not go to college, his father, Michael Maudlin, the former head of Black music at Columbia Records, was instrumental in ushering the teenaged Dupri onto the music scene. There are, in fact, numerous Black college graduates who are executives within the Hip Hop industry. It is almost a myth to suggest that in this day and age a Black person can enter and succeed in the rap music business without having a substantial amount of money and business acumen. Unfortunately, the Hip Hop community is continually fed the line that all one needs to get rich in the music industry is superior lyrical skills, or in the case of women, a pretty face. But education, particularly in the area of business, is not emphasized.

Ironically, it is the Black elites in the industry who most zealously promote the virtues of "keepin' it real" to the Hip Hop community. Many middle-class Black executives, like their White counterparts, have fetishized the ghetto as the domain of "authentic" blackness, continuing to dig deeper into its bowels to satisfy hipsters looking to be down. It suffices to say that depicting Black youth as "normal" is not a marketable concept. As observed by cultural critic bell hooks in her book, *Where We Stand: Class Matters*, "Nowadays, practically every public representation of blackness is created by Black folks who are materially privileged. More often than not they speak *about* the Black poor and working class but not *with* them, or on their behalf."[15] Although the 1990s slogan "keepin' it real" was originally a call to remember one's roots, it has been transformed into an ethos that disdains education, self-improvement, public decorum, and personal responsibility. Curiously enough, these characteristics are antithetical to the habits that successful Black executives have adopted for themselves. Hooks indicates that critics of the Black elite are often dismissed: "The Black masses are encouraged by an empowered privileged few to believe that any critique they or anyone makes of the class power of Black elites is merely sour grapes. Or they are made to feel that they are interfering with racial uplift

15. bell hooks, *Where We Stand: Class Matters* (New York: Routledge, 2000), p.95.

232

and racial solidarity if they want to talk about class."[16] In the parlance of the streets, "playa haters" (or "haters") are the only ones complaining about the successful rap artists or the Hip Hop industry.

Conclusion

In a capitalist society, businesses are organized to make profits, not to promote social ideals. Therefore, the only way that Black Americans can control their images and cultural products is to become entrenched in the ownership class of the music industry. Black Americans, as consumers, have to exert collective pressure on the record industry and on artists they believe have disrespected members of their communities. Clarence Avant, a respected music-industry veteran, says of Blacks,

> We have always been entertainers, but we have never really owned anything. Based on the number of Black artists who are successful, we should have more ownership. We are not owners because we have a combination of the wrong attitude and no money. For instance, our artists become famous, and they want to be known as "pop" stars. How can we own anything when our best assets (artists) want to stop being Black when they are successful? . . . Whoever controls the talent is going to be in the best position, but we (Blacks) do not have much time to come up with something different from what we have done before.[17]

While Mr. Avant makes some salient points, the role of ownership and control must extend beyond artists to the general Black population. Owning a chain of successful record stores, a venue that books Black artists, or a state-of-the-art recording studio are more attainable goals for the average young person than making a platinum-selling album. Black-owned businesses that impact the Hip Hop industry could encourage young people to pursue education, obtain capital, and craft plans to implement their own visions—aspirations that are not promoted to Black youth in expensive and slick rap music videos. The greater "Black community" has also fallen short by not providing alternative messages to those espoused in rap music content. The traditional institutions of the "Black community" (i.e., the churches and civil rights organizations)

16. *Ibid.*, p.98.
17. "Harvard Report on Urban Music," Section V, Personnel, Exhibit 3, p.2.

have virtually abandoned their youth, allowing hedonistic consumerism to usurp the meaningful values and ethics that for generations have fortified Black Americans. If their communities were instilling Black youth with more vision for their future, perhaps they would be less apt to see rap artists as their leaders and role-models.

At its best, rap music details, in a public space, the lives and experiences of disenfranchised Black youth; at its worst, it is nothing more than minstrelsy. Of paramount importance is the responsibility of rap music and Hip Hop culture to the "Black community," the source and inspiration for the genre—and the cash cow that the Hip Hop industry milks. While censorship is not the answer, it is an undeniable fact that urban music in general has lost the sense of responsibility and love that historically has been evident in the works of artists such as Stevie Wonder, Donny Hathaway, and Nina Simone. Much of what rap artists focus on these days is "keepin' it real" or "telling it as they see it," whereas Black music at its best provided Black Americans with a vision of the life that they should and could have. The musical aspirations of old school R&B artists were not limited to material acquisitions and often had a spiritual component. It stands to reason that in order to aspire to greater heights, one has to know that those heights exist and are indeed attainable. Rap music can definitely do more to broaden the horizons for Black youth, but the youth also require the help of engaged and committed Black citizens.

Yvonne Bynoe is president of Urban Think Tank, Inc., the first institute developed to address the economic, cultural, and political issues of concern to Americans from the perspective of the post-Civil Rights generation, also known as the Hip Hop generation. Urban Think Tank, Inc. publishes *Doula: The Journal of Rap Music and Hip Hop Culture*, the first scholarly publication on the subject. Ms. Bynoe, a graduate of Howard University and Fordham University School of Law, frequently lectures and writes on rap music, Hip Hop culture, and politics. She is currently a fellow at the DuBois Bunche Center for Public Policy at Medgar Evers College/City University of New York. ©2002 Yvonne Bynoe.

How Not to Get Jerked!
The Hip Hop Elementary Roundtable

The Heads:

Lord Finesse, MC and producer, currently signed to Penant Recordings

Mr. Dave, manager of O.C. and Payday Records label manager

Wendy Day, founder of the Rap Coalition, a non-profit group established to provide free legal assistance to hip hop artists

LS One, DJ for the platinum-selling group Onyx, currently signed to Def Jam Recordings

The Moderators:

Adam Mansbach, Editor-in-Chief and Publisher of Elementary Magazine

Danny Rudder, Elementary's Managing Editor

Do You Wanna Be in the Business?

Elementary: Let's start at the beginning. What are some of the most common mistakes that artists make in the hip hop industry?

Wendy Day: Not knowing how it works.

Mr. Dave: Not knowing how it works, and expecting too much too soon.

Wendy Day: This is a huge problem. People see artists' careers and think that they've got more money than God. Then they think, "OK, I'm gonna put out a record, it'll get on Hot 97 [WQHT-FM New York], and I'm gonna go buy a Lexus and seven different houses." That's not how it works. They don't realize that, for example, during the sixteen weeks that "Flavor in your Ear" was number one on the charts, Craig Mack was still taking the train because he had no loot yet. It takes a long time for the money to come through the system, and the artists are always the last to get paid.

Lord Finesse: I had to live off of shows for a long time.

Wendy Day: And that's when you can even get paid for shows. People expect artists to perform for free all the time.

Lord Finesse: Artists fall victim to the materials. Nine out of ten times, artists sell themselves short because they don't know what their true value in the game is. When you deal with a label, you gotta tell them straight up what you expect from them, and they'll tell you what they expect from you. You can't make any assumptions. The shit is like a date. If you just take a girl out and you ain't got your shit straight whether you're gettin' ass at the end of the night—you eat, you have fun, it's a lovely evening—then you go to make that move, and she's lookin' at you like "Eh? What you doin'? Put your drawers back on!"

It's the same thing in the industry. If you go in there and you start assuming, then at the end of the date your royalty check don't look right. It's about knowin' when you're gonna get paid, how you're gonna get paid, where your next paycheck is comin' from. The industry is ruthless. People come up to me saying, "I love to rap." Man, fuck rap. You got to know the business. Most artists don't know the business.

Wendy Day: And the worst part is, they don't care. Most artists don't care.

Lord Finesse: They don't care. They're selling their publishing rights, selling everything at the drop of a dime.

Mr. Dave: Another thing artists should know is once you get the right deal—well, there is no "right deal"—once you get a deal that you can live with, you must also understand that everything the label buys for you comes out of your pocket. I have artists comin' in and saying, "I want six different kinds of posters, ten photo shoots, and two thousand dollars for wardrobe."

All of that comes back at you at the end of the day when your album doesn't recoup and you don't get no money. Then you walk around saying, "My label jerked me." You have to know what's a necessity and what's frivolous. If you need a jacket for a photo shoot, go get the jacket and the jacket only. If you don't need no boots, don't get no boots. If you do get money from the label, put it in your pocket and save it, because you're gonna need it.

Lord Finesse: Oh yeah, you're gonna definitely need it. Another thing artists gotta learn is to be prompt; you always gotta be on time. Some artists miss their whole video shoot and wonder why their check is thirty grand short. It's cool to hang with your crew, but certain things you gotta cut back on. It's all recoupable. When that check comes in, artists are like: "Yo, what's this, what you mean seven hotel rooms!?" That's your fourteen-member crew that you took outta town with you, that bunked up in them seven rooms.

Get a Good Lawyer, So Problems Won't Pile

Mr. Dave: You need a lawyer that's objective, not someone that's buddy-buddy with everybody. But there are two sides to that. You need a lawyer that has your best interests at heart, but on the same note, you need a lawyer that's friends with the label's lawyers, because you can get more accomplished that way.

I made sure my lawyer understood that he had to look out for me before we signed any papers. When you first meet your lawyer, take him in a room, close the door, and let him understand that if he fucks your life up, you're gonna fuck his life up. A lot of people don't understand that this business is all we got. This is what we choose to do with our lives. You can give other clients down the road the dick, but if you dick me I'm gonna come see you. I'm not saying that's the way hip hop should be, but that's in any business. I don't care if you're building buses. That's the way life's run.

Lord Finesse: Your lawyer should explain fully to you what your contract is about. 'Cause usually you hand them a contract and they go, "OK, it's cool enough to sign," but they don't tell you all the twists and turns in the contract. Most artists get a lawyer who knows they're broke, but he don't really care: "Look, the check will be here next month, and that's all I can do for you." They can't sympathize with what you're going through if you're coming from the projects, or if you're coming from the hood, or whatever. When the rent is due, the rent is due.

Me, I call my lawyer on weekends. We don't even have one of those: "You're my client" relationships—it's like "Yo, you're my partner, yo what's up? How we gonna get this money this week, or this month? How we gonna attack the label to get the right things I need this year for my promotion?"

I tell my lawyer in a minute—I want a contract that you can just pick up and read. You don't even need a lawyer to tell you what's in my contract. It's a lot of flim flam, this lawyer stuff. An artist doesn't know what a standard contract is, so when a lawyer sees it he says, "Oh, this is fucked up, he was getting you for this, he was getting you for that." He don't never tell the artist, "This is a standard contract; I gotta twist a couple of things around in here, but it's gonna be all right." It's just, "Oh, it's messed up, oh, it's a lot of work here . . . hope you got money!"

Mr. Dave: A lot of lawyers just have you sign anything 'cause they don't look at you as having potential. The first piece of paper that comes through that they can get paid off of, they're like, "Sign it, hurry up." You sign it, and they get their money off the top. This whole industry ain't nothing but a big racket. The artist and the producer put their hard work and sweat into it and they're the last ones to get paid. Who get money off the top? The lawyers, the management, the distributors.

Lord Finesse: On top of that, the first thing a lawyer asks you for when you step in the office is a retainer fee. "Got my retainer? No? Oh well. I got another client comin' up in here. Call me when you get that retainer."

Wendy Day: Actually, most of the attorneys I know don't charge artists money up front. I think that if somebody does, that's the cue to walk out.

Mr. Dave: A lot of them don't, but you have to sign a retainer letter saying that if you don't pay them, they have a right to come after your publishing, royalties on your album, your shoes, everything.

Lord Finesse: You also got lawyers that tell everybody your business. If I get a deal for $500,000, I don't want the whole world to know, "My artist Finesse got $500,000 . . ."

Mr. Dave: They just put your business out there. I like my lawyer because he only deals with artists that are basically down with us. He's also dealing with a lot of rock and stuff like that, but who cares if Bon Jovi knows how much loot I'm getting? Maybe if I want to do a track with him he won't charge me that much money.

Lord Finesse: Half the lawyers don't even listen to your tape until your record comes out. They don't even care what you're doing in the studio. It's like: "Oh, you was in the studio, that's cool." They don't say, "Let me hear what your stuff sounds like."

Wendy Day: Does your lawyer listen to your stuff? Oh, wait, your lawyer's in L.A.

Lord Finesse: My lawyer listens to my shit over the phone! "I heard you was in the studio, what's your shit sound like? Oh, this is some shit here, we gettin' to it." My lawyer came from Time Warner. He used to work in a promotion position, marketing, and he saw the struggles that I went through. He got his lawyer's license and it was on after that. I think it's the best move I made in my whole life because he got me out of so many jams without that money up front. I'm where I'm at today because of him.

You Gotta Read the Labels

Elementary: Is it wise for an artist to sign with a label where the president of the label is also your manager?

Mr. Dave: It really depends on who you are. A lot of cats run to these managers at these labels because they got a name or they think, "Oh, he knows a lot of people, so I'm gonna deal with him."

Lord Finesse: There's a price for those big names. You look at those big names and say, "I'm gonna go to him or her because he's this, she's this," but when you come see that person, you ain't no dope artist or no artist that's lyrically ill—they lookin' at you as a price tag: "What can I make off of you?"

Wendy Day: I think at most labels where the label is also the manager—labels like Death Row—there's no middle person to yell at. Dave, you can't walk in and yell at Patrick [Moxey, president of Payday] and say, "Stop fuckin' O.C.," because the bottom line is he signs your paycheck.

Mr. Dave: What's unique about our situation is I knew Patrick before there was a Payday Records and I knew O.C. before I started workin' at Payday. So both of them know how far they can take me. If I am at Payday and they be like, "Yo, we want O.C. to tap dance with some pink pumps in a Macy's window," I got to walk out the door.

There is an upside to my working for both O.C. and Payday [to which O.C. is signed]. I can get things out of the label that somebody else couldn't because they wouldn't know it exists. The label will tell you, "Oh, it's not in the budget," but they can't tell me that because I have the budget in black and white. So I can say, "Instead of spending $15,000 on this conference here, why not give me the money and we can do a little commercial for [Hot 97 DJ] Funkmaster Flex?"

Lord Finesse: Management's just another form of rape. Some managers get the artist a deal, take fifteen percent off the top and then take another fifteen percent somewhere else. The rest of the work they do only gets them small fees, so why hustle to get their artist shows and clothing and commercials? That's small change compared to the $60,000 they make off the top. There ain't no more dedication with management.

Wendy Day: The attitude should be that we're building a career together.

Lord Finesse: Half these artists are so weak-minded and ignorant that they don't even understand that the management works *for* them. I've seen management take a nigga's whole budget!

You got to understand that the knowledge we drop on this tape recorder right now is what they don't want artists to know. A management that's pimpin' an artist, if that artist happen to be in a room when I'm droppin' some science, then the artist goes and flips on them—then they comin' to me like, "Finesse, what you tell them all that shit for?" It ain't my fault you didn't tell him! This hip hop shit is just like the street. If you only tell your artist half of the story, then when somebody else want to pimp him they gonna tell him a part of the story that you didn't touch on. Then your artist is not gonna trust you no more.

"You Don't Have to Go Gold or Platinum to Make a Million"

Lord Finesse: My whole moral to the hip hop situation is: You don't have to go gold or platinum to make a million, you gotta hustle. When you start hustlin', then you can get whatever you want. People be lookin' at you like, "Damn, he didn't go gold or platinum, but he chillin'." Gangstarr's a perfect example. I grew up with Premiere and Guru, chillin' in the crib with them while we was all stuck on Wild Pitch Records sayin', "One day we gonna laugh at this shit."

When I first met Ice T, I didn't even like his songs, but he's the one who pulled me off Wild Pitch and showed me what money was about. I was happy with a couple of hundreds. I did my first record for five grand at Wild Pitch. Under five grand. I mean, everybody on that project got peanuts because it was everyone's first project. I ain't even know what a recording budget looked like. Ice T scooped me up and told me, "Look, Finesse, I got $125,000 for you if you get off of Wild Pitch." "What's $125,000 for?" "That's your recording budget." "Recording budget? What's that?"

Mr. Dave: A lot of people get in the game to escape reality. A lot of guys wanna be rappers and producers and DJs because they don't want to get a real job, and they don't want to go to school to be something else. So they look at this game and be like, "Look at Finesse over there, he's livin' large and he gets up any time he wants; and look at Treach from Naughty by Nature, he drivin' a Landcruiser." Everybody wanna do it because it's quick and easy money. Now cats even want to be in the business end.

Lord Finesse: Growin' up, I had everything from paper routes to going to the store for people. I had to have a dollar in my pocket. That was just me. Whether it was gamblin', whether it was celo, whether it was chugalug or playing numbers, I had to hustle. I look at cats who go off to college for four years to come home to a ten-dollar-an-hour job. That ain't shit, that's $1200 a month. What the fuck $1200 a month gonna do for you if your rent is like $500? You gotta eat, pay bills. You gotta have cable. You aren't even in the real world today if you don't have cable.

My grandmother, she saved me from college, when I think about it. She paid for my first studio session. She schooled me to a lot of things. The family promises to send you to college when you're younger. Then when you get old everybody catches fuckin' amnesia—"Get a loan." And all that do is put everybody in debt before you even start getting paid.

There's ways to get money. I ask people all the time: If hip hop ends tomorrow, can you survive? You gotta learn a trade. Get someone to take you under their wing and teach you. If this rap shit don't take off, I'll be a fuckin' engineer. They make fifty dollars an hour just to tune music. Shit, I could do that all day and love doin' it. Rap is only a stepping stone. Don't take it like you gonna be rhymin' when you fifty, 'cause I don't. I don't care how many people are jockin' me. I'm rhymin' till I'm thirty and that's that. I'm chillin'. Niggers aren't gonna have to tomato me to get me off the stage. I know how to do production. I can get open in so many different realms in hip hop and get paid.

Give Me My Freedom: Going Independent

Lord Finesse: This whole shit is like the drug game: You gotta get yours and get out. Don't try to be kingpin of the game. When you know what you deserve, they're gonna get rid of you.

Wendy Day: Labels are corporations. They can always rob somebody else. Why give you fifteen points on your album when they can sign somebody else to a five-point deal and he thinks that he's getting all the money in the world?

Mr. Dave: The sad part is, sometimes artists have no choice but to sign a fucked-up contract. If you a dope guy and you know you a dope guy, and no one's giving you a chance, you got to get your chance right then and there.

Wendy Day: Why not put it out yourself?

Mr. Dave: To me, if you're an artist and you want to go independent, what you need to do is grab two people that you know. They don't have to have no sort of intelligence about the business, they just have to be able to add one plus one and have some money to invest. Then you go to a pressing plant and find out how much they charge to press a record up. You have some records pressed, give some to radio, and put some in record stores. Get another few cats to talk about it in magazines like this and talk to DJs.

Wendy Day: This isn't rocket science. Its not hard to figure out what the formula is: You just have to have a good team, and you have to invest your money. It's that simple. For somebody like KRS-One to not be a millionaire is unacceptable.

Mr. Dave: You'll save money if you investigate all the costs and do everything yourself. Record labels make T-shirts and say, "Oh, we paid $3.50." Really, they paid a buck and change. PolyGram be on some bullshit. They tell the artist's management, "We can't make the shirts out of house, we have to do everything in house." I tell them, "Hold up. My checks don't say PolyGram. I don't have a PolyGram ID. I can do what the fuck I want." I don't have to go through the loop to get stickers done, a poster, T-shirts. I get it done the way I want to.

Lord Finesse: And you get your shit on time.

Mr. Dave: Not only that, but people look out for you. Small businesses respect and appreciate your business. Like pressing your record. The record plant that every fuckin' PolyGram company goes through, they warp your records, put the A-side on the B-side, skip songs. And when you complain, they're like, "Oh, somebody made a mistake, we'll fix it," and hang up on you. Whereas if you go down to Pro-Discs or one of these little independents and tell them, "Yo, you fucked up my record," it's like, "Yo, I'm so sorry, I will send you an extra thousand to make up for it." And the turnaround time is better.

LS One: They'll remaster it with you right there. They'll want you to sit through the next mastering session.

Lord Finesse: It's easy to say, "Yo, let's press a record," but records cost a little bit of cheese nowadays. People press up a record and they get caught up in this sixty-to-ninety-days distribution shit. You use your last bit of savings to press up five thousand records at $2.85 a record. You would make $14,250 for those five thousand records, but even if they sell in one week you can't press any more 'cause you're out of change and you don't see any money for sixty to ninety days. Then you're fucked up 'cause your record's in demand, it's hot, and you can't press any more for sixty to ninety days. Either your record's gonna get bootlegged or someone's gonna hand you that bullshit deal: "Well, I'll press up another five thousand, but I want half."

Mr. Dave: Distribution makes the most money out of everybody in this business, because they catch you comin' and goin'. First they send out 300,000 records, then they get 200,000 returns. You gotta give them a dollar for moving that record from A to B and from B back to A.

There's a contract structure where you can buy your own returns for between a quarter and a dollar depending on who you are and how much props you got. So why would you pay somebody to move that record for a dollar, when it costs a dollar for you to buy it? You'd be better off telling the store to keep it, throw it in the ninety-nine-cent bin and make a profit. This distribution is a big game. Where do all those returns go? I never see them.

Lord Finesse: Recycled.

Mr. Dave: That's what they tell you. They say, "We got back 100,000 returns." "OK, take me to the warehouse. I want 50,000 of the returns. Take it off the top of my money." I used to do that. I used to buy returns from other companies and go across the country to little towns and say, "Look man, this record, you can get ten bucks for it. I'll give it to you for three dollars." You sell them five thousand and you makin' a two dollar profit. That's ten G's there.

Lord Finesse: [Owner of Wild Pitch Records] Stu Fine sold the rights [to the Wild Pitch library] to Japan and England. They're re-pressing all the albums but they're not telling the artists that. They don't want to see young artists get this consciousness. The stock market crashin' wouldn't be nothin' compared to how the whole industry could crash if artists got together. But it ain't gonna happen because artists are like, "If it ain't happenin' to me, I don't care." But when it happens to them, they're the ones who's like, "I had a hot record and they jerked me I'm lookin' for Wendy Day so I can get with Rap Coalition and learn how shit works."

Elementary: And then what happens when they go to Wendy Day?

Wendy Day: I pull them out of the deal by breaking the contract. It's really not difficult to break a contract.

Mr. Dave: How many artists get blackballed by the industry after you pull them out of a contract?

Wendy Day: I don't know of any. I only know of two artists that have sort of a bad reputation and that was because they chose to beat somebody down. The people who got beat down were Stu Fine at Wild Pitch and Corey Roberts at Profile. I only know of two artists that had trouble once they got out of a deal and that is because of the way they handled it.

"Soundscan is Bullshit"

Lord Finesse: Soundscan is bullshit. Say you're an artist from the projects. You underground. I put you out on my label. I don't price and position you: That means, when you walk into Nobody Beats the Wiz and Coconuts and HMV, you aren't gonna see your album with the Tupac shit or with SWV. If you ain't priced and positioned, you can't Soundscan. If you can't Soundscan, you don't come up on them *Billboard* charts, you don't even register on them listening charts that the record labels always throw in your face when you come in there. "Look, you're not Soundscanning." Well, maybe I'm not Soundscanning because y'all ain't pricing and positioning me. And even if you do Soundscan, let's say you Soundscan 20,000. You probably really sold a good 80-100,000. I'm over 100,000 for my album. You know what the Soundscan says? 24,000.

Wendy Day: It's because people were buying your album from mom-and-pop stores. Mom-and-pop don't have Soundscan.

Lord Finesse: Now, if you get smart and tell the label, "Well, I know I ain't Soundscan, but I know I sold over 100,000," then you gotta wait until the royalties come in and, "We'll show you what you sold from our book that we got for you."
   Let's say you sold 200,000. Records retail between six and seven dollars a record.

So, altogether the label made anywhere from $1.2 million to $1.4 million off of your 100,000 sales. You'll get ten percent of that. That's after videos and promotions and posters. You'll get ten percent of the $1.2 million. That's only $120,000, and you're still $180,000 in the hole. $300,000 from $1.2 million is $900,000. That's their profit. How do you still owe them something?

Wendy Day: And you have to pay them back out of your second fuckin' album.

Mr. Dave: They say, "You only sold 100,000 and that's the bad part, but the good thing is, you get another album. We're gonna give you a $100,000 budget to do this and we're gonna give you $10,000 up front."

Lord Finesse: If you get a deal like that, get as much money up front as you can. Invest it.

Mr. Dave: You never know if you're gonna put out another record. If the label doesn't want you to come out, you won't. Look at groups like Run-D.M.C., Special Ed. A lot of artists don't understand that once you sign that paper, the label has lawyers out the ass. They can keep you in litigation for years.

"We Heard Our Remix on a Tape Before I Even Had It"

Mr. Dave: Back in the day you had a whole bunch of people who expressed a desire to rap or make music. Now everyone wants to be a DJ or make a million mix tapes a day. Mix tapes fuck up the business. All these cats who are making these mix tapes and gettin' records for free should have to go out and buy them. Makin' mix tapes has gotten like radio: You gotta pay dues to get benefits. If a guy like DJ S&S who has been making tapes for years comes in and says, "Yo, let me have two records," no problem; but when a cat who I never knew before comes in and asks for two records, that's bullshit.

Lord Finesse: Mix tapes was entertaining back in the day. I was addicted to Kid Capri tapes 'cause he would kick his own rhymes and talk and shit. Half of these DJ that make mix tapes can't even rock a party.

Mr. Dave: Back in the day a guy like Ron G or Kid Capri would flip existing records so that you'd want to listen to them. You'd buy a tape not for what was on it but because of the way they formatted it. Nowadays, all I hear is, "Let me get the exclusive."

Lord Finesse: On top of these exclusives on the tape, niggas is makin' CDs now! How the fuck you gonna put my new shit on a CD when I haven't even put it out yet?

I used to do mix tapes. If it was hot, I'd be playing it on my next three tapes: I'd cut over the instrumentals, whatever. Now it's gotta stay new. Otherwise people don't buy it. I used to sell master tapes to stores for anywhere from $100 to $150. That shit is gone. I quit after I came in the store and the guy said, "Yo, 'Nesse, I usually give you $100, now I'ma give you $40 this week, 'cause I got six new DJs doin' it, and they're doin' it for $20 apiece."

LS One: You would never catch anything exclusive on my mix tapes unless its from Onyx, because that's my group. I put mix tapes out with everything that's already out that niggas is diggin'. I don't fuck with any of that exclusive shit because I'm an artist and I know what it's like. I remember when we heard our "Purse Snatchers" remix with Smoothe Tha Hustler and Trigger Tha Gambler on a DJ Cruise mix tape before I even had it, and I'm like, "This is my group, how the fuck he get this shit and now the whole world got it?"

Mr. Dave: In Japan, if you make a mix tape, you go to jail. The biggest label in the world is owned by the Japanese, and the Japanese said, "Hold up." In Japan, the only things that kids got to spend money on is music, shows, and gear. They can't strive to own a house because the country's so small that you can't buy a house unless you got a million. Kids say, "Fuck it," and spend money on CDs and tapes instead. The Japanese economy has been turned around because all these mix tapes are selling, and who's getting money for them? Some cat sitting up in his crib in New York. So they say, "Hold up, no mix tapes in the country and our records will start selling again." If America would get on some shit like that, maybe records would start selling again. All you got to do is go to the stores and arrest the ones who sell them.

Lord Finesse: These cats play your shit and act like you owe them. They come up to you and say, "I put your shit out." You put my shit out before it came out? I should put it on you, that's what I should do.

Can't Live Without My Radio

Lord Finesse: You gotta do all these exclusive special promos for the radio, too, now. It's bad enough I gotta do retail, video, all types of shit. Now I gotta sit up there and write a rhyme with this DJ's name in it—and be listenin' to all the other niggas' promos so I don't say the same rhymes? People get on some real under-the-table money shit, too.

Mr. Dave: To me, rap is turning out to be like basketball and baseball—not on the union aspect, but on the money aspect. Everybody's holdin' out for the big dollars now. I wish this whole game would go back to the way it used to be where you and your man would trade Marley Marl joints for Chuck Chillout. I would go buy an album if I liked what I heard. I wouldn't wait to hear shit on ten thousand mix tapes and on the radio!

But all these majors get in the game and they get you on the Box and MTV and all these people at radio stations don't give a fuck about you. Everyone hears it but no one buys your record. Your record might not sell shit, but mix tapes with your shit are spinning across the country. Record labels perceive every record as the same; they make every record go through the same channels. I wouldn't have a group like Onyx do the same marketing as Skee-lo because it don't work that way, but they do that.

TV and videos are only made for middle-class America. You go to places up in Wisconsin where kids go home and watch TV; hip hop is not made for these people. I'm happy if it touched those kids and they want to go out and buy hip hop records, but its not made for them. The Fugees are a perfect example. How many black kids from the Bronx went out and bought that record? Maybe about ten percent. Mostly white alternative kids are into the Fugees, so they want everyone to go that way.

Lord Finesse: They ain't even rap no more, they alternative. When you up there with a band doin' Jimi Hendrix and shit, it ain't rap no more. It's great that you combine hip hop with other forms of music, but it ain't rap no more.

Producers and Guest MCs: "Respect is a Big Factor"

Mr. Dave: We hired Jermaine Dupri to do a track for us. Jermaine Dupri didn't do it. Somebody else did it for him, and it was garbage. What it came down to was they kept half of the money and we never got a track that we could use from them. I don't use big producers. I use whoever is giving me a hit. Before you were a big producer, you had to have a hit somewhere down the line, or you had to have a dope record. So, I'm looking for the hungry kid who's running up the block talking about, "Yo, I got the next shit." A lot of artists don't know how to spend money. They think that this money is never-ending: "Oh, the company got millions; fuck it, they can afford to give me more money." It don't work like that. So what if they got ten billion dollars? All you're allotted is three hundred.

Elementary: Does hiring a guest MC for a track work the same way as hiring a producer? Let's say I'm doing a remix and I want Finesse on my joint.

Mr. Dave: If an artist signed with us says, "I want to do a song with so and so," the mistake labels make, and the mistake artists make, is that they let their management call the other management, or the label call the other label. You don't do that. You let the artist approach the artist because they got a better relationship. If you call me up and say, "Yo, I want O.C. to do something with so and so," I'm like, "I don't know that cat, never met him, I don't know his manager, nobody on his label. Fuck it, give me five or ten grand and he'll get on it."

Wendy Day: Exactly.

Mr. Dave: Whereas O.C. might be a fan of the artist, and be like, "Yo, I like your shit. I'll do it for $2500."

Wendy Day: Respect is a big factor. I mean, when Finesse worked with KRS-One, that was a respect/respect thing. They both respected each other's shit, and I'm willing to bet he didn't charge you. You probably broke him off something, but he probably wasn't charging you to do it.

Lord Finesse: Don't be too sure about that.

LS One: Onyx did songs wth Smoothe and Trigger, and with Method Man. I've known Smooth and Trigger since before they came into the rhyming life, and we've always been cool. Trigger and Khrist were signed to Def Jam, and Onyx is signed to Def Jam. So we decided, "OK, y'all do the song with us and in return we'll do a remix with y'all, so it's like an even swap. We didn't call Violator Management and ask for Trigger. I went straight to them myself. I was like, "Yo, Trig, what's the deal? We're getting ready to do this song, we want y'all to get on the remix." He was like, "What's the song?" I told him, "Purse Snatchers." They listened to the original "Purse Snatchers" on the album and they was like, "Yeah, we was talking about that song, because that's the same type of style that me and Smoothe use." "So do y'all want to get on it?" "Of course." It took like two days. We were in the studio, we did it.

Same thing with Meth. All he wanted was for us to do something with him on his new album. So that's how it went down. The second day we were doing "Purse Snatchers," Meth was in the studio, and he was mad that he wasn't on it. So him and [Onyx MC] Sticky Fingaz talked, they worked it out where we'll do a song on Meth's new album. The managers were talking behind the scenes and we were like, "We don't need all of that happening, because we took care of all of this."

Lord Finesse: It's a respect level.

Mr. Dave: Only time the label get involved with it is when it's time to sign a release, and if you got any type of props as an artist, you can get a release. And a lot of artists talk—"Yo, I'm in control of this, I'm in control of that"—and they can't even get a simple clearance to rap on a record. That will tell you who is in control of their own career.

Lord Finesse: Jive Records is like that. Jive is . . . man, they tighter than a virgin in a headlock. They put you through it. Me and Kris [KRS-One], we came to a verbal agreement. Kris is like, "I don't give a fuck about Jive, let's put it out." Boom.

Wendy Day: But Jive also hates Kris. Just like Def Jam hates Chuck D [of Public Enemy]. To clear a Chuck D voice on any record is like sticking a sharp stick in your eye, because Russell [Simmons, owner of Def Jam] hates Chuck. Then it's on some ego shit, some personal shit.

Elementary: Is that based on the relationship between the artist and the label?

Wendy Day: Yeah.

Elementary: Because the artist didn't want to get jerked?

Wendy Day: Well, it's a matter of . . . Chuck D did a record with Janet Jackson—did that ever come out?

Mr. Dave: No.

Wendy Day: OK, he did a record with Janet Jackson. Russell said, "Nah, I don't want her to use your voice." This was when she was fucking hot, a record had just come out, and Chuck was like, "I want to do this." Russell's like, "No, I'm not clearing it." And he obviously never did, because nobody's ever heard it. That's on some, "I'm going to fuck up your career"–type shit. Some "I'm tired of you, you're coming to me on some noise, I can get just as nasty as you can"–type shit.

Lord Finesse: I told my label when I first signed, I said, "I can do anything associated with Diggin' in the Crates, that's my family."

Wendy Day: You got that in writing?

Lord Finesse: No, fuck writing. That's just family, you know what I'm saying? That's who's here for me, blood and water. They'll do anything in the world for me, I'll do anything in the world for them, and ain't no contract going to stop me from getting down with my family. If I have to, I'll tear Penalty Recordings apart when it comes to my family. The only way you can survive in this game is family ties; you can't do it solo. If your label actually stops you from doing your family shit, your family will get mad at you. That will hurt your career, because when it's time to go on that tour . . . See if they'll let you go.

"New York is the Only Place in the World That's Spoiled"

Lord Finesse: Believe me, when Penalty drops me I'm coming out on my own label. If I sell a hundred thousand, you can forget it. That's half a million dollars. I could come out with six videos if I wanted to. And if I come out with six videos, what's going to stop me from going gold or platinum? The label fuckin' argues with you to give you two videos. Imagine if you got six! Everybody in the world gonna think that you larger than life.

Wendy Day: "He's got four videos, he's the man."

Lord Finesse: "Four videos, something's going on with him, just pick him up. Get him on the phone. Hello? What do you want to come here?"

Mr. Dave: That's why a lot of them Southern guys got independents. Suave. C-Bo, come on, he ain't pick up a major yet. He got three records on the charts! You know why they sell? I did a lot of research on this. New York records are over-marketed. They put out a single with three and four remixes. In the South they don't do that, they don't even put out a single. They throw the album in the store, and if you want that record, if you heard your man bumpin' it, you got to buy that whole album.

Wendy Day: And they fulfill a need. Master P knows exactly what's going to sell out in the Midwest.

LS One: In New York, they give you a B-side, a guest appearance . . .

Lord Finesse: New York is just ridiculous. New York is the only place in the world that's spoiled. In the South, records still sell by word of mouth. Here, you gotta have two singles bangin' on the radio, two videos in constant rotation, stickers the size of this table, and then it still comes back to the mix tapes.

Wendy Day: And radio's all fucked up.

LS One: Radio's monopolized by Hot 97.

Mr. Dave: There's only one radio station in town, and if you ain't playin' with them, then you ain't playin' at all.

Wendy Day: And if you want to blow up on the underground, you have to pay people to play it because they have to pay for their airtime. So you're fucked whether you come or go.

Mr. Dave: In L.A. it's the same way, so if you want to sell records you have to cater to the Midwest or the South.

LS One: But in L.A. you can sell local and go gold.

Mr. Dave: Yeah, but the radio game is still the same. The only difference is, New York artists can go out to L.A. and make money off of shows. Realistically, you are only going to know about ten people in town, so only ten people are going to get on your guest list. Whereas in New York, everybody knows you, and they show up with they man, and they cousin's friend, and they sister's uncle's brother's nephew, and . . .

Lord Finesse: Man, I get offended in New York, period. Artists have to break out of the New York state of mind. Your snipes [posters] only stay up two days if you're lucky. And do you know how much it costs to put up your snipes up in New York?

Wendy Day: A couple of G's.

Lord Finesse: You can't win in New York. People come up to me like, "Finesse, you the greatest, niggas's underrating you, you the fucking illest, I wish you all the luck in the world . . ." "Did you buy my record?" "Well, not yet . . ." "What the fuck you wishing me well for? How the fuck is you wishing me well?"

Mr. Dave: Jeru, when we would be on tour, he would go into a store and kids would be like, "Yo, I like your joint." "Yo, have you bought the album yet?" "No." So Jeru would buy it and give it to him. And I'm sure that when that kid gets money he's going to remember that day and buy the next joint. Artists have to start supporting this game, too. A guy like [Gangstarr's DJ] Premiere, he can get any record he wants free, but he still goes to Fat Beats and shops for records.

LS One: So do I. I bought two records today.

Wendy Day: And even if you're a DJ with a hot mix tape, buy the fuckin' record anyway, because first of all, you're making money; second of all, you're not paying royalties to the artist, so give them something. Buy the record so the artists get a little.

This interview originally appeared in Spring 1997 in Elementary *magazine under the title "The Artist & the Industry, or How Not to Get Jerked."*

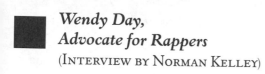

Wendy Day,
Advocate for Rappers
(INTERVIEW BY NORMAN KELLEY)

Wendy Day is the founder of Rap Coalition, a not-for-profit organization set up to help rap artists.

Norman Kelley: How long have you been doing this?

Wendy Day: Five years. I started in March 1992. I was in corporate America prior to running Rap Coalition. My background was advertising and sales, and I was very fortunate in that I made quite a bit of money. I was in Montreal at the time and I decided to come back to America, come home. I had quite a bit of money and I knew I wanted to do something to help people. I wanted to combine the money that I had with my entire business background. I have a masters degree in African-American studies and I knew I wanted to do something within the black community but wasn't quite sure as to what. I've always loved rap music since the early 1980s and I decided to take the money and start Rap Coalition. It's been five and a half years and no looking back.

Norman Kelley: Was there anything like an event or series of events that precipitated you starting the coalition?

Wendy Day: Not necessarily. It was the system that bothered me. As I mentioned, I have a degree in African-American studies and white folk have been robbing black folk since time began. So I knew I wanted to do something as a white person to sort of balance out that injustice that's been done for five hundred years. I wanted to do something that would balance that scale and I chose rap music, because it's the music I'd been listening to since the Cold Crush Brothers, since Grandmaster Flash. It's the music that has always been there for me. When I was happy, I listened to rap. When I was sad, I listened to rap. When I was tired, I listened to rap. When I was energetic, I listened to rap. So the music was my escape in my life; it was there through my saddest times and happiest times.

When I came back to the United States I knew I wanted to do something. I started studying the music business because I'm not one to jump in without learning what the climate is. I studied the music business for about eight months, and in that time period, Eric B and Rakim got jerked and X Clan got jerked, and those were two of my favorite groups—they and Public Enemy were what I was listening to. They were my favorite artists and I couldn't understand why no one stepped in to help these guys, and that's really what did it. It wasn't like one thing made me do it. It was a series of events up until that time, you know, for the past five hundred years, that led me to want to do something. But that was the straw that broke the camel's back.

Norman Kelley: How did your training in corporate America help you?

Wendy Day: The funny thing about corporate America is that you kind of learn to dance for a dollar. You learn to do what you have to do to get the job done. My background was sales and marketing and I was always very good with people. So the first thing I did with Rap Coalition was introduce very high-powered attorneys to rappers, because that seemed the one piece of the equation that was missing and the average rapper does not have access to—Madonna's attorney. So I started meeting people. I would just show up on their door steps—attorneys'—and set up meetings with them and tell them what my plans were, what I was trying to accomplish. My thinking was that Madonna's attorney makes more money that God, so chances are good that this person could probably afford to do some pro-bono work. And I also come from the belief that human nature is basically good. So somebody who had the opportunity to help somebody else probably would if that opportunity was brought to them.

I sort of acted as matchmaker between up-and-coming rap artists and very powerful attorneys. That's really what the company's first mission was. We still do that, and it's been very successful in that a lot of attorneys have taken a lot of pro-bono cases. And they are more than qualified to handle them. They are not people right out of school who don't have the time to handle it. They are very busy professionals who take one or two extra cases, in some cases five. My attorneys are handling five different pro-bono cases right now.

Norman Kelley: Have many attorneys does Rap Coalition have?

Wendy Day: About seventy.

Norman Kelley: What's the structure of Rap Coalition? Is there a structure?

Wendy Day: Yes and no. It's a loose structure. The most important aspect of the company is being able to change in order to fill needs. As the music industry changes—and it changes almost every day—so does the company, to meet those needs. We have some basic underlying principles that we go by.

Norman Kelley: Which are . . . ?

Wendy Day: Pulling people out of bad deals. Introducing people to attorneys. We have a series of educational programs, and probably as important is changing the attitude of the general public in terms of what rap music really is. That's an important one. But because the industry changes so quickly, all of the other projects are based on what the need of the day is, the need of the week, the need of the month. We have an office here in New York, an office in Chicago. By the end of the year I hope to have an office in L.A. as well.

Norman Kelley: It is interesting that you as a white person are doing this. Have you ever given any thought as to why a black person isn't or blacks themselves aren't doing this?

Wendy Day: Funny, that's usually the first question I'm asked. I think there is a problem with a white person running a black organization. I personally have a problem with that. I know my motives and I know my agenda, so if somebody has to do it and it's not a black person, I'm glad it's me. But I understand why it is a problem that a black person is not running the organization. On the flip side, there are a lot of places that my skin color gets me into and a lot of situations that my skin color gets me into. Someone from Atlantic Records is much more comfortable negotiating a deal with me than with someone who doesn't look like him or her. That's just a human nature kind of attribute. It's wrong, but it is a reality. You're dealt a certain hand in life and you play that hand.

Norman Kelley: You understand that black artists have been ripped off since the 1920s. I understand this, but why aren't today's black intellectuals or black leaders looking into this? Is it that they don't care?

Wendy Day: I don't know if they care. I know that Nelson George [a black writer who covered hip hop when it was breaking; author of *The Death of Rhythm & Blues, Buppies, B-Boys, Baps, and Bohos,* and *Hip Hop America*] cares. I know he seems to endeavor more into the film side of it. I think because this is not as glamorous, and because he has the contacts . . . He's real good friends with Russell Simmons. Why hasn't he written some sort of exposé? I'm sure he's seen it firsthand. Why hasn't he done in music what he's done in film? Maybe he has and I'm just not all up in his business. I don't know why that is, but people do know that exploitation exists.

There's no investigative journalism in music whatsoever, you know. I read *Source* magazine, I read all the magazines, even the ones you have never heard of. Craig Mack was on the cover of *Rap Pages* last month and Allen Gordon wrote an article called "Prince Among Thieves," talking about the different aspects of how he has been taken advantage of and how naïve he is. It was a great article, don't get me wrong, and I'm excited because it's a start, but it wasn't from the angle of the big bad music industry fucking over Craig Mack. It came from a stance that Craig Mack is naïve and that's the problem. It sort of blamed the victim. That seems to be the direction that criticism in music goes. People write books about the actual history of rap or the more glamorous side of things, but there is no tell-all.

Norman Kelley: Rap really became big during the mid-eighties when Run-D.M.C. proved its crossover appeal. From what I've been reading, sixty percent of those who buy rap are white kids.

Wendy Day: I bet it is a higher percentage than that.

Norman Kelley: Now, is this a matter of the tail leading the dog? Do you have black kids following someone like Puffy because he's getting paid? The question is, are these artists doing it, their particular style and content, because they want to do it, or are they responding to market demands?

Wendy Day: It's a trend. That's where the shift came. That's exactly where the shift came. It used to be that the artist would lead the market. Now, it's the market leading the artist. That's exactly the shift that occurred that inspired me to do the Rap Olympics. If we can bring the feeling of success to those who have skills rather than just those making money . . . And I'm not saying just get rid of the money-making aspect. I love that young black people are getting paid, you just don't know. I love that and I would never take that away from anybody. I just want to see the concept of success in rap music expanded a little more—not changed, but expanded to included some of the real successes.

Let's use Puffy as an example—and I'm not trying to single him out; it's just that he's in my brain right now. If Puffy were sitting here right now, today, and I said, "You know what? There's a kid in Augusta, Georgia, who's making rhymes that are creating social change," Puffy would think that's as cool as fuck. He would love that, even though he has a lot of money and he's not about that. He would love that somebody was doing that. That kid's a success—even though you don't know who he is, Puffy doesn't know who he is, and maybe even I don't know who he is. But the point is, that kid is a success. The problem is that the rest of the world doesn't see it as a success because they see Puffy as success. That's the yardstick that they are judging people by. But because of the credibility that he has, that Puffy has, because of the money he has, if he got up on a podium, like that Lotto commercial, where his voice could be heard everywhere, and said, "This kid from Rhythm and Poetry in Augusta, Georgia, is a success because he's actually keeping kids in school and keeping kids off the street or whatever social change issue he's dealing with," kids would say, "Oh, Puffy says he's a success, therefore he's a success."

Norman Kelley: Let's talk about your relationship with the Nation of Islam.

Wendy Day: I worked a lot with the Nation of Islam and when I first went to Farrakhan's house, I was ecstatic. To me, it was a symbol of success that I had achieved a level of recognition for what I do. It's pretty cool to be at a meeting at the minister's house and you're the only white person there—and he pointed that out.

Norman Kelley: Why were you there?

Wendy Day: For the Rap Summit.

Norman Kelley: What happened at that summit?

Wendy Day: Basically, we discussed that lyrical content needed to change; that the black-on-black crime that exists in the lyrics is dead, it has to go away now.

Norman Kelley: Is there a movement toward that?

Wendy Day: There has been. There has been for about two years. There has been a huge backlash against gangsta rap.

Norman Kelley: Did you think it was going to last?

Wendy Day: I thought it'd be gone two years ago.

Norman Kelley: It's still there.

Wendy Day: Sure it is. Sure it is. Especially when you leave New York. I traveled through the Midwest a lot. There's a group called the Wild West Society, and they have less than socially redeeming lyrics. The lyrical content is not positive. So when you get into the Midwest and you have people buying hundreds of thousands of politically incorrect messages, it's kind of hard to tell them to stop. How do you tell Tupac, "Don't write a song like 'Toss It Up.' Make only songs like 'Brenda Has A Baby'"? You can't. Because the buying public buys it. That's the bottom line.

Norman Kelley: How do you, as the president of Rap Coalition, deal with people like C. Delores Tucker and William Bennett, critics of rap? Have you ever met them?

Wendy Day: I have two opinions. One is my personal opinion and one is my professional opinion. As the founder of Rap Coalition, it is my job to support rap artists. Rap artists can do no wrong. When I'm out in public and somebody says, "Twisted's lyrics are wrong because he degrades black women and he talks about black-on-black crime," I will defend him to the umpteenth degree.

Norman Kelley: What would you defend?

Wendy Day: It's his right to express whatever his wants: First Amendment rights, blah, blah, blah. He's chronicling what he sees in his area of Chicago, which is called Kaytown. So he has the right to chronicle what he sees. If you don't like his lyrical content, change his lifestyle. Change the problems of the ghetto in Chicago and his lyrics will change. Then I have—Wendy-as-a-person's opinion—a problem with his lyrical content, and he knows that. I've sat down with him and said, "You know what? This shit is dead, this whole black-on-black crime thing. You have got a slave mentality. You're a lost soul and it's really pathetic." That's the personal opinion, but I would never voice that publicly. At Rap Coalition, it is my job to protect and support him. C. Delores Tucker and William Bennett are the enemies. They have never been in the situations that rap artists have been in. So I can understand why they find it odd. I understand what their goals are. I know they are trying to protect children, they're trying to protect women from misogyny. I understand that exactly. I don't have a problem with what they are trying to accomplish; I have a problem with the way they are going about it.

Norman Kelley: Which is?

Wendy Day: By attacking—attacking the messenger but not the message. If they had sat down, one on one, with a Snoop Dogg or a Tupac and tried to accomplish it that way and tried to educate Snoop on their position, I wouldn't have a problem with that. But the fact is they didn't even meet with them; they went immediately to the media and started rabble-rousing. To me, it seems that this is their agenda, but they are going about it in such a wrong way. Are they just an Al Sharpton? Are they just trying to get press? Are they media whores? That's kind of my take on it: They are media whores. Because when the cameras aren't running, what are they doing that is really making a difference? Are they really making a difference? C. Delores has been around for three years and she has accomplished less than I have in three weeks. So how dedicated is she to her cause?

Norman Kelley: How would you define the relationship between the music industry and rappers?

Wendy Day: The relationship? Rappers don't really want to be part of the industry.

Norman Kelley: Why is that?

Wendy Day: I'm not exactly sure why they don't want to be part of the industry, but they are sort of removed from the whole thing. I'm generalizing. The average rapper really doesn't want to know how the business works; they just want fame and the women; they don't even want the money, because if they wanted money they would learn how it works and learn how to manipulate that to get the money. And they don't. They don't even read the contract, for the most part.

Norman Kelley: But don't they understand that by not reading the contract . . .

Wendy Day: By the time they get here they do. By the time they get here they have been jerked. And if they are coming to my panel discussions to learn how the industry works, they are already on a superior mental plane, because they know: Study the industry, and *then* make your move. You wouldn't get on a basketball court with Michael Jordan if you didn't know to play basketball, right?

Norman Kelley: Is that what you tell some of them?

Wendy Day: Yeah.

Norman Kelley: What's their response?

Wendy Day: When they think about it, they go, "Yeah . . . you're right." If you don't study the game and, more important, how he moves, you'll never win. So why are you going to get on the court and look like an asshole? Why are you going to go to Atlantic Records and look like an asshole?

Norman Kelley: What is it that they see initially?

Wendy Day: Fame. They see a video with Jay-Z driving down the street in a Lexus. They hear Puffy on the radio every three minutes. They have a perception of this great lifestyle where you're famous and everybody loves you. Nobody hates you; everybody loves you. And you can fuck any woman you want. The president's wife? No problem. You can have her if you want her. So it's this whole misconception of more money than God and never having to worry about paying a bill. Waaaay too many women, and love from tons of adoring fans. And that's what they see and that's what they want. But it really isn't like that at all. To get to a level of Puffy is so much work. So much work. It's work and it's money. You have to have somebody behind you dumping tons of money into your project. Because you can be the greatest rapper with the best record, but if you don't have the right people working it, not getting the right publicity, not getting the right radio play, it's not going to go anywhere.

Norman Kelley: How does the music industry view rap?

Wendy Day: Let me preface this by saying this is not my opinion at all. It depends on the label. Obviously, Puffy is going to have a different view than a Craig Talbot who runs Atlantic Records, but for the most part it's "a bunch of dumb niggers," and I can see it in the deals that they offer. They front-load deals, *they* meaning record companies.

Norman Kelley: What do you mean by front-load?

Wendy Day: Front-load means they dangle money in your face. "Here's a hundred and fifty thousand dollars." They don't even talk about what you're going to get down the road. I'm generalizing again, not all labels are the same, but they say, "Okay, these guys are disposable. We'll get them to sign for a BMW or a bunch of sneakers, and a little bit of cash. We'll make a godzillion dollars and when they are not making money any more—fuck 'em. Who cares what happens to them?" And that's the perception, not just for rappers but for artists in general. Black artists in general have it even rougher because of the whole stereotype that's going on. There are stereotypes in everything. There are stereotypes about Jewish people. There are stereotypes about Middle Eastern people. But we in live a country where it is acceptable to degrade black people, and it is acceptable among both my race and black folk.

Norman Kelley: What are the typical aspects of a bad contract?

Wendy Day: First of all, there is not a typical contract. A contract is really an agreement between you and me. We sit down and you say, "Wendy, you have talent in painting toenails. So I'm going to dump five thousand dollars into you and you're going to go out and paint toenails. You've been doing it for free, but you're going to charge five dollars from now on and you're going to pay me half of everything you make until you pay me back the initial investment." That's a contract. It's not like there's a set contract for people who paint toes. Or people who lend money to people who paint toes. There is no such thing as a set contract. It's impossible to take a book like *This Business of Music* and go to the record label contract that is printed in it, then Xerox and use it, because every situation is different.

Norman Kelley: But don't record companies have standard contracts?

Wendy Day: No, they don't. They really don't. If you work for a record label, you're thinking about signing me, the rapper. There's a legal department that is going to ask me what I want or they are going to go to my lawyer, which is the preferable situation, and say, "What does this kid want?" Or they are just going to print out a contract that is as much to their benefit as possible. But each rapper comes in at a different position. Some of them have a vibe on the street and everyone knows who they are. Some of them have gotten unsigned hype in *Source*. They come at different levels. Some are straight out of school, they've never rapped a lick in their life, and they get signed. Some are Puffy's best friends. They all come in at different levels, so there are different incentives that a label has to sign them, and the contract is going to reflect that.

Norman Kelley: Is Rap Coalition trying to get a bare minimum of standardization? And if so, what?

Wendy Day: Every contract, even though they are different, includes a point system. What "points" means is this: you give me five thousand dollars to make a record and once I pay that back to you out of my royalties, I get to keep a percentage of my royalties. A good deal would be somewhere between twelve and fifteen points. That means I get twelve to fifteen percent of the net retail selling price, which, when you think about it, really sucks—but I want to be a star so I'm willing to sign to that, and that's the status quo. So a label can get away with that.

Okay, you may decide that instead of giving me twelve, to give me nine points. I've seen them as low as six. Ice Cube gave Cam six points and he signed it. Naughty by Nature gets eighteen points. They didn't start off at eighteen. I don't remember what they began with. Scarface is at thirteen. Why is Scarface at thirteen points and Naughty by Nature at eighteen points? I bet if I pull the statistics on them they sell about the same amount of units. Why is that? It's because Scarface and Naughty by Nature don't talk, but I talk to both of them and then I bring information back to both of them. I tell Scarface that they are getting eighteen. I tell them that he's getting thirteen. That's my job. My job is to educate them. What they do with that information is on them. I can't make them renegotiate their contracts. I can refer them to attorneys and accountants who can. But Scarface never will because he feels that Little Jay, his label, is working in his best interest. He doesn't have a clue. He doesn't realize it's about Jay getting rich, not Scarface getting rich. And Scarface doesn't care because whenever he needs money, he goes to Jay, and Jay just gives it to him.

Norman Kelley: And any money that Jay gives him . . .

Wendy Day: Is recoupable. When you're an artist and you pay back everything that's recoupable, you don't get to keep the masters. In fact, you don't have anything to show for it except fame. You don't get to keep shit. It is stated in almost every contract that if you leave the record label, you can't perform the songs you did for them for five years. It's usually not enforced, but what happens when the first group pisses off the labels? George Michaels pissed of the record company so badly that they may be the first ones to enforce that rule.

I have a huge problem with that whole *recoupable* element and not getting to own one's masters. I'd like to see the artists get to own their masters. I don't think the record labels should profit that much. I would like to change the laws so that you could nullify the contract if you could prove that a company was operating unfairly. I'd like the percentage to change and I don't know how far the law can go to do that. It may just have to be that we all get together and say that no one is going to sign a contract for under twelve percent. Actually, it should be higher.

I got Twisted fifty percent. He owns half his masters, he owns half of everything. And he has complete creative control. He can say, "No, I'm not doing that" on anything—on marketing, music, on how much money they spend. In fact, he did it on his first video. They wanted to spend a hundred thousand dollars, and he said, "No, I'm not spending more." He wanted to spend only fifty thousand because he knew he would have to pay it back. But he agreed on seventy-five because he didn't want to rock the boat. The point is, he felt that he saved twenty-five thousand dollars that he could put into another area—street promotions. He has a phenomenal contract. My point is, it is possible . . . it's possible. They wanted him that badly and it was the price they were willing to pay.

A version of this article was first posted on the now-defunct Word.com website on October 4, 1997, and later appeared in Gig: Americans Talk about their Jobs at the Turn of the Millennium *(Random House).* ©1997 Norman Kelley.

Death of a Nation—Where Ignorance Is Rewarded for a New Race Creation: The Niggro
BY CHUCK D

The survey might say Chuck D is a madman who might be bitter, yeah whatever, but the facts are glaringly obvious: Coon-ism is dominant when it comes to the representation of black people in the new millennium; 2000 . . . across the Mf-k'n board. I've seen a race of people reduced to mere reflections of highly financed and projected-like missiles from these same companies who fill themselves up with the idea of "it's just urban marketing." I look at television telling lies to my vision, the stations UPN (United Plantation of Niggers) and the WB (We Buffoon) Network, who will only blow a black face up that will make you laugh and make white society comfortable. I'm tired of hearing how successful this black person is or labeling him/her a "genius" just because they're continuously hilarious or have "triple-doubled" themselves to represent black people in predominately white-walled boardrooms. Yes, Amerikkka has finally Frankensteined a morphing of what/who were previously categorized as black folk into a new race: *the Niggro.*

The Niggro is rewarded by ignorance . . . an inner world within a country that has found the right formula for pimping the so-called culture and twisting its history. The Niggro cannot show intelligence in public, even to other Niggroes. If a Niggro has a degree, they're known to conceal it and not reveal their intelligence, "dumbing themselves down" because they think regular black folks ain't feelin' it. The Niggro accepts almost anything that is approved by white society. Anything that thrusts itself into "bling-bling" millionaire status, even if the credibility of black folk is flushed down the token toilet. The Niggro is lauded in *Vibe* and *Source* for its thug spirit, thus confusing it with rebellion and accepting illogic as an oath amongst young cats just to "stay in touch" or appear to be down. The Niggro follows the mentality of a thirteen-year-old to appear to be hip, instead of boldly leading the path for young cats to follow. The Niggro twists information, saying dumb things like, "Fuck it, I ain't readin' no newspapers 'cause they be lyin' an' shit," yet will wish for the day when old-school hip hop informed them . . . and go no further than that. The Niggro will rally if it comes riding on a popular trendy wave . . . but will contradict themselves with the next trendy wave. The Niggro journalists will claim they love music but know little about its history, get a token writing job, and accept most negative things taking place in the music because of its popularity.

There are Niggro rappers, singers, athletes, comedians, radio jocks, actors and reactors, executives, writers, and tons of employees sucking the corporate dicks just to pay the bills, most times at black folks' expense. The Niggro accepts "nigger ways," confusing it with the soul root of black people, just so they'll appear down and not feel guilty. The Niggro allows themselves to stay culturally screwed in the most "negroic" way and stay silent in the face of shit going down. Some white folks or other cultures with little knowledge or respect for "black legacy" will side with a Niggro because a Niggro won't ever make them feel uncomfortable about the issue of race. The Niggro asks the questions about black-on-black violence while silently contributing to some of the causes, and turning their brain off while knowing the answers. *The Niggro shows off their rewards for ignorance* to black folks and, foolishly, to everyone else while buck-dancing and out-cooning the next cat to get money to keep their created-accepted status afloat. The Niggro allows a white friend or partner to use the word "nigger" like water, even enveloping that same friend with the term. The Niggro will threaten to kill you, while never killing the "nigger" in themselves. The Niggro refuses any connection to Africa or the Diaspora. The Niggro is satisfied easily as if it's "white supremacy's pitbull." The Niggro will turn on you but never on its Amerikkkan master. The Niggro is the government's biggest COINTELPRO weapon ever . . . mutating our gifts in music, art, athletics, and sex against us—toward extinction.

In 1990 I wrote "Welcome to the Terrordome," depicting the following ten years as a *Countdown to Armaggedon*, determining our place at the base of the twenty-first century. The three categories *Negro, Nigger,* and now *Niggro* are increasingly filling out the characteristics in black people. A people lacking the basic skills to build societies in 2000+, a living panoramic genocidal flick for the world's entertainment pleasure. The new human zoo creatures for the digital age the victims of the new slavery, a matrix of mental and spiritual brain-gates and bars over our minds.

I state this because I'm weary of hearing how important hip hop is when it's a by-product of the people. Respect for the people should be paramount; instead, it's being pied-pipered by *the head Niggroes in sellout charge*. Smilin', stylin', profilin', white-lipped on their masters' dicks for the bling day. Major-owned hip hop is now about as packaged as Kraft Cheese with some suited asshole waiting for the results from the registers. Rap music is contorted to satisfy its contractual agreements, backin' its ass up into Soundscam, while the masses of black people who struggle against the one-sided racist, fascist reign are forced to be subjected to this *Million-Monkey March in Reverse*. It's hard for me to support an eighty-five-percent-white teenage audience screamin' "smoke that nigger" and call it the shit. Or maybe it is. Pop music and killin' a nigger in Amerikkka have forever been popular here. Rap music and hip hop is still a viable format for total balanced representation. That's why I support thousands of uncorrupted artists on the Web. Last week I applauded Reverend Al Sharpton and others for the Redeem the Dream March in D.C. in the stance against police brutality and racial profiling. Now, who the hell's gonna attack the genocide of mass mental brutality and racial brainwashing thru images, which result in a growing adversarial relationship between us and us?

I don't want this to be read as too psycho-deep for anyone, 'cause really I can say *fuck it* and *kiss my ass*, too. But in this Terrordome vent, I'm co-signing this wit' an attitude, but an attitude well-taken. And it's a lame excuse not to read into this because of the so-called *digital divide* widening every second, with the *Niggro cultural dam* allowing the *digital ditches* and the picking of *electronic cotton* to be dug and picked off with the soul, history, and legacy of the *lategreatblackrace* . . . clap your hands to the *Niggro* . . .

I'm out . . .

Chuck D redefined rap music and hip hop culture with a series of critically acclaimed and commercially successful albums by his group, Public Enemy. Now a public speaker and political commentator, Chuck D has hosted his own segment on the Fox News Channel and published a best-selling autobiography, *Fight the Power: Rap, Race, and Reality* (Delta, 1998). He served as national spokesperson for the National Urban League, the National Alliance of African-American Athletes, and Rock the Vote, which honored him with the Patrick Lippert Award in 1996 for his community service. A major proponent of file sharing and music on the Internet, Chuck D recently launched several e-companies, including Rapstation.com, BringTheNoise.com, and SlamJamz, an Internet-based record label.

MISTACHUCK@RAPSTATION.COM

COURTESY OF PUBLICENEMY.COM/TERRORDOME

AUGUST 30, 2000

Part

The Future of Music

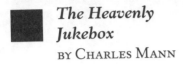

The Heavenly Jukebox

BY CHARLES MANN

Editor's note: This article originally appeared in the Atlantic Monthly *in September 2000; since that time, the Napster website has been significantly transformed as a result of further legal action by the major record labels.*

A little while ago I heard that the future of music was being decided in a nondescript office suite above a bank in San Mateo, California. I couldn't get there in time, so I asked a friend to check it out. A crowd was milling in front of the entrance when he arrived. My friend parked illegally and called me on his cell phone. There are twenty or thirty television cameras, he said, and a lectern with a dozen microphones. Also lots of police officers. I asked about the loud noise in the background. "That," he explained, "is people smashing compact discs with sledgehammers."

The compact discs contained music by the rock band Metallica. Three weeks earlier Metallica had sued a now-notorious Internet start-up called Napster, which is based on the fourth floor of the bank building. (The name comes from the founder's moniker in adolescence.) Far from being the colossus that its media prominence might lead one to expect, Napster is a surprisingly small outfit: It consists mainly of a website, about thirty-five hip, slightly disheveled employees, and a hundred or so of the powerful computers known as servers. By connecting to these computers with special software, Napster members can search one another's hard drives for music files, downloading gratis any songs they discover.

As the furor over Napster suggests, the opportunity to share music quickly and without charge has been greeted with more enthusiasm by listeners than by the music industry. Although the company's music-swapping software has only just been officially released, the service already has about twenty million regular users, and the tally is rising every day. Countless other people use Napster's brethren; the company is but the most prominent of many free-music services on the Internet. The result, in Metallica's opinion, is an outrageous pirate's Bacchanalia—millions of pieces of music shuttling around the Net uncontrolled. The group filed suit, according to its drummer, Lars Ulrich, "to put Napster out of business."

I asked my friend to visit Napster's headquarters that day because I knew that Ulrich, Metallica's lawyer, and several burly guys in T-shirts were driving to San Mateo in a black sport-utility vehicle. In the SUV were thirteen boxes full of printouts listing the user names of 335,435 Napsterites who, the band said, had traded Metallica songs during the previous weekend. Ulrich and his entourage planned to dump the boxes in the company's tiny, cluttered foyer. The people with the sledgehammers planned to shout unflattering remarks while this was taking place. Suddenly a compact man with high-tide hair and shades came to the podium: Lars Ulrich. My friend held up his phone a few feet from the drummer's face, but I could barely hear Ulrich. The catcalls were too loud.

"You suck, Lars! You sellout!"

"This is not about pounding the fans, this is about Napster . . ."

"Then why are you busting them? Have you ever even *used* Napster, Lars?"

Hooting laughter almost drowned out Ulrich's response. In an online chat with fans the previous day, Ulrich had admitted that he had never actually tried Napster. Indeed, he said later, his experience with the Internet was limited to using America Online "a couple of times to check some hockey scores." Nonetheless, his suspicions, however unfounded on experience, were entirely warranted as a matter of fact.

Within the music industry it is widely believed that much of the physical infrastructure of music—compact discs, automobile cassette-tape players, shopping-mall megastores—is rapidly being replaced by the Internet and a new generation of devices with no moving parts. By 2003, according to the Sanford C. Bernstein and Co. Investment Research Group, listeners will rarely if ever drive to Tower Records for their music. Instead they will tap into a vast cloud of music on the Net. This heavenly jukebox, as it is sometimes called, will hold the contents of every record store in the world, all of it instantly accessible from any desktop. And that will be just the beginning. Edgar Bronfman Jr., the head of Universal, the world's biggest music company, predicted in a speech in May that soon "a few clicks of your mouse will make it possible for you to summon every book ever written in any language, every movie ever made, every television show ever produced, and every piece of music ever recorded." In this vast intellectual commons nothing will ever again be out-of-print or impossible to find; every scrap of human culture transcribed, no matter how obscure or commercially unsuccessful, will be available to all.

Bronfman detests Napster. His speech likened the company to both slavery and Soviet communism. But its servers constitute the nearest extant approximation of his vision of a boundless sea of digital culture. While Ulrich spoke, I logged on to Napster. More than 100,000 people were on the company's machines, frolicking about in terabytes of music. "True fans of the talent are the ones who respect our rights," the drummer was saying. I typed in search terms: Mahler, Mingus, Method Man, Metallica . . . all were free for the taking. And all were freely being taken— users couldn't put a nickel in the machine even if they wanted to. Little wonder that the thought of such systems spreading to films, videos, books, and magazines has riveted the attention of artists, writers, and producers.

"Down in front! Down in front! . . . Metallica sucks!"

"Hey, Lars!"—a reporter. "Are you able to quantify the revenue lost?"

"It's not about revenue."

"Yeah? What's it about, then?"

In the short run the struggle is for control of the heavenly jukebox. Technophiles claim that the major labels, profitable concerns today, will rapidly cease to exist, because the Internet makes copying and distributing recorded music so fast, cheap, and easy that charging for it will effectively become impossible. Adding to the labels' fears, a horde of dot-coms, rising from the bogs of San Francisco like so many stinging insects, is trying to hasten their demise. Through their trade association, the Recording Industry Association of America, the labels are fighting back with every available weapon: litigation, lobbying, public relations, and, behind the trenches, jiggery-pokery with technical standards. Caught in the middle are musicians, Metallica among them, who believe that their livelihoods will soon be menaced by their own audiences.

At stake in the long run is the global agora: the universal library–movie theater–television–concert hall–museum on the Internet. The legal and social precedents set by *Metallica* v. *Napster*—and half a dozen other e-music lawsuits— are likely to ramify into film and video as these, too, move online. When true electronic books, e-magazines, and e-newspapers become readily available, their rules of operation may well be shaped by the creation of the heavenly jukebox. Music, according to a National Research Council report released last November, is the "canary in the digital coal mine."

This is unfortunate. Silicon Valley denizens often refer generically to writers, painters, filmmakers, journalists, actors, photographers, designers, and musicians as "content providers," as if there were no important differences among them. Yet the music industry—tangled in packages of rights that exist nowhere else, burdened by the peculiar legacies of earlier conflicts—is not like other culture industries, and digital technology is exerting different forces on it. Compared with writers and filmmakers, musicians are both more imperiled by the Internet and better able to slip past the threat. The music industry seems to have less room to maneuver. In consequence, it has been pushing for decisive judicial and legislative action. The Internet will become a principal arena for the clash of ideas that the Founders believed necessary for democracy. Allowing the travails of a single industry—no matter how legitimate its concerns—to decide the architecture of that arena would be a folly that could take a long time to undo.

"It's not about our bank accounts, it's about the thousands and thousands of artists out there who aren't fortunate enough to have the—"

"Radio is free! What about radio?"

"We have the right to control our music!"

"Fuck you, Lars. It's our music, too!"

Legislation, Litigation, Leg-Breaking

Ulrich, it seemed clear, regarded the widespread dissemination of contraband music as a dangerous new thing, another anxiety-provoking novelty from the electronic age. In fact, unauthorized music has been around as long as the music industry itself. Ulrich was not even the first musician to sue a business that he regarded as a cover for intellectual piracy. That honor may belong to Sir Arthur Sullivan, of Gilbert and Sullivan. Indeed, Sullivan's problems were, if anything, worse than Metallica's.

Like the members of Metallica, who are unusually independent of their record label, Sullivan was a careful businessman who forced the music industry to accede to his demands. In the last quarter of the nineteenth century, when Sullivan composed his operas, the phonograph was in its infancy and radio broadcasts did not exist; the chief sources of music were churches, theaters, music halls, and the pianos that were prominently featured in most middle-class parlors. All these had to be fed large quantities of sheet music. In consequence the music industry was dominated by a group of big sheet-music companies. Sheet music was immensely popular—hit pieces sold hundreds of thousands of copies. And the industry would have been even more profitable, its leaders believed, if it had not faced rampant international piracy. Bootleg Brahms and Beethoven were openly hawked on the streets of every city in Europe and the Americas. As one of Britain's most popular composers, Sullivan was a favorite target for bootleggers; he and his manager spent years fighting copyright infringement in court.

Technology, law, and culture seemed to conspire against British composers and music publishers. Improvements in printing and shipping methods had made it cheaper and easier for outlaw printers to manufacture and distribute sheet music. Worse, from the publishers' point of view, courts in many countries ruled that piano rolls (the player piano was another new invention) did not infringe composers' copyrights, because the perforations in the rolls did not look like the notes in the original printed music, and hence could not be copies of them. Building on this precedent, phonograph recordings, too, were deemed not to require licenses or payments to composers. When publishers complained, they encountered a distinct lack of popular sympathy for their plight.

One of the biggest sources of illicit sheet music in London was a limited partnership led by James Frederick Willetts, a.k.a. "the London Pirate King." The partnership was known as James Fisher and Co., although there was no James Fisher; the real principals hesitated to do business in their own names. Fisher and Co. had a simple business plan: It sold the scores for musical compositions without paying copyright holders for the right to do so. If customers ordered five hundred or more copies, the partners would prepare them to specification. "Piracy while you wait," one publisher's lawyer growled.

Is history repeating itself? At first glance the answer seems to be yes. Once again new technology has encouraged the proliferation of unauthorized music for next to nothing. Once again consumers have eagerly embraced this material. Once again complexities in copyright law seem to provide legal havens for practices detested by publishers—havens used by new businesses to give the public access to contraband music. And once again some voices are arguing that music copyright has done little but create an exploitative oligopoly that feeds on musicians and listeners alike. The way events play out today, however, may well be different from the outcome a century ago.

Sullivan fought British bootleggers but was especially outraged by their American counterparts: legitimate publishers who took advantage of a quirk in US law that denied the protections of copyright to foreign authors. The irate Sullivan filed lawsuit after lawsuit in US courts, but only dented the trade. To prevent the pirating of *The Pirates of Penzance,* he long refused to publish the score; bouncers prowled every show to stop music thieves from writing down the melodies. Tired of what he regarded as "guerrilla warfare," Sullivan paid American musicians to put their names on the scores of several operas, including *The Mikado,* and then to hand the rights back to him, thus satisfying the requirements of US copyright law. He sued American theatrical companies when the scores were pirated anyway—and lost. "No Englishman possesses any rights which a true-born American is bound to respect," one judge supposedly said. In 1900, when Sullivan died, his funeral cortège passed through London streets that were still full of scofflaw music-hawkers.

British publishers were fighting back, too. "They were losing a lot of money," says James Coover, a music professor at the State University of New York at Buffalo. "What else would you expect them to do?" As he documents in *Music Publishing, Copyright and Piracy in Victorian England* (1985), the efforts of Britain's Music Publishers' Association were at first scattershot and ineffective. The publishers tried to restrict the length of time during which people could perform sheet music before they were required to buy another copy. They asked the postmaster general to block all music shipments from the United States. They threatened to prosecute musicians who transposed songs into other keys. But eventually the publishers hit on a winning strategy: They persuaded Parliament to pass strong new anti-piracy legislation and then sought to enforce it.

The Musical Copyright Act came into effect on October 1, 1902. That day more than a thousand anti-pirate vigilantes, paid by the Music Publishers' Association, swaggered onto the streets of London, searching for and destroying illegitimate editions of "Stars and Stripes Forever," "Brooklyn Cake Walk," and "Pliny, Come Kiss Yo' Baby!" The goons became violent. Skulls were cracked, doors broken, sheet-music bonfires set. Millions of songs were seized. In addition to vigilantes, the publishers hired lawyers, who sued Fisher and Co. in 1905. Testimony was lop-sided. The publishers called more than fifty witnesses, Fisher and Co. zero. Willetts was sentenced to nine months in the clink. The light sentence annoyed the publishers, who had gone to considerable expense to prosecute him.

Nonetheless, the trial was successful, Coover told me recently: By showing the teeth in the new copyright law, the publishers "scared off" the great majority of music black-marketeers. The pirate trade quickly collapsed, done in by a determined blend of legislation, litigation, and leg-breaking.

Today's music industry, like yesterday's, initially faced unfavorable laws; like yesterday's industry, it induced the legislature to revamp them and then went after infringers with a legal club. The first attempt to prosecute someone who released copyrighted material on the Internet, in 1994, collapsed embarrassingly when the judge threw out the charges—existing case law said that infringement had to be associated with financial gain, and the material had been given away. The No Electronic Theft Act, passed in 1997, closed this loophole. The Digital Millennium Copyright Act, passed in 1998, further strengthened the industry's hand—it banned attempts to circumvent copy protection. With the help of what Edgar Bronfman of Universal recently described as a "Roman legion or two of Wall Street lawyers," the Recording Industry Association of America has for the past two years sued or threatened to sue websites that contain copyrighted songs, universities that allow students to trade tunes on their computer networks, consumer-electronics companies that produce digital music players, online-music services that lack proper licenses, and, of course, Napster. *A&M Records, et al.* v. *Napster,* an RIAA-backed suit by seventeen record companies, was filed in December, ninety-four years after charges were brought against Fisher and Co.

Some of the lawsuits have been successful, most notably a proceeding against MP3.com, a site that, among other things, lets people listen through the Internet to music they own on compact discs. (The company did not obtain the requisite licenses to provide this service.) Napster has suffered serious legal setbacks. Nonetheless, it is widely believed that this time around, laws and lawsuits will not be enough. Although the British were able to preserve their traditional way of selling music at the beginning of the twentieth century, nothing comparable will be possible at the beginning of the twenty-first—the Internet, as the new-economy magazines like to say, has Changed Everything. Hillary Rosen, the president of the RIAA, conceded to me that "there are not enough lawyers in the world to sue all the people we'd have to sue." (As it is, the association sends as many as thirty threatening letters every day.) Stop fighting to preserve the past, Rosen counsels record labels. It can't be done. The costs of manufacturing and distributing online music are so low that record companies will be forced to offer their wares on the Net. Instead of fighting the trend, she says, the industry should "embrace the opportunities" provided by the Internet. Don't try to stop the flow of zeros and ones—rechannel it!

Rosen's advice is predicated on the belief that the labels can find a way to make music files effectively uncopyable—a belief that many Internet-security experts regard as an illusion. "If people think that building higher walls and nastier barbed wire around desirable product [on the Net] is going to prevent people from getting it, they're only fooling themselves," contends Dan Farmer, a computer-security researcher for EarthLink, a big Internet service provider. Farmer strongly believes in protecting artists' copyrights; indeed, he consulted for the plaintiffs in *A&M Records, et al.* v. *Napster.* But in a time when a single click can spread a work around the world, he and others ask, how can anyone imagine that it is possible to control distribution?

In an e-mail exchange I asked Farmer what would happen if all content migrated to the Net, as many publishers promise, but none of it could be paid for, as many technophiles promise. Would this mean the collapse of the music labels, the movie studios, and book publishers? Given publishers' past successes, such an apocalyptic resolution seemed unlikely. But watching the lists of song titles on Napster drop down my screen like the slats of a venetian blind made it easy to imagine. Farmer quite properly replied that economics wasn't his field. He restated his belief that there was really not much to be done about it. Then he added, in what I imagined were the apologetic tones of someone forced to give bad news, "I can see why people get worried about this stuff, though."

Joe Average Becomes Jane Hacker

Arguably, the person most responsible for the present turmoil in the recording industry is an Italian engineer named Leonardo Chiariglione, and he is responsible only by accident. The director of the television research division at Telecom Italia's Centro Studi e Laboratori Telecomunicazioni, the Italian equivalent of the old Bell Labs, Chiariglione led the development of a standard means for converting recorded sound into digital form, which is now called MP3. The tale of the development of MP3 explains both how the music industry stumbled into its current predicament and why technophiles believe that the industry's attempts to control online copying are doomed to failure.

The International Organization for Standardization, based in Switzerland, is the world's premier standards body, establishing conventions for everything from the dimensions of letter paper to the size of screw threads. Chiariglione approached the organization—and a sister agency, the International Electrotechnical Commission, also based in Switzerland—about putting together a working group to arrive at standards for digital video and audio, both of which were on the horizon. The Moving Picture Experts Group (MPEG) met for the first time in May of 1988. Twenty-five people attended. Not one of them was from a record company. "Some of them came later, when the group became larger," Chiariglione says. "But at the time—well, nobody *knew,* you see. Nobody, I promise you, had any idea of what this would mean to music."

Converting pictures and sounds into zeros and ones creates files that are too large for most computers and networks to work with easily: A single second of music from a compact disc takes up 175,000 bytes. Researchers have invented methods of shrinking this information without losing its identifying qualities, much as shorthand shrinks written language while leaving its sense intact. Codecs, as these methods are called, take advantage of quirks in human perception. (*Codec* stands for "coder-decoder.") Because the ear can discern certain frequencies more clearly than others in particular situations, codecs can slice away the tones people don't perceive, decreasing the size of music files without greatly affecting the sound. "You'd think that people would notice if you pulled out half the sounds in their favorite music, but they don't," says David Weekly, an independent programmer who is writing an online book about digital audio.

Chiariglione's group asked for candidate audio and visual codecs. One response came from the Institute for Integrated Circuits of the Fraunhofer Gesellschaft, a group of forty-seven laboratories in Germany that helps companies develop marketable products from university research. In the 1980s a research team from the institute and the University of Erlangen developed a codec that let high-quality music be transmitted over ordinary telephone lines, fine-tuning it by encoding music, including a Suzanne Vega song, hundreds of times and listening to the results. The codec could shrink music files by a factor of twelve or more with little loss of quality. With the Fraunhofer-Erlangen team's help, Chiariglione's group laboriously incorporated the codec into its first audiovisual standard, MPEG-1. Completed in 1992, MPEG-1 described three separate but related schemes—"layers," in the jargon—for converting sound into a pattern of ones and zeros. Layer 1 and Layer 2 were intended for high-performance applications; Layer 3, a buffed-up version of the Germans' ideas, was intended for devices that handle data relatively slowly, such as today's personal computers. MPEG-1, Layer 3 is what is now called MP3.

To show industries how to use the codec, MPEG cobbled together a free sample program that converted music into MP3 files. The demonstration software created poor-quality sound, and Fraunhofer did not intend that it be used. The software's "source code"—its underlying instructions—was stored on an easily accessible computer at the University of Erlangen, from which it was downloaded by one SoloH, a hacker in the Netherlands (and, one assumes, a *Star Wars* fan). SoloH revamped the source code to produce software that converted compact-disc tracks into music files of acceptable quality. (The conversion is known as "ripping" a CD.)

This single unexpected act undid the music industry. Other hackers joined in, and the work passed from hand to hand in an ad-hoc electronic swap meet, each coder tinkering with the software and passing on the resulting improvements to the rest. Within two years an active digital-music subculture was shoehorning MP3 sites into obscure corners of the Net, all chockablock with songs—copyrighted songs—that had previously been imprisoned on compact discs.

No one was more surprised than Chiariglione. The main application the experts group had foreseen for MPEG-1, of which MP3 is a part, was CD-i, a now-uncommon form of interactive compact disc developed by Philips and Sony to put games and educational programs on television sets. But on the Net little is predictable. The development of MP3 software happened with the burbling, self-organizing spontaneity that is one of the global network's most salient characteristics—and the ultimate source of the music industry's digital dilemma.

Napster was incorporated in May of 1999, and released its software in preliminary form three months later. It quickly caught on, spawning imitations and variants, commercial and nose-thumbingly uncommercial: Wrapster, Napigator, Gnutella, Scour Exchange, CuteMX, iMesh, eCircles, FileSwap, Gnarly!, MP123, NetBrilliant, OnShare, Angry Coffee—even, mockingly, Metallicster. Much of the software is hard to find, slow, buggy, and unfinished, requiring so much perseverance that one might expect only adolescents to use it. Adolescents, as it happens, are the labels' biggest market, and indeed, the infelicities of the user experience have not deterred them from ripping and trading CDs on these services. Estimates of the number of MP3 files on the Net range from just under a hundred million to more than a billion. Some students, blessed with the fast Internet links common at universities, have thousands of songs on their computers. In April 2000 the Bernstein Investment Research Group warned that within three years the industry could lose as many as one out of six CD sales to Internet piracy.

"The sharing may be technically illegal, but there's no way to stop it," says Whitney Broussard, a lawyer at the music-law firm of Selverne, Mandelbaum and Mintz. "Already the entire body of important musical works is in compact-disc format—unencrypted digital copies" that are freely convertible into MP3 files. MP3 itself can't be retrofitted to enforce copyrights, because today's ripping and playing software wouldn't be able to comprehend the add-ons. Similarly, CD players can't readily be changed to make copying impossible; indeed, a trial release in Germany of copy-protected CDs foundered in early 2000, because some consumers couldn't get them to play. As for halting the spread of MP3s ripped from CDs, Broussard says, "It's too late."

Furthermore, the industry is not simply fighting an unorganized group of college kids. In an illustration of Lenin's remark about capitalists selling the rope with which to hang themselves, businesspeople are lining up to profit from activities they officially decry.

The trade association for record stores, the National Association of Recording Merchandisers, trumpets on its website its support of "aggressive efforts to fight piracy." And yet the National Record Mart, an association member that owns more than 180 record stores, announced last March—in an if-you-can't-beat-'em-join-'em move—that it would buy MP3Board.com, a company that runs a website that searches for and posts links to illicit music files. When the RIAA tried to shut down MP3Board.com, in May 2000, the company sued, demanding that the court preemptively rule that its service is legal. (The labels countersued in June.) Perhaps more startling, Scour.com, a rapidly growing start-up with a Napsterlike service called Scour Exchange, is bankrolled in part by Michael Ovitz, agent and manager to the stars. A search on Scour for Robin Williams, a client of Ovitz's management company, turned up more than fifty copies, all available for downloading, of comedy routines from Williams's recordings.

Beset by a growing mass of enemies, the labels and dozens of other companies—retailers, consumer-electronics firms, information-technology companies, trade associations, dot-coms of various persuasions—have been meeting to create what is uneuphoniously known as the Secure Digital Music Initiative. The goal is to create security measures that will permit the industry to release music on the Internet without fear of its spreading uncontrollably. Unlike the bulk of today's online music, SDMI music will be playable only on software and hardware that follows SDMI rules about copying. It will be as if CDs could be played only on special stereo systems that cannot be hooked up to tape recorders. Most important, customers won't be able to trade downloaded SDMI music on Napster and its ilk. More accurately, customers will be able to shuttle files around Napster freely, but the SDMI protection will control the circumstances under which the files can actually be played. In theory, SDMI will return control of the music to the industry—a necessary precondition, in Bronfman's view, for the "huge creative and industrial efforts" required to build the heavenly jukebox and the planetary sea of content that will follow it.

The head of SDMI is an engineer with considerable experience with large, fractious groups: Leonardo Chiariglione. Despite his efforts, the initiative has been plagued by feuding and foot-dragging. SDMI members include both record stores and e-commerce sites that hope to drive them out of existence, record labels that want to shut off free music, and hardware manufacturers that are rushing scores of Walkman-like MP3 players to the market, and such active legal antagonists as Napster and the RIAA.

But even when SDMI music finally becomes available, it "just won't work," according to Gene Hoffman, an SDMI participant who is the president of the online music store EMusic.com. "There's no way it will do the things they want it to do, which is to lock up this kind of content."

Encoding computer files in a way that prevents unauthorized copying is a form of cryptography. No matter how SDMI encodes a song, explains Martin Eberhard, the CEO of Nuvomedia, which manufactures electronic books, it must be listened to in unscrambled form, which means that somewhere on the computer the song exists in "plaintext," as cryptographers call it. The decrypted stream of data can be captured, in the digital equivalent of putting a tape recorder in front of stereo speakers. "It doesn't matter how good the cryptography is," Eberhard says. "Once [the music] is decrypted, you just bypass the cryptography and re-rip the music into an MP3."

SDMI employs the further protection of embedding digital watermarks in the music. SDMI software looks for the watermarks; if they have been altered, which happens if the music is illicitly decrypted, the software refuses to play the music. But watermarking, too, is vulnerable to attack, according to Bruce Schneier, an Internet-security consultant who is the author of *Secrets and Lies*, a disquisition on the pitfalls of computer networks that is being published this month. "At the moment, the techniques are hard to do," he says. But the Net is very good at bringing down the bar. "You always have two kinds of attackers—Joe Average and Jane Hacker. Many systems in the real world only have to be secure against Joe Average." Door locks are an example: They're vulnerable to expert thieves, but the chance that any one door will encounter an expert thief is small. "But if I am Jane Hacker, the best online," Schneier says, "I can write a program that does what I do and put it up on the Web—click here to defeat the system. Suddenly Joe Average is just as good as Jane Hacker."

In 1999 Microsoft released a new version of Windows Media Audio, an equivalent to MP3 that the company touted as secure: Songs in the format could be restricted to a single personal computer. Within hours of its release somebody with nothing else to do slammed together a program, archly called "unfuck," that intercepted the decrypted data and stripped away the restrictions. Hours after that the program was available on websites around the world, from one of which I recently downloaded it. "If your stuff is on everybody's desktop, people will try to tinker with it," Gene Hoffman says. "You're giving the whole world a chance to crack your cryptography on machines that inherently make that easy to do."

These difficulties are not restricted to music. Contemplating the apparently ineluctable growth of the global network, book publishers and film studios see themselves rushing toward a digital dilemma of their own. Like the record labels, they recognize the overwhelming speed, ease, and cheapness of online distribution. At the same time, they fear—with good reason—that what has happened to the music industry will happen to them. On March 14, 1999, Stephen King electronically released a novella, *Riding the Bullet*, in a format that was readable only by using designated electronic books or special software. Just three days later a plaintext version appeared on a website in Switzerland. Remarkably, the crackers troubled themselves to break the code even though Amazon.com and Barnes and Noble were offering the authorized version at no charge.

Film studios use what is called the Content Scrambling System to encrypt digital video discs. In 1999 at least two groups of European hackers raced to break the CSS encryption; the better software, DeCSS, was released on the Web in October. It was used by yet another band of hackers to create a new compression scheme, called DivX, that can shrink feature films to six hundred megabytes—small enough to be traded, Napster-style, by people with ultra-fast connections. The software, which is distributed from a website ostensibly based on a group of islands in the Indian Ocean, is hard to use, unreliable, and popular; a week after the release of *Mission: Impossible 2*, I found DivX copies on the Net. Meanwhile, the movie industry has been trying to suppress not only the hundreds of websites around the world that host unauthorized software but also the much larger group of sites that link to them. Because new DeCSS and DivX sites pop up as rapidly as the old ones are taken down, the studios are facing a grim, unwinnable contest of legal Whack-a-Mole.

Given the huge number of MP3 files already in existence, the explosion of file-sharing software, the willingness of companies to try to profit from illicit copies, and the likelihood that SDMI will be circumvented, it seems reasonable to suppose that the music industry will never be able to restrict copyrighted material on personal computers connected to the Internet. Nor will print publishers or video or film producers. The content industry therefore has two possible courses of action. One is to prepare for a world in which copyright plays a much smaller role. The other is to change the Internet. The first alternative is problematic, to say the least. The second could be much worse.

They're Paying Our Song

Every year Austin, Texas hosts South by Southwest, the nation's biggest showcase for independent rock and roll. Hundreds of bands play in the city's scores of enjoyably scruffy bars, which are thronged by young people with the slightly dazed expression that is a side effect of shouting over noisy amplifiers. When I attended the festival in the spring of 2000, I was overwhelmed by the list of bands—almost a thousand in all, most of them little-known hopefuls. I had no idea how to sort through the list for what I would like. Luckily for me, I ran into some professional music critics who allowed me to accompany them, which is how I ended up listening to the Ass Ponys late one night.

Led by a husky singer and guitarist named Chuck Cleaver, the Ponys crunched through a set of songs with whimsical lyrics about robots, astronauts, and rural suicide. At the back of the room, beneath an atmospheric shroud of cigarette smoke, was a card table stacked with copies of their most recent CD, *Some Stupid With a Flare Gun*. By the bar stood a tight clump of people in sleek black clothing with cell phones the size of credit cards. With their Palm hand-helds they were attempting to beam contact information at one another through the occluded air. They didn't look like local students, so I asked the bartender if he knew who they were. "Dot-commers," he said, setting down my beer with unnecessary force.

Silicon Valley had overwhelmed South by Southwest. In a festival usually devoted to small, colorfully named record labels with two-digit bank balances and crudely printed brochures, the slick ranks of the venture-capitalized were a distinct oddity. It was like a visitation from a distant, richer planet.

Music, especially popular music, has been a cultural bellwether since the end of World War II. Swing, bebop, blues, rock, minimalism, funk, rap: Each in its own way has shaped cinema, literature, fashion, television, advertising, and, it sometimes seems, everything else one encounters. But the cultural predominance of the music trade is not matched by its financial import. Last year the worldwide sales of all six hundred or so members of the Recording Industry Association of America totaled $14.5 billion—a bit less than, say, the annual revenues of Northwestern Mutual Life Insurance. As for the tiny labels at South by Southwest, many of the dot-coms in attendance could have bought them outright for petty cash.

After the show I asked Cleaver if he was concerned about the fate of the music industry in the Internet age. "You must be kidding," he said. With some resignation he recounted the sneaky methods by which three record labels had ripped off the band or consigned its music to oblivion, a subject to which he has devoted several chapters of an unpublished autobiography he offered to send me. (He had nicer things to say about his current label, Checkered Past.) Later I asked one of the music critics if Cleaver's tales of corporate malfeasance were true. More than true, I was told—they were typical. Not only is the total income from music copyright small, but individual musicians receive even less of the total than one would imagine. "It's relatively mild," Cleaver said later, "the screwing by Napster compared with the regular screwing."

Although many musicians resent it when people download their music free, most of them don't lose much money from the practice, because they earn so little from copyright. "Clearly, copyright can generate a huge amount of money for those people who write songs that become mass sellers," says Simon Frith, a rock scholar in the film-and-media department at the University of Stirling in Scotland, and the editor of *Music and Copyright* (1993). But most musicians don't write multimillion-sellers. Last year, according to the survey firm Soundscan, just eighty-eight recordings—only .03 percent of the compact discs on the market—accounted for a quarter of all record sales. For the remaining 99.97 percent, Frith says, "copyright is really just a way of earning less than they would if they received a fee from the record company." Losing copyright would thus have surprisingly little direct financial impact on musicians. Instead, Frith says, the big loser would be the music industry, because today it "is entirely structured around contracts that control intellectual-property rights—control them rather ruthlessly, in fact."

Like book publishers, record labels give artists advances on their sales. And like book publishers, record labels officially lose money on their releases; they make up for the failures with the occasional huge hit and the steady stream of income from back-catalogue recordings. But there the similarity ends. The music industry is strikingly unlike book publishing or, for that matter, any other culture industry. *Some Stupid With a Flare Gun*, for example, contains twelve songs, all written and performed by the Ass Ponys. From this compact disc the band receives, in theory, royalties from three different sources: sales of the disc as a whole, "performance rights" for performances of each of the twelve songs (on radio or MTV, for instance), and "mechanical rights" for copies of each song made on CD, sheet music, and the like. No real equivalent of this system exists in the print world, but it's almost as if the author of a book of short stories received royalties from sales in bookstores, from reading the stories to audiences, and from printing each story in the book itself. The triple-royalty scheme is "extraordinarily, ridiculously complex," says David Nimmer, the author of the standard textbook, *Nimmer on Copyright*. Attempts to apply the scheme to the digital realm have only further complicated matters.

As a rule, the royalty on the CD itself—typically about $1.30 per disc before various deductions—goes to performers rather than composers. After paying performers in advance against royalties, as book publishers pay writers, record labels, unlike publishers, routinely deduct the costs of production, marketing, and promotion from the performers' royalties. For important releases these costs may amount to a million dollars or more. Performers rarely see a penny of CD royalties. Unheralded session musicians and orchestra members, who are paid flat fees, often do better in the end.

Paying back the record label is even more difficult than it sounds, because contracts are rife with idiosyncratic legal details that effectively reduce royalty rates. As a result, many, perhaps most, musicians on big record labels accumulate a debt that the labels—unlike book publishers—routinely charge against their next projects, should they prove to be successful. According to Whitney Broussard, the music lawyer, musicians who make a major-label pop-music compact disc typically must sell a million copies to receive a royalty check. "A million units is a platinum record," he says. "A platinum record means you've broken even—maybe." Meanwhile, he adds, "the label would have grossed almost eleven million dollars at this point, netting perhaps four million."

As a standard practice labels demand that musicians surrender the copyright on the compact disc itself. "When you look at the legal line on a CD, it says 'Copyright 1976 Atlantic Records' or 'Copyright 1996 RCA Records,'" the singer Courtney Love explained in a speech to a music convention in May. "When you look at a book, though, it'll say something like 'Copyright 1999 Susan Faludi' or 'David Foster Wallace.' Authors own their books and license them to publishers. When the contract runs out, writers get their books back. But record companies own our copyrights forever."

Strikingly, the companies own the recordings even if the artists have fully compensated the label for production and sales costs. "It's like you pay off the mortgage and the bank still owns the house," says Timothy White, the editor-in-chief of *Billboard*. "Everything is charged against the musician—recording expenses, marketing and promotional costs—and then when it's all paid off, they still own the record." Until last November artists could take back their recordings after thirty-five years. But then, without any hearings, Congress passed a bill with an industry-backed amendment that apparently strips away this right. "It's unconscionable," White says. "It's big companies making a naked grab of intellectual property from small companies and individuals."

The other two kinds of royalties—performance and mechanical rights—go to songwriters and composers. (The Ass Ponys receive these because they write their own songs; Frank Sinatra did not, because he sang mostly jazz standards.) Songwriters receive performance-rights payments when their compositions are played in public—executed in concert, beamed over the radio, sprayed over supermarket shoppers from speakers in the ceiling. Individual payments are calculated through a complex formula that weighs audience size, time of day, and length of the composition. In the United States the money is collected primarily by Broadcast Music Incorporated and the American Society for Composers, Authors, and Publishers, known respectively as BMI and ASCAP. Mechanical rights derive in this country from the Copyright Act of 1909, which reversed earlier court rulings that piano rolls and phonograph recordings were not copies of music. Today the recording industry pays composers 7.55 cents for every track on every copy of every CD, pre-recorded cassette, and vinyl record stamped out by the manufacturing plants. The fee is collected by the Harry Fox Agency, a division of the National Music Publishers' Association, which represents about 23,000 music publishers. In 1998 performance and mechanical rights totaled about $2.5 billion.

Because US labels, publishers, and collecting societies do not break down their cash flow, it is difficult to establish how much of the $2.5 billion American songwriters actually receive. But in an impressively thorough study, Ruth Towse, an economist at Erasmus University in Rotterdam, ascertained that in Britain from 1989 to 1995 the average annual payment to musicians was $112.50. Musicians in Sweden and Denmark made even less. Although the system in the United States is different, the figures, as Towse drily observed, "do not suggest that performers' rights considerably improves performers' earnings."

A few composers—the members of Metallica, for instance, who perform their own songs—do extremely well by copyright. But even some of the country's most noted performers and composers are not in this elect group. Among them was Charles Mingus, who wrote and played such now-classic jazz pieces as "Goodbye, Pork Pie Hat" and "Better Git it in Your Soul." According to Sue Mingus, his widow and legatee, "Charles used to joke that he wouldn't have recognized a royalty check if it walked in the door." She meant royalties on record sales; Mingus did receive checks for performance and mechanical rights. But when I asked what Mingus's life would have been like without copyright, she said, "It would have been harder. He took copyright very seriously. But what kept him going financially was that he toured constantly." Few rock performers have this alternative: Their equipment is so bulky and expensive that their shows can lose money even if every seat is sold.

Musicians, who are owed many small checks from diverse sources, cannot readily collect their royalty payments themselves. Similarly, it would be difficult for radio stations to seek out and pay every label and publisher whose music they broadcast. In consequence, there are powerful incentives to concentrate the task into a small number of hands. Further driving consolidation is the cost of marketing and advertising. Promotion is expensive for book publishers and movie studios, too, but they aren't trying to place their wares on the shrinking playlists of radio-station chains and MTV. Because singles effectively no longer exist, playlists are not based on their sales; songs on the radio function chiefly as promotional samples for CDs. Instead, playlists are based on criteria that people in the trade find difficult to explain to outsiders, but that include the expenditure of large sums for what is carefully called "independent promotion"—a system, as Courtney Love explained, "where the record companies use middlemen so they can pretend not to know that radio stations . . . are getting paid to play their records." Although Love didn't use the word, the technical term for paying people to play music is *payola*.

Payola wasn't always illegal, and similar schemes still aren't in many industries: consumer-products firms, for example, pay supermarkets "slotting allowances" to stock their wares. According to the author and historian Kerry Segrave, one early payola enthusiast was Sir Arthur Sullivan, who in 1875 paid a prominent singer to perform one of his compositions before music-hall audiences. Until his death Sullivan sent a share of his sheet-music royalties to the singer.

Although the payola market thrived in the vaudeville era, it did not become truly rapacious until the birth of rock and roll. Chuck Berry divided the royalties from his hit "Maybellene" with two DJs. Dick Clark, the host of *American Bandstand*, had links to a record company and several music publishers. After a chest-thumping congressional investigation, highlighted by appalled evocations of the evils of rock and roll, anti-payola legislation was passed in 1960. The labels outsourced the practice to "independent promoters," a loose network of volatile individuals with big bodyguards and special relationships with radio stations. Millions of dollars went for payola—much of it recouped from artists' royalties. A second wave of investigations, in the 1980s, did not end the practice.

At present the music industry is dominated by what are called the five majors: Warner, Sony, EMI, BMG, and Universal. (Warner and EMI have announced plans to combine; the joint label would become part of the merged America Online and Time Warner.) The majors control about eighty-five percent of the market for recorded music in this country. They do this by routinely performing the paradoxical task of discovering and marketing musicians with whom a worldwide body of consumers can form relationships that feel individual and genuine. "You want to fill up stadiums with people who think that Bruce Springsteen, the voice of working-class America, is speaking only to them," says David Sanjek, the archives director at BMI and a co-author, with his late father, of *American Popular Music Business in the 20th Century* (1991). "The labels are often incredibly good at doing this."

Music critics frequently sneer at the practice of manufacturing pop concoctions like Britney Spears and the Backstreet Boys. But in this way the labels helped to create Elvis, the Beatles, and the Supremes—musicians who embodied entire eras in three-minute tunes. As Moshe Adler, an economist at Columbia University, has argued, even listeners who grumble about the major-label music forced on them are probably better off than if they had to sort through the world's thousands of aspiring musicians on their own. But this benefit to consumers comes at a cost to musicians. Records that are hits around the world inevitably draw listeners' attention from music by local artists that might be equally pleasing. "The money is made by reducing diversity," Adler says.

For better or worse, the star-maker machinery behind the popular song, as Joni Mitchell called it, is the aspect of the music industry that would be most imperiled by the effective loss of copyright to the Net. If the majors can't reap the benefits of their marketing muscle, says Hal Varian, an economist and the dean of the School of Information Management and Systems, at Berkeley, "their current business model won't survive." The impact on their profits could be devastating. Musicians have much less to lose, and much less to fear.

Elton John Gets Mad

To many musicians, the threat to the majors posed by the Net is more than counterbalanced by the promise of the heavenly jukebox. Ultimately, many music pundits say, listeners will simply pay a monthly fee and download whatever music they want. Music will no longer be a product, acquired in a shrink-wrapped package, in the vision of Jim Griffin, the co-chairman of Evolab, a start-up that is attempting to create a wireless version of the jukebox. Instead it will become a service, almost a utility. Consumers will have ready access to more artists than they do now, but will pay less for music; musicians will no longer be forced to cover exorbitant production costs, and will be able to reach audiences more easily than ever before. "Musicians will get paid," Griffin promises. "But to the consumer, music will feel free—just the way cable TV feels free once you've paid the fee."

Huge obstacles stand in the way of this attractive vision. Legally, downloading a song can be construed as being simultaneously a sale (someone is buying the song), a broadcast (the song is being transmitted over the Internet), and a mechanical copy (the buyer is making a copy on a hard drive). Pooling the world's music would require negotiating copyright licenses with dozens of collecting societies (ASCAP, BMI, Harry Fox, and the like) here and abroad, hundreds of record companies big and small, and thousands of independent music publishers. One would also have to obtain licenses from the patent-holders on the codec and the developers of the copy-protection software, if any is used. The entire musical output of the world may well end up on Napster or its equivalent before the lawyers finish.

This possibility may not prove completely disastrous. In the past, creators who have lost revenue they should have received from intellectual property have been able to find other ways to support themselves, even if under reduced circumstances. Musicians will still be able to charge for performances, sell T-shirts, and make personal appearances at the launch parties of new dot-coms. Some may follow the singer-songwriter Todd Rundgren's lead and send subscribers regular shipments of music for a fee. Others will use the Net to introduce listeners to their music with the hope of then charging for more. More than a million people downloaded music by the band Fisher from MP3.com, and as a result the band was signed by a major in early 2000.

Such plans are not limited to pop groups. Symphony orchestras have been losing record contracts as labels cut back on releases whose sales potential are small. In June 2000, sixty-six symphony orchestras and opera and ballet companies, among them some of the nation's most prominent, announced that they were joining together to build audiences by distributing their music over the Net. Musicians will explore services like MP3.com's DAM, which charges fans a fee to burn songs from unsigned bands onto custom-made CDs; the musicians and the website split the proceeds. The company also pays bands to let their work be syndicated to restaurants and other establishments as hip background music. David Bowie, ever inventive, has sold bonds based on his future earnings. The singer-songwriter Aimee Mann, regarded by her label as uncommercial, successfully released a CD over the Internet. Limp Bizkit announced plans for a national tour of free concerts, with the band's fee picked up by a corporate sponsor—Napster.

In addition, businesses will probably still have to pay: They can be sued more readily than individuals for playing illicit music. And advertisers, broadcasters, film companies, websites, and other companies will always be interested in music. "Music draws a crowd," Griffin says. "And there are a lot of reasons that companies are interested in crowds. Look at the JVC Jazz Festival in New York, or Budweiser sponsoring the Rolling Stones." These firms sponsor music not to sell compact discs but because music provides an environment in which to put across a message. "Maybe Coke will find a way to integrate itself directly into the shows," says Hal Varian, the Berkeley economist. "Or they'll release the music free on the Internet, except that it will be wrapped in a commercial."

Varian is untroubled by the thought of corporate-sponsored music. What difference does it make if the Spice Girls are marketed by Coca-Cola or by Virgin Records, soon to be a subdivision of AOL Time Warner? The difference is that Virgin must recoup its costs from the sale of CDs and cassettes, whereas Coca-Cola can write off the whole undertaking as an advertising expense. If it hired experienced marketers, Coca-Cola, which has annual revenues much higher than those of the entire music industry, would be far better able to promote music than any individual label. If Virgin cannot make money from the sale of music, it will either be hired by Coca-Cola—or Nike, or Ford, or Frito-Lay—or be replaced by it.

Even if they lost their supremacy, the labels would still have ways to make money. Their expertise in production and marketing would still be valuable. And their control over the copyrights on music of the past would still generate licensing revenues from advertisers, broadcasters, and other businesses. Indeed, the proliferation of Internet radio and music-subscription services may create a windfall for the labels' music-publishing arms. But there is little doubt that in a world where individual listeners can ignore copyright rules, the labels will lose their dominant position.

Surprisingly few performers and composers would mourn the fall of the majors. The hostility musicians routinely express toward their industry is unlike anything in book publishing or even in Hollywood. Elton John, who has sold more than sixty million records and won four Grammies, is like a Stephen King or a John Grisham of music. It seems fair to say that neither writer would, as John did in March on the *Today* show, vehemently denounce publishers as "thieves" and "blatant, out-and-out crooks." The major labels were now "just laughing all the way to the bank," he said.

"But they won't be laughing very soon, because when the music on the Internet comes in, the record companies will all be crying."

When I tried to describe this rosy picture of artistic self-sufficiency on the Net to the science-fiction writer Bruce Sterling, he was able to contain his enthusiasm. In 1993 Sterling became one of the first writers to post a book in its entirety on the Internet. The effort was part of a time "when writers really had the idea that with all this great technology they could bypass the Man and go directly to the public," he told me. "Hell, I believed it—sort of, I guess. And you know what we all found out? It never works. Either you spend all your time marketing yourself, in which case you don't actually write, or you hand over the marketing to your website guy or the new Internet entrepreneur who's going to take care of it all for you, and they then become your new boss."

Some artists may do well under the new system, Sterling said. Some won't. But, as he points out, the current attempt to weigh the results of the loss of effective copyright assumes that the majors will sit by passively as their role is usurped. They won't, of course. As they did in the past, they'll fight with every available weapon. And sooner rather than later they'll go after the Internet itself.

Fear and Greed

When I was younger, I was briefly in a rock band. Some of its members were not completely devoid of musical talent; alas, I was not one of them. As often occurs in such situations, I was assigned to the drums. Eventually the other members decided that having no ability to keep a beat was even more of a handicap on the drums than on other instruments, and I was replaced by someone who also couldn't play drums but at least had the potential to learn.

I recently obtained a tape we made in performance. Because I wanted to learn more about digital music, I decided to make a project of converting the songs on the tape into MP3 files. After considerable fussing I was able to listen to my younger self on the tinny little speakers that flank my monitor. The experience failed to provoke regret about the road not taken. In fact, it provoked little thought of any kind until a few days later, when I loaded up Gnutella.

Gnutella is software that (again!) is being developed by a loose band of young people with a lot of spare time. (The name Gnutella comes from a combination o

"Nutella," a thick chocolate-hazelnut spread presumably favored by the program's developers, and the GNU Project, a free-software group.) Like Napster, Gnutella allows people to search one another's hard drives for pieces of music; unlike Napster, Gnutella lets its users swap pictures, movies, and texts.

After the Gnutella window came up on my screen, I saw that its users were sharing about a million megabytes' worth of pictures, sounds, programs, and texts. And then, to my shock, I saw that somebody was trying to copy my band's music.

Because the last thing I wanted was to reveal this stuff to the world, I quickly slammed the program shut. After double-checking to ensure that Gnutella wasn't running, I sat in my chair, somewhat unnerved. I was safe—should I run for public office, my opponent would not be able to use the music to ridicule me in attack ads. But who had tried to copy it, and how had they found it? A few minutes later I figured it out. I had stuck the MP3s in a directory with other MP3s. Because I couldn't remember the names of the songs we played, I had awarded whimsical names to the computer files of those songs. Some of the names were variants on the names of famous rock tunes. A Gnutella user searching for the originals had come across mine and tried to download one of them.

In this small way I walked in Lars Ulrich's shoes. The impetus for Metallica's legal attack on Napster was the circulation on the service of rough drafts of "I Disappear," a single from the soundtrack of *Mission: Impossible 2*. With the volatile promiscuity of the Internet, unfinished versions had been copied hundreds of times, depriving the group of control over its own work and, possibly, of some sales. When the musicians complained, they were astounded by the angry reaction. Trying to stop what they viewed as the forced publication of private material, Metallica—rebellious rock and rollers for twenty years—suddenly found themselves accused of censorship and toadying to corporate America.

Did the band in fact lose money, in addition to control? Ascertaining the financial impact of file-swapping is difficult—indeed, the discussion quickly verges on the theological. Because not everyone who downloads a song would otherwise have paid for the compact disc, one can't simply multiply the number of illicitly traded CDs by the average price of a CD to estimate the economic impact of unauthorized copying. So pro- and anti-sharing advocates rely on indirect data. In May, Reciprocal, a start-up in New York that hopes to make money from secure downloads, released a study showing that CD sales at stores near colleges—thought to be hotbeds of Napster users—had slipped slightly, whereas overall CD sales had risen. Scoffing, pro-Napster forces pointed out that now, when MP3 is supposedly destroying the music business, the industry is selling more compact discs than ever before. Such sales increases, in the view of John Perry Barlow, an advocate of sharing and a former lyricist for the Grateful Dead, are the logical outcome of music-swapping, which exposes audiences to new music. Counterargument: It is simply the demographic boom in the number of teenagers that is propelling the rise in music sales. Counter-counterargument: In the spring of 2000, new records by Eminem, Britney Spears, and 'NSync were easily available on the Internet, yet buyers mobbed stores for all three; *No Strings Attached* by 'NSync sold 2.4 million copies in its first week—more than any other album in history.

To Ulrich, such claims have merit but fail to address a central question. "Why would people pay for music if they get it for free?" he asked outside Napster. "We're very lucky—we have all the money we need. But what about the musicians who are just getting started? How are they going to survive?"

The back and forth exemplifies the "fear and greed" that drive the struggle over online music, according to P. Bernt Hugenholtz, of the Institute for Information Law at the University of Amsterdam. Publishers of all kinds of material fear the unpredictability of the Internet, he argued at a conference in London in 1999. Their apprehension leads to campaigns of "aggressive, almost paranoid lobbying for increased copyright protection in the digital environment." In turn, the lobbying scares the digital elite, who fear that "the Internet, once hailed as the ultimate vehicle of democracy and empowerment, will succumb to the evil forces of monopoly and capitalism."

For "content industries," fear turns directly to greed with the realization that digital technology provides opportunities to extract money from consumers in ways never before attempted. Consider Stephen King's electronic novella, *Riding the Bullet*. Not only was it "printed" and distributed for next to nothing, but in theory the book could not be copied from one computer to another—owners of *Riding the Bullet* could not lend it to their friends. Editors often guess that four or five people read every "hard" copy of most popular books and magazines; digital technology offers the captivating possibility of forcing the freeloaders to pay up.

Users feel greed, too. Every person to whom I introduced Napster, Gnutella, Scour, and the other services was tempted to use them. (Because I make my living from copyright, I tried to restrict my downloading to music I already own or that is out-of-print. Although that is probably illegal, I figured the artists wouldn't mind.) At first I thought that most adults would never put up with the uncertainties of illicit downloads—the bad rips, the cut-off transmissions, and the defects of the MP3 codec itself, which are distinctly audible in sustained pure notes. But according to a survey funded by the Pew Charitable Trusts, more than forty percent of all music-grabbers are thirty or older. Indeed, it is hard to imagine asking people to forgo the twin pleasures of downloading anything they want without paying and coming up with intellectual justifications for doing it. "Information wants to be free." "The labels are thieves." "Everything's going to the Net anyway."

Seeing itself as under threat, each side lashes out at the other. Record labels, invoking the image of the suffering genius in the garret, speak of the need to protect artists. But the copyrights involved are all too often owned by enormous companies. Users, too, see themselves as powerless victims of corporate overreaching. But one of the features of the Internet, as the development of MP3 shows, is that small groups of people can greatly disturb large organizations.

Gnutella is an example. The initial version of the software was written by pro-grammers at a subsidiary of America Online called Nullsoft. On March 14, 2000, Nullsoft put a preliminary version of the software on the Web. America Online, one recalls, is merging with Time Warner, the owners of Warner Music, one of the five majors. The appearance of Gnutella apparently displeased AOL, and the program vanished within hours. But during that time thousands of people downloaded the program, and thousands more tried but were blocked by traffic. Eight days later someone I don't know e-mailed me and several hundred other people a copy of Gnutella's source code, which could be used to re-create the program. Because the code was copyrighted by America Online, actually using it would have been legally fraught. I didn't have to worry, because in another e-mail I was told the address of a website where volunteer coders had posted a version of the software they had created without using the original source code. This new version was the one I was using when someone tried to download my music.

In part, Gnutella was a response to the legal threats against Napster. In Napster every user's searches are shuttled through a central hub—the company's server room. The service can be shut down by unplugging the hub. Similarly, because all the searches are directed to Napster's Internet address, college computer administrators can reject all requests to send and receive data to and from that site, thus blocking it completely. With Gnutella, the users' computers are all connected directly to one another. Gnutella is therefore much less vulnerable to legal action—there's no central entity to sue. The reason the software was written is evident from the anonymous tutorial that accompanied the first version. The decentralized nature of the software, it explained, "makes it pretty damned tough for college administrators to block access to the gnutella service . . . [and] almost fucking impossible for college [administrators] to block the free uninhibited transfer of information . . . Am I making myself painfully clear? I thought so."

Gnutella has many potential uses, but today it is primarily a vehicle for sharing illicit music, pirated software, and pornography. The last is especially prominent. Although Gnutella is usually discussed in connection with music, the most common search term users type in must surely be "Pamela Anderson video." Without much trouble I was able to find pirated versions of most of the software on my computer, complete with identifying codes necessary for installation; many versions of a take from the French television show *Dimanche* in which the camera operator cruelly zooms in as Britney Spears falls out of her dress; a complete set of Yo-Yo Ma's latest version of the Bach solo-cello suites; cheat files for a computer game named Obsidian that my son and I never finished playing because it was too long; a plaintext copy of *Riding the Bullet*; twelve of Shostakovich's fifteen string quartets, most of them performed by the Borodin; and a preliminary version of a DivX software kit for ripping and playing DVDs.

It defies belief to expect that publishers will passively let this continue. As Lawrence Lessig of Harvard Law School points out, the structure of the Internet is set by software and federal law, both of which can always be rewritten. Applying this insight straightforwardly to Gnutella leads to the suggestion that the music industry ask Congress to ban music-swapping or even add stringent legal controls on decentralized file-sharing applications.

Could the government really clamp down? According to Dan Farmer, the computer-security researcher, it will always be possible to disguise the use of such services by encryption. Such arguments have repeatedly proved true in the past, but they do not take into account the possibility that law enforcement, spurred by industry, might go after infringers much harder than it has before. "Silicon Valley is constantly saying that the government is irrelevant and powerless," Lessig says. "But that's because most people there have never seen it get serious."

Today, Internet service providers are shielded from responsibility for the traffic they bear. Just as my telephone company is not legally liable if I make criminal plans on the phone, my Internet service provider is not implicated if I trade unauthorized music on the Net. But if providers were required by law to monitor actively for the use of Gnutella, people would be less likely to use it. "If the police started arresting people and seizing their computers," says Robert Kohn, a cofounder of EMusic.com, "music on the Internet would not seem quite so free." Worried about the future of free speech, a computer activist in London named Ian Clarke is leading an effort to create a network called FreeNet that would guarantee anonymity, no matter what. But it, too, could conceivably be prohibited, and if it comes to anything, surely we will see attempts to do so. The Net, Bronfman promised in July, "will not be able to survive if it becomes a haven for illegal activity. Copyrights must be protected online."

The trouble is that the legal charge is being led by the recording industry, which—in addition to having the most to lose—has a tradition of tight copyright control and rough dealings that is not shared by other media. Given the special circumstances of the industry, this tradition is comprehensible. But it doesn't qualify the labels to set the rules for the global forum. To music companies, prohibiting online anonymity, something Bronfman has suggested, may make sense. But print publishers should feel differently about letting people read and write without revealing their identities. Too many editors know how important anonymity was to Soviet protest literature, and how profitable some of that writing was in the West. Similarly, the movie industry should be careful of the legal precedents set in music. If Napster wins its lawsuits, DivX movies may slip into legality.

Equally important, other culture industries potentially have less to fear from unbridled distribution than the music industry. The Secure Digital Music Initiative will be broken, argues Martin Eberhard, the e-book manufacturer, not so much because of the Internet but because of the combination of the Internet and personal computers. Computers can simultaneously play and re-record music for future distribution, whether or not the music was initially encrypted. Single-purpose machines like CD players and electronic-book readers cannot do this without retrofitting that is beyond the capability of the vast majority of computer users—it involves tinkering with hardware components. If electronic books, magazines, and newspapers are distributed through the Internet not to computers but only to specialized reading devices, they will be much less vulnerable to copying. If Hollywood stops licensing DVD technology to computer manufacturers, the studios will gain some of the same protections; and they will also continue to be able to count on money from ticket sales. For the record labels it's too late. They can't take back compact discs and the millions of CD machines that can play them.

Musicians, who share so little of the wealth from music copyright, might even do better in a world of unrestricted copying, by performing, selling merchandise, offering subscriptions, and the like. Writers, filmmakers, and other content providers who have fewer ways to recoup may well be more vulnerable to the Net. These losses, though, lie only in the future.

The potential lack of economic harm is especially significant in light of the importance of copyright to democracy. According to most legal scholars, the writers of the Constitution viewed copyright in utilitarian terms. By granting a temporary monopoly on distribution to creators, the Founders hoped to stimulate the creation of new ideas. "The creator was rewarded for a little while, but then the idea passed into the commons, where people could do what they liked with it," Lessig says. Now, he says, the campaign against piracy is pushing toward "a massive increase in regulation over the distribution of culture, which is inconsistent with the conception of the commons that lies at the root of democracy." In the American tradition artists, writers, musicians, and audiences work together, creating the intellectual ferment that has helped this country adapt to change for more than two centuries. "People hear the cries of the industry about piracy, which are real and justifiable," Lessig says. "But they don't realize that simply giving the industry what it wants will have an impact on the entire public sphere."

Except for the music industry, the campaigners against Internet piracy are working well in advance of the problem. Many of the music-industry lawsuits have been decided rapidly, without extensive fact-finding; many did not even require the companies to show that they had been harmed. The Digital Millennium Copyright Act, which is being used to sue Napster, contains elaborate provisions governing the Secure Digital Music Initiative, even though music files that are fully SDMI-compliant don't yet exist. "People are always scoffing that the technology moves so much faster than the law," P. Bernt Hugenholtz of the University of Amsterdam told me, "but that's ridiculous. In fact, the law is moving faster than the technology, which is both ironic and a very bad sign. I'll tell you one thing. All academics I've ever met—

no matter what their political stance—agree on one thing: All this Internet-related legislation is very, very premature."

He sighed. "You'd think they'd at least see what the car looked like before trying to drive it."

Charles C. Mann is a correspondent for the *Atlantic Monthly*. His article about copyright in the Internet age, "Who Will Own Your Next Good Idea?" (September 1998), was a finalist for a National Magazine Award. This article originally appeared in the *Atlantic*, September 2000.

Music and New Technology: Making Music in the Digital Age
BY WILLIAM PHILLIPS

On July 6, 2000, in a federal district court, the Recording Industry Association of America (RIAA) won an injunction against the file-sharing website Napster, which was ordered to shut down.[1] (Earlier in the year, Napster had been sued by the heavy metal band Metallica and rap artist Dr. Dre.) In the music "revolution" of the Internet, a crucial battle seemed to have been won by the music industry. At issue was the industry's claim that the Napster service, by providing a central means by which music fans could link their computers together to share and swap music files, had helped to perpetrate copyright infringement on a massive scale. US District Judge Marilyn Hall Patel, ruling in the case, apparently agreed. Although an appeals court subsequently revised the lower court's decision, allowing the service to continue operating, it nonetheless required the service to block access to copyrighted songs, which had largely the same effect, drastically reducing the service's offerings and popularity. For now, it would seem, the idea of freely sharing music over the Internet is at a standstill.[2]

The Napster case and its attendant controversy is at the heart of the new "revolution" in music technology that has been fueled by the emergence of digital technology and the growth of the Internet. While there are a variety of issues at stake in the debate over the digital distribution of music, they all stem from the fact that the new technologies allow artists and music fans to participate in the activities of music duplication and distribution, activities that have long been the exclusive domain of the music industry. As a result, the story of the impact of the new technology is largely one of power struggles and changing relationships between the industry and artists, between artists and fans, between the industry and consumers. The issues themselves are varied: intellectual property rights and the question of whether downloading music files constitutes "stealing"; to what degree the major record labels' status as

1. Usnews.com, "Napster: When the Music Died" (February 17, 2001).
2. George A. Chidi Jr. "Napster Reportedly Wants Microsoft's Anti-Piracy Technology," *TheIndustryStandard.com* (May 14, 2001).

middlemen/distributors is imperiled; how and at what cost music fans will be able to download music. None of these issues or questions are easily addressed or answered, since there are so many factors and players involved in determining their ultimate outcome. For example, powerful media corporations with both money and political influence at their disposal; musicians, whose interests are sometimes with and sometimes contrary to those of the recording industry; and music fans, whose habits both enrich and threaten the livelihood of the music industry. In addition, there are the lawmakers whose power to draft legislation (such as the Digital Millennium Copyright and No Electronic Theft Acts) will also significantly shape the ways in which consumers will ultimately access music in the digital era. Finally, technology itself, which is constantly evolving, will play its own role in shaping the future of music and its distribution. In the following essay, I will attempt to explain some of the ways in which these factors are working together to change the face and business of popular music.

Technologically Speaking

While there are many factors involved in the current "music revolution," there are two crucial technological innovations that are central to it. These are *digitization* and the Internet. Digitization refers to the fact that all forms of information and entertainment media—recorded music, photographic and other images, video, and written text—can now be translated into zeros and ones, the binary code of computer language. The significance of this development can hardly be overestimated, since it now allows the unlimited copying of any such text or song or video in the form of a computer file potentially at no additional cost after the initial copy has been created. For instance, once a music track has been converted from a CD to a computer music file, copies of the song file can be reproduced and transferred from one computer to another at no additional cost. As a result of digitization, then, the actual costs of digitally reproducing music and other media texts—the "second-copy costs," in the parlance of economists—have effectively dropped to zero.

The second technological development central to the music revolution is that of the Internet itself. Where digitization undermines the record industry's monopoly on reproduction of music, the Internet does the same for the *distribution* of music. The development of digitization and the Internet, of course, go hand in hand, as the computers linked together to form the Internet communicate by exchanging information in the form of binary bits of the zeros and ones.

MP3 is by far the most popular digital format for music on the Internet. While MP3 software was first released in 1992, it wasn't until three or four years later—with the coming of the Pentium chip and 56K modems—that hardware capable of taking advantage of MP3 became available and it began to take off as a popular online format. Beginning as a college-based, underground phenomenon, MP3 steadily moved into the mainstream, and by July of 1998 had become so popular that the term "MP3" had overtaken "sex" as the most common search term on the World Wide Web.[3] And, according to *Wired* magazine, MP3 files were being downloaded from the Internet at a rate of seventeen million a day.[4]

In 1999 college student Shawn Fanning, frustrated at the sporadic availability of MP3s on the Internet, developed a software program called Napster. Napster, a type of software known as "peer-to-peer" (P2P), not only enables users to search the Internet to find MP3s of their choice, but effectively turns every user's own computer into a virtual server, that is, a source of MP3s as well. When a music fan uses that software to search the Web, he or she is essentially accessing the computers of other users of the software. Upon finding the music file that it is seeking, the program then downloads a copy of it onto the seeker's computer hard drive. Fanning made the software freely available on the Net, and it quickly caught on. In May of 1999, Fanning and a friend, Sean Parker, along with Fanning's uncle, venture capitalist John Fanning, formed Napster Inc. in an attempt to profit from the Napster phenomenon.[5] Still using the basic Napster concept, they established an easily accessible website for the service that had the effect of taking the concept from the underground to the mainstream. In coming aboveground, however, it also made itself a target for the recording industry, and in December 1999, the RIAA filed an injunction against the service for copyright infringement.

Several years ago, using software programs that surf the Net twenty-four hours a day looking for pirates, the RIAA began locating websites that offer unauthorized music for downloading and issuing cease-and-desist letters demanding that the material be removed.[6] But the RIAA has had more than just threats at their disposal.

3. Warren Cohen, "They Want Their MP3," *US News and World Report* (July 26, 1999): p.43.
4. Vito Peraino, "The Law of Increasing Returns," *Wired* (August 1999): pp.144–145.
5. P.J. Huffstutter. "Fine-Tuning a Digital Revolution," *Los Angeles Times* (December 25, 2000): p.1.
6. David Grad, "MP3's Collegiate Criminals," *New York Press* (September 1, 1999): p.16.

A law passed in 1997, the No Electronic Theft Act (NET), made it a felony to reproduce or distribute copyrighted works, even if it is done without a commercial purpose. The distribution over the Web of ten or more copyrighted works with a value of more than $2500 carries a penalty of up to three years in prison and a fine of up to $250,000.[7] According to Frank Creighton, the head of the RIAA's antipiracy division, the law and the agency's efforts seem to be paying off. "We're finding sites with fewer songs available for download," he noted, "which means illegal sound recordings are becoming harder to find."[8]

While there is a question as to whether the RIAA's claims of piracy were overblown in the first place, there is little question that the government is giving the music industry greater tools for the prosecution of digital pirates. A case in point is the prosecution of Jeffrey Levy, a University of Oregon senior. Levy pleaded guilty to making thousands of pirated software programs, movies, and music recordings available on his website. In a statement regarding Levy's legal battle, the first prosecution under the NET Act, US Assistant Attorney General James K. Robinson noted that Levy's case "should serve as notice that the Justice Department has made prosecution of Internet piracy one of its priorities. Those who engage in this activity, whether or not for profit, should take heed that we will bring federal resources to bear to prosecute these cases. This is theft, pure and simple."[9]

Another bill passed in 1998, the Digital Millennium Copyright Act, offered the industry yet another legal tool for the pursuit of pirates by providing for the "expedited subpoena process." This act gives the RIAA access to the account information of Internet service providers, information that previously had been off-limits—again, allowing for easier prosecution of those operating "pirate" websites.[10]

Less successfully, the RIAA in 1998 sued Diamond Media, the makers of the "Rio," a Walkman-like device that plays MP3 files. While the RIAA claimed that the device was "intended to encourage piracy," Diamond successfully argued that the Rio was merely a storage device, and the court agreed. The Rio has effectively upped the ante in the MP3 debate, since it represents the move of MP3s from the computer (and the dorm room) to the world of consumer electronics.

7. Ibid.
8. Ibid.
9. Ibid.
10. Ibid.

Piracy, Copying, and the Distribution of Music Files

A central claim of the record industry, as we have seen, is that the copying and distribution of music files that MP3 enables constitute "piracy." From the industry's
perspective, this type of music sharing represents the criminal appropriation of
their intellectual property. The comments of Steven Marks of the Recording
Industry Association of America—the industry's lobbying group—exemplify this
attitude: "There's a spirit on the Internet that lends itself to people thinking they
can take everything for free. But it's hard to argue with the basic fact that if you're
ripping music off of a CD and putting it onto the Internet, it's theft. It's no different from walking into a store and taking something without paying for it."[11] Of
course, there is a difference between putting the contents of a CD on the Internet
and stealing a CD from a store, in that, in the latter example, the store owner is left
with one less CD than he had before. Part of the problem with MP3 (for the music
industry) is that the metaphor of intellectual property becomes more and more
abstract. This makes the claims of copyright infringement seem to lose something
of their legitimacy with some music fans. According to an article in *Time Digital*,
up to seventy-five percent of college students are music "pirates." And while some
may be unaware of the legal issues involved, many seem simply not to care. "They
grew up ripping off the latest Microsoft software," author Karl Greenfeld notes,
"why should the music industry's software be any different?"[12] And as one user
observed: "We are violating laws, but the laws are painfully obsolete."[13] As the
practice of duplicating copyrighted materials becomes normalized as a result of the
spread of digital technologies, it may become more difficult to support the legitimacy of intellectual property rights in general and of copyright in particular. As
industry analyst Dan Lavin notes, "Morality is what the community consensus
decides is morality."[14] It may then become harder, as time goes by, to get people to
see what is actually "wrong" with duplicating copyrighted materials.

Even in those more egregious cases where an individual sets up a webpage of
unauthorized MP3 files for downloading, accusations of piracy and its accompany-

---

11. David Weiss, "MP3: The Real Deal," *Musician* (April 1999): pp.38–42.
12. Karl Taro Greenfeld, "You've Got Music," *Time Digital* (February 22, 1999): pp.9–10, http://www.pathfinder.com/time/dig-
ital/reports/mp3/index.html.
13. *Ibid.*
14. *Ibid.*

ing losses may not be all that convincing. The industry currently claims it's losing millions to online piracy, but such claims are hard to prove. As one observer has noted, the fact that an MP3 website had 2.5 million visitors in a given month does not necessarily mean that this represents "2.5 million legitimate CDs unsold, in the way that 2.5 million orders for CDs from a dodgy pressing plant in China might."[15] The premise that every downloaded music file represents a lost sale is a weak one at best and was first advanced when the industry panicked at the introduction of another device of mechanical reproduction: the cassette recorder. "Home taping is killing music!" proclaimed the warnings printed on record-album sleeves—a warning accompanied by the skull and crossbones of the pirate's flag. But, as it turns out, home taping didn't kill the music. Popular music scholar Simon Frith has called this claim "the substitution effect," and notes that it rests on inadequate evidence, deduced primarily "from record sales figures rather than from an investigation of the consumer choices that lie behind them."[16] In fact, Frith found that the little public research that had been done on the subject suggested that just the opposite was the case: that home taping involved "a particular commitment to music," and was done by those people who actually bought the most records.

Musicians

For the most part, musicians have taken to the Internet much more readily than the record industry as a whole, since it has given them a variety of new tools with which to manage their careers. Before the advent of the Internet, most musicians seeking professional careers in popular music set their sights on obtaining a contract with an established record label, since only a record company could finance their recording, mass-produce it, distribute it, market it, and promote it. With digital technology and the Internet all of this is changing: The artist can now perform many of these functions.

To begin with, in addition to giving us the Internet and MP3s, digital technology has also facilitated the development of affordable, professional-quality, home-recording equipment. And it is now possible, and increasingly common, for aspiring artists to produce their own high-quality recordings without having to pay for expensive studio time or have a record label finance them.

15. Ham Khan, *New Statesman* (November 6, 1998): pp.43–44.
16. Simon Frith, "Art Versus Technology," *Media, Culture, and Society*, v.8, n.3 (July 1986): pp.263–279.

As significant as the power of digital production may be, however, it is in the distributive power of the Internet that the musical artist is most liberated from the traditional record company. With a website, any musician or act can establish a worldwide presence. They can make all of their songs available as free MP3 downloads, aiming to get their music out to the greatest number of listeners, making promotion and the growth of their fan base their first priority. They might otherwise offer just a track or two as free MP3 downloads, or in streaming format such as RealAudio, in order to give potential fans a sample of their wares—and then offer more music that can be downloaded for a fee. In addition, a website can provide pictures, videos, news, or other information about an act. This is a means of reaching the public without being dependent upon either the mass media or a record company's publicity department. In short, if we see the artist as an "entrepreneur," as one writer notes, "running a business founded on creating and selling copyrights and generating economic activity from writing, performing, and recording," the development of the Internet can help in many ways to "grow" these areas of activity.[17]

All of this bodes well for the increasing independence of both signed and unsigned artists in the digital age, although there may be differing degrees to which they can take advantage of these opportunities. While an established act with a well-known name will have little trouble bringing traffic to its website, a lesser-known artist has a greater challenge. But even for unknowns, most of whom would never obtain a major-label contract, the Internet is providing unprecedented opportunities to expand their audience beyond the confines of their hometown crowd. A number of websites now abound that serve as clearinghouses for independent and unknown artists. While the best known of these is MP3.com—which now boasts over a million music files from tens of thousands of artists—some of the other online players include Peoplesound.com, Besonic.com, Vitaminic.co.uk, Musicunsigned.com, Popwire.com, and Garageband.com. Although these sites share a mission of bringing unknown acts to the Internet, they differ in their specific approaches, with Musicunsigned and Popwire, for instance, seeing themselves more as dedicated A&R sites that attempt to connect unsigned acts to the major labels.

For the unsigned artist, the new opportunities offered by digital technology and

---

17. Conrad Mewton, *All You Need to Know About Music and the Internet Revolution* (London: Sanctuary, 2001).

the Internet are radical and powerful, yet not really controversial, since the artist in question is a free agent, able to pursue his or her digital destiny without interference. In the case of the artist with a record deal, the contract itself may limit an act's online activities. As a result, the case of signed artists who attempt to use the Internet to further their career raises some of the most compelling issues regarding the new technology and the music industry. Perhaps the most significant of these concerns control of copyright.

The Separation of Authorship from Ownership

When Chuck D and Public Enemy decided to put their album *Bring the Noise* on their website in 1998, they considered the action equivalent to sending out promotional copies of a CD. Their record label, PolyGram, took a dimmer view and threatened legal action, claiming that they controlled the copyright to the tracks and demanding they be taken down.[18] Tom Petty and the Beastie Boys have had similar encounters with their labels.

One might wonder how it is that a record label is able to use copyright *against* an artist, since copyright, in principle, originates with the *creator* of a work. The answer lies in the power that accrues with those who control the means of artistic and cultural production and distribution. This concentration of power leads to what copyright scholar Ronald Bettig has called a "separation of authorship and ownership."[19] That is, authors and other media creators who copyright law is intended to protect rarely remain the owners of the copyright to their own work. This, Bettig argues, is due to the fact that "the owners of the means of communication are able to appropriate the creative labor of others as a result of their control over access to the marketplace. To get published, authors [and recording artists] must generally surrender their ownership rights to the fruits of their labor."

What Bettig is referring to here is the fact that copyright is regularly *transferred* to the publisher (in this case the record company) of the work, who then has the exclusive right to market and sell the artist's work. Since record companies have long had a monopoly on the distribution of music, they have been able to dictate the terms under which the transfer of copyright takes place. While proven stars like Michael

18. Jesse Freund, "Listen Up", *Wired* (March 1999): pp.138–39.
19. Ronald V. Bettig, "The Enclosure of Cyberspace," *Critical Studies in Mass Communication*, 14 (1997): pp.138–57.

Jackson or Bruce Springsteen are able to command million-dollar contracts and generous royalty rates in return for their copyrights, most other artists must settle for the terms set by the record companies. The control that record companies have had over the industry and over artists as a result of their copyright ownership may in part be responsible for a certain amount of resentment on the part of some artists toward the industry. This feeling may be leading many of them to embrace the liberating nature of MP3 and the Internet. With the possibility of digitally distributing their music from a website over which they have control, there exists a means by which musicians and authors can "publish" themselves. So the necessity of turning over copyrights under terms dictated by record labels is now, theoretically at least, past.

In addition, with the industry's rhetoric about copyright infringement focusing on the moral issue of "artists' rights" being violated, a variety of musicians have become outspoken about the degree to which the industry itself has been less than fair about these rights. A number of organizations have recently been formed to represent artists, including the Future of Music Coalition and the Recording Artists' Coalition (RAC). The latter recently gave testimony to Congress noting that artists' interests have not been adequately represented in the debate over digital rights, and that the RIAA, while speaking of the rights of musical creators, actually represents the interests of the major record companies, whose standard contracts regularly exploit artists.[20]

In his congressional testimony, RAC founder and former Eagle singer Don Henley characterized the industry's standard contract terms as "unconscionable," and noted that they allowed a record company to recoup the expenses of recording, promoting, and marketing an artist out of that artist's royalties. As a result, Henley claimed, it is possible for an artist to sell half a million copies of an album "and still not make a single dollar in royalties." Courtney Love, too, has been outspoken on this issue, calling for the formation of a new recording-artists union and for collective bargaining, in order to make the standard recording artist contract fairer to artists (see Love's letter to fellow musicians later in this volume). Love cites the cases of black artists TLC and Toni Braxton, both of whom she contends were forced to declare bankruptcy in order to get out of onerous contracts that reportedly

20. Statement of Don Henley on behalf of the Recording Artists Coalition before the Committee of the Judiciary, United States Senate, April 3, 2001, http://www.artistsagainstpiracy.com/henley-statement.html.

paid them royalties of less than two percent on albums that sold millions of copies. [Note: RIAA lobbyists managed to add a clause into the recent bankruptcy reform bill passed by Congress that makes it more difficult for artists to declare bankruptcy and free themselves of their contractual obligations. This, even though less than one-tenth of one percent of recording artists declare bankruptcy, as compared with the one percent of Americans who declare bankruptcy annually.[21]] As a result of such economic realities, it is not unusual for signed artists to make less of their money from record royalties than by touring and selling merchandise.

This may explain why a number of artists seem to have few qualms about giving their music away on the Internet, and seem to subscribe to the view of Esther Dyson, John Perry Barlow, and other pundits of the Internet who claim that the nature of digital replication calls for new business models in which the free distribution of content stimulates other revenue-generating opportunities such as live performances and merchandise sales.

Several artists have already begun to operate on this or related assumptions, severing or limiting their ties to the traditional record company and distributing their music primarily over the Internet, often for free. Public Enemy now offers their music this way, through their website Rapstation.com, which also hosts hundreds of other acts. Chuck D is arguably the most fervent champion of music on the Internet, and at the same time the most vocal critic of the organized music industry. Believing that the growth of online music distribution and MP3 in particular will force the industry to change the way that it does business, he notes, "It's the end of the industry as we know it. They can't think like they've thought before; they have to come to the table. This is a technology they can't pimp, and that's a problem."[22] For artists like Prince—who is so prolific that his record company would not release his music as often as he would have liked—the Internet provides a mode of distribution that can keep up with his own pace of creativity. As Chuck D observes, "The Internet is saving the group, the artist, the songwriter, and the producer. Can you imagine the amount of product that sat gathering dust, never released? It's back to the days when you cut a record one day and put it out the next."[23] Other artists who have embraced the Internet model of music distribution,

1. Justin Pritchard, "Fine Tuning: Provision in Bankruptcy Bill Puts the Squeeze on Musicians," http://www.opensecrets.org/newsletter/ce55/03tuning.htm.

2. David Weiss, "MP3: The Real Deal", *Musician* (April 1999): pp.38–42.

3. Conrad Mewton, *All You Need to Know About Music and the Internet Revolution* (London: Sanctuary, 2001).

releasing whole albums and more online, include Courtney Love, David Bowie, and the Smashing Pumpkins.

Of course, not all artists are at odds with their labels, and the degree to which established artists see the industry's interests as their own often seems to shape, if not determine, their attitude toward the MP3 revolution. In a scenario such as Metallica's lawsuit against Napster, in which the interests of the artist are seen to be synonymous with that of the industry, it is often the relationship of the artist with its audience that suffers. Rap artist Dr. Dre, who joined in Metallica's suit, is perhaps emblematic of a number of rap performers who have been vocal in their opposition to the "free" music revolution that the Internet has spawned. It has become quite common on urban radio stations to hear rappers railing against the evils of "bootlegging" with MP3s, or to see their supporters on the street wearing T-shirts that proclaim, "You bootleg us, we break your leg." While this resistance to music-file "sharing" may be due to the fact that MP3s are seen to threaten the newfound economic power that the rise of hip hop has brought to black performers and producers, there is nonetheless something ironic in hearing such vehement protection of intellectual property rights from artists whose genre was built on the (often illegal) sampling of others' copyrighted tracks.

Whether particular artists feel threatened or liberated by the Internet and digital distribution may well be determined by the degree to which they share common interests with their record company. The important thing is that for those who do not, there is now an effective alternative for getting their music to the public. As artists begin to experiment with new options, even those who are lucky enough to choose the traditional route may be able to negotiate from a stronger position than they could before the introduction of the new technology.

Consumers

Perhaps more than any other player, it is the music consumer who is driving the Internet music "revolution," with the sheer magnitude of users making MP3 the phenomenally popular format that it is. Experts estimate that Napster alone has had some thirty to fifty million users for its service, who have downloaded music files by the *billions*.[24] While the music industry has been fairly successful in blocking Napster's operation and that of other unauthorized musical providers, and is ready-

24. Chidi, "Napster Reportedly Wants."

ing its own authorized music file services, it is the unauthorized sharing of music files that has garnered such favor with the public.

What, then, does music file–sharing offer the music fan? Basically, it presents at least five advantages over traditional retail distribution. First, it offers an extremely wide selection. Napster CEO Hank Barry recently noted that just before the service was forced to block copyrighted songs, there were 375 million music files available to users of the service.[25] And since the songs are converted from CD to MP3 by fans, the process of selection is done on the basis of fan interest rather than corporate predictions about what is likely to appeal to the largest audience. Hence, the variety of MP3s on offer has tended to be a more broad and eclectic one than the typical record store, with not only the latest chart-toppers, but also more esoteric fare, from converted 78rpm jazz sides to out-of-print eighties new wave and obscure classical tracks.

Second, due to the fact that MP3 is a single-song format, fans have greater flexibility in how they assemble their song collections. If they are only interested in certain songs from a particular album, they can simply download those. Most music fans are aware of the phenomenon of buying an album on the strength of a song or two, only to find that the rest of the album does not meet the same level of quality. One of the appeals of downloading MP3s has been the ability to select choice songs and eliminate the "filler."

Third, related to this track-by-track selection is the fact that even for interested fans that are inclined to ultimately purchase retail CDs, the Internet gives them an opportunity to "taste"—to listen to music that they might not otherwise be familiar with. Without the restrictions of retail price or homogenized radio programming, computer-equipped music fans have had an unprecedented opportunity to develop new musical appreciation. Conversely, this has also given musical acts a unique opportunity to broaden their own fan base.

Certainly another aspect contributing to the appeal of Internet music is convenience. The ability to obtain new music without having to leave one's home has no doubt been an important factor in making the process so popular.

Last, and certainly not least, has been the matter of price—or the lack thereof. While all of the above factors have undoubtedly contributed to the phenomenon of online music distribution, the fact that it has been free may well be the most compelling—and the most threatening to the music industry.

25. "Embattled Napster CEO Speaks to Librarians About Copyright Issues," http://www.siliconvalley.com/docs/news/tech/080689.htm.

All of these factors have made the downloading of music files an extremely popular process, but as Napster itself prepares to go legit following a number of damaging lawsuits, and other industry-backed services prepare to come online, how successful they will be may well hinge on the extent to which they are able to replicate these factors. Already in the case of Napster we have seen the importance of selection: Since the spring of 2001, when the service began blocking access to copyrighted material, there has been a thirty-six-percent dropoff in downloads from the site. According to the Internet research firm Webnoize, 1.59 billion files were downloaded from the site in April, a figure down from 2.49 billion in March and 2.79 billion in February.[26] When the service changes over to a subscription model, it will be interesting to see whether charging a fee will affect its ability to regain its popularity.

Even while the number of songs available on the Napster system is declining, other similar file-sharing programs are still available on the web. Gnutella, Aimster, Freenet, and Open Nap are all similar peer-to-peer programs that allow the as-yet-unblocked sharing of music files. But while Napster required users to log in to a central website, these other programs operate independently of a central server, making them difficult, if not impossible, to police or censor. Although such programs will probably not achieve the high visibility that Napster has, they may well continue to provide access to a wide variety of MP3s for those music fans adventurous enough to seek them out.

The Recording Industry's Models

While there are other "legitimate" music sites (i.e., legally sanctioned by the music industry) available to consumers, they have tended to either focus on lesser known and/or unsigned artists (MP3.com) or have only provided access to a limited number of copyrighted music files (emusic.com). Consequently, the ninety percent of recorded music controlled by the five major record companies has largely remained unavailable in authorized form online, a fact that gave Napster the opportunity to fill the void. But that will soon be changing, as the majors begin to develop their own services online. At the time of this writing, at least three new online music services are about to be launched by the major labels, most of them in alliance with services that already have an Internet presence. The software firm RealNetworks has forged a

26. Chidi, "Napster Reportedly Wants."

partnership with the music divisions of AOL Time Warner, Bertelsmann, and EMI known as *MusicNet*.[27] Universal Music Group and Sony Music Entertainment have joined with Internet portal Yahoo to start a music site.[28] And there is the new Napster that has made arrangements to offer Bertelsmann acts online and is seeking permission to carry other labels' music as well.[29] In addition, Microsoft is rolling out its MSN *Music Site*, which, while not immediately offering music itself, will provide tools for searching for songs over the Internet.[30]

While all of these online services will differ somewhat in terms of actual content and specific pricing schemes, they will all share some general features that are likely to characterize the new standard model of digital distribution for music on the Web, at least in its music industry–approved guise. For one thing, they are all likely to adopt a *subscription* model, with users paying monthly or yearly for the privilege of downloading either a set or an unlimited number of tracks, depending upon the fee. There will most likely be a per-song pricing option as well. MP3s, however, will not be a part of the equation. Instead there will be a copy-protected format that will limit what users will be able to do with a file once they pay for and download it. When Napster eventually rolls out its new subscriber service, they will reportedly be foregoing MP3s in favor of Microsoft's Windows Audio sound-file system.[31] A music file downloaded from the new Napster will thereby only play on the user's computer, and the user will not be able to burn it onto a CD or share it with others.[32]

These services will go a long way toward fulfilling the industry's desires for a "secure" mode of online distribution, although questions remain regarding just how appealing consumers will find them. Much will depend, of course, upon the pricing schemes developed. If music fans are able to pay a reasonable fee for unlimited access to the music of their choice, they may well take to the new services, even if their ability to play them on other machines or share them with others is eliminated. But if the prices seem excessive and/or the music files are only able to be played for a limited number of times (as some in the industry are suggesting such a "licensing" scheme), consumers may well balk.

27. "Going Straight," *The Economist* (April 7, 2001).
28. "Changing Their Tune," *Electronic Engineering Times* (April 16, 2001).
29. "Going Straight."
30. "Changing Their Tune."
31. Chidi, "Napster Reportedly Wants."
32. "Going Straight."

PART 5

Technology: The Music Revolution's Wild Card

One thing that needs to be understood with regard to the dynamics between technology and the music business is that there are a number of sources of technology itself, and that the various providers of technology do not all share the same motivations or goals. As a result, these technology producers often play conflicting roles as they attempt to serve the needs of some players (music fans, for instance), while foiling the plans of others (record companies). On one hand, there are the programmers and hackers who have emerged with the technology of the Internet itself, whose activities are often guided by a non-commercial ethos ("information wants to be free," goes the legendary hacker motto). They are the source of such free software programs as (MP3 player) Winamp, (file-sharing programs) Gnutella, Napster, and the distributors and popularizers of the MP3 format itself. Committed as they are to the widespread distribution of free software technology that empowers users, they are important figures in the dynamics of digital technology.

On the other hand, there are the more traditional commercial manufacturers of hardware (stereo systems, personal listening devices, computers) and software. Their commitment is not so much a public one as a private one: serving the commercial market for their goods. While they are all interested in profiting from the world of digital music, they sometimes adopt different strategies that can have unforeseen consequences. For instance, when Sony and other major manufacturers hesitated in producing personal listening devices for MP3s, and instead marketed ones that utilized the music industry's preferred copy-protected format, the players failed to sell. This left the door open to upstart Diamond Media, whose MP3-playing Rio device became a hit. Although the music industry sued Diamond, charging copyright infringement, the courts OK'd the device's sale, observing that it was merely a playback device. The success of the Rio, then, has been both a result of the user-friendly nature of MP3s and a factor in the format's continuing popularity. The example of the Rio serves to illustrate how the realm of technology is something of a wild card in the world of digital music. As the music industry presses for the development of copy-protected standard formats, there may well remain market incentives for manufacturers to support the open format of MP3 as well. And even as commercial software developers attempt to devise music-file formats that are encrypted and cannot be copied, it is likely that the hacker community will find ways to hack the software and/or convert such files into the open MP3 format and make them more widely available.

One troubling development, though, is the seeming willingness of computer hardware and software manufacturers to heed the concerns of the copyright industry and design their own products to incorporate safeguards against unauthorized copying. The latest version of Microsoft's ubiquitous Windows operating system now comes with something called the "Secure Audio Path," which is capable of keeping an audio file encrypted until the moment it reaches a computer's sound card.[33] More insidious is a new technology called Content Protection for Recordable Media (CPRM) that's being jointly developed by Intel, IBM, Matsushita, and Toshiba. Currently being proposed as a new standard for computer hard drives, CPRM is a mechanism that controls the copying, moving, and deletion of digital media on a user's computer or digital playback device.[34] With CPRM, the debate over copyright infringement could well become moot, as the ability to make unauthorized copies of digital media would be removed from the average computer.

Ultimately, though, as a result of the dynamic nature of technology and the players creating it, it is quite difficult to anticipate just what our digital future will ultimately look like. And when we factor in the actions of music fans and those of policymakers, the picture hardly becomes clearer.

Conclusion: The Future of Music Technology

Even if the music industry is successful in establishing a copy-protected standard for the digital distribution of music, there will remain a number of unresolved issues. For one thing, it will not necessarily mean the end of "free" music on the Internet. While major-label music may be issued in other formats, MP3s will likely remain, since they so well suit the purposes of independent musicians, who have little to gain from preventing the free distribution of their music over the Internet. For these and other musicians, MP3s will continue to function as a means of increasing their fan base and opening up other sources of income.

Another issue is that of price. Although there have been no explicit mentions of

33. *Ibid.*
34. Andrew Orlowski, "Everything You Ever Wanted to Know About CPRM, but ZDNet Wouldn't Tell You . . ." *The Register,* http://www.theregister.co.uk/content/2/15718.html.

pricing for subscription models of distribution, the price per song that has been commonly mentioned (ninety-nine cents) seems unnecessarily high. Given that most CDs have upwards of twelve songs on them and can usually be found for thirteen to fifteen dollars apiece, charging a dollar per download seems exorbitant—especially when one considers that the costs of distribution, pressing, and retailing have largely been eliminated. Such concerns, however, may prove moot, as most consumers seem to be aware of the basic economics involved, and as the commercial services come online, the market may well force an adjustment in charges.

Finally, of all these issues, perhaps the most significant is that of copyright itself. This issue in the digital age is far from adequately resolved, and is likely to loom even larger as the digital duplication and distribution of books and movies becomes technically feasible. In the rhetoric of the music industry, and even to a certain extent artists themselves, copyright is often referred to as a bona fide private-property right, when this is not quite the case. The first intended beneficiary of copyright law is not the creator but the *public*. While copyright does provide incentive for creativity, it does so as a *means* to enrich the public sphere, not as an end in itself. Part of the reason why copyright originally had a short fourteen-year term was so that works would enter the public domain quickly and become available to those who could not afford them initially.

While we no doubt need to find ways to continue providing incentives for artists and authors to create in the digital age, we now have at our disposal the digital technology that can make works of music, art, literature, and entertainment available to anyone with a computer and a modem. That we are using copyright law to thwart that process, rather than to encourage it, seems to go against the original public-interest rationale of copyright law. The battles over the distribution of music on the Internet show that copyright law, which is intended to minimize the scarcity of creative works in society, is in fact being used to preserve that scarcity. We need to make sure that creators continue to be rewarded for their work, but we also need to find better ways to unleash the tremendous democratic potential of digital technology as we move into the twenty-first century.

William Phillips, a former professional musician, is a doctoral candidate at New York University, where he teaches in the Department of Culture and Communication.

Online Entertainment and Copyright Law: Coming Soon to a Digital Device Near You

TESTIMONY OF THE FUTURE OF MUSIC COALITION
SUBMITTED TO THE SENATE JUDICIARY COMMITTEE, APRIL 3, 2001
BY JENNY TOOMEY, MICHAEL BRACY, WALTER MCDONOUGH,
AND KRISTIN THOMSON

Summary

The Future of Music Coalition is a not-for-profit think tank that advocates for new business models, technologies, or policies that will advance the cause of artists. We firmly believe that the music industry as it exists today is, at a very basic level, anti-artist, and that any serious examination of a digital future must take into account the structures in place in our analog present. While the final solutions to the challenges in this space will be driven in many ways by technology and the market, there are a number of critical policy decisions in front of Congress that could make a significant difference in the lives of artists. These include:

1. Competition for collection and distribution of the digital royalty
2. Direct payment of the digital royalty to the artist
3. Fostering of non-commercial space on the radio and on the Internet
4. Ensuring artists have the right to keep their recordings in print

The Future of Music Coalition remains eager to work with any organization that shares our concern for improving the conditions for artists in these exciting times.

Introduction

More often than not, the debate over digital music distribution has left artists and their representatives sitting on the sidelines. Even today's hearing has omitted many of the organizations that have been driving the debate and have stood alone in proposing concrete and coherent solutions to the questions that the Senate is posing.

The Future of Music Coalition (FMC), for example, took the unique step of bringing together more than six hundred music-industry leaders, technologists, consumers, musicians, academics, and composers (including Senator Orrin Hatch) to discuss these very issues this past January at Georgetown University. Unless the Senate and other governmental organizations include artist organizations, like the FMC, in public discussions about the future of digital music, the public cynicism that has made peer-to-peer a phenomenon will continue to grow.

Increasingly, the public believes that artists are not compensated fairly. This perspective is then used as a justification for file sharing of copyrighted materials. If the average teenager believes that her favorite artists will not receive compensation for their creations, it gives her the excuse to use peer-to-peer file-sharing services that have no mechanism in place to compensate the artist. This is the crux of an enormous problem.

The Recording Industry Association of America (RIAA) has a confusing track record. It has publicly stated that the organization does not represent the interests of artists, but rather the interests of the major record companies. It has also stated that it is trying to protect recording artists and their creations through litigation against Napster and MP3.com. Still, there has been no public explanation as to how the recording artists will participate in the large sums that have been generated by the settlements and/or judgments from these cases.

The Senate must ask the difficult questions: How are the artists being paid now, and how will they be paid in the future? In other words, each time that a settlement is reached or a new lawsuit is filed, the Senate must ask: How will the artists be compensated when there is a final adjudication? Prospectively, the Senate should look at each of the digital music distribution issues and conflicts through this prism of artistic compensation.

The System is Broken

Any serious examination of the digital future of downloadable music needs to take into account the fact that the music industry in America is fundamentally broken. In 1999 less than one percent of the total number of albums released sold more than 10,000 copies.[1] Commercial radio airplay is often sold to the highest bidder through a

---

1. David Segal, "They Sell Songs the Whole World Sings: Mass Merchants Offer More Convenience, Less Choice," *Washington Post*, February 21, 2001, p.A1.

shadowy network of "independent radio promoters,"[2] while attempts to create new non-commercial Low Power FM stations have been gutted by Congress.[3] The dreams of stardom chased by many are met head on with the sad reality that an estimated seventy-five percent of releases from major labels are not even currently in print, leaving artists with a huge debt to the record companies that they have no means to pay back. Meanwhile, technology companies seem content to roll out new business models and technologies without giving serious thought to how these technologies will impact artists' traditional revenue streams.

Elevating the Artists

The Future of Music Coalition is a not-for-profit think tank whose sole mission is to elevate artists into the middle of this debate. The FMC aims to increase knowledge about the current industry and advocate in favor of specific solutions—including policy solutions and business models—that will improve artists' ability to succeed in a notoriously (if not artificially) constrained industry. We strongly believe that an artist's agenda and a consumer's agenda are one and the same.

Ultimately, the new music industry will be defined in relation to innovations in technology and the marketplace. It is important to recognize that neither of these forces is neutral. There are a number of critical policy decisions that will determine how the market evolves, and artists need to participate in those decisions. The FMC proposes four simple steps that will not only increase artist compensation but will also grow the size of the music market, thereby creating new jobs and new sources of capital for investment. Each of these proposals will not only effectively create new opportunities in our industry but will also enhance the shareholder value of each of the publicly traded major record labels. This is truly an opportunity to nurture and to grow the recording industry and the performing artists that make it all possible.

1. Competition in Collection of Digital Royalty

SoundExchange is the name of an organization created by the Recording Industry Association of America (RIAA) that is poised to become the sole mechanism by

2. Eric Boehlert "Pay for Play," *Salon*, March 14, 2001.
3. Stephen Labaton, "Congress Curtails a Plan for Low-Power Radio Stations," *New York Times*, December 19, 2000, A1.

which all webcasting royalties will be collected and dispersed to all musicians. The Future of Music Coalition believes that artists must have the right to choose between competing collection agencies, similar to the robust competition between ASCAP, BMI, and SESAC for analog performance royalties.

The Future of Music Coalition has stated a number of reasons why SoundExchange should not be the sole collector:

A. It is partisan.

It is clearly inappropriate to force independent musicians who have consciously worked outside of the major-label system, and who compete with that system daily, to now go to an organization that was created by the major labels in order to collect their independently generated royalties.

B. The data is too valuable.

It is also our opinion that the transfer data (who is playing what songs, how many times, etc.) is valuable and should not be owned or controlled by the RIAA.

C. The RIAA cannot be trusted to represent artists' interests.

We believe that if the major labels are allowed any discretion in the manner by which webcasting royalties are collected, divided, and paid out, they will certainly exert influence in a way that benefits themselves and their constituents. Here it might be wise to remember the recent "work for hire" controversy that implicated the RIAA for requesting (and getting passed) a "technical amendment" that changed the substance of the Copyright Act to the detriment of recording artists. This change allowed record companies to claim ownership of sound-recording copyrights *forever*; previously these copyrights reverted to the creators after thirty-five years.

Thankfully, the "work for hire" clause was identified, fought, and ultimately repealed due to the efforts of a coalition of recording artists and musicians' rights groups. Still we think it would be unwise to allow such recently identified "foxes" as the RIAA or their agents at SoundExchange to be the sole guardian of the newly established "hen house" of digital royalties.

2. Direct Payment of Artists' Forty-five Percent of Webcasting Royalties Through the DMCA

The language of the Digital Millennium Copyright Act needs clarification to ensure artists are paid their royalties directly.

The Problem

As it stands now, some parties believe the DMCA language states that the entire one hundred percent of any webcasting royalty should be paid first to the copyright owner (usually the label), who is then required to pay forty-five percent to the performer and five percent to the unions.

Other parties suggest that ambiguity in the language of the DMCA implies that artists should be paid their forty-five percent directly.

The Solution

To eliminate further confusion and to guard the artists' right to their forty-five-percent share of the webcasting royalties, the FMC proposes an amendment to the Digital Millennium Copyright Act (DMCA). Modeled after the so-called writers' share paid by ASCAP, BMI, and SESAC, the FMC amendment would establish that recording artists be paid directly their forty-five-percent share of all Digital Performance Royalties for Sound Recordings (DPRSR). The FMC believes that this is the first step in acknowledging recording artists as stakeholders in the use of music on the Internet.

Why Should This Be Done?

As it stands, the digital webcasting royalties are set to be administered exclusively by SoundExchange, a partisan collective created by the labels. Recently, SoundExchange offered to pay the artists their forty-five-percent share directly—but only for the first year.

The FMC believes this is a smokescreen of false generosity. It is hardly a foregone conclusion that the money is currently controllable by the labels. If the law was meant to state that the artists get paid their forty-five percent directly in perpetuity, who is SoundExchange to offer the same deal for a diminished period of only one year?

What is at Stake?
A. Fear of Cross-Collateralization
If these royalties go first to the copyright owner, the labels may then attempt to cross-collateralize this new money against any of the artists' accumulated label debt. If royalties are diverted in this manner, the overwhelming majority of major-label artists would not see any webcasting royalties whatsoever.

B. Fear of Obfuscation
As it stands, very few artists who work through the major label system pay off their "expenses" and earn royalties. Often those artists that do recoup only learn of that fact after auditing the label. It would be dangerous to subject webcasting royalties to the same non-transparent formula that already underserves musicians in the terrestrial world.

C. The Future is Interactive—We Should Plan for That Now
FMC believes that it is critical that the stakeholders work together to attempt to make these statutory licenses apply to both interactive and non-interactive web uses. Impending technological advances (Tivo, etc.) already allow for interactive uses of non-interactive streams on the back end. Thus, it is fair to suggest that the future of music and all "innovative" business models will be interactive.

If we do not address the issue of a fair statutory rate for interactivity now, we run the risk of a future where only non-interactive and dated business models pay the fair forty-five-percent statutory rate to creators—while all other interactive and forward-thinking business models pay artists in a manner that is subject to the same nebulous contractual rate that pays artists far less.

Here it is important to remember that an artist's contract royalty rate is not statutory, transparent, nor public. Traditional contract royalties begin at a much smaller "eleven to thirteen percent" and allow for that royalty amount to be further diminished through a process of unfair deductions that are standardized within the industry.

To understand this royalty reduction, multiply an eleven-percent royalty rate by eighty-five percent for a "free goods" deduction. Then multiply it by seventy-five percent for a "packaging" deduction. Then multiply it again by seventy-five percent for a "new media" deduction. After this process of deduction, an eleven-percent royalty is effectively reduced to less than six percent.

Non-interactive webcasting royalties pay artists forty-five percent. Interactive webcasting royalties are subject to contracts. They pay artists six percent. At a difference of thirty-nine percentage points, clearly, artists stand to fare far better under a statutory rate than one that is contractual. Therefore, FMC suggests that it would greatly benefit the majority of artists if the statutory rate were applied to both interactive and non-interactive webcasting licenses.

3. Support for Non-commercial Speech in Broadcasting and on the Internet

In general, music is programmed for one of two reasons: to aggregate the largest possible audience in hopes of charging larger rates to advertisers (the commercial model), or because a piece of music is important enough that a broadcaster thinks it should be shared with its audience (the non-commercial model). Obviously, artists and consumers benefit from the widest number of possible outlets for their music.

Therefore, beyond taking a look at potentially illegal "pay-for-play" practices in commercial radio, or creating new community-based platforms like Low Power FM, there needs to be a means by which less expensive (or graduated) licenses can be granted to community-based webcasters in the same manner that the performing rights organizations—BMI, ASCAP, SESAC—license community-based terrestrial stations at a less expensive rate.

While it is critical that webcasters compensate creators for the value of their music, we should recognize the important contribution that community-based stations make in exposing music fans to a broader variety of music.

Why is This Important?

In order to webcast legally, a majority of independent Internet radio programmers have signed the Statutory Licensing Agreement and agreed to back-pay royalties at the "statutory rate" from the date of that signature, once the rate is established.

It has been over two years since some of these webcasters have signed the agreement, yet the rate is still undecided! There are obvious and grave concerns among independent and community-based webcasters that they will be forced out of business on the day that they are presented with a back-dated bill that is beyond their means.

If this happens, the FMC fears, we will soon find the infinite space of the World Wide Web dominated by the same hit-driven, bottom-line mentality that currently dominates the finite terrestrial bandwidth and underserves the majority of musicians and consumers.

Consolidation of the Terrestrial Bandwidth

The commercial radio bandwidth is no friend to the majority of musicians, nor, for that matter, the majority of consumers. In 2001 the overwhelming consolidation of the commercial radio ownership has concentrated control of terrestrial radio into very few dominant hands.[4] The predominance of super-duopolies (more than seven radio stations in a market owned by one company) and the resulting drive to create additional super-duopolies, has resulted in reductive, consolidated, market-driven programming and far less bandwidth space for niche or independent broadcasting on the radio dial. Both of these factors have had a grave impact on the ability of musicians to get their music in front of a listening audience.

Concentration of Radio Playlists

Commercial radio playlists seem dominated by a "once-removed" process of independent radio promotion that requires overwhelming investment to place songs on commercial radio. If this is true, then over eighty percent of musicians who do not choose to release records through the major label system are effectively locked out of the publicly owned but commercially licensed airwaves. It would be a disservice to artists and consumers to see this same unfair structure replicated on the web through a process of prohibitively expensive webcasting and licensing fees.

4. "Automatic" License for Out-of-Print Recordings

Major labels commonly acknowledge that a majority of their back catalogue is currently out-of-print. This phenomenon harms both musicians, who lose potential record sales, and consumers, who find their variety of musical choices artificially diminished.

In order to address this problem, record contracts in some countries contain "reversion clauses" which allow for the return of the copyright to the creator (musician) if a title has remained out-of-print for an established period of time. Reversion

---

4. Lydia Polgreen, "The Death of Local Radio," *Washington Monthly*, April 1999.

clauses frame the relationship between artist and label as an equal one where both sides have responsibilities and accountability.

In the United States there is no such reversion clause and, therefore, very little recourse for musicians who have signed away their copyrights to a label that is unwilling to keep those records in print.

In order to address this problem, FMC is advocating for the creation of a compulsory or "automatic" license to enable musician signatories (or their heirs) the unquestionable legal right to license their back catalogue sound recordings (at a fair statutory rate) from labels that have allowed these recordings to go out-of-print.

Copyright as Ante

It is standard industry practice to require musicians to sign away the rights to their copyrights in order to participate in the major-label system. This means that ultimately musicians will have little to no control over the availability of their records for sale. Since mechanical royalties paid to artists from record sales make up a large portion of musicians' income, it seems wholly unfair that they would have no recourse when their records are purposefully allowed to remain out-of-print.

Artists and Recoupment

Danny Goldberg of Artemis Records recently indicated that most major-label artists need to sell more than 200,000 copies in order to pay back their debt to the label.[5] However, according to Soundscan data, only one percent of records released in 1999 sold more than 10,000 copies,[6] a number far short of Mr. Goldberg's projection. Using these statistics, we can assume that the overwhelming majority of major-label musicians are in debt to their labels. Understanding that major labels routinely let artists' material fall out-of-print, as noted above, there are even fewer opportunities for artists to recoup.

Napster's Newest Fans

In the physical world, record store and warehouse shelf-space is finite and valuable, but the virtual marketplace does not have the same physical limitations. The fastest-growing demographic segment using Napster is adults over the age of twenty-four.

5. Danny Goldberg, "The Ballad of the Mid-Level Artist," included in this volume.
6. Segal, "They Sell Songs."

Research reports have confirmed that one of the major reasons that they are doing so is to access commercial recordings that are no longer commercially available. The FMC believes that allowing recording artists to make all of their recordings available to the public will lessen the public dependence on Napster, stimulate new record sales, and help achieve our goal of putting more money into the pockets of both recording artists and record labels.

Conclusion

Clearly, the music technology space is a difficult area for policymakers to negotiate, with evolving technologies and market forces shifting constantly. That being said, the Future of Music Coalition has identified four specific areas of concern that Congress should address:

1. Competition for collection and distribution of the digital royalty
2. Direct payment of the digital royalty to the artist
3. Fostering of non-commercial space on the radio and on the Internet
4. Ensuring that artists have the right to keep their recordings in print

We firmly believe these four major items will make a tremendous difference to the lives of artists nationwide, and we look forward to collaborating with other interested parties to help build the structure that will sustain a middle class of musicians in America.

FOR MORE INFORMATION, VISIT WWW.FUTUREOFMUSIC.ORG.

Artist Rights and Record Companies:
A Letter to Fellow Recording Artists
by Courtney Love

March 2001

Dear Fellow Recording Artists,

I'm writing to ask you to join the chorus of recording artists who want us all to get a fair deal from the record companies. R.E.M., the Dixie Chicks, U2, Alanis Morrissette, Bush, Prince, and Q-Tip have called me with their support and we need your participation as well.

There are three basic facts all recording artists should know:

1. No one has ever represented the rights and interests of recording artists as a group in negotiations with record companies.

2. Recording artists don't have access to quality health care and pension plans like the ones made available to actors and athletes through their unions.

3. Recording artists are paid royalties that represent a tiny fraction of the money their work earns.

As I was working with my manager and my new attorneys on my lawsuit with the Universal Music Group, we realized that the most unfair clauses in my contract applied to *all* recording artists. Most importantly, no one was representing artists in an attempt to change the system.

Recording artists need to form a new organization that will represent their interests in Washington and negotiate fair contract terms with record companies.

Here's what you should know:

There is No One Who Represents Recording Artists

Recording artists don't have a single union that looks out for their interests. AFTRA (American Federation of Television and Radio Artists) has a contract with major labels for vocalists and the AFM (American Federation of Musicians) has a contract for non-singing musicians and session players.

If you're in a band, your singer is represented by a different union (AFTRA) than the rest of your group (who are represented by the AFM). AFTRA negotiates contracts for TV and Radio performers. They don't pay very much attention to the recording business; it's not their priority. The AFM acts like band members are sidemen and session players because that's mostly whom the union represents.

Record companies like this system because neither union represents all artists. AFTRA and AFM only negotiate session fees and other minor issues for the singers or the "sidemen."

Who looks after our interests in Washington? Until very recently, congress believed that the RIAA spoke for recording artists. The RIAA (Recording Industry Association of America) is a trade group that is paid for by record companies to represent their interests. The Napster hearings last summer and a few other issues have let Washington know that *no one* speaks for recording artists right now. We have their attention and must act quickly to make sure artists have a voice.

Recording Artists Don't Have a Safety Net

Compare yourself to actors and baseball players. Like the music business, the film and the sports industries generate billions of dollars in income each year, but those industries offer far better benefits to the men and women who create their wealth.

The Screen Actors Guild (SAG) offers a fantastic health care plan to its members. That health plan is paid for by the contracts that SAG has negotiated with film studios. The baseball player's union has negotiated a pension plan that ensures that *no* major league player ever finds himself without an income.

Why shouldn't recording artists get the same benefits?

Recording Artists Don't Get Paid

Record companies have a five-percent success rate. That means that five percent of all records released by major labels go gold or platinum. How do record companies get away with a ninety-five-percent failure rate that would be totally unacceptable in any other business?

Record companies keep almost all the profits. Recording artists get paid a tiny fraction of the money earned by their music. That allows record executives to be incredibly sloppy in running their companies and still create enormous amounts for cash for the corporations that own them.

The royalty rates granted in every recording contract are very low to start with and then companies charge back every conceivable cost to an artist's royalty account. Artists pay for recording costs, video production costs, tour support, radio promotion, sales and marketing costs, packaging costs, and any other cost the record company can subtract from their royalties.

Record companies also reduce royalties by "forgetting" to report sales figure, miscalculating royalties, and by preventing artists from auditing record company books.

Recording contracts are unfair and a single artist negotiating an individual deal doesn't have the leverage to change the system. Artists will finally get paid what they deserve when they band together and force the recording industry to negotiate with them *as a group*.

Thousands of successful artists who sold hundreds of millions of records and generated billions of dollars in profits for record companies find themselves broke and forgotten by the industry they made wealthy.

Here a just a few examples of what we're talking about:

Multiplatinum artists like TLC ("Ain't 2 Proud 2 Beg," "Waterfalls," and "No Scrubs") and Toni Braxton ("Unbreak My Heart" and "Breathe Again") have been forced to declare bankruptcy because their recording contracts didn't pay them enough to survive.

Corrupt recording agreements forced the heirs of Jimi Hendrix ("Purple Haze," "All Along the Watchtower," and "Stone Free") to work menial jobs while his catalogue generated millions of dollars each year for Universal Music.

Florence Ballard from the Supremes ("Where Did Our Love Go," "Stop! In the Name of Love," and "You Keep Me Hangin' On" are just three of the ten number-one hits she sang on) was on welfare when she died.

Collective Soul earned almost no money from "Shine," one of the biggest alternative rock hits of the nineties, when Atlantic paid almost all of their royalties to an outside production company.

Merle Haggard ("I Threw Away the Rose," "Sing Me Back Home," and "Today I Started Loving You Again") enjoyed a string of thirty-seven Top 10 country singles (including twenty-three number-one hits) in the sixties and seventies. Yet he never received a record-royalty check until last year, when he released an album on the indie punk-rock label Epitaph.

Even Elvis Presley, the biggest-selling artist of all time, died with an estate valued at not even $3 million.

Think of it this way: Recording artists are often the writers, directors, and producers of their own records. They write the songs, choose the producers and engineers who record their music, hire and oversee the photographers and designers who create their CD artwork, and oversee all parts of video production, from concept to director to final edit.

Record companies advance money for recording costs and provide limited marketing services for the music that artists conceive and create. In exchange, they keep almost all of the money and one-hundred percent of the copyrights.

Even the most successful recording artists in history (the Beatles, the Eagles, Nirvana, Eminem) have been paid a fraction of the money they deserved from sales of their records.

This is a very big and very important project and we're in the early days. Here's what we're looking for:

1. Artists who are willing to speak to the media to publicly lend their support to the idea that recording artists need an organization that represents our interests in Washinton and with the record companies. We also would like you to tell your managers and attorneys that you support this cause and that you expect them, as your representatives and employees, to do the same.

2. Anyone who can tell us specific stories about how artists have been ripped off by record companies like the ones I told above. We're going to have to educate the public and the media and congress, and the only way we'll do that is by giving them examples they can relate to.

Now is the time for action. Artists like Garbage and 'NSync have have joined me in questioning bad contracts and have also gone to court to change the system.

Record companies have merged and re-merged to the point where they can no longer relate to their artists. Digital distribution will change the music industry forever; artists must make sure they finally get their fair share of the money their music earns. We need to come together quickly and present a united front to the industry. Your managers and attorneys will probably tell you not to rock the boat and not to risk your "relationship" with your record company by taking a stand.

Most attorneys and managers are conflicted. Almost all entertainment law firms represent both artists and record companies. Lawyers can't take a stand against record companies because that's where they get most of their business. Even the best managers often have business relationships with labels and depend on record companies to refer new clients. Think about Eddie Vedder and Pearl Jam's stand against TicketMaster. Everyone knew he was right and yet no other artist took a public stand against a company that we all knew was hurting our business, because our managers and attorneys told us it would be a bad idea.

Attorneys and managers are your employees. Make sure they know how you feel and that you want them to publicly support the idea that the terms of recording contracts are unfair and cover too long a time period. You also want them to support an organization that will negotiate health and pension benefits for all recording artists.

Artists have all the power. They create the music that makes the money that funds the business. No one has ever harnessed that power for artists' collective good.

And remember something equally important: Actors had to fight to end the studio system that forced actors to work for one employer, and baseball players had to strike to end the reserve clause that tied a player to one team for his entire career. Even though "experts" predicted economic disaster once actors and athletes gained their freedom, both the film business and baseball have enjoyed their greatest financial success once their talent was given its freedom.

Join us now in taking a public stand. Your name will help get the attention that artists' rights deserve. If you're willing to speak to the media or testify before Congress, you can help make our goals a reality. Do it for yourself, for your children, and do it for the artists who inspired you to make music in the first place.

E-mail us at: Artists@theredceiling.com. Give us your stories and your support. Tell us we can add your name to the list of artists who support this organization. And let us know how to contact you directly as we move forward on this project.

If you're interested in learning more about my case with Universal, visit my manager's website: www.theredceiling.com. You can download a copy of our cross-complaint and press releases that describe the issues we're taking to court.

Thanks in advance for your support.

Best regards,
Courtney Love

Courtney Love is a singer/guitarist and actress. With her band Hole, she released the multimillion-selling albums *Celebrity Skin* and *Live Through This.* Love sent this letter out to fellow recording artists in March 2001.

Also From Akashic Books

The Big Mango by Norman Kelley
270 pages, paperback
ISBN: 1-888451-10-8
Price: $14.95

She's Back! Nina Halligan, Private Investigator.
"Want a scathing social and political satire? Look no further than Kelley's second effort featuring 'bad girl' African-American PI and part-time intellec tual Nina Halligan—it's X-rated, but a romp of a read . . . Nina's acid takes on recognizable public figures and institutions both amuse and offend . . . Kelley spares no one, blacks and whites alike, and this provocative novel is sure to attract attention . . ." —*Publishers Weekly*

We Owe You Nothing: Punk Planet, the Collected Interviews
Edited by Daniel Sinker
334 pages, paperback (6" x 9")
ISBN: 1-888451-14-9
Price: $16.95

"This collection of interviews reflects one of *Punk Planet's* most important qualities: Sinker's willingness to look beyond the small world of punk band and labels and deal with larger issues. With interview subjects ranging from punk icons Thurston Moore and Ian MacKaye to Noam Chomsky and representatives of the Central Ohio Abortion Access Fund, as well as many other artists, musicians, and activists, this boo is not solely for the tattooed, pierced teenage set. All of the interviews are probing and well thought out, the questions going deeper than most magazines would ever dare; and each ha succinct, informative introduction for readers who are unfamiliar with the subject. Required reading for all music fans." —*Library Journal*

News Dissector: Passions, Pieces, and Polemics; 1960-2000
by Danny Schechter
297 pages, trade paperback
ISBN: 1-888451-20-3
Price: $16.95

"Danny Schechter, a kind of journalist without borders, has shaken up pub broadcasting, among many other media institutions, in the course of his career as a self-styled 'News Dissector' and human rights advocate . . ." —*The Nation*

Falun Gong's Challenge to China: Spiritual Practice or "Evil Cult"?
A report and reader by Danny Schechter
287 pages, trade paperback
ISBN: 1-888451-27-0
Price: $15.95

"The only book-length investigative report on this severe human rights cris that is affecting the lives of millions. "[Schechter] offers a persuasive analys of this strange and still unfolding story . . ." —*New York Times*

Spy's Fate by Arnaldo Correa
305 pages, hardcover
ISBN: 1-888451-28-9
Price: $24.95

"Arnaldo Correa is one of a handful of Cuban writers whose work is finally making its presence felt in the United States. In *Spy's Fate* he gives us a courageous book that offers a true insider's view of the new Cuba: the Cuba that has emerged since the fall of the Soviet Union; the Cuba that neither the United States government nor Fidel Castro wants you to know about."
—William Heffernan, Edgar Award winning author of *Red Angel*

Adios Muchachos by Daniel Chavarría
245 pages, paperback
ISBN: 1-888451-16-5
Price: $13.95

"Daniel Chavarría has long been recognized as one of Latin America's finest writers. Now he again proves why with *Adios Muchachos*, a comic mystery peopled by a delightfully mad band of miscreants, all of them led by a woman you will not soon forget—Alicia, the loveliest bicycle whore in all Havana."
—Edgar Award-winning author William Heffernan

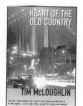

Heart Of The Old Country by Tim McLoughlin
216 pages, trade paperback
ISBN: 1-888451-15-7
Price: $14.95

"Set in a crummy corner of present-day Bay Ridge, Brooklyn, this sweet, sardonic and by turns hilarious and tragic first novel opens with a no-hoper named Michael going through his motions . . . The novel's greatest achievement is its tender depiction of Michael as a would-be tough guy, trying to follow his father's dictum of 'Give them nothing,' while undergoing a painful education in the real world."
—*Publishers Weekly*

These books are available at local bookstores. They can also be purchased with a credit card online through www.akashicbooks.com. To order by mail, send a check or money order to:

Akashic Books
PO Box 1456
New York, NY 10009
www.akashicbooks.com • Akashic7@aol.com

(Prices include shipping. Outside the US, add $3 to each book ordered.)